THE SHI‘IS OF SAUDI ARABIA

Fouad Ibrahim

THE SHI'IS OF SAUDI ARABIA

SAQI

London   San Francisco

ISBN 10: 0-86356-903-X
ISBN 13: 978-0-86356-903-6

This edition published 2006 by Saqi Books

A full cip record for this book is available from the British Library
A full cip record for this book is available from the Library of Congress

Manufactured in Lebanon

SAQI
26 Westbourne Grove, London W2 5RH
825 Page Street, Suite 203, Berkeley, California 94710
www.saqibooks.com

Contents

Acknowledgments

I have incurred many debts in writing this book, and benefited a great deal from the comments of others. I am grateful to them all for their generous assistance, which has made this work possible.

I am indebted to the copious assistance and guidance of my dear supervisor, Dr Kate Zebiri. Her full support and commitment throughout all the stages of writing this book has strengthened and informed my determination. I am so grateful for her encouragement, essential comments and excellent suggestions about the approaches, objectives and language of my thesis.

I want also to acknowledge the difficult job of editing done by Miss Rachel Scott. I thank her also for the suggestions and comments she offered.

Special thanks to the many friends who kindly and promptly responded to my requests for information, interviews and questionnaires. In particular, I want to thank Mr Ja'far al-Shayeb, who generously provided me with valuable information about the Shi'is in the Eastern Province, and for his immediate assistance and participation in the questionnaire held during the *hajj* 2000.

Finally, thanks to my precious family for all the patience, love and care they offered me throughout the years. A special thanks to my dear wife, whose support and help were essential in providing the time and peace of mind needed for this study.

Introduction

The study of Shi'i political Islam has captured the attention of a wide range of scholars from different disciplines throughout the last two decades. In this work I hope to highlight the evolution of the political and intellectual discourse of the main Shi'i religious opposition in the Eastern Province of Saudi Arabia since 1975. I focus particularly on the dominant Shi'i religious opposition (the Islamic Revolution Organization, or *Islahiyya* Movement), founded in 1975. From its initiation, it was affiliated with a Shi'i Islamic movement in Iraq, called the Movement of Vanguards' Missionaries (*Harakat al-risaliyin al-tala'*, founded in 1968 in Karbala, an Iraqi Shi'i shrine city.

A number of Shi'i political Islamic movements appeared in the wake of Iran's Islamic revolution in 1979 and scholarly research since then has concentrated mainly on Shi'ism in the context of Iranian events and literature. The analysis of Shi'i movements has become, to some extent, stereotypical and generalized, and failed to take account of the disparate internal social, cultural and historical factors that contributed to the political formation of the Shi'i communities in other regions. Fortunately, the studies of Graham Fuller and Rend R. Francke of the Shi'i Arabs have drawn attention to the missing elements in previous approaches to Shi'i political movements, by demonstrating that they are independent entities and not fifth columns created by Iran to serve its own ends.

There remain few works on the Shi'i opposition in the Eastern Province. Those that exist can be divided into three categories: works on the Shi'is in the Gulf, noting their socio-economic conditions and their suffering in the face of state discrimination; works on the Saudi Shi'is, which, though valuable for their historical background, are generally based on external observation and

other published material, which omit discussion of the activities, strategies and
political views of the Shi'i political organization's emergence in the late 1970s,
and some of which present or perpetuate errors of fact or interpretation; and
works on the Saudi Shi'i opposition, which have contributed to understanding
of the political conditions of the Shi'is but have failed to take into account
the time when the *islahiyya* Movement had already dissociated itself from the
revolutionary past and leaned towards moderation.

Thus, the main gap in the literature is the study of the main factors
contributing to the transformation of the *islahiyya*'s discourse. In attempting
to bridge this gap, I refer to five types of sources: the so-called internal
literature (*adabiyyat dakhiliyya*) of the Movement, which consists of a package
of private treatises written by the leaders of the Reform Movement for the
purpose of indoctrinating members of the movement; personal interviews
with the leaders of the Reform Movement as well as with influential members
who joined the movement from a fairly early period; the published works of
the ideologies of the Movement of Vanguards' Missionaries (MVM); my own
experience and observations as a former member of the Central Committee
of the Reform Movement; and academic articles on the Shi'is in Saudi Arabia
and the Gulf in general.

The private archive of the Reform Movement to which I refer contains
valuable information regarding the political and intellectual discourses of the
Movement. It also contains reports, letters and notes written by the leaders of
the Movement and the members of the Central Committee, particularly in
the period of dialogue with the Saudi government between September 1993
and July 1994. The publications of the Reform Movement in the period 1989
to 1993 were of considerable importance as they reflected the new rhetoric
and political views of the *islahiyya* Movement. They include the monthly
magazine *al-Jazira al-'Arabiyya* (The Arabian Peninsula), based in London
from January 1991 until August 1993. Among other publications of the
movement (e.g. *Arabia Monitor*, *al-baqi'*, *ahl al-bayt*), *al-Jazira al-'Arabiyya*
is the prime mouthpiece of the Movement's reformative agenda; it also
represents its views towards the political situation in the Saudi realm during
the Gulf crisis. This also includes the historical narrative and religious and
cultural aspects of the period reflected in the publications and activities of
mu'assasat al-baqi' li 'ihiya' al-turath (Baqi' Establishment for the Revival of
Heritage). Further, the publications of '*rabitat 'umum al- Shi'is fi al-Sa'udiyya*'

(the Pan-Shiʿi Association in Saudi Arabia) are a primary source for the study of the cultural authenticization of the Shiʿis.

I extended my research by conducting interviews with the founders and other leading members of the Reform Movement, notably Shaikh Hassan al-Saffar and Shaikh Tawfiq al-Saif, who provided valuable information on the circumstances, factors and objectives of the Islamic Revolutionary Organization (IRO) in its first phase, and also about the political and intellectual transformations of the Reform Movement's discourse. Their views help one to understand the transformation of the ideology from revolution to reform. They also reflect the conflicting stances on such issues as the principle of the Islamic state, the adoption of the military option as a means of political change, freedom of expression, pluralism and the relationship with despotic regimes and other political groups, notably leftist ones.

Although the Reform Movement was formally dissolved in December 1993, it maintained a certain identity that could be described as a political and intellectual trend, which is distinct from other trends within both the Shiʿi community and the political forces in the country as a whole. There is considerable literature on the *islahiyya* Movement in the national context, to which I have made copious reference.

Throughout two decades of membership of the *islahiyya* Movement, I joined in various activities, which enabled me to gather unlimited information and access private sources that are exclusively available for members, including sensitive information to which only members of the Central Committee have access.

My own personal interest in this topic can be traced back to the uprising of the Shiʿis in the Eastern Province in 1979. I come from a relatively small town close to the oilfields, called Safwa, and on Thursday 9 Muharram 1400 (28 November 1979) nine of its inhabitants lost their lives. I had been among the crowd who rampaged the streets in response to the killing of a local teenager by the National Guards during a demonstration in Qatif city, the night before. In this bloody incident, I saw my cousin lying on the ground, shot dead; he left behind nine children, aged from two to twelve years. It was this tragic episode that triggered my intense interest in the status, identity and rights of the Shiʿis in this country, on the one hand, and, on the other, the attitude of the Saudi government towards the Shiʿis.

During summer 1984, I travelled to Syria, where I joined the MVM. In the first stage, I went through an introductory programme, which centred mainly on indoctrinating new members with religious precepts, ideology and the political agenda of the MVM, and at the same time enabled the leaders of the MVM to decide whether entrants were eligible to become members of the Movement, a process that normally took between one and two years.

Having met the requirements to become formally a member of the MVM, I joined the news reporting section of the Movement, first as a trainee and then, after a couple of years, as one of the senior editors of *al-shahid* (Martyr) magazine, the first Arabic magazine in Iran after the revolution in 1979. The magazine, which was widely circulated both in Iran and around the globe, espoused the Islamic revolution in Iran; it also called upon Muslims elsewhere to follow the Iranian revolutionary model and decried Arab regimes that had relations with the United States, the symbol of international despotism and tyranny, according to Ayatollah Khomeini.

The magazine, though owned by the MVM, was initially financed by the Iranian government. In the prevailing climate of pragmatism in Iran in the middle of the 1980s, the magazine was financially dependent on the donations of the Shi'is in the Gulf. However, the importance of *al-shahid* waned as more and more Arabic magazines and newspaper came into being, and simultaneously more restrictions were imposed on the management of *al-shahid* by the Iranian leadership.

In 1987, the magazine revealed its political identity as the organ of the MVM, dissociating itself from the Iranian regime. As a consequence, *al-shahid* lost its universal tenor and became restricted to publishing taped sermons, interviews, articles and/or parts of books authored by the leaders of the MVM.

From 1984 to 1988, I became familiar with the political and intellectual activities of the MVM. As a senior member of the Movement, I was exposed to the private literature of the MVM, including the internal magazine, *al-'Arabi*, which covers various issues such as the ideology and strategy of the MVM as well as political assessment of current imperatives and periodical reports by leading members from different sites. I also had access to a vast collection of pamphlets written by the leader of the MVM, Muhammad Taqi al-Mudarresi, and other leaders, setting out the world views, ideology and strategy of the Movement.

In September 1988 I took a major step towards complete commitment

to the Shi'i 'creative resistance', as Mamoun Fandy called it. Armed with a
new understanding of the mechanism of opposition and the possibilities of
promoting new ideas that were essential to engaging in a struggle for freedom
and democracy, I decided to dedicate myself to the cause of the Shi'is in the
Eastern Province.

I joined *al-Thawra al-Islamiyya* magazine, the voice of the Islamic
Revolution Organization (IRO), and served as its editor until 1990, when the
Movement began to take a more moderate line. While in Syria I was able to
access the private literature of the IRO, and communicated closely and often
with Shaikh Hassan al-Saffar, the leader of the IRO.

In October 1991, I went to London and joined the team of a new magazine,
al-Jazira al-'Arabiyya, a manifestation of the new reformative orientation of
the movement, which replaced the IRO with the Reform Movement. With
the election of Tawfiq al-Saif as general secretary of the *islahiyya* Movement,
London acquired a great deal of importance, as he and a number of leading
members of the *islahiyya* opted to live in the city. The political, journalistic and
human rights activities carried out by the *islahiyya* in London between 1990
and 1993 carried considerable weight and their effects extended to nearly all
of western Europe.

In an attempt to create a broad and effective network of relations, the
islahiyya wing in London adopted a new moderate political discourse suited to
the Western multicultural environment, thus paving the way for the *islahiyya*
members in London confidently to voice their grievances and demands.
Evidently, *al-Jazira al-'Arabiyya*, the organ of the *islahiyya*, had strong ties with
a number of quality papers in London such as *The Guardian*, *The Independent*,
the *Financial Times* and the *Sunday Times*; it also had good relations with
such magazines as *The Economist*. In addition, the London branch of the
International Committee for Human Rights in the Gulf and Arabian Peninsula
(ICHR–GAP) maintained firm and mutually respectful relations with human
rights organizations operating in London such as Amnesty International and
Article 19. Both increasingly relied on the reports and information provided
by the ICHR–GAP regarding human rights conditions in Saudi Arabia. For
instance, Article 19, which is concerned with freedom of expression around
the world, in 1991 issued a report entitled *Kingdom of Silence*, based almost
entirely on work done by Tawfiq al-Saif, General Secretary of the *islahiyya*,
and Hamza al-Hassan, editor of *al-Jazira al-'Arabiyya*.

Journalism and human rights activities were not the only experience of the *islahiyya* in London. Political relations, organizational arrangements, fundraising and seminars were also central parts of the *islahiyya*'s agenda. As a member of the Central Committee, I have been involved, with other members, in formulating the policies of the *islahiyya* in London.

As managing editor of *al-Jazira al-'Arabiyya* from August 1992, I became almost obsessed with the new reformative themes in the *islahiyya* discourse, such as freedom of expression, political and religious plurality, women, labour and minority rights, the rule of law, the constitutional state and the democratic system of government. These issues were central to the *islahiyya* discourse towards the end of discussions with the Saudi government and even after the accord was reached in September 1993.

Although the present study has much in common with already published works, these have failed to cover the historical context, particularly in the period between 1975 and 1993 when the discourse of the Reform Movement underwent significant changes. Understanding these changes requires a thorough reading not only of the published works, taped sermons and statements made by politically motivated leaders or influential members of the Movement, but also of the internal literature that records the Movement's ideology and strategy.

Overview

This book is divided into seven chapters.

The first chapter, 'The Shi'is in the Eastern Province and Saudi Rule', presents an overview of the political and economic implications of Shi'i geography and demography. It also highlights the state's discriminatory policies towards the Shi'i community. Thus, in the first chapter I endeavour to outline the complexities of the Shi'is' relationship with the Saudi state during the last two hundred years, focusing on recent times. Examination of the factors, forces and circumstances involved in this relationship helps one to understand the potential unrest of the Shi'i regions in the Eastern Province. Within this context, I study the forms of discrimination practised by the Saudi government and Shi'i reaction, along with the evolution of Shi'i protest until it reached its final manifestation in the *islahiyya* Movement in 1979.

The second chapter deals with 'Shi'i Identity in the Eastern Province'. While I am fascinated by the works of scholars of social science, ethnicity and nationalism, these issues are not so relevant here. I am more interested in the way in which scholars of these disciplines present the problem of identity, how it evolves, what components are involved in creating it, and what choices of identity are available for the Shi'is. I have gained some understanding of this from the work of such scholars as Bryan R. Wilson, Meredith B. McGuire, C. Fried, Ernest Gellner and Walker Connor. I aim to examine how the Shi'is prioritize their multiple identities and, more importantly, to explore the oppositional tendency among the Shi'is. In my view, those who do not identify themselves as Saudis are more inclined towards opposition than those who regard themselves primarily as Saudi.

Intimately related to this subject is the issue of national identity, which is a second context within which the issue of Shi'i identity should be discussed. However, discussing national identity is possible only if one focuses on state-building ideology, which assists in understanding the formation of Saudi identity. This dualism is necessary in order to gain insight into the elements and also the paradoxes of Shi'i identity.

In the third chapter, 'The Emergence of the Shi'i Islamic Movement (1960–79)', I focus on the political and intellectual climate within which the MVM arose and on the organizational activities, literature and goals of the Movement. Here I introduce discussion of the prime topics (Islamic *umma*, implementation of *shari'a*, Islamic government, *jihad* and social protest, Islam and *jahiliyya* and so on) that have been widely debated by Islamic movements as a whole, ranging from the *ikhwan* mother group and the Tahrir party, to the Da'wa party and even to Iranian Islamic trends. By considering such concepts, these movements have formulated their strategy of change, which has enabled them to achieve their ultimate goals.

Between 1960 and 1979 the main concern was the restoration of Islam and Shi'ism to social life and, hence, the reaffirmation of the validity and continuity of Islam and Shi'ism as an ultimate option for Muslims in their present and future lives. The chapter focuses on two aspects: the comprehensiveness of Islam versus comprehensive *jahiliyya*, and the new interpretation of the Shi'i tradition.

This chapter also includes an overview of the intellectual influence of Mawdudi, Sayyid Qutb and Shari'ati on the MVM. Comparison of the works of these inspirational figures with the writings of the leaders of the MVM shows that their impact was significant.

The fourth chapter, 'The Revolutionary Decade (1979–89)', analyses the circumstances, impetus, discourse, leaders and aims of the Shi‘i uprising in the Eastern Province in November 1979. The so-called *intifada* marked a major shift in Shi‘i opposition, and its impact on the manifestation and crystallization of the Shi‘i opposition is of great importance.

The Shi‘i uprising contributed to the development of religious and political awareness within the Shi‘i community, and while it deepened the confrontation with the Saudi regime it also created an opportunity for the Shi‘i opposition to gain various forms of support from Shi‘i groups inside and outside the country.

Here I will also consider certain consequences of the *intifada*, the responses of the state towards the Shi‘is' demands, and, in return, the opposition's responses to repressive government measures against the leaders of the Shi‘i opposition. As any form of protest was officially banned, a group of Shi‘i activists was compelled to leave the country and then publicly announce the formation of the Islamic Revolution Organization as a Shi‘i opposition group in Saudi Arabia. What were its ideology, strategy, views and activities, and how did it succeed in recruiting members, in mobilizing supporters, in communicating with the Saudi Shi‘is and in transmitting its religious and political message?

The impact of both the Iranian revolution and the Islamic Action Organization in Iraq, with which the Saudi Shi‘i opposition is associated, must not overshadow other factors contributing to the *islahiyya*'s adoption of the revolutionary option. In order to evaluate the rationale behind such an option, I attempt to study and analyse the revolutionary discourse of the Saudi Shi‘i opposition with reference to the writings of the IRO and interviews with its leaders.

Chapter Five, entitled 'From Revolutionary Option to Reformative Alternative (1989–93)', presents the problems associated with the transformation of the *islahiyya*'s discourse in 1990. In this chapter I endeavour to give insight into the new strategy and discourse of the *islahiyya*. It appears that the political and intellectual literature of the *islahiyya* projected a dual image of its purpose and function. Despite its assertion that Islam is a source of inspiration and legitimacy, there is frequent reference to Western political notions and human rights perceptions. I highlight a series of transformations that reflect the Movement's new orientation.

My discussion of the transformation of the *islahiyya*'s discourse to moderation makes extensive reference to academic works. I look into some contemporary writings that suggest some useful ideas about the changing strategies and tactics of opposition groups, including the various forms of resistance of underprivileged groups.

Chapter Six, 'The Accord (1993)', presents a detailed review of the accord between the Saudi government and the leaders of the *islahiyya* Movement, which took place in September 1993. The first question I deal with, from a Shi'i religious standpoint, is that of the legality of dialogue with rulers. What were the circumstances and results of the agreement and how did the Shi'i and the national government respond to the success or the failure of the agreement?

In this chapter I also consider the motives behind the Saudi government's decision to initiate such a direct dialogue with the Shi'i opposition, and devote particular attention to the issues involved in the dialogue, and to what the dialogue achieved and what promises it made. Did the Saudi government commit itself to the promises towards the *islahiyya* leaders and how did the *islahiyya* leaders view this dialogue with the government? Their subsequent reactions are also considered here.

Finally, Chapter Seven presents a central theme, namely the 'Accommodation and Evolving Attitudes (1993 – the Present)'. The return of the *islahiyya* Movement to the country marked a turning point in the relationship between the Shi'i community and both central government and the local authorities in the Eastern Province. I examine how the *islahiyya* Movement accommodated its political and intellectual discourse after its return to the country, and how the government responded to the Shi'is' fundamental demands.

In this chapter I also compare the Saudis' strategies towards the Shi'is and towards other opposition groups, both secular and religious, in order to understand how the government deals with its internal rivals and whether it applies one method to all opposition groups regardless of their sects, regions and ideologies, or whether it exercises different options.

The political and intellectual discourse adopted by the leaders of the *islahiyya* Movement, which was elaborated in their publications, reflects a significant shift in its political objectives. Was the *islahiyya* Movement really inclined towards accommodation? Was it a real strategy or merely a Shi'i manoeuvre, or *taqiyya*?[1] What, moreover, were the government's responses and initiatives towards the *islahiyya* attitude? Did the government implicitly or explicitly express its willingness to ameliorate the social and economic conditions of the Shi'is? Was the government willing to revise its policies towards the Shi'is, in order to build a new basis for a secure and stable relationship?

Here I examine the new phase of the relationship between the Shi'is and the government, not only because it represents the apex of a long-term confrontation between the Shi'is and the Saudi regime, but also because it reveals the Saudis' political attitude towards opposition movements. I focus on the responses and reactions of the Shi'i opposition to the government's performance in the aftermath of the return of its members, and on the alternatives that were made available for the *islahiyya* in order for it to realize its demands. This opens the way for further research on the relationships, disputes and issues between the Shi'is and the Saudi government.

Among the conclusions I reach in this book, the most important is that the opportunities created by the experience of the groups need to be observed and that the understanding derived from such experience needs to be appreciated as a vital part of the study of opposition groups as a whole. For the Shi'i opposition in the Eastern Province, the transformation to moderation has helped to eliminate many obstacles that have impeded the Movement in the past, so that it can play an active part in Saudi national politics. Although the accord did not correspond to what the Shi'is in the Eastern Province hoped to gain, the change in internal circumstances following the attacks of 9/11 and the war in Iraq has created a new climate that has meant the Shi'i issue is one of the top priorities on the Saudi government's agenda. It has also helped the Shi'is to be more open in voicing their grievances and demands inside the country. It could be argued that the new epoch the country has entered since 2001 could make the Shi'is a major factor in any future political reshuffle.

ONE

The Shiʻis in the Eastern Province and Saudi Rule

The importance of the study of the Shiʻis opposition in Saudi Arabia stems from a number of facts. First, the Shiʻis reside in the most strategically crucial area of the kingdom, the Eastern Province, which contains most of the oilfields in the country, including Ghawar and Qatif, the largest oilfields in the world. Second, from the perspective of international security and world trade, the Shiʻi in the Eastern Province contribute to the country's economic and political stability, both regionally and internationally. Their regions provide around 90–95 per cent of the country's income and 15 per cent of the world's oil markets,[1] and Shiʻis labour has constituted between 40 and 60 per cent of the oil industry's workforce.[2] Third, the Saudi Shiʻis reside in a region near to three Gulf states with a Shiʻis majority, namely Bahrain (with over 65 per cent of the overall population), Iraq (with nearly 60 per cent) and Iran (with nearly 90 per cent).[3] Furthermore, thanks to their ethos, religious outlook and political potentiality, the Shiʻis as a distinct sect represent the greatest dissenting element in the Kingdom.[4]

Although reliable official figures are lacking, it is widely believed that Saudi officials regularly underestimate the number of indigenous Shiʻis concentrated in the Eastern Province, for political, security and socio-economic reasons.[5]

The most recent estimates of the Shiʻis population are similar. According to an anti-Shiʻa group, the Shiʻis (including the Ismailis and Zaidis) number 970,452, or 5% of the total population of 19,409,058.[6] In 2000, the US State

Department estimated that the Shi'is, numbering 900,000, live mostly in Eastern Province.[7] Although many indications suggest that the number of the Shi'is is even greater than these estimates, the figures show that the Shi'is of al-Hasa and Qatif constitute the largest Shi'is community in the Arab Gulf states except for Iraq. Moreover, they make up the largest Shi'is community in the Arab world, except for Iraq and Lebanon.[8]

Thanks to their numbers and to strategic geography, the Shi'is are an important factor in Saudi politics and the region as a whole. The historical background of the Shi'i relationship with the Saudi state throughout the last two hundred years serves to help us understand the potential unrest in the Shi'is regions in the Eastern Province.

Wahhabism: An Ideology of Conquest

The emergence of the Wahhabi revivalist movement in Najd in 1745 and its related developments marked a new epoch for the Shi'is and nearly all the communities in the Arabian Peninsula as a whole, in which their history, political fate and responses have been shaped.

The impact of Wahhabism on those communities is best interpreted as a pursuit of dominance with an excessive use of religion as a pretext. We should not be misled by the dichotomy within Islam when we consider the tensions created by the Wahhabi movement in the Arabian Peninsula. Indeed, this movement afflicted nearly all Muslims in the Arabian Peninsula and elsewhere in the Islamic world.

Angelo Codevilla, a professor of international relations at Boston University, has realized that the war within Islam is more serious for Muslims than for the rest of the world, because the Wahhabi ideas imply irreconcilable enmity against other Muslims first, and then against others.[9]

In its early stages, the Wahhabi ideology was prone to violently reproducing the seventh-century model of Islamic *umma*. This daunting and ambitious pursuit was founded on a solid world view that the impurities and evil practices of the present Muslims need to be eradicated and replaced by the norms of true Islam, as comprehended and interpreted by the pious ancestors to whom the Wahhabis adhered, such as Imam 'Ahmad b. Hanbal, Shaikh al-Islam Ibn Taimiyya, Shaikh Ibn Qaim al-Jawziyya and others.

This ideology comprises two intertwined tendencies: first, the excommunication (*takfir*) of nearly all non-Wahhabi Muslims, let alone non-Muslims, which represents the world view of Wahhabism;[10] second, the radical change of the universe through a series of invasions with the aim of reviving the Islamic *umma*.

The al-Saud's state is thus founded on excommunicating the neighbouring communities in order to legitimate invading their lands, occupying their regions and confiscating their possessions. The tendency of expansionism, being inherent in Wahhabi ideology, is, by extension, also a feature of the Saudi regime.

In the conventional interpretation of Islamic tradition, war against associationists is a religious duty that must be carried out by the faithful people in order to implement God's *shariʿa* and to establish the Islamic *umma*.[11] Applied to the Wahhabi ideology, this principle could permit war to be waged against all Muslims of impure faith.

According to the Iraqi sociologist Ali al-Wardi, contrary to Ibn Sanad al-Basri's view that the Wahhabis' practice of excommunication (*takfir*), among other factors, led to their failure (i.e. in the second Saudi phase), this tendency created the legitimate pretext to invade and fight their adversaries, promising an abundance of booty that they had never dreamed of. Without such a pretext, the tribal Bedouin would not be tempted to embrace the *daʿwa*. According to al-Wardi, the *daʿwa* opened the way for the invasion of neighbouring regions instead of invading their own brethren, and this, according to religious teachings, allowed them to accumulate booty on earth in addition to the promised rewards in heaven.[12]

The ideology of conquest as I describe it here is associated with Shaikh Muhammad Ibn ʿAbdulwahab, who came from a remote region of Arabia, namely al-Durʿiyya village in Najd region. He was impressed by the alleged deviations from Islam of the Ottoman Sultans, Hijazi Sherifs, Shammar leaders of Hail and the Shiʿis in Hasa and Qatif. He wrote that Islam, above all, is a rejection of all gods except God, and a refusal to allow others to share in that worship that is due to God alone. *Shirk* (polytheism), he maintains, is evil no matter what the object, whether it be king or prophet or saint or tree or tomb. Thus the Wahhabi army destroyed the tombs of the Prophet's companions because they had become objects of veneration. Shaikh Ibn ʿAbdulwahhab claims that 'most of humanity is manipulated by Satan [...] It is clear that the earth is filled with major *shirk* and worship of idols (*authan*).[13]

Accordingly, Shaikh Ibn ʿAbdulwahhab instructed his followers to dissociate themselves psychologically and physically from the *jahili* society in which they lived and migrate to the alternative society that was about to be founded in al-Durʿiyya, its 'kernel' (*dar hijra wa Islam*), a land of migration and Islam. This implies that the fulfilment of Islam is conditional upon migration to the new society.[14] He clearly stated that 'migration is a religious duty, and is of the most good deeds, and is the cause of maintaining the religion of worshipper and preserving his faith'.[15]

For this, Najd was regarded as the land of migration (*hijra*), since a group of Muslims migrated to it and settled there following the dictates of the Imam. And those who settled in Najd were accredited as migrants (*muhajiroun*).[16] As we follow the implications of the term *hijra* and the context in which it was applied, we may find that *hijra* was a prelude and crucial step towards staging *jihad* where both *hijra* and *jihad* become intertwined. Indeed, the sequence of events clearly suggests that there could be no *jihad* without *hijra*.

With regard to the settlement (*hijra*), which implies migration from the land of *shirk* to the land of Islam, Shaikh ʿAbdulrahim al-Shaikh, a descendant of the founder of Wahhabism, states that:

> What needs to be learned is that as injustice and disobedience prevailed, almighty God has sanctioned migration for preserving [this] religion and securing the spirits of believers against evils not intermixing with the people of sins and disobediences, so to distinguish the people of obedience and faith from the denomination of decay and antagonism, and thus the banner of Islam would rise [...]. Without migration religion would neither be able to rise nor God to be worshipped; it is also impossible without migration to denounce *shirk*, oppression and evil.[17]

As a consequence, many of the followers of Shaikh Muhammad Ibn ʿAbdulwahab migrated to the new home and joined the nascent community of true believers where military campaigns were mobilized and unleashed against the neighbouring regions. This would not have been possible unless the founder of Wahhabism divided the world into two camps: the land of Islam (*dar Islam*) and the land of War (*dar harb*), that is, the land of *mushrikin* including nearly all Muslims, with the exception of his followers.

In response to a refutation of the Wahhabi *takfir* precepts by Dawood Bash, the Ottoman viceroy in Baghdad from 1817 to 1831, Imam Muhammad Ibn Sa'ud affirmed these precepts and labelled the Ottoman subjects *mushrikin* and *kuffar*.[18] Likewise, Shaikh Hamad b. 'Atiq (1812–1883), a renowned Wahhabi scholar during Faisal b. Turki's reign in the second Saudi phase, accused the two Holy Cities of Islam of *shirk*.[19]

Abd al-'Aziz b. Sa'ud, surprisingly, expressed a similar opinion regarding the inhabitants of Mecca, whom he regarded as *mushrikin*:

> Why, if you English were to offer me one of your daughters to wife, I would accept her, making only the condition that any children resulting from the marriage should be Moslems. But I would not take of the daughters of the Sharif or the people of Mecca or other Moslems whom we reckon as *mushrikin*. I would eat of meat slain by Christians without question. Ay, but it is the *mushrik*, he whose worship of God is sullied by association with others (e.g. objects or creatures apart from God), that is our abomination. As for Christians and Jews, they are 'People of the Book'.[20]

He also claims that:

> Praying to the *Ka'ba* or to the prophets and saints; harlotry; usury; and the various types of oppression and ignorance of the *sunna* are *bid'a* against the Qur'an and are to be found in the land of *shirk*. Even the person of meanest intelligence knows that this country is judged to be condemned as a land of *kufr* and *shirk* especially if they [its inhabitants] show hostility to the people of *tawhid* and are doing their best to eliminate them from the lands of Islam. This *shirk* does not come from the people of the town. It is said that this comes from pride or ignorance ... *Shirk* remained because of 'Amr b. Luhayy.[21]

It has become clear that *takfir* is combined with the concept of *jihad* and invasion, since *jihad* could be justifiable only by excommunicating the targeted communities.

The house of Sa'ud became the shelter of the Wahhabi version of Islam and it was upon this that they based their legitimacy. Thus Wahhabism became the state religion. It has been exploited against other creeds and regions for political reasons. Thus it could be argued that without Wahhabism, the Saudi royal family would not be legitimately ruling the present Saudi Arabia.

According to this evidence, the Wahhabi ideology of conquest is directed against nearly all Muslims, be they in the Arabian Peninsula or elsewhere. This ideology continued to be the instrument of mobilization throughout Saudi political history.

Impact of Wahhabism on the Shi'is

The Shi'is in Eastern Province are Twelver Shi'is who adhere to a designated line of succession from the Prophet Muhammad, starting with Ali, the son-in-law of the Prophet and extending to his ancestors through his son Hussain, who was martyred in Karbala in 61 AH. Their differences with the Wahhabi Sunni Muslims, who form the dominant group in the country, though not the majority of the population, are theological ones. The principal difference is over the doctrine of *tawhid*.

The main criticism levelled against the Shi'is is that they intermingle the worship of God with the veneration of saints, his servants. However, the actual dispute is over the issue of succession to the Prophet. The Wahhabi, like all Sunni Muslims, reject the Shi'is claims. This dispute caused a split between the Sunni Muslim and the Shi'is Muslims, leading to deep-rooted tensions between the Shi'is and both the Saudi state and its religious ally, the Wahhabi establishment.

Domestic tensions and sectarian unrest in Shi'ite areas began with the formation of a sectarian-based state in Najd. The Wahhabi–state alliance in 1744 between the Najdi ruler Muhammed Ibn Sa'ud and religious reformer Shaikh Muhammed Ibn Abdul Wahhab (b. 1703) led to the formulation of a state ideology.

The Shi'is in the oil-rich Eastern Province were subject to discriminatory measures. They were treated as second-class citizens and were deprived of their fundamental rights. Consequently, the Shi'is' sense of deprivation created what might be described as a unity of the deprived, which was subsequently exploited in oppositional activities against the Saudi regime.

Under the banner of al-Sa'ud, Wahhabism advocates the doctrine of *tawhid*, that is, the unity of God. In accordance with this doctrine, Shaikh Muhammad

Ibn 'Abdul al-Wahhab stresses the absolute devotion of servants to the worship of God. This entails dissociation between the creature and the Creator in terms of invocation (*tawassul*), veneration of saints (*taqdis al-awliya'*) and intercession (*shafa'a*). From the Wahhabi point of view, the practices of the majority of Muslims have been embroiled in polytheism, in the sense that they worshipped stones and trees.[22] Shaikh Ibn 'Abd al-Wahhab claims that, 'The first of those who introduced polytheism (*shirk*) into the *umma* were the *rafida* [the Wahhabis' pejorative term for the Shi'is] who invoke 'Ali and others to realize their needs and to alleviate their sufferings.' They consider this an ample justification for declaring *jihad* against their regions and confiscating their possessions and hence forcing them to embrace what they deemed the religion of the *sunna* and *jama'*, namely, those who followed and implemented the prophetic traditions of the Hanbali school.[23]

Spurred on by Shaikh Ibn 'Abdul Wahhab's teachings, the Najdi forces constantly launched raids on the eastern coast of the Arabian Peninsula.[24] From the Saudi standpoint, the invasion of al-Hasa in 1791 was, according to Wahhabi historian Ibn Ghannam, aimed at 'purging its regions of idols (*asnam*) and images (*authan*)'.[25] Consequently, the Saudi–Wahhabi conquerors destroyed Shi'is houses of worship (e.g. mosques and *hussainiya*s) as well as domed tombs and all other objects of Shi'is worship. The Wahhabi conqueror, Sa'ud the Great (*al-kabir*), gave his orders to impose a Wahhabi infrastructure and to 'launch comprehensive campaigns aimed at the indoctrination of the Shi'is population'.[26] Indeed, Sa'ud strove to implement the dictates of Wahhabi Islam by any means.

In 1801–02, the Saudi–Wahhabi forces expanded their military operations beyond the borders of the Arabian Peninsula and moved into Iraq. Sa'ud led the forces towards Karbala, the shrine city of the third Imam of the Shi'is, Hussain. According to the famous Saudi historian Ibn Bishr:

> The Muslims [Wahhabi–Saudi troops] headed towards Karbala where they gathered and scaled the walls of the city. They stormed the city and killed the majority of its inhabitants in markets and houses, and destroyed the dome built on what is claimed to be the tomb of Hussain. They also confiscated all possessions including money, weapons, clothes, furniture, gold and silver and so on. This booty was divided up and distributed among the troops.[27]

While there were relative lulls in the second Saudi realm (1824–91) owing to the general weakness of the state,[28] the sectarian attitude of the Saudi ruler, Turki (r. 1824–34), towards the Shi'is in al-Hasa remained unchanged. In order to gain the loyalty of the community in al-Hasa and consolidate his rule in the region, he attempted to pacify the Shi'is.[29] However, all evidence suggests that the Shi'is suffered heavy economic burdens as a result of high taxes imposed on their crops.[30]

During Faisal b. Turki's reign, Shaikh 'Abdulrahman b. Hassan Al al-Shaikh of the Wahhabi *'ulama* urged him to scrutinize the beliefs of the people of al-Ahsa and Qatif and investigate their Islam. He instructed him to force the Shi'is to comply with the teachings of Wahhabi Islam.[31]

With the rise of the third Saudi state in 1902, 'Abdul 'Aziz al-Sa'ud (best known as Ibn Sa'ud) expressed his desire to recapture al-Hasa and Qatif. Before the Saudi–Wahhabi raids, Ibn Sa'ud sent a letter to Qatif notables threatening them 'with an attack and with the destruction of lives, the plunder of properties and violation of their honour' if they attempted to hinder the advance of his forces. In response, the Shi'is of Qatif declared themselves inclined to submit peacefully and obey Ibn Sa'ud.[32] Shi'is notables and the *'ulama* in Qatif and al-Hasa sent a letter to the Turkish Deputy (*qa'im maqam*) in al-Hasa ordering him to surrender to Ibn Sa'ud.[33] According to a prominent Shi'is *mujtahid*, Shaikh Ali Abu al-Hassan al-Khunaizi (1874–1944),[34] the people of Qatif received convoys of Ibn Sa'ud headed by 'Abdul Rahman Ibn Sfwailim, who became the viceroy of Ibn Sa'ud in Qatif. Al-Khunaizi records that he entered al-Qatif 'like an absentee from his homeland, returning to it without fighting'.[35]

Although the Shi'is of al-Hasa and Qatif surrendered peacefully to Ibn Sa'ud's rule, they were repressed. At the outset, Ibn Sa'ud assembled the Shi'is *'ulama* of al-Hasa and told them that they should recognize him as their Amir and conform to Wahhabi precepts. Furthermore, he appointed a new governor for Qatif, and imposed four main terms on its residents, as follows:

1. The Shi'is of Qatif should concede in writing that Qatif belonged to the ancestors of Ibn Sa'ud.

2. Fourteen notables of Qatif should go and meet Ibn Sa'ud to pledge allegiance and to contribute money to him.

3. Each village in the Qatif region should offer ten men to join Ibn Sa'ud's forces when needed.

4. A ban on export of vegetables to Bahrain.[36]

In the face of the severe measures inflicted on them, the Shi'is 'ulama felt forced to compromise in order to survive as a socio-religious community, yet they seem to have attempted to assure the religious rights of the Shi'is. According to Shi'is sources, an agreement was worked out between Shaikh Mussa Abu Khamseen, a Shi'is religious leader in Al-Hasa, and Ibn Sa'ud, following the fall of al-Hasa in 1913. Ibn Sa'ud is said to have guaranteed the religious freedom of the Shi'is in exchange for loyalty and obedience to his rule.[37] Although the agreement is neither preserved in document form nor acknowledged by the sons of Ibn Sa'ud, there is consensus among the Shi'is 'ulama and notables regarding the main issues upon which both sides agreed.

Nevertheless, the Shi'is population were subjected once more to systematic persecution and coercive Wahhabi proselytism at the hands of Ibn Sa'ud's ideological army, the *ikhwan*. The Shi'is had not been, according to Ibn Sa'ud's testimony, allowed to hold religious readings in their *hussainiyas*. Penalties of the severest nature had been imposed on those who disobeyed, and the *ikhwan* murdered several unfortunate Baharinahs men of the Shi'ish community of Qatif.[38]

Contrary to Ibn Sa'ud's allegations that the Shi'is' religious and economic conditions had been alleviated after 1922, a Shi'is petition in March 1923 shows that the religious freedom that the people of al-Hasa and Qatif had enjoyed before the occupation of al-Hasa was ended. This is also evident in their appeal to British personnel at that time to exercise influence on Ibn Sa'ud to 'stop religious molestation against the Shi'is'.[39] Furthermore, a British official source in February 1924 states that on more than one occasion in 1923 there were 'distinct signs of considerable discontent with his [Ibn Sa'ud's] rule, particularly among the merchants of Hassa' as a result of 'oppressive taxation'.[40]

Fatwa of 1927

Shortly after the annexation of the Hijaz and the completion of his geographical expansion in the Arabian Peninsula, Ibn Sa'ud's relationship with the *ikhwan* began to deteriorate drastically. The *ikhwan* leaders felt that they no longer were the chosen warriors and the sword of Islam, as Ibn Sa'ud used to describe them, and thus they should 'return loot taken or make restitution'.[41] The leaders decided to rise up against Ibn Sa'ud. In 1926 a conference was held in al-'Artawiyya attended by the leaders of the *ikhwan* from Mutair, 'Utaibah and 'Ajman tribes, the backbone of Ibn Sa'ud's army. They reached an agreement to espouse God's religion and to declare *jihad* against the infidels in the neighbouring countries. At this conference, the *ikhwan* overtly voiced their criticisms of Ibn Sa'ud. Among other grievances, they charged him with 'failing to force the Shi'is of al-Hasa and al-Qatif to adhere to the religion of the *sunna* and *jama'*, the Wahhabi Islam'.[42]

In response, Ibn Sa'ud returned to Najd from the Hijaz to meet *ikhwan* leaders and chiefs in Riyadh in January 1927. He reaffirmed his devotion to the *shari'a* and his commitment to implement it. The meeting ended with the issuance of a *fatwa* by the *'ulama,* in which the *ikhwan*'s prime objections were dealt with. With regard to the Shi'is of al-Hasa, the *fatwa* stated that:

> The *rafida* of the Hasa be obliged to surrender to true Islam and should abandon all their defective religious rites. We asked the Imam, Ibn Sa'ud, to order his viceroy in al-Hasa, Ibn Jiluwi, to summon the Shi'is to Shaikh Ibn Bishr, before whom they should undertake to follow the religion of God and his Prophet and to cease the invocation of the saintly members of Ahl al Bayt, and to abandon other innovations in their public assemblies, and to conform to the rule of prayer five times daily in the mosque. Prayer callers (*mu'dhin*) are to be sent. The people are also to study the three principles of the Wahhabi tenets; their houses of worship are to be destroyed and those that object to this will be exiled.
>
> With regard to the Shi'is of Qatif, we have advised the Imam to send missionaries and preachers to certain districts and villages, which have come under the control of the true Moslems and in which *shari'a* laws should be put in effect.[43]

In contrast to the view that the *fatwa* was never implemented,[44] numerous reports confirm that serious measures were inflicted on the Shi'is in an attempt to force them to follow the dictates of the Wahhabi *'ulama* in accordance with the stipulations of the *fatwa*. According to the India Office Records, the

Shi'is of Qatif sent a letter on 20 July 1927 to the deputy ruler of Bahrain, complaining of their treatment at the hands of Ibn Sa'ud, who forced them at prayer times to follow one of the Imams whom they called a 'boy'.[45] Further, a petition signed by over 500 men[46] was addressed to the Shaikh of Bahrain, Hamad Ibn 'Isa al-Khalifah, in June 1927. According to the petitioners, 'Abdul 'Aziz bin Sa'ud has, unfortunately, brought pressure to bear upon us which cannot be tolerated and to persecute us in a manner unprecedent [sic]'. The petitioners implored the ruler of Bahrain to protect them from 'their evils and to ward off their molestation', asserting that they had lost 'religious freedom and might lose [...] rights and property as well'.[47] In the hope of appeasing the *ikhwan* leaders, Ibn Sa'ud had sent a legion of Wahhabi preachers among the Shi'is of al-Hasa to oblige them to conform to Wahhabi Islam.[48]

The far-reaching implications of the *fatwa* need to be highlighted. One was that it reaffirmed the standardization of the alliance between Muhammad Ibn Sa'ud and Shaikh Ibn 'Abdul Wahhab. In other words, the *fatwa* was deeply rooted in the legitimating ideology of Saudi rule, meaning the preservation of Wahhabi doctrinal aims. According to the *fatwa*, Ibn Sa'ud's rule should be based on a set of clearly perceived aims, especially the emphasis on *tawhid* and denouncing the practices of the polytheists. This implies that the legitimacy of Ibn Sa'ud's rule relied primarily on how he treated the polytheists, particularly the Shi'is. According to the Wahhabi activists in the last two decades, the legitimacy of Saudi rule rests, in practice, on its position toward the Shi'is.

Two examples of those who challenged the legitimacy of Saudi rule will help explain the paramount importance of the *fatwa* in this connection. First, Juhiman al-'Utaibi, the leader of the Holy Mosque revolt in November–December 1979, wrote a treatise entitled *Al'imara wa al-bay'a wa al-ta'a* (Rulership, Allegiance and Obedience), in which he excoriated the Saudi rulers for 'harboring the polytheists, the Shi'is and the Rafida'. He condemned the Saudi rulers who like to call their state 'the state of *tawhid*'. 'It unites the Muslims with the Christians and polytheists; it recognizes their religions, like *rawafid* [the Shi'is]; it fights those who disagree with them; and kills those who kill the *mushrikin* who invoke Ali and Hussain'. He revived the *ikhwan*'s prime grievance, namely, preventing 'The propagation of *tawhid* in neighboring regions, notably in Iraq, where Mushrikfn invoke Ali, Fatimah, Hassan and Hussain'.[49]

Second, in 1993 a memo was sent by Shaikh Nasir al-'Omar, an eminent neo-Salafi activist, to the Committee of the Senior 'Ulama (*hai'at kibar al-*

'ulama) concerning 'The penetration of the Shi'is in all spheres of the state of the two holy mosques'. This memo attempted to draw the attention of the government to the alleged increased prominence of the Shi'is in education, trade, agriculture and missionary activities. As we are going to refer to this memo in the following chapters, it is necessary to indicate that it aims to remind both the 'ulama and the government that a tolerant stance towards the Shi'is would inevitably endanger the legitimacy of Saudi rule.[50] Shaikh al-'Omar denounces the Shi'is as follows:

> They demand recognition of Shi'ism as a legitimate judicial school, call for freedom of religion and sanctity of their religious places, demand the right to build *hussainiya*s, to teach Shi'ism in their schools, to publish Shi'is books, and for the government to end the state's campaign against Shi'ism.[51]

Clearly, one criterion by which government actions are judged is how devoted it would be to enforcing Wahhabi doctrines in the conquered regions. However, the willingness of the Saudi rulers was always restrained by the fierce resistance of the non-Wahhabis, notably the Shi'is.

Faced with rising murmurings in Shi'is regions, Ibn Sa'ud decided to repeal the new religious sanctions imposed on the Shi'is[52] and ultimately the Wahhabi *mutawwi'yn* (or *mataw'a* in Saudi popular terms) were ordered to withdraw from Qatif. The Shi'is *mujtahid*s, in return, issued a *fatwa* 'Decreeing that the Shi'is in Qatif should obey King Abdul 'Aziz and that the use of force against them be prohibited'.[53] This *fatwa* was issued following the eruption of a revolt in al-'Awamiyya village led by a *mujtahid*, Shaikh Muhammed al-Nemr, in 1928.[54]

As a result, the *fatwa* could be considered as a legitimating tool that encouraged the Wahhabi community to inflict discrimination and hardship on the Shi'is, since they dominated the government apparatus. The *fatwa* legitimated physical attacks by the *mutawwi'yn* to prevent the Shi'is from practising their religious ceremonies and rites.

Religious and Political Ends

Perhaps the majority of the scholars of Saudi Arabia incline to distinguish between two clearly divergent lines within the Saudi realm, particularly in regard to attitudes towards the Shi'is. The *ikhwan* insisted on using all possible means to impose the Wahhabi version of Islam on their subjects and to prevent the Shi'is from conducting their religious rites both privately and publicly. Ibn Saud and his cousin Ibn Jiluwi, whom he appointed the first governor of Hasa, sought to pursue a different policy.[55] According to Jacob Goldberg, the attitude towards the Shi'is in Hasa fluctuated between these two positions, reflecting an ongoing struggle, both political and ideological, between Ibn Saud and the *ikhwan*.[56] This has also been manifested in the open confrontation in 1926 and related incidents thereafter.

Goldberg's analysis could help justify the Saudi political standing rather than explain it. The extent to which the Saudi rulers implemented the demands posed by the *ikhwan* was greatly dependent upon the political aims of the Saudi rulers. Thus, the distinction between the latter and the *ikhwan* and, by extension, the Wahhabi *'ulama* reflects the disparate approaches to the Shi'is question. In the context of the *fatwa*, the Wahhabi religious community appeared to have opted for a more radical policy to be imposed on the Shi'is, meaning that they either fused into the Wahhabi body or were totally uprooted from the country. On the other hand, Ibn Sa'ud, being more politically motivated, favoured a kind of policy that would consolidate his rule, a calmer policy that would not cause internal and external tensions. He tried both the carrot and the stick. Although such a policy did not satisfy the Wahhabi senior *'ulama*, it formed the basis for the systematic persecution of the Shi'is in later periods.

Moreover, it has been repeatedly argued that the Wahhabi *'ulama* are the main driving force behind the persecution of the Shi'is.[57] This view, indeed, could serve the Saudi rulers, who like to be absolved of any responsibility for the grievances of the Shi'is, the blame for which – in Shi'is *'ulama* eyes – they have consistently placed on the Wahhabi *'ulama*.[58]

Here we turn to the balance of power between the Wahhabi *'ulama* and the Saudi rulers throughout the three Saudi realms. It is apparent that in the third state, 'the Wahhabis' use of the Sa'uds became far less important than the Sa'ud use of the Wahhabis'.[59] Thus, it could be argued that Ibn Sa'ud has played a primary role in the radicalization of the *ikhwan* in order to achieve his political ends. For this, he instilled in the *ikhwan* a hatred of the Shi'is. This view seems to have been adopted by the British personnel in the Persian Gulf. A memorandum to the Political Resident in the Persian Gulf on 18 February 1924 states that:

> Although bin Sa'ud has in the past always represented himself as being
> the only restraining influence on these wild tribesmen [the *ikhwan*], in
> actual fact he lost no opportunity to encourage fanaticism, as it kept the
> *ikhwan* together and constituted his strength.[60]

This is also evident in the heated debate between Ibn Sa'ud and *ikhwan* leaders
Sultan Ibn Humaid and Faisal al-Dwaish, which took place in March 1929.
The *ikhwan* leaders reminded Ibn Sa'ud of the fact that he stated that Iraq as
a Shi'is state 'must ultimately be destroyed, and that everything taken from
her people is halal'.[61] Ameen Rihani asked Ibn Sa'ud whether he deemed it
a religious duty to declare war against *mushrikin*. Ibn Sa'ud denied it and
mentioned the Shi'is as an example.[62] Taking both these examples into account,
it would be a plausible conclusion that Ibn Sa'ud's harsh attitude towards the
Shi'is is anchored in the Wahhabi tenets.

Politics of Sectarian Discrimination

Many students of Saudi Arabia agree that the Shi'is in Saudi Arabia were and
still are on the lowest rung of the country's economic and social scale, and were
always victims of systematic discrimination.

Before considering the various forms of discrimination inflicted on the
Shi'is in Eastern Province, we need to review the socio-economic and religious
conditions of the Shi'is. These conditions have no doubt played a very
important role in the process of politicization and political activism among
them and have created an atmosphere in which Shi'is opposition originated.
In order to understand the Saudi politics of discrimination towards the Shi'is,
we need to focus briefly on two major sources, religion and state.

Some might argue that Islam is the key factor contributing to the
discriminatory policy against the Shi'is. This is a misunderstanding. The fact
is that the dominant group within the Saudi state is unwilling to recognize
religious plurality in the country and thus puts the rights of the Shi'is and
the non-Wahhabi Sunnis at risk. The alleged belief is that Wahhabis represent
al-firqa al-najiya (the Saved Faction) and the true Islam encourages them
to monopolize power and wealth in the country, whereas the Shi'is are
to be denied the status of Muslims and are thus liable to be politically and
economically downgraded.

It could be argued that the Saudi kingdom has been created to represent minority interests (al-Sa'ud and the Wahhabi community). The population is divided into underprivileged and overprivileged groups; this would happen only in the absence of a legal framework that would ensure individual liberties and group rights. In a country like Saudi Arabia, individuals and groups do not always rely upon the law to achieve and secure their interests, partly because the state has failed to transform itself into a state of law or, in other words, an actual guarantor of the rights of individuals and groups. Rather, they would invoke other illegal means to attain and maintain their own rights. Consequently, discrimination varies from one area to another and from one group to another, and also from one segment to another within the same group. For example, discrimination against Imami Shi'is in Saudi Arabia varies from Qatif to al-Hasa and to Medina. The Shi'is in Qatif, for example, perform their religious ceremonies in 'Ashura; their preachers wear religious dress; the prayer caller (mu'adhin) pronounces the third testimony, namely ''ashhadu 'anna 'aliyan waliu allah' (I certify that Ali is God's Viceregent). The Shi'is in al-Hasa, on the other hand, avoid the third testimony and their preachers eschew wearing the traditional turban ('emma' or 'emama). As for the Imami Shi'is in Medina, the picture is entirely different. Their mosques and hussainiyas were destroyed.[63] Moreover, they are denied the right to 'Proclaim their faith or to perform their rituals openly; they may not declare their call to prayer, and must not wear the traditional turban.'[64] They were also prohibited from constructing mosques or hussainiyas; rather, they were allowed to assemble for prayer only in a so-called majlis or sala (hall).[65]

The varying degrees of discrimination may correspond with the constraints imposed upon the Shi'is in these regions by the Saudi authorities. In order to obtain rights not given by the state, the Shi'is had to resort to options that were not necessarily recognized by the state or enshrined in state rules.

The failure of the state to extinguish potential divisions and discriminatory attitudes among the groups constituting the population of the Saudi state stimulated some disadvantaged groups (e.g. the Shi'is) to make use of social protest to attain their goals. Indeed, the Saudi state's affirmative action against the probable internal rivals, notably the Shi'is and the Hijazis, contributed to reproducing religious, social and political differences around the country. This is vividly reflected in the symbolic language of the people, which reflects the hierarchical order in the country. In one version of this symbolic language, the economic and political status of regions comprising the Saudi state is classified in accordance with the telephone area codes, as follows: Central Province (01), Western Province (02), Eastern Province (03) and so on. Another categorization is based on sect, using the local electric voltage. The Shi'is are typed as 110 volts whereas the Sunnis are typed as 220 volts. These measures indicate that the Shi'is are placed in the lowest stratum of Saudi society. Both examples exhibit the discriminatory politics adopted by the Saudi regime, in terms of financial and budgetary allocations and public appointments. Najd receives the greatest proportion of public and government funds allocations.[66]

Economic Deprivation

Robert Lacey maintains that, 'If the Eastern Province had never been conquered by the Al Sa'ud, its massive oil wealth would have made it a prosperous state in its own right – richer than any other country around the Persian Gulf.'[67] However, according to a report issued by the Minnesota Lawyers International Human Rights Committee in 1996:

> The Eastern Province is one of the most impoverished regions in Saudi Arabia. Compared to other regions in Saudi Arabia, the government has spent less on construction projects, roads, medicine and education in the Eastern Region [...] Shanties were commonplace until the early 1980s, and Shi'is cities and towns still lack the modern medical facilities available in cities like Riyadh and Jidda. It was not until 1987 that the Saudi Government built al-Qatif Hospital – the first modern hospital in the Eastern Province.[68]

With the advent of the oil era, notably following the rapid increase in oil prices in 1973, the Shi'is, along with their regions Qatif and Hasa, have become economically powerless. They have experienced long-standing persecution at the hands of their rulers. The economic calamity of the Shi'is in Eastern Province has been a major source of tension and confrontation between the Shi'is and the Saudi regime since 1913. The occupation of al-Hasa led to a drastic deterioration in the economic conditions of the Shi'is. During Ibn Sa'ud's reign, the Shi'is suffered greatly from a harsh taxation policy.[69]

Although that socio-economic equality among groups does not exist anywhere, some argue that the degree of inequality can range from severe to relatively mild.[70] The recruitment of a large number of Shi'is into the oil industry should be carefully assessed. The decision to recruit Shi'is appears to have taken into account the rudimentary infrastructure of the state, namely, the lack of transport, poor communications and harsh living conditions, all of which discouraged many people from migrating to the oil areas.

What should be emphasized is that, although the Shi'is constituted about 50 per cent of Aramco's workforce until the 1970s,[71] they never felt that they were benefiting from the oil wealth as much as their compatriots, the Sunni majority.[72] They were excluded from occupying high-ranking positions equal to their Sunni counterparts. Although some Shi'is workers have acquired long-term experience in the oil industry and contributed to the development of Aramco's producing and trading capacity, they were, with very rare exceptions, debarred from reaching high managerial levels in the company.[73]

While the Shi'is were and still are, with rare exceptions, excluded from fields such as the armed forces, the National Guard, security and even civil aviation, Aramco was the major employer of the Shi'is. Aramco's 'colour-blind' employment policy was not, as might be claimed, based on moral principles but merely on necessity. According to a former chairman of the company, 'It did not specifically favour the employment of Shi'is, but simply resorted to the only convenient source of domestic labour.'[74]

However, it should be said that before the process of 'Saudization' began in 1982, sectarian factors were not detectable in the allocation of jobs in the administrative body of Aramco. There were two reasons for this. First, the American-based management has generally speaking adhered to relatively unbiased criteria regarding the allocation of jobs, promotion and relocations. Second, the rise in state revenues before 1982 had little effect on the Shi'is in terms of economic discrimination, in the sense that the Shi'is hitherto had benefited from the economic boom in the country, though not equal to the Wahhabi Najdis or to Sunnis in the country as a whole.

In recent years, tribal as well as religious factors played a strong role in allocations of jobs in Aramco. Individuals from certain tribes such as Qahtan and 'Utaiba or from the Wahhabi sect have had preference. The Shi'is mainly benefit from official and virtually institutionalized indifference, for example in the banking sector. The reason is that Wahhabis are prevented by their religion from working in this sector. The Wahhabi *'ulama* regard banking transactions as contravening the *shari'a* because they are based on interest.[75]

Apparently, the Shi'is have sought equality as a solution to their problem with the government, but their quest for equality particularly with the Wahhabi Najdis is thwarted. The Wahhabis regard the Shi'is as inferior to the People of the Book (*ahl al-Kitab*), such as the Christians and Jews, who enjoy a special place because they are monotheists, whereas the Shi'is are believed to be heretics or apostates.

Consequently, most of the Shi'is are on the middle and lower rungs of the Saudi socio-economic ladder. Their areas are distressed and suffer from the minimal infrastructure needed for any community, while other areas, notably the Wahhabi ones, have flourished rapidly on economic, urban and industrial levels.

According to a *fatwa* issued by Shaikh Muhammad Ibn Ibrahim, the Shi'is, deprived of the status accorded to the Sunnis, are forever excluded from receiving state booty (*fay*), and the ruler should not allocate any portion to them whatsoever unless they overtly abandon their beliefs.[76]

The discovery of oil in Shi'is regions added new elements to the discriminatory policy against the Shi'is in Eastern Province. Kostiner has noted that 'the newly acquired oil revenues were not shared fairly with Shi'is communities'.[77] While Aramco transformed most of the country into prosperous and flourishing areas, the Shi'is towns lagged behind. Owing to insufficient budgetary expenditure and long-term investment, the towns and villages of Hasa and Qatif remained neglected and underdeveloped in contrast with towns like Dammam, Jubail and Khubar.[78]

Until the late 1970s, Shi'is areas suffered from the lack of both an appropriate infrastructure and basic public services – decent schools, hospitals, clinics, paved roads, sewage, in addition to poor electrification and water supplies. Some of their most serious grievances related to provision in education, employment and health services. Shi'is petitions show that these grievances date back to the late 1940s.[79] The disproportionate lack of Shi'is appointments in education and health services appears to have nourished a sense of resentment among them that has lasted until the present time.

In this context, we should bear in mind that the period 1974–82 was the golden era of the welfare state in Saudi Arabia, when a sharp increase in oil revenues was coupled with a relatively small population.

However, the Shi'is' petitions cast great emphasis on the role of Ibn Jiluwi, the often harsh governor of the al-Hasa province,[80] who blocked the development of Shi'i areas. When the Five Year Plans started in 1970, the government allocated less money for public services and urban infrastructure to the Shi'i towns than to the Sunni ones. According to a Shi'i petition presented to Crown Prince Fahad (the former king) in 1977, the Shi'i notables alluded obliquely to Ibn Jiluwi's role, saying, 'If there is one of the officialdom who holds power but does not want good for us, who makes us suffer [...] then we have bestowed our hope on the sons of King Abdul Aziz, particularly King Khalid and your highness'.[81]

During the *intifada* of November–December 1979, a famous caricature was circulated showing a vast camel standing across the country: it was feeding in the east, it was being milked by a merchant in the west, and the milk was being handed to a slothful character sitting in the middle, namely Najd.[82]

Religious Discrimination

The general attitude of the Saudi government and the religious establishment derived from the religious stance of the Wahhabi sect towards the Shi'is, who were denied the status of Muslims.

A number of instances illustrate the religious restrictions that were imposed upon the Shi'is. The Shi'is are not allowed officially to become butchers, as this work 'must be peformed by a true Muslim', according to a *fatwa* issued by the Committee of the Religious Jurisdiction and Guidance. Meat and chicken prepared by Shi'is butchers is conisdered *haram* and not to be eaten, since the slaughter 'was not done by a Muslim, whereas the Shi'is are apostates and *mushrikin*'.[83] By the same token, the Shi'is are not to be married to Muslims, because the Qur'an states that a Muslim may marry a non-Muslim woman who is from *ahl al-Kitab*, but she cannot marry other non-Muslims, namely the Shi'is.[84]

These *fatwas* were widely repeated and circulated within the Wahhabi community. Shaikh Abdullah Ibn Jibrin, a member of the Senior *'ulama* Council, stated that, 'The sheep slaughtered by a *rafidi* [a Shi'i person] is not considered *halal,* as the *rafida* in general are *mushrikin* associationists.[85] Many documented reports show that serious efforts were made to put the *fatwa* into effect.[86] Indeed, the Minister of Municipal Affairs, Ibrahim al-'Anghari, issued a decree based on directives from the former Grand Mufti, Shaikh Ibn Baz, ordering that all municipalities and state councils throughout the country must undertake legal slaughtering, which must not be performed by the *rafida* and Qadiyaniyah.[87]

In a pamphlet entitled 'A Hundred Questions and Answers about Charitable Activity', sponsored by the Islamic Rescue Bureau (*Hay'at al-Ighatha al-Islamiyya*), al-Hasa directed a question to Shaikh Abdullah Ibn Jibrin about help for the needy among the innovators (*al-mubtadi'un*). In the pamphlet, which has been widely circulated in a predominantly Shi'is region, the Hasa, Shaikh Ibn Jibrin comments:

> It is not allowed [for a Muslim] to help the innovators unless they rid themselves of their defective beliefs; if they belong to the Rafida who do not accept the advice to relinquish their bad deeds and insist, instead, on declaring *kufr* against the Companions [...], then they should thus not be supported.[88]

Another example is a four-volume work printed inside Saudi Arabia in 1996 by Nasir b. Abdulakarim al-'Aqil, a prominent religious scholar and preacher and a senior lecturer in theology at Imam Muhammad b. Sa'ud University in Riyadh. The work contains a variety of accusations, attacks and harsh criticisms, but what is noticeable is the denial to the Shi'is of the status of Muslims. 'The Shi'is have departed from the [Muslim] community in terms of doctrine and practice'.[89] These accusations were repeated by 'Abud b. Ali b. Dere, a Wahhabi lecturer at the College of Shari'a and the Islamic Principles, which is affiliated with Imam Muhammad b. Sa'ud University. The author labelled the Shi'is a deviant faction, characterized by extremism, violence and terrorism.[90]

In addition to these examples, we note that the religious rights of the Shi'is are denounced, for example, they are not allowed to perform religious practices, to build mosques and *hussainiya*s, to publish or import religious books, and so on.

In this regard, three major issues are to be highlighted: education, legal affairs and religious culture.

The vital field of education falls within the scope of the missionary project of Wahhabism, which regards the country as a whole as an area for Wahhabi proselytism, in which all groups should be assimilated into the the Wahhabi sect. The Saudi regime has exploited education to this end. The Shi'is have been deprived of the right to teach in schools on the basis of their religion. In a letter to the minister of education on 15 May 1966, the Grand Mufti, Shaikh Muhammad Ibn Ibrahim, expressed his deep concern that some Shi'is individuals were assuming teaching posts in the schools of Medina. He appealed to the minister to verify the news before action was taken.[91]

The Shi'is students in government schools are obliged to learn Wahhabi doctrine, which overtly and harshly denounces the Shi'is. A government-issued textbook entitled *Tarikh al-Dawla al-Islamiyya* (The History of the Islamic State), taught to students at secondary school, defines Shi'ism as 'a renegade denomination in which conspirators against Islam take refuge.'[92] In another textbook entitled *Kitab al-Tawhid* (The Book of Monotheism), taught to eleventh-graders in government schools, the author stresses that, 'The people of Sunna and Jama' condemn the *Rawafid* [the Shi'is] whose doctrine was the first innovation [*bida*] in Islam.' Shi'is children are taught that their 'sect arose at the hands of hypocrites and atheists to undermine Islam and to defame the Prophet.'[93] Simultaneously, the Saudi authorities banned the publication of a refutation of this book written by a Shi'i scholar, Shaikh 'Abd al-hadi al-Fadli.[94]

Another textbook entitled *al-Thaqafah al-Islamiyya* (The Islamic Culture), taught to the fourth-graders in the state-owned King Abdul 'Aziz University in Jeddah, defines Shi'ism as being 'the shelter for those who aim to destroy Islam, or who endeavour to introduce the tenets of Jews, Christians, Zoroastrians and Hindus into Islam.'[95] Some Shi'is students who attempted to refute the accusations at the conclusion of a lecture in which this textbook was read were imprisoned.[96]

It should be remembered that religious education represents a substantial part of the government schools' curriculum and Wahhabi doctrines are taught in local schools and universities. The teaching of Shi'is literature and history, by contrast, is banned even in schools that are predominantly Shi'is. Furthermore, the Shi'is are denied the right to have religious schools (*hawzas*) or to conduct educational programmes to teach Shi'is doctrines to their children. The Mubaraz Hawza, which had been illegally and secretly operating since 1983, was closed down in the late 1990s, and some of its teachers and students were arrested.

In legal matters, the Shi'is' legal codes and practices were abandoned shortly after the occupation of al-Hasa in 1913. According to Article 6 of the 1926 constitutional instrument, all rules that did not conform to Hanbali legal precepts would be abandoned. Shi'i as well as other Sunni legal codes were officially disapproved. And in 1928, the Supreme Judicial Council of the country passed a resolution to ensure that courts in civil transactions comply with Hanbali sources.[97]

Although the Shi'is judges in Qatif and al-Hasa operating during the Ottoman rule were reappointed after the occupation of the region, their authority had been circumscribed and they lacked equal footing in the judiciary. Until the late 1960s, the state banned Shi'is judges (*qudat*) from engaging in jurisdictional matters publicly, and they were thus compelled to use their houses for the purpose without any financial commitment from the Saudi authorities. Moreover, they were not authorized to produce judicial opinions inferred from the four Shi'i general principles (Qur'an, Sunna, Consensus and Reason), which are not recognized by the state.

During King Khalid's reign (1975–82) a royal decree was issued sanctioning the establishment of a Shi'i court, though it was limited to such matters as endowments, inheritance, marriage and divorce. However, the court's deeds had to be verified and approved by the Wahhabi legal courts (*al-mahakim al-shari'iya*) in order to verify whether these deeds were or were not 'identical with the Islamic *shari'a*'.[98] Several petitions sent to the king and high-ranking princes seeking a broader authority for Shi'i judges met with a lukewarm reception from the royal family. In fact, the subsequent restrictions on the Shi'i judicial authority suggest that both the royal family and the religious establishment were inclined to abandon Shi'i courts altogether.[99]

Moreover, the Shi'is have no legal status comparable to the Sunnis, particularly the Wahhabis. The legal system treats the Shi'is differently from the Wahhabis in that the testimony of a Shi'i, who is regarded as a heretic by the Wahhabi religious establishment, is discounted in Saudi courts of law. In the case of a dispute between a Shi'i and a Sunni, the Shi'i testimony will be rejected, whereas the Sunni's will be taken as valid.[100]

The Saudi authorities have suppressed Shi'i cultural symbols and practices, religious ceremonies and historical legacy. The general sense among the Shi'is is that the regime is deliberately aiming to eliminate all traces of Shi'i culture.[101]

The governors of al-Hasa have persistently declined the Shi'i petitions in which they seek permission to maintain mosques and *hussainiyas*.[102] Nearly all Shi'i mosques and *hussainiyas*, although funded by the Shi'is, are considered illegal by the Saudi authorities and some have been destroyed or closed down during the last two decades.[103] Until recently, the Shi'is have been prevented from openly performing their religious activities.

Because of the severe building restrictions, many Shi'is in the 1980s and 1990s employed devious means to obtain building permits for mosques and *hussainiyas*, passing them off as wedding halls or community centres.[104]

By contrast, a report issued by the ministry of endowments for the year 1418/19 (1998–9) mentions that there are 37,850 mosques (*masjid*) and 3215 prayer houses (*musala*) in the country, nearly all of them funded by the government.[105] Furthermore, the head of the ministry's branch and the sponsor of the mosques in the Eastern Province acknowledges that the ministry 'supervises 4000 mosques and prayer houses in Eastern Province'.[106]

In addition, the Saudi government has financed the construction of 1510 other mosques around the world, including in Western Europe and the United States,[107] whereas Shi'i mosques number fewer than 150 in Eastern Province, all of them privately funded. Shi'is prayer callers (*mu'dhin*) are not allowed to perform their own prayer call (*'adhan*) on threat of severe punishment, according to a decree issued by the religious police.[108]

Many more examples of cultural discrimination could be given. A royal decree was issued during King Faisal's reign prohibiting the appellation of Abdul Hussain, Abdul Rasoul or Abd Ali. Those who already bore such names were obliged to change them.[109]

Shi'a religious culture is banned in Saudi Arabia. Shi'is religious books and audio cassettes are not allowed into the country; those caught possessing such items are arrested and charged a fine on each book.[110] According to a report issued on 10 August 1989 by Amnesty International, Zahra Habib al-Naser, a 40-year-old woman, died as a result of torture. She had been arrested at the Saudi-Jordanian frontier when the Saudi police found a photograph of Ayatullah Khomeini and a Shi'is prayer book in her possession.[111]

The Shi'is are also not allowed to publish books on their history, culture and religious leaders. In the mid-1960s, the Saudi government condemned a Shi'i scholar, Shaikh Abd Allah al-Khunaizi, to death for writing a polemical book about the Prophet's uncle, Abu Talib. Against the common Sunni belief, the author, like most Shi'is, is of the opinion that Abu Talib embraced Islam and became a sincere believer of the Prophet's message. The book, *Abu Talib Mu'min Quraish* (Abu Talib: The Quraish's Believer), seems to have provoked the Wahhabi *'ulama*, who denounced the author and sanctioned his death for contravening Islamic doctrine.[112] Although the death penalty was abandoned following the mediation of the Iranian Shah, the publisher was ordered to cease circulating the book.

The Shi'is are normally permitted to carry out religious ceremonies in 'Ashura and Ramadan, yet many Shi'is preachers and activists are liable to be imprisoned or interrogated following the conclusion of each religious occasion.[113] While Shi'is preachers are harshly treated by the security police (al-mabahith) and debarred from refuting the accusations against the Shi'is doctrines, the Wahhabi 'ulama and preachers have the exclusive freedom to decry, disown and excommunicate the Shi'is publicly. According to a fatwa issued in September 1987 by the Permanent Committee for Scientific Research and Jurisdiction (Al-Lajna al-Da'ima lil Buhuth al-'Ilmiyya wa al-'Efta'), 'a Muslim is prohibited from following the Imami Shi'is, the Zaiydis and other similar people of innovations ('ahl al-bida')'.[114]

Yet more worrying is the Wahhabi 'ulama labelling the Shi'is as murtadin (apostates), which in itself legitimates waging war against them and expropriating their properties. In October 1991, a member of the Committee of Senior 'ulama, Shaikh Abdul Allab b. Abdul Rahman al-Jabrin, issued a fatwa prompting the Saudi rulers to slaughter the Shi'is because they are equivalent to apostates.[115]

Successive reports issued by Human Rights Watch confirm that the government discourages religious freedom and practices. The organization stated in 2001:

> The government heavily restricted religious freedom and actively discouraged religious practices other than the Wahhabi interpretation of the Hanbali school of Sunni Islam [...] The mutawwi'yn also policed the public display of religious icons and public worship or practice of religions other than Wahhabi Islam [...] Official intolerance extended to alternative interpretations of Islam, and members of Saudi religious minorities continued to be harassed or detained for the peaceful practice of their faith. Shi'is Muslims [...] faced discrimination in employment as well as limitations on religious practices. Shi'is jurisprudence books were banned, the traditional annual Shi'is mourning procession of 'Ashura was discouraged, and operating independent Islamic religious establishments remained illegal.[116]

Reports in 2002 and 2003 assert that the human rights record on freedom of expression and religious freedom remained unchanged, noting (2003), 'The government did not respect the rights of religious minorities in the kingdom, whether these communities were Saudi or expatriate'.[117]

Political Exclusion

According to A. M. Thernstrom, the effect of discrimination is '[n]othing more than a disproportionately low number of minority officeholders'.[118]

The Shiʿis are under-represented in the upper echelons of government, notably ministerial and ambassadorial offices.[119] They are also not employed by state armed forces or state security bodies. Indeed, the Shiʿis are excluded from nearly all administrative positions. In the Eastern Province, where they represent the majority of the indigenous population, the Shiʿis are barred from positions such as that of a governor in a town, village or even settlement (*hijra*), head of a municipality or police station or dean of a department in a state-owned university; Shiʿis in al-Hasa are even prevented from holding positions such as deputy headmaster in an elementary school.[120]

Their lack of political power lies at the heart of integration. Allowing the Shiʿis to share power in government and enjoy a certain degree of autonomy are considerations that have never concerned state policy makers, and as a result the Shiʿis have remained politically estranged. Indeed, as there is a close connection between political integration and loyalty to the state, their integration could be regarded as the measure of the extent to which the Shiʿis are loyal to the state.

The inclusion of a Shiʿi member in the long-awaited *majlis al-shūra* (established in March 1992) was interpreted by R. H. Dekmejian as a 'tacit recognition of the Shiʿis'.[121] Furthermore, he calls the inclusion of two Shiʿi appointees in the 1997 *majlis* a signal of 'the state's ongoing policy of accommodating the Shiʿis'.

In practice, the government has made no real gesture towards the integration of the Shiʿis into state structures. The formulation of the three ruling orders, the Basic Order (*al-nizam al-asasi lil hukm*), the Consultative Council (*majlis al-shūra*) and the Provinces Council (*nizam al-manatiq*), which were issued by King Fahad in February 1992, reflects clearly the state's affirmative action. The sixty members of the Consultative Council were selected on the basis of regional, tribal and sectarian considerations. An analysis of the Council membership in the first round shows that the Eastern Province gained five seats, among which only one was taken by a Shi'i member; the Hijaz won seventeen seats; the Southern Province had five seats; the Northern Province had two seats, whereas the number gained by the Najd exceeded half of the total. The Shi'is share in the second round (1997), in which there were 90 members, and the third round (2001), with 120 members, remained unchanged, with only two members. In proportion to the total Shi'is population, which is 5 per cent at its lowest estimate, six Shi'i members should have been appointed to the Council.

If, hypothetically, the Shi'is percentage does not qualify them for political participation in central government, then what about local government? According to conservative estimates, the Shi'is represent 33 per cent of the total population in the Eastern Province, but in the regional council, which consists of twelve members, they have only two members, about 15 per cent of the total.

Scholars of nationalism remind us that communities whose integration into the political and economic system is largely tenuous do not conceive themselves as members of the nation in which they live, much less in a state without nationalistic traits.[122] The politically alienated Shi'is are in this position, not only resisting any sense of belonging to the Saudi state but also calling for its overthrow.

However, the performance of the *majlis al-shūra* during the last two rounds shows that it failed to gain momentum among the population. The main reason is that the council was not effective, in that it did not assure all groups of equal status and fair shares. Besides, the marginal role of the Council in the decision-making process, countering the unfettered authority of the king, caused deep frustration among nearly all groups. The *majlis al-shūra* was established essentially to convey a message to the external world and not to respond to internal demands.

The Saudi-Wahhabi hegemony over al-Hasa and Qatif has determined the Shi'is' status religiously, economically and politically. The bitter confrontation with the Wahhabi revivalist movement in 1747 had far-reaching consequences that have shaped their history, ethos and political attitude.

With the emergence of the third Saudi realm in 1913, the Shi'is refrained from military resistance and favoured, instead, peaceful submission to the conquerors. Aiming to consolidate his rule in the region, Ibn Sa'ud inflicted severe discriminatory measures against the Shi'is religiously and economically.

The proclamation of the Saudi state in 1932 signalled a perpetual persecution and reduction of the status of the Shi'is owing to the sectarian nature of the ruling class and the religious establishment, which was bent on complete domination. Although subjects of the Saudi state do, nominally, enjoy equal status, the prevailing attitude of the rulers shows that discrimination against the Shi'is persists. Under the auspices of the Saudi royal family, the religious excommunication of the Shi'is by the Wahhabi *'ulama* legitimated all forms of discrimination against them. It could be said that the Wahhabi religious position helped prepare the legal ground for the government to show no serious commitment to Shi'is fundamental rights.

Between 1913 and the end of the 1970s, the Saudi discriminatory attitude towards the Shi'is manifested itself in economic deprivation, the prohibition of public religious ceremonies, severe restrictions on building mosques, *hussainiya*s and religious schools, urban and social marginalization and ultimately political exclusion. The inevitable consequence of the Saudi's harsh attitude towards the Shi'is is that the tensions between the government and its Wahhabi loyalists, on one side, and the Shi'is, on the other, were always liable to reach their height during the big religious occasions, notably *'Ashura* days, which always call for a strong police profile. After the *'Ashura* procession, it is commonplace for a group of Shi'is to be arrested, interrogated and tortured, while religious books, taped sermons and photos are confiscated, and those who are caught possessing these materials are fined.

Islamic practice generally is limited to that of the Wahhabi order, which adheres to the Hanbali school of the Sunni branch of Islam as interpreted by Muhammad Ibn Abd Al-Wahab. Practices contrary to this interpretation are discouraged, including those of non-Wahhabi Sunnis.

While the government supervises almost all mosques in the country and funds their construction, maintenance and operations, the Shi'is are barred from obtaining government funds to build their mosques or from funding their own mosque building.

In a word, the Shi'is' fundamental rights are considered a direct challenge to both Wahhabi doctrine and the legitimacy of Saudi rule.

Clearly, there are ample reasons for the Shi'is in the Eastern Province

and in the country as a whole to oppose the government and to challenge
its policies. Accordingly, many discontented Shi'i individuals have protested
against the regime and joined resistance groups to lobby the government to
cease its discriminatory measures against the Shi'is.

TWO

Shi'i Identity in the Eastern Province

The context within which Shi'is identity was formed has two aspects. The first is the Shi'i context, in which individuals gain the 'them and us' feeling. The second is the national context, in which individuals, being citizens of a country, share broader traits. The extent to which this dualism is involved in the formation of Shi'is identity depends greatly on a wide range of cultural, religious and political interactions.

This section endeavours to gain insight into themes that are involved in the formation of Shi'i identity in the Eastern Province. It also will study the way in which the Shi'is developed their sense of distinctiveness and how they created their alternative society, generating individuals' sense of belonging, loyalty and commitment or their withdrawal, protest and revolt.

Shi'i Religious Particularism

In Saudi Arabia the focus for identification varies. It may be territory (e.g. Najd, Hijaz, 'Asir, Sharqiyyah), religion/sect (e.g. Shi'i Sunni in a broad sense, and Hanbali/Wahhabi, Ja'fari, Isma'ili, Maliki, Shafi'i in a narrow sense) or tribe ('Unayzah, Shammar, Qahtan, Ghamid, and so on). Some groups, nevertheless, may be identified with all of these traits, such as the Shi'is Isma'ilis.

Generally speaking, individuals tend to bear and use more than one form of identity. They may present themselves as members of a tribe, family, country, region, town, religion, sect, party, and so on. Circumstances always influence individual identity choices. At certain times, an individual will focus on a singular identity because it fully reflects his peculiar character; in some cases, he may avoid using this identity because it may cause him trouble. Identity becomes most important when a group identity is countered by another group identity. For instance, the Wahhabis' insistence on imposing their creed has encouraged other groups to adhere to their own. In this case, the Shi'is' sense of identity manifests itself as an 'us against them' sentiment. This could be clearly seen during the rising tide of sectarianism following the Iranian revolution in 1979, when the need for a Shi'is identity was given added urgency.

Over a relatively short time, the Shi'is in the Eastern Province incorporated a set of elements into their identity. Apart from their religious affiliation, a range of intrinsic and exogenous features contributed to the formation of the Shi'is collective consciousness. These included dialect, dictums, popular legends, economic activity, customs including style of dress and mode of wedding parties and social and familial values. These characteristics have been woven into the fabric of the Shi'is identity.

The question that we pose here is: how did the Shi'is develop their collective consciousness? To answer this question, it will be useful to shed some light on certain attributes that distinguish the Shi'is in the Eastern Province from other groups.

The Role of the Sect

Twelver Shi'ism forms the common ideology of the Shi'is in Eastern Province, and this is the type of Shi'ism that is seen in their religious gatherings, daily collective prayers, collective rituals and social and cultural peculiarities.

Shi'ism, it could be said, is an ideology that has an immediate appeal because it provides those who hold it with answers to perennial issues relating to the origins, destiny and, ultimately, the meaning of life. This implies that Shi'ism is an agency of salvation. According to Bryan R. Wilson, two points are worth noting in this connection: first, the conditions for the attainment of salvation imply a range of taboos and injunctions for everyday living; and, second, the realization of life in obedience to those strictures is also in itself seen as at least a partial achievement of salvation. Thus, the sect becomes a location for the experience of salvation as well as an agency of promise.[1]

Another essential social aspect of Shi'ism is found in the practical commitments that are placed on Shi'i individuals towards their community, such as participation in religious ceremonies, festivals and funeral rituals, and contribution to fund-raising in addition to the regular giving of religious alms (the Fifth *khums*, the Tenth *zakat* and the Vows *nudhurat*).

Since Shi'i Islam is, in the minds of its members, a source of most social norms and values, Shi'i individuals should be aware of their responsibility towards these norms and values. They represent the sacred space that should be maintained and protected by the entire group. The sacred space of the Shi'i sect covers the whole of their realm: every symbol, practice, belief, dogma and even myths fall within the scope of the sacred. According to Durkheim, 'as far as religious thought is concerned, the part is equal to the whole; it has the same powers, the same efficacy'.[2] In this respect, the Shi'is in Saudi Arabia as a whole have shown no compromise regarding their principles and no infringement of the taboos that they maintain. This may be clearly noted during the *hajj* season. Unlike the Iranian pilgrims, the Shi'is in the Eastern Province do not commit to Khomeini's *fatwa*[3] which summons the Shi'is pilgrims to pray behind the Wahhabi prayer Imam of the Holy Mosque. Their rejection of this edict has, however, nothing to do with religious deviance but, in reality, shows that they assess compliance with the *fatwa* as a disruption of their distinctiveness and simultaneously a concession to their rival sect.

It should be emphasized that Shi'ism in the Eastern Province does not necessarily stand against Sunnism as such, but rather against Wahhabism, although the latter claims to represent the true Sunni community. This may be clearly seen in the amicable relationship between the religious and intellectual elites of the Shi'is and the Sunnis living in the Eastern Province and the Hijazi Sunnis. Beyond their own realm, the Shi'is prefer to identify themselves as Muslims rather than Shi'is. From a sociological perspective, minorities find appeal in a broader belonging because it rids them of a sense of weakness and vulnerablility. On the other hand, the Shi'is adhere to their sect (Shi'ism) when facing real or conceived threats from other sects. In this respect, Saudism and Wahhabism, from the Shi'is perspective, form one entity, combining sectarian and regional elements.

The question then arises whether the Shi'is are ready to adopt a broader religious identity, since many people readily change their ethnic identity if they can benefit by doing so. Walker Connor notes, however, that no example of significant assimilation can be cited as having occurred since the advent of the age of nationalism and the propagation of the principle of self-determination.[4] Rather, people prefer not to incorporate a new identity, because they fear this will lead to the effacement of their private identity and will often not assure all groups of equal rights and responsibilities. The Shi'is are unlikely to fuse into the state identity because it may force them to abjure their beliefs and, at the same time, would not change their political status as an underprivileged group.

Although the disadvantages of being part of the Shi'is community in Saudi Arabia outweigh the advantages, the Shi'is have not relinquished their identity. In fact, those who look at identity merely as an agency of utility ignore its moral and psychological aspects. Many members of ethnic groups even sacrifice their lives as a result of expressing their loyalty to their group.

The actual foci of the Shi'is sense of identity can be interpreted within Durkheim's central concept of a 'meaning system'. 'The unity of the group is expressed and enhanced by its shared meanings. The group's meaning system, in turn, depends on the group as its social base for its continued existence and importance'.[5] The application of this concept to the Shi'is in the Eastern Province shows that the *hussainiya*, for example, is not merely a place of religious activity but, in essence, expresses a fundamental link between the Shi'i meaning system and those who hold it. In this capacity, religious rituals and symbols are, at root, representations of the Shi'is, which Durkheim has termed 'collective representations'. These practices, according to Durkheim, are 'to strengthen the bonds attaching the believer to his god, and they, at the same time, really strengthen the bonds attaching the individual to the society of which he is a member'.[6]

The *fatwa* issued by the Wahhabi *'ulama* in January 1927, to force the Shi'is to abjure their doctrine and to re-enter Islam, was followed by severe measures against the Shi'is aimed at abolishing the Shi'i *hussainiya*s and mosques. It met vehement resistance from the Shi'is and thus ended in complete failure.

Unlike the Shi'i Isma'ilis in the south, the Imami Shi'is fought against any form of assimilation. Yet what distinguishes the Isma'ilis from the Imamis is that the former organized themselves on a tribal basis. In other words, the Isma'ili sect is closely associated with an ethno-tribal element exemplified in the Yam tribe. Being an esoteric sect, the Isma'ilis succeeded in adapting themselves to the existing system without relinquishing their ethno-religious identity. Consequently, the impact of the state and the continued Wahhabi propaganda campaigns had little effect on the Isma'ilis. In fact, very few were absorbed into the Wahhabi camp. Conversely, in the past few years, the Isma'ilis have tended to assert their markers of distinctiveness by revitalizing their historical, social and religious legacy in the Najran region. The incidents in this area in April–May 2000 reveal that there has been a strong Isma'ili revitalization movement in a manner reminiscent of the Shi'i religious novels. Like the Shi'is Imamis in the Eastern Province, they decided to celebrate the martyrdom of the third Imam, Hussain, in public, a decision that provoked both the government and Wahhabi religious propagandists. Such a move came at a time when Wahhabi propaganda directed almost exclusive attention to this region, with the aim of converting the Isma'ilis to the Wahhabi sect.[7]

Religious commemorations have, indeed, become the tools by which both the Imami and Isma'ili Shi'is manifest their private identities. Similarly, Shi'i sectarianism offers individuals an effective mechanism by which they organize themselves and preserve their distinctiveness. The variety of cultural and social interactions within the Shi'is community helps them to withstand real or perceived opposition from the dominant group. Like nearly all sects, Shi'ism secures its distinctiveness by asserting exclusivity. The Arabic term *jama'* denotes a distinct group to which its members refer. In the Shi'i context, individuals identify themselves and recognize each other by the phrase *min al-jama'*, meaning 'from the Shi'is inner group'. However, nearly all groups, regardless of their religious and ethnic origins, use similar phrases to assert their difference.

Religious boundaries between the Shi'is and the non-Wahhabi Sunnis in the country are sometimes sharp and sometimes fuzzy. For example, both the Shi'is and the Shafi'is and Malikis in Hijaz differ from the Wahhabi sect, in that they commemorate the Prophet's birth festival,[8] and in their belief in the reverence and intercession of the *ahl al-bayt*.[9] In other respects, however, the gap between the two sects remains unbridgeable, for example regarding traditional issues such as the designated Imamate, the infallibility of the Imams and a wide range of collective religious activities. Among the Shi'is, 'the strength of ethnic allegiance is always a function of participation in ethnic group activities.'[10] Moreover, sectarianism has stimulated the Shi'is to create their own institutions (e.g. *hussainiya*s, mosques, publishing houses, magazines, social clubs and cultural centres, and even political parties), by whatever mechanisms are available both internally and externally, in order to articulate their groupness. This has all occurred when they have failed to organize themselves formally, i.e. by making use of the official framework for social and group activity, because of the lack of freedom of expression in the country.

The Role of 'Ulama

The collective mobilization and sense of cohesiveness and belonging among the Shi'is derives from a certain set of forces, of which the 'ulama are the most important. They represent the socio-religious embodiment of the Shi'is, to which many achievements may be attributed, albeit they have, with the exception of sporadic incidents, shunned direct political involvement. The Shi'is 'ulama may have been politically quiescent before the Iranian revolution in 1979 but the political implications of their religious role are remarkable. Their insistence on the maintenance of the collective ritualistic practices of the Shi'is, despite the restrictions imposed by Saudi rulers and the Wahhabi 'ulama, impeded attempts at assimilation.

The Shi'is 'ulama, being well versed in Shi'i Islamic law and tenets, have devoted their efforts, first, to disseminating the Shi'i traditions and teachings among the Shi'is and, second, to defusing Wahhabi accusations against the Shi'is, namely, that they are heretics and polytheists. Simultaneously, they have made every possible attempt to urge the Saudi rulers to reassure the Shi'is of their religious rights. Most crucially, the Shi'is 'ulama have, by preserving religious conformity, ultimately saved the Shi'is from any possible internal fracture. Recent Shi'is activism can be traced back to the earlier efforts of the 'ulama.

Earlier, during the infancy of the Saudi state, the Shi'is 'ulama persistently withstood forced assimilation into the Saudi-Wahhabi polity. Their devotion to their community was behind the existence and growth of the Shi'i symbolic system, by which the Shi'is in the Eastern Province articulate and reaffirm their collectiveness and distinctiveness. Despite the restrictions imposed on them, they insisted on reviving religious ceremonies that have collective expression such as the commemoration of the Shi'is Imams' dates of birth and death. They also asserted the relations between laymen and the 'ulama in terms of endowment, marriage and divorce, familial disputes and so on, which secure Shi'is unity.

The role of the Shi'is 'ulama in the Eastern Province grew significantly with the solidification of the role of the marji'iyyah in the Shi'is realm. Though a relatively new concept, the marji'iyyah (which appeared at the turn of the twentieth century) had quickly gained great momentum among the Shi'is.[11] While the marji' has been depicted in the past as a mere transmitter of the Prophet's and the Imams' injunctions and directives, subsequent developments show significant changes in the marji's role, once it began to gain political weight.

As the Shi'is in the Eastern Province failed to create their own marji', they were religiously obliged to follow the precepts of marji's in Iraq or Iran.[12] Those marji's provide not only spiritual leadership to their followers, but also, according to recent transformations, political guidelines and juristic precepts to their imitators (muqallidun). Thus, the Shi'i individual should seek the legal opinion of the marji' in nearly all aspects of life.

In 1941, a written legal inquiry was sent to Sayyid Abf al-Hasan al-Asfahani, the marji' taqlid at the time in Najaf, by Shaikh Mansfr al-Marhfn, an eminent scholar in al-Qatif. The inquiry asked whether it was legal to abandon allegiance to Ibn Sa'ud. The marji' al-Asfahani sent a reply in writing, saying that it was not, but Saudi border guards confiscated the letter on the Saudi–Iraqi border. When Ibn Sa'ud read the reply, he ordered his men to arrest Shaikh Mansfr and his son Shaikh 'Ali, and for them to be subpoenaed in Riyadh. Though Ibn Sa'ud was pleased with al-Asfahani's fatwa, he threatened to kill Shaikh Mansfr and his son if they raised such questions with the marji'.[13] Being the absolute autonomous ruler, Ibn Sa'ud would not tolerate an autonomous religious domain that might compete with him for the loyalty of his citizens.

Regional Factors

Although the Shi'is in the Eastern Province share common descent with some families from different tribes and regions, geographic circumstances play a large part in the formation of Shi'is identity. The Shi'is are concentrated in distinct territorial locations. Although the population in the Eastern Province is divided into Shi'is and Sunnis, both sects never live in the same village. The Shi'is live in tightly knit villages and do not marry into or mix with the Sunni community[14]. Evidently, al-Qatif region is overwhelmingly inhabited by the Shi'is. Very few Sunni communities live there, most of them being concentrated in their own distinct areas such as Umm al-Sahik, Rahimah, Da'rin, 'Enak and al-Zur. Although relations between the two communities have frequently been tense, mainly because of socio-economic factors, improvements in living conditions and the consolidation of the Saudi state seem to have brought some calm, although divisions still exist.

In spite of their scattered distribution and demographic changes, which came about following the process of urbanization within the al-Hasa region, the inhabitants of al-Hasa can be easily distinguished into Shi'i and Sunni areas[15] and sectarian boundaries still exist. However, the distinction between the Shi'is and the Sunni in the al-Qatif region appears to be very sharp in comparison to al-Hasa, where peaceful co-existence between the two communities has long been apparent.

Starting from the early 1970s, many Shi'is of al-Hasa migrated from the villages to the towns, especially to Dammam (the commercial centre and capital of the Eastern Province), Riyadh and some other regions, while the Shi'is in al-Qatif clung to their ghetto. The difference may be attributed to the tolerance the Shi'is in al-Hasa experienced as a result of their intermixing with the Sunnis. Neither the Shi'is nor the Sunnis in al-Hasa have qualms about entering into mutual business partnerships. In addition, the Shi'is in al-Hasa, unlike their co-religionists in al-Qatif, are not politically motivated. For the Shi'is in al-Hasa, religion is separable from business, from politics and from the public domain, whereas the insistence on the synthesis between these polarities is a big issue for the Shi'is in al-Qatif.

The 'ulama of al-Hasa did not insist on adherence to Shi'i symbols, such as wearing the religious dress, in particular the turban ('emama), or even the utterance of the third testimony (ashhadu 'anna 'Aliyan waliu allah), while the 'ulama in al-Qatif were not willing to compromise on such matters. The difference is that the Shi'is in al-Hasa do not conceive their identity in this way; rather, they express it through adherence to Shi'i doctrines and a wide range of collective social and religious practices and commemorations. The Shi'is in al-Qatif, by contrast, view these issues as integral parts of their collective identity and dignity.

Despite all this, the difference in attitude between the Shi'is of al-Hasa and of al-Qatif does not necessarily reflect the degree of religiosity of each community. Religious commitment among the Shi'is in al-Hasa is deeply rooted and incorporates many mystic and spiritual elements, whereas religiosity among the Shi'is in al-Qatif takes a more rational and political form. Their religiosity is a response to external factors, namely Wahhabi sectarianism, the Islamic movement in Iraq and Egypt and the Islamic revolution in Iran.

This is not to argue that there is a sharp dichotomy between the two communities. The aim here is to examine the impact of regional factors upon the Shi'is' sense of identity. Al-Qatif, al-Hasa and the Eastern Province at large are not mere locations inhabited by a group of people, but represent a space of communication and interaction between the Shi'is. Within this space, Shi'is individuals demonstrate their cultural distinction, social cohesion and, moreover, their political resentment. Here they also unite in opposition to their assumed enemy, which is the source of their deprivation and vulnerability.

The separateness of the two spaces (the Eastern Province and the other regions) is inherent in the Shi'is' sentimental construction. This may be easily applied to the Shi'is in al-Qatif, who resist any call to migrate to other regions. It is common for Shi'is jobseekers from al-Qatif to decline offers of work in other regions, because they do not want to be socially estranged. At the King Sa'ud University in Riyadh most Shi'is students do not mix with other students, but stay together in an isolated group where they feel secure.

Social Solidarity

Social solidarity is derived not only from a shared religious consciousness, but also from familial ties, shared interests, values, customs and crises. On the social level, the participation of individuals in collective rites, such as daily collective prayers, occasional sermons (e.g. for the festival of the birthdays of the Prophet and the Imams), religious commemorations (e.g. *'Ashura*) and funeral rituals exhibit Shi'is social solidarity. They are, at root, symbolic expressions of group unity and 'participation in religious ritual is experience of the transcendent force of society itself'.[16] When such activities are manifested publicly, they reflect the commonalities the Shi'is share, a common memory, history and fate, by which the Shi'is can distinguish themselves from others.

The sense of groupness among the Shi'is also has a part to play in matters such as marriage and makes it nearly impossible for an individual to divest himself of membership of the group. Most Shi'i families have traditionally insisted that their children marry within the Shi'is community. Nearly all Shi'is firmly decried the very rare cases of intermarriage with the Sunni community, notably the Wahhabis, that have occurred in recent decades, and mobilized collectively against what they regarded as an unforgivable transgression.

Moreover, the continuous threats posed by the state religious establishment against the Shi'is have made most Shi'is members refrain from examining, let alone criticizing, the doctrinal aspect of the sect, for fear that this will be interpreted as a step towards undermining the identity and unity of the Shi'is. According to Durkheim, 'If a belief is unanimously shared by a people, then [...] it is forbidden to touch it, that is to say, to deny it or to contest it. Now the prohibition of criticism is an interdiction like the others and proves the presence of something sacred'.[17]

Individuals – in any sect faced with threats from within or without – are expected to defend the unity of their community. While reaffirming their distinct boundaries, sects customarily use the maximum religious energy to secure their internal consensus.

This brings us, once again, to the field of ethnicity as an analytical tool by which we might explore such reactions. In this respect, the sense of the Shi'is' religious particularism may be understood as 'the conscious awareness of threatened or real crisis and the need which this crisis both stimulates and by which it is resolved'. The 'crisis' here refers to 'exilic anxiety, the fear of separation, of isolation, of being cut off'.[18]

In the case of the Saudi Shi'is, the major source of crisis and impulse to ghettoization come from a sense of exclusion from the larger community, intensified by Saudi affirmative action. This response, however, also corresponds to that of a Shi'i teaching that summons the believers, during the occultation of the Twelfth Imam, to commit to the principle of dissimulation (*taqiyya*) and waiting (*intizar*). The Shi'is are obliged to distance themselves from illegitimate rulers, namely, those who are neither Imams nor designated by the Imams. Though this principle began, rapidly, to erode after the Shi'i Islamic resurgence in Iraq, Iran and the Gulf, it has continued to influence their religious consciousness.

In sum, the Shi'is in the Eastern Province represent a religious particularism, which can be identified with the ethnic network, where individuals express their membership through regular participation in collective actions; with ethnic association, which is the political expression of the Shi'is; and finally with territory, which distinguishes the Shi'is region from other regions.

Therefore the Shi'i sect has transformed itself into a sort of alternative society, in which individuals have maintained their mutual interests, views and dogmas. Within this ghetto, the Shi'is community demonstrates its solidarity and promotes its collective political visions and demands.

The Shi'is and the Question of National Identity

The present Saudi state was established in a region that, throughout its history, had never experienced centralized political power. The Arabian Peninsula embraced numerous tribal, religious and regional polities; Saudi Arabia is thus 'a collection of families and diverse ethnic and religious groups which were united through conquest by 'Abd al-'Aziz ibn Sa'ud during the first quarter of the century'.[19] This political unity did not extend to their deep-rooted traditions and feelings of belonging. The communities of present Saudi Arabia represent a plural society, with no shared social origins, religious outlooks, historical symbols, dialects, social customs and values, or any collective memory and cultural consciousness.

Jacob Goldberg claims that 'Saudi Arabia's indigenous population is more homogeneous and cohesive, ethnically and religiously, than that of any Arab state. The Shi'is community is the only major exception to this homogeneity'.[20] Likewise, James Piscatori thinks that 'with the possible exception of the Shi'is [...] ethnic and religious differences have not been very important and have not complicated national unity.' He adds, 'By and large the kingdom is homogeneously Arab and Sunni.'[21]

This view rests on the assumption that Saudi Arabia is divided into two categories: a Sunni tribal majority and a Shi'is sedentary minority. According to Joseph Kostiner, 'the majority of the population in the Saudi core areas Najd, al-Qasim, and al-Ahsa was nomadic'.[22] This statement is not based on fieldwork, but rather on assumptions. First, it has been assumed that these regions are not real core areas in the country. Until the 1950s, Mecca was the only city in the country consisting of 100,000 inhabitants (most of whom were settled), Riyadh and Jeddah numbered 80,000 each.[23] The population is at its most dense in the Southern Province. Second, the majority in al-Hasa was not nomadic at the turn of the twentieth century, as Kostiner claims. According to J. G. Lorimer, the total settled population in al-Hasa in 1915 was 101,000, whereas the total nomadic population was 57,000, most of whom migrated from Najd.[24] Although no official statistics are available, it is widely known that the Shi'is, who are classified as a sedentary community, represent 50 per cent of the total population of the al-Hasa region.

With respect to the alleged religious homogeneity of the Saudi state, we should look into the deep and complex social, cultural and religious differences in the country. To speak of religious homogeneity in Saudi Arabia is like speaking of a homogeneous Muslim community throughout Islamic history. Religious divisions manifest themselves more easily than other kinds of divisions, if only because religion forms the sharpest and most distinctive characteristic between different groups.

Likewise, we must consider the assumption that a majority–minority categorization can be applied to Saudi Arabia.[25] Though it greatly depends on how each group perceives itself, Saudi social scientists apply the term 'minority' to those who came from Africa during the pilgrimage seasons and eventually opted to reside in the two holy cities of Mecca and Medina. In Medina, for example, there are some minorities who reside in Manshiyah and Bab al-Kusah. Though most members of these minorities obtained Saudi nationality, ethno-cultural constraints prevented them from integrating into Saudi society. In their ghettos, these minority groups maintain their own social traditions, language, customs and cultural background.[26] The Wahhabi polemicists, however, tend to apply the term 'minority' to the Shi'is to indicate that their society or region is inferior to the majority, the Sunnis.[27]

However, this does not imply that the rest of the population represents a cohesive and homogeneous society. On the religious level, the Sunni–Shi'i categorization is not adequate when one examines the heterogeneity in both the Sunni and the Shi'i communities. According to Salamé, 'The Sunnis, although they represent the overwhelming majority of the population, are by no means unified. Despite the constant pressure of Wahhabism, the four recognized Sunni schools continue to exist in the country.'[28] Likewise, the Shi'is are not a homogeneous community; there are the Imami Shi'is in the Eastern Province and Medina; the Isma'ilis and Zaidi Shi'is in Najran, in the south, and also segments of the Kaysaniat Shi'is in Yanbu'. Thus the alleged religiously homogeneous majority is a myth, in the sense that sects are not necessarily pure religious entities but each sect stores the regional, social and religious pecularities of its members. The fact is that Saudi Arabia, like the Lebanon, could be considered as a state of religious minorities, among which the Wahhabis represent the dominant minority.

On the ethnic level, it should be noted that nomadic and tribal communities are concentrated in the Najd, whereas urban and sedentary communities mainly inhabit Hijaz and al-Hasa. Although these regions were nominally integrated into the political geography of the state, they are culturally, psychologically and sociologically divergent. Empirically, Najd, Hijaz, ʻAsir and so on are still regions alien to the Shiʻis in the Eastern Province, and vice versa. When a Shiʻi individual goes to Jeddah or ʻAsir, he does not feel that he shares the same socio-cultural traits as the local community; likewise, when a Hijazi comes to the Eastern Province, he does not think of that region as part of his realm. It is evident that the Saudi employees from other regions working for Aramco prefer not to link themselves with the Eastern Province. Those who were granted lands and loans from the company to build houses in areas dominated by the Shiʻis usually make financial arrangements with their fellow employees, notably the Shiʻis, through which both benefit from Aramco's offers. Despite the Saudization of Aramco in 1982–3, when the gates of employment were opened wide for the Saudis and thus large numbers were recruited into the company, the Shiʻi regions did not see a significant demographic change. Indeed, employees from Hijaz, Najd, ʻAsir and other provinces opted to earn money with the aim of building houses in their own regions, many of them considering their stay in the Eastern Province as an exception.

Historically speaking, the clear-cut distinction between regions is deeply established, and can be traced back long before the inception of the Saudi state. In Hijaz, for example, the roots of regionalism are linked to the history of Islam and to the people who resided in it. When ʻIbn Saʻud's troops conquered the Hijaz, the seeds of regional cleavage were implanted, because of the sharp distinction between the Najd and the Hijaz, culturally, socio-economically and even politically.

According to one Hijazi scholar, 'While Najd was a tribal society, al-Hijaz was an urban, relatively sophisticated society.' And when Ibn Saʻud invaded al-Hijaz, he found himself faced with what has been described as 'a dual kingdom – on one hand, the isolated desert and the backward towns which simple theocracy could rule, and on the other, the holy land with its window on the world, where subtlety was needed'.[29] This analysis was expounded by J. B. Killy in 1980 using a similar statement.[30] The alternative, then, was to pursue very subtle and long-term policies in order to reconcile the two poles, to win the allegiance of both the nomads (*badu*) and the urban dwellers (*hadar*). Yet, the *ikhwan*, who deemed those who do not conform to their beliefs to be 'polytheists', rejected the reconciliatory alternative, which they called 'a sinful weakness'. As Saudi rule failed to integrate the Hijazi community fully into the state, 'the rule of Ibn Sa'ud was considered by the Hijazis to be an external rule that was just to replace another external rule, that of the Ottomans'.[31]

Indeed, the Hijazis' regional consciousness represented a fierce challenge to the Saudi dynastic state. Thus, following the defeat of the 'Ashraf polity in 1925–6, Ibn Sa'ud intensified his efforts to integrate the Hijaz into his state, in the hope of diminishing the sense of distinctiveness among its people. From Ibn Sa'ud's political point of view, the integration of Hijaz was vital for shifting the centre of power from the coast to the desert.[32] Ibn Sa'ud's central pursuit was to found a state based on a common loyalty to the al-Sa'ud dynasty and Islam, as shaped by the Wahhabi traditions. What measures have been taken to cultivate these two essentials as a basis for national identity, and how have other groups and regions responded to these measures? In short, how did these components affect the formation of the Saudi national identity?

Saudi-Wahhabi Nationalism

Nationalism, being a new arrival in the Saudi realm, is still a difficult issue. Since the country lacks unified political traditions and culture to which individuals can refer in order to deal with the controversy over the theoretical and practical aspects of this notion, interpretations are subject to individual and group judgements. From the standpoint of the Wahhabi *'ulama*, nationalism is equivalent to the Arabic word *qawmiyya*, which corresponds to the concept of *al-'asabiyya al-jahiliyya*, meaning a sort of bond which prevailed in the pre-Islamic era, based on primordial ties (i.e. kinship, tribe, family and so on).[33] Nationalism would thus, inevitably, contradict the notion of the Islamic *umma*. But if nationalism takes the meaning of *wataniyya*, that is 'patriotism', then the debate would appeal to the state (*al-dawla*) rather than the nation (*al-umma*). Whatever the political and religious interpretation, it may be impossible to find nationalism in this country, as it is understood in social science literature.[34]

It appears that the royal family imposed a certain interpretation of nationalism on their subjects, namely, loyalty to the king and the royal family.

According to this interpretation, the king is the sovereign and is identified as the Imam (religious leader), to be mentioned in daily prayers.[35]

The crucial dilemma facing the Shi'is in terms of their national sentiment is connected to the stereotypical perception of the Shi'is as a source of schism within the Muslim *umma* or a dissident movement that is against the status quo in the Islamic world. This depiction seems to have gained more currency following the Iranian revolution, when the Shi'is were portrayed as an Iranian satellite on Saudi soil. As a result, they are perceived as a threat to national cohesiveness.

This depiction is not necessarily derived from the present attitude of the Shi'is, but largely perpetuates the historical picture of dichotomy, that is, the confrontation over the issue of succession to the Prophet and the Shi'is' rejection of the legitimacy of the Sunni government. The Wahhabi insistence on using the term *rafida* (rejectionists), meaning those who refuse to recognize the legality of the first three caliphs (Abu Bakr, Omar and 'Uthman), recalls the historical legacy that places the Sunnis on the government side and the Shi'is on the opposition side. This interpretation implies that the Shi'is' loyalty to a Sunni government will always remain doubtful. Furthermore, since the Shi'is are able to conceal their faith, they will be looked on as the nest in which opposition groups breed. Therefore, while the Shi'is have built their own identity, the Wahhabis have also contributed to this process, and have used this to justify the total exclusion of the Shi'is.

However, the conventional approach to the question of nationalism and hence national identity emphasizes the close association between nationalism and the inception of the state. Understanding this issue requires an anatomical analysis, by which we can address the dialectical relationship between a sense of nationalism and the principles of the Saudi state.[36]

Wahhabization of the State

Scholars of Saudi political history, such as James Piscatori and Ghassan Salamé, tend to promote a paradigm with which they aim to explore the identity fostered by the Saudi royal family. According to Piscatori, Ibn Sa'ud evolved a transnationalist force, with the aim of integrating tribes into the state and legitimizing his control over a disunited territory,[37] whereas Salamé argues that the Saudi regime tried to foster what he terms *supra-tribal identity* among the tribes.[38] However, these terms represent none other than the Wahhabi

Islam that Ibn Sa'ud and his successors endeavoured to use as a unifying force for the whole population. In his article about the formation of the Saudi identity, Piscatori argues that, 'the efforts to structure a transnational force, Islam, helped to integrate the tribes and to encourage a transtribal identity; transnational values were helpful in legitimating the control of the Saudi elite over disunited territory.'[39] He concludes that Ibn Sa'ud exploited Islam to 'create an elementary identity' and a 'greater authority', by which he controlled the tribes.[40]

What should be emphasized in this respect is the type of Islam that has been pursued, and to whom it was applied. Perhaps, to an outsider, Islam may seem to be the magical glue that has unified the whole country. We should distinguish, however, between different varieties of Islam, for example, Islam as a mere text enshrined in the Qur'an and the Sunna, and Islam as school of thought, sects, dogmatic and hermeneutic trends, jurisprudence and political ideology. In short, a distinction should be made between tradition (*al-nas*) and independent judgement (*al-ijtihad*) in identifying Islam. Islam has never meant the same thing to all peoples and at all times, but may be defined differently according to time and place. Saudi Arabia is no exception to this rule.

Whereas a 'standard' Islam no longer exists, the prevailing Islam is a human one, which has been subjected to a series of changes, owing to varying degrees of individual and group awareness. Islam is not only a scriptural religion, but is what Muslims perceive it to be. Furthermore, each sect claims that it holds the truth, and that its interpretation is correct while the other's is corrupt, and from here the cycle of dichotomization starts.

In spite of the continuous efforts by the Saudi government to forge a singular interpretative framework for Islam through a united legal code, these efforts contributed to deepening the differences between the Wahhabi community and other sects, both Sunni and Shi'i. Religion is thus anything but a unifying force in Saudi Arabia. We should distinguish between the role of religion in regional and national frameworks. Because religion has successfully united the Najdi tribes, many scholars have assumed that this was the case in the other regions. However, religion was a dividing force in other regions, where it was clothed in the uncompromising Wahhabi version of Islam, aimed at 'purifying' the Arabian Peninsula from the 'associationists', a suggestion that met with fierce resistance.[41]

As Ibn Sa'ud strove to pursue a religious standardization with recourse to the imposition of a singular legal code derived from Hanbali jurisprudence, he placed a major obstacle in the face of other sects to be integrated into the state. The Shi'is and, to a lesser extent, the Malikis and the Isma'ilis were not recognized as legal sects.

Although Ibn Sa'ud acknowledged the existence of sectarian pluralism, including, in addition to the four traditional Sunni sects, the Imami and Zaidi ones,[42] he approved the proposal presented in 1926 by the juridical committee consisting of a group of Wahhabi 'ulama. The proposal states that, 'all courts should follow the legal code derived from Imam 'Ahmad bin Hanbal's precepts'.[43] Ibn Sa'ud's prior acknowledgment was interpreted as a political tactic aimed at pacifying the Hijazis, who were accustomed to sectarian pluralism, at a time when his grasp on the region was shaky. But once he had succeeded in subjugating the whole Hijaz he autocratically imposed the Hanbali legal code in Hijaz. Such a step appealed to the Wahhabi 'ulama, who did not regard other sects as truly Islamic.[44]

In response, other sects had to seek different means in order to maintain and practise their legal codes. If they did not, they had to commit to the Hanbali judgements. Although Ibn Sa'ud approved the Ottoman policy regarding the Shi'is' independent courts, their authority was drastically curtailed and became inconsequential. From an official judicial perspective, the precepts of the Shi'is judges are not recognized by the Wahhabi-based religious establishment. Although Shi'is courts are confined to matters such as marriage, inheritance and endowments, all verdicts must be approved by what is called *al-mahkama al-shar'iyya*, that is, the Legal Court, which is dominated by the Wahhabi *'ulama*. The decline in the authority of the Shi'is judges remains a central issue, being an essential element in national identity, and will inevitably entail the subordination and the delegitimization of other sects. As Wahhabism was officially imposed as a state religion, the Wahhabi *'ulama* have acquired an autonomous role in all religious matters. Their *fatawa* are the tools by which the state excommunicates its enemies, and by which it attains its legitimacy.

The most traumatic experience for the Shi'is came from the attempts of the Wahhabi *'ulama* to impose their version of Islam on other sects. In the early years of Saudi rule, the Shi'is, being classified as polytheists, were forced to renew their allegiance to Islam, and were excluded from professing their ritualistic practices in *hussainiya*s; they were also forced to pray in the Sunni mosques.[45] The treatment of the Shi'is by the Wahhabi *mutawwi'yn* was humiliating. Apart from Ibn Sa'ud's commitment to the Wahhabi *'ulama's fatwa* regarding the ordinances pursued against the Shi'is in al-Hasa, Ibn Sa'ud ordered his viceroys in al-Hasa and al-Qatif to force the Shi'is *'ulama* to resubmit to Islam, at the hands of the Wahhabi *mutawwa'*, Ibn Bishr, in 1927. Many were also compelled to utter the Two Testimonies (*al-shahadatain*) before the Wahhabi *mutawwa'*. In addition, in 1927 Ibn Sa'ud appointed a praying Imam for each Shi'i village in al-Hasa and al-Qatif. In response, the Shi'is sought help from the British administration in the Gulf to put pressure on Ibn Sa'ud to cease these oppressive policies.

This seems to be the obvious starting point for studying the national consciousness of the Shi'is, the group consciousness that is passed on from father to son. According to Ghassan Salamé, the Shi'is 'will not soon forget the Wahhabi fanaticism which has oppressed them for two centuries, nor their own religious affiliation, which has frequently cost them their lives'. These tragic memories must have stimulated them to 'maintain strong ties with the Shi'i centers, such as al-Najaf, in southern Iraq, Qum in Iran, or Bahrain, where their co-religionists make up the majority of the population and enjoy a relatively better status.'[46] Furthermore, the frequent attacks against the Shi'is have helped perpetuate their cohesion, while diluting any countervailing influence of political and cultural Wahhabism. As a result, attempts to impose Wahhabism on the Shi'is have not only failed to assimilate them into the alleged national identity, but have also encouraged them to cling strongly to their own identity.

Likewise, discrimination against the Shi'is on religious grounds has enhanced their unity and given their identity a religious colour. 'Discrimination against a particular feature of one's identity,' say Fuller and Francke, 'reinforces that feature in relation to others.'[47] It could also be argued that the formation of Shi'is identity was a reaction against the attitude of the Wahhabi men of religion.

The governmental education system is the most important domain within which a clash of identities occurs. Since Shi'is children are obliged to study the Wahhabi version of Islam in government schools, they are instructed to join parallel religious schemes set up by both their families and the Shi'i religious elite, through which children become immune to what they have learned in school. The major objective of these parallel schemes is to create the we–they cognitive framework in Shi'is children from an early age. Thus, 'children come to think of themselves as part of the in-group and share their group's way of perceiving the rest of society.'[48] Although the modern state relies heavily on the education system for the maintenance and supervision of its social infrastructure, this system has proved ineffective in fostering loyalty to the Saudi state. Consequently, Shi'is children and, most probably, children from other sects are encouraged from an early stage to distinguish between the doctrinal boundaries of Shi'ism and Wahhabism. The problem of this dualistic orientation appears to have been resolved by regarding scholastic religious materials as mere exam materials, that is, Shi'is students are supposed to study and revise them in order to pass the final exams, but not to believe in them. On the other hand, children are supposed to imbibe Shi'i doctrines, particularly the doctrine of the Imamate, or the rightness of Ali for the succession of the Prophet, through parental religious rearing and regular attendance at the *hussainiya*s and mosques.[49] Eventually, Wahhabism came to be looked on by the Shi'is as one of the state weapons against its subjects, and not, as was claimed, as a central element of national identity-building.

Symbolization of Saudi Monarchy

The earliest instances of the tendency among the al-Sa'ud to symbolize the royal family can be traced back to the confrontation with the *ikhwan* Movement, which began to challenge the legal basis of Ibn Sa'ud's rule in 1927. He was quoted as saying: 'Two things are essential to our state and our people [...] religion and the rights inherited from our fathers'.[50] This statement reflects the ideological basis of the Saudi state and, simultaneously, the substantial components of national identity, in which private identities should be assimilated. The efforts of al-Sa'ud, the major unifying force of the country, were geared towards fostering a national consensus around the royal family's right to rule.

However, the impact of the aforementioned components varies from one place to another. In Najd, for example, the consolidation of Ibn Sa'ud's rule was aimed at defusing tribal loyalties. Ibn Sa'ud's supra-tribal leadership was enhanced by assuring the welfare and security of the tribes' members, by which he won the allegiance of the Najdi tribes.

On the other hand, heavy fiscal burdens imposed on the Shi'is in the Eastern Province for the building of Ibn Sa'ud's state had a negative impact on the Shi'is' loyalty to the state. These fiscal burdens were exploited in order to subsidize the settlement of Ibn Sa'ud's tribal allies. To consolidate his rule in Najd, the resources in other regions were employed to rebuild a new network of alliances through subsidies for agriculture and industry, grants for housing and land, installation of water supplies, financial incentives for marriage, and so on. These privileges were, in essence, aimed at buying the loyalty of the Najdi tribes and assimilating them into the state. Thus, the Najdi tribes began to regard Ibn Sa'ud as their indisputable leader, since he alleviated their economic hardship and ultimately elevated their status to that of the most privileged group in his state.

The picture in other regions is totally different, however. Other communities did not receive the kind of benefits the central region received from the Saudi state. Thus, many groups have viewed the Saudi state as the ultimate embodiment of the community of the central region, and also as a resolution to internal dilemmas in the central region.

The view, therefore, that 'the ruling family did not attempt to undo' the identities of groups, but 'tried to create overarching loyalties based on a common social and religious community'[51] is entirely inaccurate. The reverse, in fact, is true: the ruling family strove to undermine private identities but, on the other hand, failed to create an alternative national identity for the conquered groups. Yet, it is true that within the process of the consolidation of the state, traditional tribal identities began, gradually, to lose their influence in favour of an imposed identity.

This brings us to the common argument regarding the definition of the nation-state. If the ideal nation-state is one that brings together all the members of a single national group, and no one else, into a unified political structure, then neither Saudi Arabia nor any other nation quite meets that ideal. However, the term 'nation-state' has come to be applied indiscriminately to all states.[52] Between these two extremes, there lies a more realistic definition of nation-state, namely, a state that takes its character from the largest number of its citizens.

Is it sufficient for a state to incorporate the fundamental elements of territoriality, effective government and peoplehood to be recognized as a nation-state, as J. Piscatori argues?[53] If so, then why did many nation-states disintegrate with the collapse of the USSR, whereas some nation-states, such as East and West Germany and South and North Yemen, were reunited into one nation? The answer is that the stated elements are characteristic of the state, but not of the nation-state.

A particular point of contention here is that Saudi Arabia lacks national traits, meaning that if there is no state, then there is no geopolitical framework by which groups are bound. Ernest Gellner argues that 'nationalism emerges only in milieux in which the existence of the state is already very much taken for granted'.[54] Against this is the view that the state is the natural outcome of the nation; it expresses its general will, its cultural and social attributes, its historical legacy and, finally, its present and future pretensions. Countries such as Egypt, Syria and Yemen, which possess very rich national heritages, have not experienced great difficulties in terms of building states, though they each have had their own history. Conversely, countries such as the six GCC (Gulf Cooperation Council) members, which have very limited political experience and national cultures, are states founded by the use of military force and/or foreign support.

One means of assessing whether or not Saudi Arabia is a nation-state is the common history that the native population supposedly shares.[55] The Shiʿis, like other excluded regions, tribes and sects, do not recognize themselves as being part of the history of the Saudi state, because this is a history built on their subjugation and defeat and ignores their cultural peculiarities. They are not represented in the state's symbols, rituals and celebrations. Apart from Najdis in the central region, groups find it nearly impossible to take part (except in a formal and sycophantic way) in celebrations of the unification of the kingdom by Saudi citizens in other regions, because they do not feel that the process of unification was meant to realize their aims: it is not their unity, but the Najdis'. On such days of celebration it is the Najdi traditional symbols such as the Najdi popular dance (ʿarda), tent, dress, cultural heritage and even songs and poems that are on display.

The Saudi state strove to impose and develop its private identity, symbols, rituals, history and, to a certain extent, dress and dialect on all regions and groups. From the outset, the ruling family insisted on amalgamation between nationalism and the adoption of these traits. The authoritative, transcendent and paramount nature of these traits was meant to prevail, so that they would form the basis for national identity. However, the ambition was not fulfilled. The crux of the identity crisis in the country is the invocation of private traits (Najd, Wahhabism, and al-Saʿud) in order to create a national identity.

Moreover, the regime assigned distorted meanings to a series of general concepts, such as fatherland (*watan*), loyalty (*wala'*) and citizenship (*al-muwatana*). The *watan* is a very new notion in the country. It is certainly true that, 'the concept of fatherland to which one owes primary allegiance is contradictory to the spirit of Islam which places its emphasis upon the universal community of the fatherland rather than upon national groups'.[56] Thus the *watan* means recognition of the Saudi kingdom as a geopolitical entity and a rule to which citizens are obliged to offer loyalty.

On the other hand, socio-political scientists have agreed that the concept of citizenship may be applied in all countries, as it is the only basis of collective identity and the only general bond, and all other social relationships are private, personal and familial.[57] The elements of citizenship are defined in terms of specific sets of rights and social institutions through which such rights are exercised. These principal elements of citizenship are civil, political and social rights. The civil element of citizenship is composed of rights necessary for individual freedoms; the political element consists of the right to participate in the exercise of power through parliament and the like. Finally, the social element of citizenship is made up of the right to the prevailing standard of life and the social heritage of the society.[58]

What may be understood from the definition of citizenship cited above is that everyone in the state has equal status and equal access to power and resources, and is equal before the law: there would be no pariahs, outcasts and/or underprivileged groups. Realistically, people cannot be loyal to the state for the sake of loyalty alone. Indeed, people can attest their loyalty only in connection with the responsiveness of the government to perceived needs and interests; its treatment of citizens and their grievances; and the integration of individuals and groups into state structures. When the state cannot or will not provide for the basic needs of its people, then there is no real belonging to this broader entity, and a sense of separation or isolation will almost inevitably develop.

The sub-loyalties of the Saudi subjects, with all their intricate differences, were certainly considered a hindrance impeding the process of citizenship, yet the same is true in nearly all world states. Every state presides over heterogeneous groups, and it is the role of the state to integrate them by creating an enveloping whole while at the same time complementing private identities. In the Saudi case, the state, in the eyes of many, notably the Shi'is, existed to serve the members of the preferred identity, which consisted of the royal family and its Najdi tribal and religious allies.

Does national identity represent an imperative issue for the Saudi-Wahhabi state? In other words, do the al-Sa'ud feel a pressing need to create a collective/public/national identity? And when and in what milieu does identity become an issue?

Before attempting to answer these central questions, we should consider the Saudi-Wahhabi's dominant psychological position vis-à-vis other regions, sects and tribes. It could be argued that, like all conquerors, the Saudi-Wahhabi leaders tended not to develop a national identity, which would require them to accept, at least in theory, the principle of sharing political and economic resources with their subjects. This may be evident in Ibn Sa'ud's proclamation of his right to rule, which he 'inherited from his fathers'. Furthermore, the creation of a national/collective identity requires the acceptance of the principle of equality among all citizens. Yet this principle contradicts both the religious and political ideology of the Saudi state. On the religious level, the Wahhabi 'ulamas claim that they represent the true Islamic model, the people of monotheism (*ahl al-tawhid*), and their message is to purge the tenets of associationists in the Muslim *umma* (the Shi'is, the Sufis and so on). They cannot therefore dispose equally towards believers and polytheists. On the political level too, the Saudi rulers, who forcibly subjugated a vast area of the Arabian peninsula to build a state in the name of the Saudi dynasty, cannot readily invite their subjects to share the political power for which they have sacrificed themselves. Members of the al-Sa'ud are above all other citizens including Najdis in all matters, including legal and financial ones.

National identity was thus manifest in the trinity of Wahhabi sectarianism, Najdi territorialism and Saudi authoritarianism, though this identity has failed to persuade the Saudi subjects to give up their traditional loyalties. The Saudi state will thus remain a heterogeneous state, harbouring potential threats to its unity, unless changes are made in the ideological discourse of both the state and its religious allies.

The Role of Modernization

According to the old theory, modernization dissolves traditional, cultural and ethnic distinctions between communities. Modern institutions should replace and transcend the traditional social formations (e.g. tribes, families and, by extension, sects). However, modernization seems to have failed in terms of the process of detribalization in Saudi Arabia.

The role of modernization in forging a national sense of identity among the Saudis was constrained by internal social, cultural and political complexities. In spite of the efforts made by the royal family to exploit modernization in order to fuse traditional loyalties into a national identity, by integrating a large number of groups and regions into the nascent state, regionalism, tribalism and sectarianism remained relatively strong. As Joseph Malone wrote in 1966, 'the people continued to think of themselves as Nejdis, Hejazis or Asiris', whereas in al-Hasa, one often heard the expression '...after bin Jilawi [the first governor of the Eastern Province] Nasser', and consequently 'a unified Saudi state and a national consciousness [were] far from being realized'.[59] In 1977, Levon Melikian examined regional sentiments among Saudi students. He wrote:

> Saudis from al-Hasa (the Eastern Province) were described by Saudis from the other three provinces (Najd, Hijaz, and 'Asir) as revolutionary, downtrodden, industrious, nationalist, practical, and sectarian. Those from Hijaz (the Western Province) were identified as mercantile, nervous, hospitable, artistic, sociable, and progressive. Saudis from Najd (the Central Province) were described as reactionary, conservative, religious, hospitable, sectarian, and miserly; whereas those from Asir (the Southern Province) were labeled as being poor, simple, ignorant, patient, generous, and backward.[60]

Although such stereotypes may be inaccurate, the description reflects some of the sentimental differences among Saudi citizens. It also proves the state's failure to foster a national discourse superseding private discourses, be they sectarian, regional or tribal.

In 1997, another Hijazi scholar emphasized the ethnic diversity and cultural distinctiveness in Saudi Arabia. She notes that:

> regional consciousness exists between Najdi tribal members and Hejazi urban settlers, exemplified by how they refer to each other. The more heterogeneous Hejazis, for example, are often called *baqaya hujjaj* (literally 'remnants of pilgrims') or *tarsh al-bahr* (flotsam of the sea),

while Najdis are called *badu* (Bedouin) or *shuruq* (Easterners).[61]

Furthermore, she maintains that internal diversity and heterogeneity are clearly reflected in the form of 'different dialects, specific religious rituals, different food, and regional dress, and are especially evident in the absence of interregional marriage'.[62]

Nevertheless, we should admit that modernization has changed the regional, sectarian and tribal perceptions of the people, which have passed through significant changes, each one incorporating new functional meanings. For the new Hijazi regionalist, regionalism could mean self-government or federal rule, while tribalism could be interpreted as a vehicle for its members to have access to jobs, the market and high posts. Shi'ism itself has witnessed organizational change, and ultimately individuals perceive it through different contexts, which owe something to the transformations that occurred under modernization programmes. This includes political Shi'ism, which was adopted by new generations who have been exposed to modern education, culture and values. It could be argued that revolutionary Shi'ism was, to a certain level, associated with the modernization process.

Although economic development is the most vital process by which people integrate into the state, its success is highly dependent on the degree to which people participate in it. While the Saudi royal family opted for partial technical modernization, namely, urbanization, industrialization and the institutionalization of the state, other aspects such as political modernization were ignored entirely. This selectivity seems to have provoked even the new Salafi activists who, being the product of quasi-modern universities, such as Imam Muhammad b. Sa'ud University, Islamic University in Medina and Umm al-Qura University in Medina, have levelled harsh criticisms against the ideological aspects of modernization such as secularism, democracy and liberalism.

The series of sermons delivered during the the Gulf crisis in 1990 by prominent Salafi activists (e.g. Salman al-'Awdah, Safar al-Hawali, Nasir al-'Omar and others) criticized what they termed *al-hadathiyfn* (the modernists), who dominated the state institutions.[63] Thus, in the Wahhabi religious community, modernization is producing groups that are deeply rooted in their religion and who at the same time make use of extreme rhetoric against modernization and modernists in the country. As a response, the royal family appears to have given the Salafis an influential role in standing against liberal tendencies, insofar as this role contributes to realizing the political ends of the al-Sa'ud dynasty. The common explanation is that this is essential for maintaining the religious values of society.[64]

Although modernization appears to have significantly contributed to the consolidation of the state, it has also created a new climate, in which political formations burgeon. The state has succeeded in curtailing the influence of both traditional and modern forces to a very limited extent only. This was evident in the 1950s and 1960s, and again in the last two decades, when the country witnessed incidents triggered by new forms of tribal and religio-ethnic groupings. The occupation of Mecca in 1979 revealed that a high number of 'Utaiba tribesmen were among those who occupied the *Haram*. Again, in the 1990s, the decline of state power during the Gulf crisis spurred both traditional and modernist groups to voice their political demands. The contents of the petitions that these groups presented to the king revolved, in essence, around the crisis of national identity. Their demands centred on the expansion of political participation, decentralization of the political system, equality among all citizens regardless of racial, dynastic, sectarian and social affiliations, and the reform of the judiciary, education and information systems.[65]

As the government failed to meet the people's political expectations, the crisis of national identity deepened. During the last decade, tribal, regional and sectarian tendencies began to flourish remarkably. Writings about tribes and regions have begun to appear in both local and external markets. Books about tribes such as Shammar, Banu Khalid and al-Jiluwi, regions such as Ha'il, Hijaz and 'Asir, and even towns and villages such as 'Awamiyah, Safwa and Tarout are commonplace.

Such tendencies are seen not only in those who are politically or religiously motivated but also in modern Saudi academics who live abroad, such as Mai Yamani, Madawi al-Rashid and Sorrya al-Torki. Yamani's book *Cradle of Islam* (2004) reflects the cultural, social and religious peculiarities of the Hijazi society and affirms the identity of the Hijaz against the attempts of the Saudi rule to undercut their cultural capital.[66] Al-Rashid[67] has written about the al-Rashid tribe to which she belongs, while al-Torki has focused on then 'Unayzah tribe.[68]

If modernization has introduced essential changes to the Saudi state, then it has also offered new meanings, tools and a discourse by which groups may reinforce their identities and fight against the state's exclusionary attitude.

As a result, modernization, in terms of communication, transportation and the media, has succeeded in curtailing the cultural and religious influence of the dominant group. For the Shi'is, modernization has ended their cultural isolation. They can travel in relatively large numbers to Iraq, Iran, Syria and other parts of the world to learn more about their sect. They can also listen to the radio, watch television and read newspapers, magazines and books, in order to know more about the world, including their own.

The impact of modernization on the Shi'is' political consciousness was relatively strong during the 1950s and 1960s, when groups of the Shi'is joined the nationalist and socialist parties, but minimal in altering the relationship between the Shi'is and the regime. On the religious level, neither the Shi'is' nor the state's position on doctrinal matters shifted. In Saudi Arabia, Shi'ism represents an agency of protection and a religious identity for the Shi'is vis-à-vis the state religion, Wahhabism. It is not the task of Shi'ism to secure the material needs of its followers; indeed, they have to seek different means to fulfil those needs. Thus, although the modernization process was the hand-maiden of the Shi'is' economic integration into the state, the Shi'is did not necessarily repudiate their loyalty to their religious and group values.

Modernization in terms of the institutionalization of the state was perhaps the most effective mechanism for integrating all groups (including the Shi'is in the Eastern Province, Medina and Najran) into the Saudi state. Aramco played a pivotal role in integrating a large number of the Shi'is into the Saudi oil industry. However, the Shi'is were excluded from the ministerial body and from most administrative positions in municipalities, local government and domestic authorities. Until recently, the position of headmaster in schools whose students are overwhelmingly Shi'is was not allotted to a Shi'is.

The pervasive shared sentiment among the Shi'is was created out of a sense of distinctiveness and powerlessness, as well as growing concerns about unfair treatment and the legal, economic and politically discriminatory strategies of Saudi rule.

Wahhabi Islam and loyalty to the royal family were the two pillars on which rested a national identity among the population. Although these two elements may have appealed to those who joined Ibn Sa'ud's troops and contributed to the realization of his political ends, they represented, from the perspective of other regions and groups, an implicit abandonment of their peculiar characteristics.

Some scholars of Saudi political history have laid heavy emphasis on the role of Islam in the unification of the country, without considering its religious heterogeneity, which made it impossible to use Islam in this way. As a result, the invocation of a transnational identity such as Islam failed to go beyond the boundaries of the Wahhabi Najdi community.

Although the groups that compose the country were integrated through political domination of the Saudi-Wahhabi allied forces, the unification of these groups owes its existence to external factors such as force and not to a collective will that emanated from themselves. Such groups have clung to their traditional identities and have withstood attempts by the dominant group to destroy them.

While a widely accepted and defined sense of nationalism has not yet evolved, the official Saudi understanding of this notion is that individuals should be loyal to the royal family. That is to say, nationalism was perceived by the al-Sa'ud as a blind commitment to the rules and regulations of the state. While nationalism in the West alleviated tensions between different groups and became an umbrella for all regions, the Saudi regime used it to reinforce its identity. Although the exploitation of nationalism contributed to the consolidation of the al-Sa'ud's rule, the rulers failed to develop a sense of national consciousness among the native population. Thus, the future of this alleged national identity is tied to the future of the royal family.

Modernization played a pivotal role in nation building and also in social and political realignment among various groups. The Shi'is, though, clung to their doctrinal orientation, while modernization helped them reformulate their sense of belonging and self-awareness and their political expectations.

Whatever the reasons behind the political and socio-cultural exclusion of the Shi'is, their identity developed at the expense of a national identity. This identity developed partly as a result of discriminatory policies by the state, and partly from cultural, social and doctrinal impulses. Both orientations have incited a large number of the Shi'is to organize themselves and voice their discontent against the exclusionary attitude of the state.

THREE

The Emergence of the Shi'i Islamic Movement (1968–79)

The Intellectual Phase: 1968–79

During the last two decades, Shi'i Islamic movements have been the object of much extensive and erudite study by Western and Muslim scholars, yet scant attention has been paid to the period before the emergence of militant Islamist groups. This is probably because it was a less 'heated' period compared to the revolutionary stage that followed the Iranian revolution of 1979.

In this chapter, I will refer strictly to the *harakat al-risaliyin al-tala'*, which means literally 'the Movement of Vanguards' Missionaries' (MVM). Apart from Iraq, the Movement included groups from Saudi Arabia, Bahrain, Kuwait and Oman. Until 1980, there was no clear-cut distinction between these groups. They formed a unified body. Throughout the 1980s, the MVM played a significant role in the politics of at least three countries, namely Iraq, Saudi Arabia and Bahrain, where many supporters joined and participated in MVM activities including religious learning programmes, newspapers and magazines, Islamic centres, preaching, fundraising and military training and operations.

Up to the end of 1990s, MVM was regarded as the second largest Shi'i Islamic movement in the Arab world after the *da'wa* party. Surprisingly, however, no single scholarly work has so far been dedicated to the study of the MVM. My purpose here, therefore, is to study in detail the discourse,

ideological foundations and agenda of this Shi'i Islamic movement in the three
decades before the Iranian revolution.

The MVM was founded in 1968 in Karbala, a Shi'i shrine city in Iraq,
under the patronage of the nascent *marji'taqlid* (religious authority) Ayatullah
Sayyid Muhammad Mahdi al-Shirazi (1928–2002). Al-Shirazi was the *marji'*
of millions of Shi'i Muslims in Iraq, Iran, the Gulf States and elsewhere in
the Indian subcontinent. In 1971 he was exiled to Lebanon by the Ba'thist
regime of Iraq. He later stayed in Kuwait until 1979, when he migrated to the
holy city of Qum, Iran, following the foundation of an Islamic Republic led by
Ayatullah Khomeini.

Al-Shirazi was born in the holy city of Najaf, Iraq. He belonged to a
distinguished scholarly family that has produced prominent scholars and
marji' taqlid, whose political and intellectual influence was tremendous both
in Iraq and Iran. Two of the best-known leaders are Grand Ayatullah Mirza
Hassan Shirazi, leader of the 'tobacco' movement in Iran in 1891, and Grand
Ayatullah Muhammad Taqi Shirazi, the leader of the 1920 revolution in Iraq
against British colonization. The Shirazi's father, the late Grand Ayatullah
Mehdi Shirazi, was a highly respected scholar and the *marji'* of his time.

Al-Shirazi was considered a mentor and inspiration to many Shi'is Muslims
around the globe. He made extensive contributions in various fields of religious
learning, ranging from jurisprudence, theology, politics, economics and law to
sociology and human rights, and reportedly authored more than 1200 books,
among them the 150-volume encyclopaedia of Islamic jurisprudence.[1]

Along with his father, al-Shirazi, aged nine, settled in the holy city of
Karbala, Iraq. After primary education, the young Shirazi continued his
studies in different branches of learning under his father's guidance as well as
those of various other eminent scholars and specialists.

Al-Shirazi's school of thought advocates the fundamental and elementary
nature of freedom in mankind. He calls for freedom of expression, political
plurality, debate and discussion, tolerance and forgiveness. He strongly believes
in the consultative system of leadership and calls for the establishment of the
leadership council of religious authorities.[2] He also nurtures the concept of
universal Islamic government encompassing all the Muslim countries. These
and other ideas are discussed in detail in his books.

In the mid-1950s, cultural and socio-religious activities began to draw in a
wide segment of the local community in Karbala. Religious learning centres,

popular sermons, magazines, books and social gatherings were the means by which individual and popular support were mobilized. These activities culminated in the formation of an organized movement, the aim of which was to propagate the message of Islam and enforce the dictates of the *shari'a*. Its ultimate end was to create *insan risali*, meaning a human imbibed with the Islamic message; *umma mu'mina* a faithful nation; and *hadara Islamiyya*, an Islamic civilization.[3]

Confrontation with the Iraqi regime by members of al-Shirazi's entourage forced the movement to seek refuge in Kuwait in 1970. Although Muhammad al-Shirazi is the spiritual leader and *marji' taqlid* of the members of the MVM, Muhammad Taqi al-Mudarresi is regarded as the actual leader and ideologue of the movement.

Muhammad Taqi al-Mudarresi was born in the holy city of Karbala in 1945. He started his religious learning at a young age and continued his advanced studies under his uncle, Grand Ayatullah Sayyid Muhammad Taqi al-Mudarresi, among others. He was exposed from an early age to the literature of enlightened Shi'is intellectuals in Iran such as Jalal al-Ahmad and 'Ali Shari'ati and Sunni intellectuals in Pakistan and Egypt such as Muhammad Iqbal, Shaikh Abu 'Ala al-Mawdudi (Pakistan), Shaikh Hassan al-Bana, Sayyid Qutb and Yusuf al-Sebai (Egypt). He acquired such expertise in Islamic thought that he became renowned in Shi'is religious circles in Karbala as a distinguished thinker. He generated a school of thought anchored in Shi'is traditional sources and aimed at producing a progressive version of Shi'ism based on new interpretation of the doctrines, history and legal systems of Shi'i Islam, in order to help establish the basis of Islamic revival.[4]

In 1968 al-Mudarresi was nominated by Ayatullah al-Shirazi to be the leader of the MVM, for his distinction in leadership and political credentials. In his quest for a political and popular base, he, together with other founding fathers of the Movement, made every possible effort to form a broader network of organizational cells throughout Iraq and the Gulf region.

Between 1970 and 1979, the MVM poured much energy into expanding its activities along the western coast of the Gulf region. Pamphlets and taped sermons were distributed among the Gulf Shi'is, mainly in Kuwait, Saudi Arabia, Bahrain and Oman, with the aim of winning the popular and financial support of the Shi'is in the Gulf states, from whom thousands of youths were recruited. In Bahrain, for instance, a large number of those subscribing to the leftist parties, notably the Popular Front and National Liberation Front, shifted to the MVM.

Shaikh Hassan al-Saffar, the renowned Saudi Shi'i speaker, political activist and founding father, together with Shaikh Tawfiq al-Saif, of the Islamic Shi'is opposition movement in the Eastern Province, joined the Movement in Kuwait and became one of its leading figures. He made a significant contribution to the proliferation of the MVM's literature, taped sermons and writings, as well as to the introduction of al-Shirazi's *marji'iyyat* (religious authority).

The Islamic Revolution Organization (IRO), which came into being in 1975, was, from its inception, affiliated with the MVM. Its discourse, world view and programmes are indistinguishable from those of the mother movement. As the IRO had no robust structure in its formative years of 1969 to 1979, we will consider here the literature of the MVM and the writings of al-Saffar during this time. First, however, we need an overview of the origins and circumstances of the MVM. Although Islamic movements have some common roots and concerns, the causes of their resurgence are manifold and differ from country to country.

The MVM emerged in a very complex political climate. Since the formation of the Iraqi state in 1920, the Shi'is, who constituted the majority of its population, played a marginal role in politics; indeed, they were a 'shadowy group'. In the 1920s, the Shi'is initiated an attempt to create a full independent state, but it was abortive and a Sunni king ascended to the throne. Subsequently, the Shi'is *'ulama* retreated from politics, confining themselves to scholastic activity.

With the rise to power of Abdul-Karim Qasim in 1958, latent secular ideologies were nourished by the prominence of Nasser's charismatic leadership and the flowering of nationalist sentiment in the Arab world. Secular ideologies, including Arab nationalism, communism and Ba'th socialism, were the dominant ideologies between 1954 and 1967. They inspired millions of Arabs to dream of comprehensive unity, economic prosperity and political pluralism, though such ambitious goals have never been realized. Furthermore, the nation-state in Iraq proved a failure in tackling the common problems associated with poverty, illiteracy and inequity.

As a result, Arab nationalism was destined to fall into a decline, an ideological defeat followed by a military one in 1967. The MVM emerged as a response to the failure of the secular ideologies to fulfil the dreams of the Arabs.

As in many Arab countries, the MVM drew on the vocabulary of Islam in order to voice its resentment against the comprehensive crisis in the Arab world. On the ideological level, there were persistent attacks against communism in Iraq and elsewhere in the Arab world, including Saudi Arabia. With the crushing defeat of the Six-Day War, the MVM, like Islamic movements elsewhere in the Arab world, blamed the Arab secularists and said that Israel had won the war because of its adherence to its religious roots. Many works opposing communism and its related ideologies were published during this period.

As the Islamic revival began to crystallize and take a certain shape in the mid-1970s, the discourse, world view and agenda of the MVM became identifiable. Generally speaking, its task, as a revivalist movement, was to reinterpret Islam, on the grounds that Islam encompasses all the issues that secular ideologies have raised and failed to answer. It is, at heart, as John Esposito observes, a quest for authenticity, identity and tradition.[6] This movement appears also to be part of a broader worldwide movement, in which people who are disaffected with their government and who feel threatened by the erosion of traditional values turn to religion as a source of identity.[7] In other words, the Islamic revival is a reassertion of cultural identity, formal religious observance, family values and morality, and, finally, it is the most effective source of resistance.

Another factor contributing to the emergence of the MVM is the perceived failure of the Shi'i traditional *marji'* and *hawza* in facing the common problems of the Shi'is in various parts of the Islamic world. The emergence of the MVM can be seen as a reaction to the inertia of the religious cultural sphere in Shi'is communities, as reflected in the perceived failure of the religious learning centres (*hawza*) to arrest the penetration of Western ideologies and cultural forms; to formulate programmes to overcome the ideological challenges facing the Shi'is; or to address socio-economic and political problems.

A third factor, which is more applicable to the Saudi Shi'is, is the uneven distribution of wealth, making material inequities and social imbalances greater and more visible. The sense of deprivation and discrimination among Saudi Shi'is has spurred groups of them to join the MVM, with the aim of challenging the discriminatory policies imposed by the Saudi regime.

The MVM's Ideology

What Islam does the MVM aim to revive? What type of Shi'ism does the MVM espouse? And what were the aims of the MVM during the important period 1968–79?

The literature of the MVM falls into two main types. The first type concerns Islam in general, and in it the ideologues of the MVM emphasize the comprehensiveness and validity of Islam, just as their Sunni counterparts do. The second type concerns Shi'ism, specifically, the sort of Shi'i Islam that contrasts with popular or traditional Shi'ism.

Comprehensive Islam Versus Comprehensive Jahiliyya

Throughout history, Islam has never ceased to be a determinant force in the life of Muslims. For the laity, Islam is a spiritual resource, a system of beliefs and values, and, as Durkheim calls it, an expression of social cohesion and identity. For rulers, Islam is a source of legitimacy by which they attain what Max Weber describes as the 'conflict-management capability' and, more important, by which they justify their existence and hegemony over their subjects. Finally, for the 'ulama, it provides a source of knowledge and spiritual authority.

Nevertheless, in the last century, Islam has been 'overshadowed by authoritarian states that have propagated secular ideologies and values'.[8] In response, Islamic revivalist movements, such as the Muslim Brotherhood in Egypt (founded in 1928) and *Jama'at-i-Islami* in India (founded in 1932), heralded the view that Islam is 'a comprehensive ideology for personal and public life, the foundation for Muslim state and society'.[9] This cliché has been expounded by nearly all Islamic revivalist movements that have come into being in the second half of the twentieth century, many of which have attempted to turn this assertion into a reality.

The MVM is the first Islamic movement to devote a great deal of its activities to actualizing this ambitious task. The ideologues of the MVM, including its spiritual leader and *marji' taqlid* Muhammad al-Shirazi, endeavoured to develop new themes of Islam, as well as ideas already promoted by Islamic revivalists in the nineteenth century, such as Jamal al-Din al-Afghani (1839–1897) and Muhammad 'Abduh (1849–1905).

Among the Shi'i *mujtahids*, Ayatullah al-Shirazi produced the first juristic encyclopaedia of Shiʿi Islamic history. It consists of 150 volumes encompassing a wide range of issues, from matters related to worship (ʿibadat) and conduct (muʿamalat) to modern issues such as the state, environment, management, traffic, economics, sociology, human rights, trade and business, media, psychology, medical science, freedoms, development and so on. It is asserted that all these issues are covered by the shariʿa.

Likewise, Muhammad Taqi al-Mudarresi, the leader of the MVM, wrote a series of books about various aspects of Islam. These books include: *Al-fikr al-Islami* (Islamic Thought); *Al-mantiq al-Islami* (Islamic Logic); *Al-qiyada al-Islamiyya* (Islamic Leadership); *Al-fiqh al-Islami* (Islamic Jurisprudence); *Al-tarikh al-Islami* (Islamic History); *Al-baʿth al-Islami* (The Islamic Renaissance); *Al-tashriʿ al-Islami* (Islamic Legislation); and *Al-maʿhad al-Islami* (The Islamic Institute).

Following the ideas of Qutb, another influential ideologue and famed speaker, Hadi al-Mudarresi,[10] a younger brother of Muhammad Taqi, in the early 1970s wrote pamphlets entitled *Al-Islam Manhaj al-Hayat* (Islam ... a Complete Programme for Life; Beirut, 1973); *Hadha al-Din Lil-Qarn al-Wahid wal-ʿIshrin* (This Religion Is for the Twenty-first Century; Beirut, 1988); *Al-Islam Abadan* (Islam ... for Eternity; Beirut, 1974); *Al-Alam Yabhathu ʿAn Khalas* (The World Seeks Salvation; Beirut, 1988); and *Al-Islam wal-Ideologiat al-Munawia'* ... *ela Ayn?* (Islam and Counter-Ideologies ... Where are they Heading to?; Beirut, 1974); in which he asserts the validity and comprehensiveness of Islam.

What are the implications of al-Shirazi's and the al-Mudarresi brothers' works? First, the authors' central aim is to prove that Islam possesses all answers to all questions, that, in the famous slogan of the Muslim Brotherhood, Islam is the solution; it is self-sufficient and deals with all issues, past, present or future. Second, the label *Islami* alludes to religious particularism, in the sense that it regards this version of 'Islam' as the only legitimate one, unlike other interpretations.[11] Third, the emphasis on the comprehensiveness of Islam entails delegitimizing other ideologies, and will inevitably lead to a stark clash with them.

The increased emphasis on the original sources of tradition (Qur'an and Sunna)[12] to educe precepts to modern problems is, in essence, an attempt to show that Islam is not only a 'belief of heart', but also a defined programme for individual and social life. These sources, as repeatedly asserted, encompass issues ranging from the compensation of a minor wound (*irsh al-khadsh*) to what humanity needs until the day of resurrection. Muhammad Taqi al-Muddaresi contends that the Qur'an not only specifies what people must believe and how they should behave, but also that it 'formulates irrevocable solutions for the problems of humanity'.[13]

It could be argued that there is a conspicuous difference between Muslim scholars with respect to understanding and interpreting the Qur'anic verses and Sunna, as well as to the experience of the Prophet's Companions. This diversity among Muslim scholars is unavoidable, since there is neither a fixed, accepted corpus of *hadith* nor monolithic principles that may be invoked for inferring religious precepts.

However, emphasis on the original sources of Islam is by no means a backward step towards restoring a seventh-century model. In fact, the literature of the MVM exhibits clearly that it is a future-oriented movement. For instance, Muhammad Taqi al-Muddaresi argues against the view endorsed by the majority of Islamist revivalists that, as every day passes, humanity moves towards a catastrophic end, on the basis of the famed tradition that, 'the best era is that of the Prophet, followed by the era that follows him'. By contrast, al-Muddaresi contends that human history is in a state of frequent evolution:

> The Islamic (*risaliyya*) culture is progressive and integrative, thus the last Prophet was the best because he was chosen to fulfil the message of his predecessors, the prophets, and he paved the way for humanity, so every *umma* is obliged to extend further towards integration, to reach an era where absolute justice prevails.[14]

This view seems to reverse the common perception that the seventh century is a normative era that should be revived and emulated; but it is at odds with the repeatedly expressed views of the ideologues of the MVM. There is, for instance, great emphasis on the notion that Islam is a doctrine and programme encompassing all facets of life, i.e. the social, political, economic, moral and so on, be they in the past, present or future.[15] There is of course a contradiction between the view of the inevitable evolution of the human historical movement and the positon that Islam is the last revealed message that stores the solutions for humanity until the end of time.

We now turn to the attitude of the MVM towards existing Muslim society, which will determine the discourse adopted by the movement and the mechanisms of change it advocates.

The literature of the MVM on this issue, both public and private, is inconsistent, apparently because of the about-turn in MVM thought in the late 1970s. It is clear, however, that the fundamental position of the movement is similar to that of Qutb, whose writings had a strong impact on the ideas and visions of the MVM's leaders.

Terms such as *jahili* and *ridda* were used frequently and loosely by Qutb and fused into the discourse of the MVM, although their connotations and implications should be considered carefully, since they were first used in a context that was heavily embroiled in the political situation in Egypt.

The term *jahiliyya* is commonly defined as a state of ignorance in the Islamic classical sense and refers to the pre-Islamic period. With the spread of Islam, *jahiliyya* became part of history, since the Meccan pagans surrendered and embraced Islam in the year 9 AH.

In the last five decades, Muslim scholars and revivalists have become distressed by the widening gulf between Islamic values, institutions and practices, on the one hand, and the emerging postcolonial nation-states that have spurned innate religious sentiment, on the other. The secular-oriented states such as Egypt, Syria and Iraq are often bitterly accused of having disparaged moral and religious values and injunctions. In such tense circumstances, the concept of *jahiliyya* saw its second birth.

Qutb's *Milestones* (*Ma'alim fi al-tariq*) was the most influential work of the late 1970s. The ideas, methodology and even vocabulary of the work caught the attention of the ideologues of the MVM. Based on personal experience and meetings with leading members of the movement, Qutb's works were circulated in Shi'i shrine cities, notably Karbala and Najaf, in the 1950s–1970s. For the members of the MVM, *Milestones* became part of an internal programme, which members were obliged to study.

Milestones was written for the awaited vanguard, whose task is to re-root Islam in the lives of all Muslims and to uproot *jahiliyya* practices, values and institutions. This call has been accepted by a wide spectrum of Islamic revivalists throughout the Islamic world, some of whom emerged in response to his call.

Further, Qutb sought to answer some focal questions, such as why Islam is the best formula for humanity; why Western civilization has failed to 'present healthy values for the guidance of mankind';[16] and how Muslims can re-establish Islam in the way Prophet Muhammad did.

According to Qutb, the answers to these questions are possible only if Muslims are bound by Islamic criteria; and the whole environment prevailing in the universe is a *jahiliyya*. He understands *jahiliyya* not in its traditional sense as a historical phenomenon, but as a state that will appear when it meets similar conditions to those of the pre-Islamic period, regardless of time and place.[17] Moreover, he believes that the modern *jahiliyya*, though similar in nature, differs from the first in terms of its comprehensiveness:

> Our whole environment, people's beliefs and ideas, habits and arts, rules and laws, is *jahiliyya*, even to the extent that what we consider to be Islamic culture, Islamic sources, Islamic philosophy, and Islamic thought are also constructs of *jahiliyya*.[18]

Jahiliyya represents, Qutb argues, a system of belief, values and institutions. Against the traditional and narrow Islamic sense, *jahiliyya* is not merely ignorance in the path of God, but is, in essence, a counter-sovereignty in its broadest sense. It manifests itself in socio-political orders in which men impose power over other men, in order to adjudicate principles of conduct that are not derived from divinely based sources. Eventually, *jahiliyya*, as Qutb defines it, is the sovereignty of humans over humans. Whether in its old or modern form, Qutb argues that *jahiliyya* is antithetical to the sovereignty of Islam.

Taking his ideas to the extreme, Qutb argues that the true Muslim community vanished from existence on earth the moment the laws of God were suspended, and laws, regulations, habits, standards and values were derived from a source other than that of Allah. As such, the whole world, including the Islamic part, 'is steeped in *jahiliyya*, and all the marvellous material comforts and high-level inventions do not diminish this ignorance'.

Based on certain verses in the Qur'an, Qutb promotes the concept of *jahiliyya* to assign a certain role to a Muslim vanguard in a *jahili* environment. This vanguard resembles that of the period of the Prophet Muhammad's mission, when he had intermittent contact with existing society, as a step towards redressing the imperfections and moral corruption of the *jahiliyya*.[19]

An overview of the literature of the two major Shi'i movements (*al-da'wa* and MVM) shows that Qutb's concept of the *jahiliyya* provided a context within which the ideologues of both parties formulated world views, strategies and religious discourse.

Hizb al-da'wa, for instance, have had a bewildering experience with regard to its final verdict on existing Muslim society. In 1966, a prominent leader of the *da'wa* stated: 'the society in which we live is not Islamic; rather it is saturated with Western spirit and thought.' He reiterated this view, saying, 'our movement has risen on the basis of a belief that our society is not Islamic.' However, the later generation of leaders of the *da'wa* abruptly stemmed these statements made by the founding fathers, in the hope of arresting the growing criticisms against such a radical position within the party.[20] Indeed, as the *da'wa* fled Iraq in the late 1970s, its views, positions and even strategies drastically changed. In the early 1980s a major debate took place between different wings in the party over the question of what the *da'wa*'s position should be towards existing Muslim communities. According to the so-called *bayan al-tafahum*, the Communique of Understanding issued in 1982, the dispute over the question was settled in favour of those who believed that the exisiting *umma* was Islamic.[21]

One private pamphlet by MVM asked whether they lived in an Islamic society and answered the question by suggesting three main attributes of Islamic society: the collective commitment to the good, or *khair*, based on the principle of propagating virtues and prohibiting vices; the observance of prayer and religious alms (*zakat*); and obedience to religious leadership. The pamphlet concluded that the Islamic society of the day is not heading towards God, but towards materialism.[22] 'The majority of our youth do not observe prayer, and the majority of Muslims do not pay the prescribed tithe.'[23] Consequently, 'the existing society is apostate [*murtadd*].' Like Qutb, the pamphlet distinguished between two forms of *jahiliyya*: the first occurred before the advent of Islam, when the sins of *jahili* society were excusable because of the absence of divinely ordained guidance, but today's society has no excuse before God, since He has fully accomplished the message of Islam, while the Prophet(s) and Imams have exerted their best efforts to guide humanity.[24]

Like Qutb, the MVM sees the current environment as similar to that of the pre-Islamic period. According to an unpublished treatise:

Before the Islamic society deserted faith (*yartadda*), the whole of life was based on Islam, namely state, family, school and other social institutions ... But today, following the invasion of Western civilization and the proliferation of infidel trends armed with ideology, money and weapons, the situation has turned upside-down. Everything is now based on un-Islamic norms.

The apostate to *jahiliyya* has changed all the characteristics of our religious life; social institutions have led individuals to infidelity and libertinism, and not to faithful commitment.[25]

Thus it is the task of the MVM to build the nucleus of Muslim society, by removing *jahiliyya* idols and values and re-orienting individuals towards the principle of *tawhid*.[26] As such, Islamic revivalism in the minds of the ideologues of the MVM is the rebellion of the Muslim against a corrupt society.[27] Ultimately, Islam is a message that aims at 'undermining the *jahili* construction inside and outside the human body, and replacing it with a perfect Islamic civilizational construction'.[28]

Clearly, this radical stance reflects the perceived socio-religious realities of the 1960s and 1970s, when Muslim society was believed to be lacking religious consciousness, observance and commitment to the injunctions and prohibitions of Islamic law, as a result of the proliferation of what used to be called *al-tayyarat al-ilhadiyya*, namely secular and communist currents. The ideologues of the MVM most probably used Qutb's radical terms in order to illustrate the perils of the separation between religion and society.

In order to bring the existing *jahili* society to Islam, there must be what Qutb calls a 'Muslim vanguard', armed with the message of God. This task is related intimately to the communal role of the believer, whose responsibility is not limited to securing his own faith, but extends to the faith of the whole people.[29] Thus, the title 'The Movement of Vanguards' Missionaries' echoes Qutb's call to set up a movement that claims to walk in the footsteps of the Prophet in the *jahiliyya* period and bears the task of eliminating the roots of the *jahiliyya* and restoring Islamic values, institutions and legal codes to the Muslim peoples, who are portrayed as *jahili*.[30]

Thus the early writings of the ideologues of the MVM start from fundamental questions related to the basic doctrines of Islam. Does God exist?[31] How many gods are there? What are the attributes of God? What does worship imply? It then extends to the justice of God, the messages and apostles of Allah, the divinely ordained guidance of the Imams, the day of resurrection, human acts, predestination, fatalism, virtues, vices and so on.[32]

Another central theme of the MVM is refutation of the secular notion of religion. In a privately published pamphlet, its ideologues assert that Islam is a religion of life.[33] The MVM rejects the idea advocated by secular intellectuals that religion is an individual matter. It emphasizes the fusion of individual religious observances with the social message of Islam.

This new interpretation of Islamic traditional concepts established a base for a great deal of writing by the ideologues of the MVM, which convey the message that Islam is a social message; an economic revolution; a school of thought; a political system; and a comprehensive and universal message of reform. It is interesting to note that the internal literature reduces prophets to social reformers, though their message of reform is based on the principle of *tawhid*. While little is said about the purely religious mission of the prophets, great importance appears to be placed on their social message, which consists of three major principles: justice, truth and freedom.[34] These principles represent the main objectives of the MVM. Indeed, the MVM's ideological reading of the history of religions and prophets is meant to justify its activities, as will become clear when we focus on this new interpretation of Shi'ism.

In the final analysis, the major objective of the MVM prior to 1980 was to restore Islam to Muslim social life, in the sense that it aimed to reactivate the role of religion in the social domain and present Islam in a more modern framework, with the aim of attracting the largest possible segment of Shi'is Muslim society.

The Reactivation of Shi'ism

Shi'i Thought and History
Before the foundation of a revolutionary-oriented state in Iran in 1979, Shi'ism leaned towards political quietism, as most Shi'is jurists had, for many centuries, denied the temporal authorities, awaiting the end of time, when al-Mahdi would reappear.

The collective political resignation of the Shi'is shortly after the occultation of the twelfth Imam has shaped Shi'is thought for nearly ten centuries. While no kind of Shi'is religious state was attempted by the *'ulama* until 1979, Shi'i jurists and theologians promoted traditional legal and mystical concepts to justify the quietist attitude of the Shi'is. Certain parts of the *shari'a* (e.g. *jihad*, *zakat*, Friday Prayer and *hudud*) were to be abandoned until the reappearance of the Mahdi,[35] and, likewise, concepts such as dissimulation (*taqiyya*) and waiting (*intizar*) provided incentives for an isolationist tendency among the Shi'is, which led to the depoliticization of Shi'ism. These doctrines appear to have created a milieu in which mystic and Hellenic-oriented teachings were integrated into the Shi'i system of belief. Thus, the view that several common theological characteristics unite Sufism and Shi'ism is, to a great extent, correct, as Sufi monasticism supports the Shi'i messianic doctrine, as well as its passivity and resignation.[36]

Despite significant developments in the eighteenth century, namely the *usuli* dominance, which led to the rapid growth of the rational tendency within Shi'i Islam and the crystallization of the religious establishment, the interpretation of tradition was, to a great extent, confined to the juristic field.[37] In fact, the Shi'is *mujtahid*s succeeded in overcoming the major obstacles that debarred them from producing legal precepts relating to matters of worship (*'ibadat*) and conduct (*mu'amalat*). With the exception of sporadic attempts to unite religion and politics in the eighteenth century, there was a tacit agreement on the separation between what belongs to God and what belongs to Caesar. Thus, messianic teachings remained intact and effective among the Shi'is until the first half of the twentieth century. Furthermore, institutionalized control over the laymen (*muqallid*s) and the consolidation of the *mujtahid*'s authority curtailed the potential possibilities of altering the doctrinal constructs of Shi'ism.

The hierarchy of the *'ulama* strove to maintain the unity of the Shi'is community by requiring allegiance to themselves, not only in juristic matters but also in nearly all religious matters. As a consequence, the highly influential relationship of the *mujtahid*s to their *muqalid*s became more institutionalized, and *taqlid* became the barometer for the gathering of followers who are obliged to emulate the legal precepts of the *mujtahid*s. It is this uneasy relationship that explains the quietist *'ulama*'s domination of the Shi'i religious establishment.

However, the renowned jurist Sayyid Kadim al-Yazdi formulated a chapter of emulation (*taqlid*) and reasoning (*ijtihad*) that formed the infrastructure for the later jurists to develop the concept of religious authority of the *marji'*. As a result, the *marji'iyyat* encompasses all religious and social issues. Although the Najaf *marji'iyyat* was traditionally anti-*wilayat al-faqih*, it enjoys an authority almost equal to that of the advocates of the absolute guardianship of jurists. Armed with allegedly divinely ordained authority, it possesses the power of legalization and de-legalization of nearly all acts of the laymen.

Consequently, up until the Iranian revolution, there is little to choose in the attitudes about inherited messianic teachings and beliefs between the traditionalists (*akhbaris*) and the rationalists (*usulis*).

Here we shall describe the attempts of the MVM to liberate Shi'ism from the clutches of quietist thought.

Reform of the Shi'i Learning System

From the outset, the MVM aimed to form a parallel religious authority to the traditional and long-standing one in Najaf. In doing so, it endeavoured to build its own *marji'iyyat* and network of learning centres, agents (*wukala'*) and emulators, and also to formulate its own curricula, political movement and ideology.

The ideologues of the MVM attempted to redress what they believed to be the defects in the religious learning systems in the Najaf *hawza*. In this section we will consider further the underlying ideas that were articulated by the leading ideologues of the MVM.

Muhammad Taqi al-Mudarresi emphasized the need to develop the curricula of the Shi'is *hawza*. In his critique of the prevailing education system, al-Mudarresi raised a series of questions concerning the devotion of the men of *hawzas* to the classical sciences and their total neglect of the modern sciences.[38] In his view, the Church's rejection of modern sciences was the main cause of atheism (*ilhad*). Apparently, the comparison between the attitude of the church and that of the *hawza* points to a specific situation in Iraq. What al-Mudarresi aimed to convey by this comparison was that the spread of anti-religious ideologies, particularly communism, was merely the result of the *hawza*'s refusal to integrate modern sciences into the religious education curricula.

What determines the dynamics of the religious education system, in al-Mudarresi's view, is its flexibility in accommodating changing conditions. The responsibility of the *'ulama* is not to reproduce the problems and solutions of predecessors or to pursue solutions to problems that do not exist. He believes that the men of the *hawza* are in need '[of those] who are acquainted with both politics and religion, so as to provide a religious vision to [our] political problems; of those who know economics and possess religious visions, so as to suggest solutions to [our] economic problems; of those who know modern culture and its currents in education, sociology, literature, and art, so as to provide [us] with effective results'.[39] In short, al-Mudarresi advocates what he calls *waqi'iyat al-tashri'* (realistic legislation).[40]

Al-Mudarresi insists on liberating religious disciplines from old philosophies and related branches of knowledge, notably Greek logic and mysticism. He argues that these disciplines have had a destructive impact on Shi'i faith and thought. Through philosophical studies, he argues, gnostic doctrines, Hellenic theories and Sufi monastic traditions were integrated into the *hawza*'s curricula at the expense of the authentic teachings of Islam and the infallible Imams. Al-Mudarresi wrote a number of books, entitled *Al-mantiq al-Islami* (Islamic Logic), *Al-fikr al-Islami* (Islamic Thought) and *Al-'irfan al-Islami* (Islamic Mysticism), to refute those philosophical theories, which he regards as intruders to Islamic thought. These theories, he argues, were formulated by Greek philosophers such as Aristotle and Plato, and subsequently expounded by Muslim philosophers such as al-Hallaj, Ikhwan al-Safa', Ibn 'Arabi, Ibn Sina and al-Farabi, who did not base their theories on revelation and scripture. In his belief, the philosophical theories taught in the *hawza* spawned the proliferation of defective doctrines such as the unity of being, determinism and fatalism, most of which lead to *shirk* in a religious sense and resignation in a socio-political sense. Al-Mudarresi was reluctant to publish *Al-'irfan al-Islami*, lest it provoke Khomeini, a prominent advocate of philosophy.

In an attempt to debunk the apologetic philosophies that have penetrated Islamic thought, he argues that a philosophy such as that of the unity of being is responsible for confining human will. Like Shaikh 'Abduh, al-Mudarresi argues that this philosophy aims to unify good and evil, creator and creature. As a result, worshipping Allah or idols would be the same, since everything belongs to one autonomous entity, and thus abandons the boundaries between right and wrong, good and evil, responsibility and irresponsibility, and so forth.[41]

Al-Mudarresi's critique stretches to concepts such as metaphysics, asceticism, mysticism and supplementation (*du'a'*), which transformed, with the passage of time, into shackles, leading to the dominance of what he calls an 'apologetic culture' (*thaqafa tabririyya*). He argues that the *umma*, exhausted by internal wars, invented this culture to justify its escapism. By the same token, he refutes Sufi asceticism, which he regards as an 'abandonment of responsibility'.[42]

Indeed, unlike Shari'ati, al-Mudarresi was not an iconoclast, though he was at war with what was, and sought to create what ought to be. Al-Mudarresi detested the persistence of outmoded tradition, and upheld his Islam with reference to traditional sources, but with a different interpretation. Indeed, al-Mudarresi, again unlike Shari'ati, was reluctant to take on this daunting task openly, and thus used a pseudonym for his critical writings, to avoid possible friction with the Shi'i traditional scholars and *hawzas*.

Overall, al-Mudarresi's attempts to formulate alternative and competitive Islamic theories failed to inspire both the students of traditional *hawzas* and those of the *hawza* he sponsored; many of them adhered to the curricula enforced by the highly influential and recognizable *'ulama* in the *hawza*. The probable reason is that the works he produced did not conform to the learning order in the traditional *hawza*, in addition to their unsuitability for higher studies in the *hawza*. A closer look, for example, into *Islamic Logic* and *Islamic Thought*, written by al-Muddaresi, shows that they are too basic for those who aim to continue their higher studies in the *hawza*. More importantly, these books are not compatible with other disciplines students learn in the *hawza*, such as *usul al-fiqh*, the principles of jurisprudence, which is closely related to logic, as taught in the Shi'i traditional *hawza*.

Apart from the classical disciplines taught in the Shi'i traditional *hawza*, students of *al-Rasfl hawza* were taught subjects such as Qur'anic studies, Islamic history, classical literature, writing, politics and Islamic culture (*al-thaqafa al-Islamiyya*). Some courses, such as politics and literature, were based on works translated or written by secular Arab authors, particularly Palestinian, though delivered by lecturers subscribing to the MVM. The aim behind the *hawza* was to produce individuals who have the capacity to spread the type of Islam and Shi'ism adopted by the MVM among the Gulf Shi'is. Indeed, al-Mudarresi transformed the *hawza* into a missionary centre for those who were recruited to propagate the religious-political message of the MVM.

As regards religious studies, al-Mudarresi may be considered a reformer, but from without. In other words, since he did not belong to the traditional hierarchy, the efforts he exerted were impeded by the *'ulama* and a large segment of the students of higher studies in his *hawzas*, whether in Kuwait or in those *hawzas* that were established after his migration to Iran in 1979. The students believed that al-Mudarresi's attempts were not based on a comprehesive assessment of religious seminaries and curricula, since the latter have a genealogy that may be traced back over two centuries.[43] This implies that changing the learning system requires a new infrastructure for the *hawza*'s education system; and this task cannot be achieved without collective effort.

Reinvention of Shi'i Tradition

Contemporary Shi'ism's intellectual transformation from quietism to activism took place outside the realm of the *hawza*. The advocates of Shi'i reform do not subscribe to the religious hierarchy; rather, they have been exposed to secular ideologies, mainly socialism.

Two important currents dominated the contemporary history of Shi'ism, first in Iran and then elsewhere in the Middle East. These currents are anti-Westernization. The spokesman and pioneer of the first was Jalal al-Ahmad (d. 1969), a former Tudeh member who coined the expression '*gharbzadaghi*', to 'denote and condemn those who were awestruck, intoxicated, or bewitched by the West'.[44] The expression has been widely used by an enthusiatic audience among the generation of youth who are against Western imperialism and internal dictatorship. Jalal al-Ahmad's writings gained added attraction when he promoted Islamic themes, albeit with a Marxist flavour. It is highly likely that al-Ahmad is the first contemporary Shi'i writer to try to devise a certain type of revolutionary Shi'ism. The impact of Jalal's thought on the Shi'is *'ulama* may be observed in the favourable comments from Imam Khomeini, and in the wide circulation of his famed work *Gharbzadaghi*, which has been translated into Arabic.[45]

The other current was led by Dr 'Ali Shari'ati (1933–1977), the ideological father of the Iranian revolution. Expanding on Jalal's idea of *Gharbzadaghi*, Shari'ati portrayed the Iranian intellectual as a fake copy of his European counterpart, acting as a 'guide' to neo-colonialism.

Since Jalal al-Ahmad died in the late 1960s, Shari'ati occupied the intellectual space of Iran for less than a decade. Though he left few coherent and systematic written works, his published talks were rich in ideas, ideals and spirit. The impact of Shari'ati's revolutionary thought, socio-religious analysis and politico-religious visions on Shi'i Islamic movements, be they in Iran, Iraq or elsewhere, is undeniable. His synthesis of religion with modernity was received positively by both the educated youth and religious activists. Though many of the men of the *hawza* despised Shari'ati in public, quite a large number of them were mesmerized by his attractive speeches and rhetoric.

An examination of Shari'ati's thought must focus on the Shi'i themes that

Shari‘ati tried to develop, and how his methods, visions and ideas influenced the ideologues of the MVM. Shari‘ati preached a return to the kind of Shi‘ism preached by the first three Imams, ‘Ali, Hassan and Hussain, which aimed at reviving the perceived meanings, symbols and traditions of the original version of Shi‘ism. However, Shari‘ati's progressive thought will remain under investigation, since many of his ideas are derived from neither the Shi‘i cultural legacy nor canonical sources, but are to a considerable extent influenced by his socialist tendency and leanings.

Sickened by the dictatorship in his country and the political aloofness of the *ulama*, Shari‘ati entered the realm of religious thought in order to promote a paradigm of an ideal Islamic society, relying on the argument presented by Max Weber (1864–1920) about the 'ideal type' of society. Shari‘ati sought to define the fundamental factors for the change and transformation of human societies. This seems to have had added urgency for the ideologues of the MVM, who struggled to change the corrupt situation and set up an Islamic society. In Shari‘ati's view, the fundamental factor for the change and transition of society is its people. He argues that Islam is the first social school of thought, which considers the people to be 'the basis and fundamental factor of society and history as well as responsible for the divisions within history and society'.[46]

Shari‘ati's influential philosophy of history is the most distinguishing feature of his school of thought. He believes that at any point in history, humanity is destined to undergo a class struggle. Shari‘ati argues that class struggle takes a static form, that is, a struggle between a chain of polarities: Divine and Satan, rich and poor, good and evil, true and false, oppressors and oppressed, and so on. He maintains that the struggle between Cain and Abel symbolizes the perpetual conflict between two contradictory fronts.[47] Imam Hussain's revolt was the most vivid example of this dualistic conflict, in which the oppressed, exemplified by Hussain, rose to eradicate the tyrannies of the oppressor, Yazid.

The emphasis on the episode of Karbala helps to eliminate the impasse in Shi‘i thought. Shari‘ati's philosophy of history, as summarized in the eternal confrontation between classes, was expounded by many Shi‘is scholars. In the literature of the MVM, however, Shari‘ati's concept of class struggle within society is clothed in religious language, and so takes the title 'the struggle between the truth (*haqq*) and falsehood (*batil*)'. According to one private treatise, 'Since Cain killed Abel [...] struggle never ceased to dominate the relationship between individuals.' It is, in other words, a 'struggle between *haqq* and *batil*', starting with Cain and Abel. In each period of time persons and poles are disguised differently, but the essence and objective remain the same.[48] This implies that human beings have no choice but to follow the path either of Cain or of Abel. Shi'is ideologues reinterpreted traditional and historical incidents in the light of this historic vision, ultimately reconstructing the Shi'i system of belief.

The ideologues of the Movement contend that prevailing Shi'i Islam is not a pure form of religion, but a collection of inherited social traditions, legends, imported philosophies, etc., besides religious formal practices and teachings. Thus it is important to rid Shi'i Islam of alien doctrines and tenets. The MVM was the first Shi'i movement in the Arab world that attempted to exercise some sort of critique of traditional Shi'i Islam.

Al-thaqafa al-risaliyya (The Message-Oriented Culture) was the most courageous self-criticism of its kind among the Arab Shi'is. Written by Muhammad Taqi al-Mudarresi and published in the mid-1970s, the book forms the most important source of the Movement's religious ideas. It attempts to answer the questions, why are the Shi'is backward and what are the root causes of the dilemma within Shi'i Islam?

The author claims that Shi'i culture is itself responsible. It is 'the corrupt culture that invaded and dominated the minds of the Shi'is, and thus produced pseudo-sacred values and defective intellectual methods'. This culture, al-Mudarresi argues, is not the genuine form of Shi'i Islam. He critically discusses certain concepts that are considered integral parts of the Shi'i theological legacy. Among the concepts he aims to tackle is that of occultation or *ghayba*.

Like Shari'ati, al-Mudarresi looks at occultation from two different angles: first, its negative social impact on the Shi'is community, which was dormant, passive and socio-politically disabled; and second, its negative political impact on the Shi'i jurists, who kept aloof from politics. Occultation, he postulates, 'is neither a passive waiting for the advent of a rosy future, nor a leadership vacuum'.[49] In other words, it is not a state of stagnation, but a process of rehabilitation and sacrifice. As can be noted, this view is in stark contrast to the traditional belief in the occultation of the twelfth Imam. Al-Mudarresi, being exposed to the progressive thought of Shari'ati and the Muslim Brotherhood of Egypt, sought to rediscover Shi'i tradition.

Another aspect of the critique focuses on jurisprudence and legal reasoning.

Al-Mudarresi argues that Shi'i jurisprudence failed to produce modern legislation and precepts that are suited to modern life. Shi'i jurists, he argues, have made little effort to fill what Sayyid Muhammad Baqir al-Sadr has coined *manteqat al-faragh*, the empty quarter in jurisprudence, in which jurists are supposed to produce precepts on issues being raised at different times. The author poses a question about the lack of legal precepts regarding the issues of the time, *al-hawadith al-waqi'a*, or what was recently termed *al-masa'il al-haditha* or *al-haditha*, i.e., the Islamic view of the liberal capitalist and socialist economic systems; its view of various schools of modern psychology and sociology, and so on. Furthermore, he emphasizes the role of the Qur'an in addressing both minor and major issues of life.[50] These views seem to be contradictory, since the call to fill the empty quarter contradicts the allegation that the Qur'an encompasses all topics.

It is clear that al-Mudarresi's critique of the popular conception of Shi'i Islam is similar to that of Shari'ati, in the emphasis it gives to the negative impact of metaphysical ideas and philosophies such as fatalism, determinism and so on, and doctrines such as intercession, cold mourning (*al-huzn al-barid*) and passive waiting, all of which Shari'ati discussed in his public sermons in *Hussainiyyat Irshad*, either tackling them or reinterpreting them, in an attempt to promote a Shi'i revolutionary paradigm. Like Shari'ati, al-Mudarresi contends that these philosphies and doctrines impeded the progress of the Shi'is, making them backward on social, economic and poltical levels.

Although al-Mudarresi reveals the shortcomings and stagnation of Shi'i jurisprudence, he does not tell us how it is possible to produce legal precepts that are not based upon traditional sources, without having recourse to the apologetic culture he strives to debunk. If apologetic culture, as he explains it, is the type of interpretation of a religious text that reflects a particular inclination of a person, then this may be applied to the new interpretation of Shi'i tradition, since this interpretation does not necessarily comply with Shi'i traditional sources.

Taqiyya and Intizar: from Passivism to Activism

Shari'ati's revolutionary discourse transformed the doctrine of *intizar* into an ideology of social protest. He distinguishes between two types of *intizar*, negative and positive. Negative *intizar* sees salvation and the establishment of a just rule as the sole responsibility of the Imam, while positive *intizar* is, in essence, a revolution. Contrary to the conventional view, Shari'ati contends that *intizar* is the belief that the universal revolution will take place at the end of time. That is to say, *intizar* is implicitly a refusal of the oppressor's rule, and responsible believers must play a part in revolting against this rule and replacing it. In fact, Shari'ati reversed the implication of *intizar*, to place the responsibility of reform and change on believers, so that the result would be the 'Mahdi, who is waiting for us'.[51] Believers should, then, be prepared for his reappearance, so as to put an end to the dualities and the binary system that has ruled human history, so there would be no ruler and ruled, poor and rich, oppressor and oppressed.

Through this revolutionary interpretation, which twisted around the most inert doctrine in Shi'i Islam, namely *intizar*, Shari'ati successfully paved the way for traditional scholars to find an ideology of protest and salvation in Shi'ism. For the ideologues of the MVM, these new revolutionary interpretations would transform its discourse, world views and strategies. Shaikh Hassan al-Saffar, responding to Shari'ati's translated works in Arabic, raises questions about the role of the laity at the time of occultation: does the occultation mean a ceasefire between truth (*al-haqq*) and falsehood (*al-batil*)? And if *al-batil* is active, is it the role of *al-haqq* to remain passive and confined? He contends that Islamic teachings urge believers to preach the message of God and propagate virtues and prohibit vices. The task of the believer, then, is to prepare the ground for the Mahdi to reappear, by propagating Islamic values and principles and forming the nucleus of an Islamic society, which the Imam aims to realize. Al-Saffar claims that when believers begin working towards implementing the message of God on earth, then the Imam will appear to fulfil the task.[52]

Obviously, this interpretation contrasts with Shi'i traditions and the expositions of the prominent Shi'i *'ulama* in the tenth century. Based on the tradition about *taqiyya*, the latter called their Shi'i followers to adhere to the principle of waiting (*intizar*), limiting themselves to performing religious observances (*'ibadat*) until the reappearance of the divinely ordained Mahdi.

A Revolutionary Reading of Islamic History
The history, symbols and doctrines of Shi'i Islam underwent a sharp transformation in the second half of the twentieth century. The Shi'i legacy has been revolutionized, reinterpreted and modernized. The ideologization

of Shi'ism began to colour the works of Shi'is activists, spurred by domestic political circumstances and the religious sentiments and slogans that appeared on the horizon shortly after the 1967 war.

Since a reinterpretation of Shi'ism would serve the cause of change, Shari'ati distinguishes between two types of Shi'ism: Black Shi'ism and Red Shi'ism, or Safavi Shi'ism and 'Alawi Shi'ism. Black/Safavi Shi'ism is the type that becomes a tool the ruler uses to oppress the ruled. It encourages the passive waiting of the populace for the reappearance of the saviour, and also the shedding of tears and mourning on the days of 'Ashura, without apprehending the profound message conveyed in Hussain's martyrdom.

Shari'ati's unprecedented analysis of Shi'ism has had a great impact upon a large number of Shi'i activists, both in Iran and outside. In distinguishing between the two versions of Shi'ism, he aims to develop a paradigm of Shi'ism that is the religion of martyrdom. He holds that historical Shi'ism was an ideology of protest, beginning with 'Ali's refusal of the council's election of Abu Bakr until the pre-Safavid times. With the advent of the Safavid era in 1497, Shi'ism leaned towards quietism. In vigorously denouncing Safavid/ Black Shi'ism, Shari'ati was, indeed, attacking prevailing Shi'i doctrines, beliefs and rituals. The fact is that the Black Shi'ism that Shari'ati attacked was nothing other than the version practised by the great majority of the Shi'is in his time, and the version he devoted much effort to replacing.

Shari'ati's presentation of Shi'i history is not sound and scientific. It is subject to ideological motivation and selectivity. He has sketched a historical map of Shi'ism that is contrary to the view accepted by modern scholars. The latter are agreed that Shi'ism was, from its inception at the time of Ja'far al-Sadiq, quietist, and remained so until recent decades, during which Shari'ati himself was among the first Shi'i ideologues to transform it into a revolutionary ideology.[53]

Those with ideological tendencies are selective in approaching various topics that fall within the scope of their activities. Shi'is Islamist revivalists seek anecdotes from classical sources to fortify their perceptions and goals, even though these anecdotes might, in many cases, contradict sound reports and traditions.

Nonetheless, it is clear that Shari'ati's revolutionary interpretation of Shi'i history appears to have captured the attention of the ideologues of the MVM. Influenced by Shari'ati's thought, Shi'ism is defined in their writings as an 'integrated revolutionary culture [;] it delineates a sketch of the struggle of the deprived (*mahrumin*) and the downtrodden masses (*mustad'afin*)'. In another definition, Shi'ism is 'the genuine revolutionary sect that served the cause of the *umma*'.[54] The definitions and the terms used echo Shari'ati's class analysis. Indeed, the Qur'anic terms incorporated in Khomeini's discourse and then widely used by Shi'is activists were first employed by Shari'ati, who strove to promote an Islamic class perspective as well as a Shi'i revolutionary ideology.[55]

The MVM reinterprets the history of Shi'ism in a way that reflects Shari'ati's ideas about Shi'ism as a populist movement. In the literature of the 1970s, the MVM tended to promote the view that government/political power is not an ultimate objective of Shi'ism. On the contrary, they argued, the latter emerged to oppose political power and to defend the rights of the masses. In this respect, the MVM cites Hussain's revolution as something that can be emulated. One private pamphlet describes Hussain's revolution as a 'red revolutionary reform', a term echoing Shari'ati's Red Shi'ism.[56]

In the late 1970s, Muhammad Taqi al-Mudarresi, delivered a series of lectures in an attempt to reinterpret the history of Shi'ism, which subsequently appeared in book form in 1982. The author depicts Shi'i history as a flow of revolts, one following the other. Even quietist Imams, such as Muhammad al-Baqir and Ja'far al-Sadiq, were revolutionized according to this new interpretation of Shi'i history.

Likewise, Shaikh Hassan al-Saffar attempts to reinterpret the history of the *ahl al-bayt* and infallible Imams. He rejects the view that the Imams are utopians who cannot be emulated. He contends that this view reflects the defeatist tendency dominating the backward generation of Muslims, most of whom have tried to justify their aloofness with regard to corrupt realities. He argues that the history of the Imams that has been handed down emphasizes their tragic, supernatural and miraculous nature, while their social and political roles have been to a great extent either misinterpreted or discounted.[57] In his view, the Imams are the embodiment of divine values and ideals, particularly resistance and sacrifice, and these values are signposts for humans to follow.[58]

Clearly, this view of the Imams corresponds with Shari'ati's view, in which he condemns the popular conception that the Imams are 'pure, sacred and preternatural souls, superhuman beings who are the only means of approaching and having recourse to God'.[59]

'Ashura: The Revolutionary Paragon

It was Shari'ati's school of thought and revolutionary presentation of the episode of Karbala that diverted the attention of the Shi'is away from the passive and tragic aspect of the incident towards a revolutionary and active one. Undoubtedly, no Shi'i scholar had previously considered the universal dimensions of Hussain's martyrdom in the way that Shari'ati did. Furthermore, no one, including Khomeini, had considered the term *shahada* (martyrdom) in the way that Shari'ati did.[60]

For Shari'ati, Hussain is not only a martyr but also the ideal man, a universal emblem and historical symbol who has sacrificed his soul for the sake of the oppressed throughout human history. By the same token, Hussain's action in Karbala was a 'prototype for all societies and all cultures'.[61] As such, Hussain represents the prophets from, using Shari'ati's Persian expression, '*Adam ta Khatam*', that is, from 'Adam to the Seal of Prophets' (Muhammad). According to Shari'ati, Hussain is the standardbearer for the struggle of history in the story of mankind, and Karbala is the battlefield that links various fronts, various generations and various ages.[62] Shari'ati is the first Shi'i intellectual to transform martyrdom into an ideology, culture and goal.

For the Saudi Shi'is, the popular conception of Karbala is identical to that of the Shi'is in Bahrain, Iraq, Iran and elsewhere in the Islamic world. Inspired by Shari'ati's pamphlet *Shahadat* (Martyrdom), Shaikh Hassan al-Saffar, widely recognized as an adept preacher and author of dozens of books about the Shi'is in the Gulf, started in the mid-1970s to portray the episode of Karbala in a more revolutionary and modern way. Al-Saffar, who lives in an overwhelmingly Sunni and anti-Shi'is state, namely Saudi Arabia, strove to convey a specific message to his audience, with reference to the events of Karbala. In an attempt implicitly to liken Saudi rule to that of the Ummayads, al-Saffar reinterprets the historical circumstances that led to Hussain's revolt using a quasi-modern method and concepts. Al-Saffar emphasizes the root causes of Hussain's revolt, which he attributes to what he calls *barnamaj jahili*, that is, the *jahili* programmes imposed by Mu'awiya b. Abi Sufyan, the father of Yazid. These programmes, al-Saffar argues, consist of four points: first, fragmentation of Islamic society as a result of tribal and sectarian discrimination; second, repression and abandonment of freedoms; third, uneven distribution of wealth; and fourth, monopoly of power.[63] Interestingly enough, al-Saffar, who cautiously avoids explicitly provocative statements against the Saudi regime, dresses up his political message with references to the Umayyad era.[64] Thus, his audience is supposed to comprehend the indirect signs and rhetoric of his sermons. In this, as in most of his other books, he invokes tradition to support ideas that are already there.[65] M. Amir-Moezzi argues that 'militant Shi'ism has continued to justify its activities religiously by the case of Imam al-Husayn and the battle of Karbala with out-of-context use, as ideological necessities suggest, of some of al-Husayn's words and actions'.[66]

Al-Saffar devotes his book to discussing the revolutionary option of the Shi'is to realize their ultimate aims. He begins by stressing that true faith entails a rejection of oppression, of surrender to evil and of passivity towards tyrannies and deviation. Thus the goals of revolution would be as follows: destroying the despotic rule; reform of the *umma*; the propagation of virtues; and the prohibition of vices.[67]

Taking it to the extreme, Hadi al-Mudarresi, a leading figure of the MVM, contends that the objectives of Imam Hussein's revolt were as follows: building *umma risaliyya*, or 'a nation with a mission', that is, a nation invested with the message of believing in God and committing to His laws and precepts as a sole source of legislation; ridding 'Islamic civilization' of deviation (*inhiraf*); and saving it from collapse (*suqft*).[68]

These pamphlets include tacit political statements conveyed to the audience in the guise of the Karbala story. Furthermore, their vocabulary, rhetoric and analytical methods echo leftist revolutionary thought. More importantly, the Karbala episode is turned into a myth in the popular imagination, and a legitimating ideology by which the ideologues win support.

Divine Sovereignty: An Approach to the Shi'i State

The ideology of the MVM is that of *wilayat al-faqih*, or jurist guardianship. I will argue here that Mawdudi's works played a primary role in encouraging the ideologues of the MVM to pay great attention to the issue of *wilayat al-faqih*. Without Mawdudi's theory on *hakimiyya*, the promulgation of *wilayat al-faqih*,[69] which appeared in the first half of the eighteenth century, would not have had such wide currency among Shi'is activists before Khomeini's appearance on the political scene, since the works of Shi'is jurists in the period between 1825–1960 did not shed light on Naraqi's work.[70] However, since the Shi'is 'ulama both in Iraq and Iran read Mawdudi's theory on *hakimiyya*, some of them searched for a genuine Shi'is theory equivalent to that of Mawdudi.

Mawdudi's thesis would not have attained as much celebrity in the Arab world without Qutb's elaboration and advocacy.

When Mawdudi's works were translated into Arabic and subsequently entered the Egyptian market, Qutb, though imprisoned, sought solace in Mawdudi's ideas.[71] In the concept of *hakimiyya* he seems to have found the missing piece of his world view. He took the idea further and it became the cornerstone of his school of thought. Qutb believed that *hakimiyya* is an intimate attribute of divinity, which in turn entails the unity of rituals with Islamic law (*ittihad al-sha'ira bi-l shari'a*).[72]

Based on the pivotal principle of Islam (*al-tawhid*), Qutb argues that:

> The whole of this religion forms a unity: worship and human relations [*mu'amalat*], doctrine and conduct, spiritual and material matters, economic and moral, this world and the world to come, all of these are well coordinated parts of an integrated mechanism.[73]

Unlike Mawdudi, Qutb rejects any form of reconciliation between Islam and temporal concepts, which imply a mixture of a system made by God with a system made by man. Muhammad Taqi al-Mudarresi, among the first modern Shi'is advocates of *wilayat al-faqih*, appears to have opted for Qutb's exposition of *hakimiyya*. For instance, he retrieves Qutb's tacit condemnation of Mawdudi's political theory, theo-democracy, yet from a Shi'i point of view. As he states:

> There is, undoubtedly, a corrupt root in any form of democracy, whether we call it 'Islamic' or *jahiliyya*, insofar as people are to be entitled to elect a ruler regardless of the person, manner of election, or conditions sanctioned by the religion (i.e. Islam) [...] which will consequently lead to the dominance of fancies and caprices (*ahwa'*; *shahawat*) in the life of the *umma*.[74]

Although Qutb rejects interference of a class of people, or a group, party or organization, or even an individual in the realm of legislation, on the basis that such an interference would usurp the rights of Allah to legislate for the people, it is not clear whom he means by 'those who legislate', since there is no embedded hierarchical body in Sunni Islam. For al-Mudarresi, on the other hand, the enigma surrounding this issue would be readily eliminated, once the concept is applied to the Shi'i school of thought. From the Shi'i perspective, al-Mudarresi argued, the people have no sovereignty such as they have in the democratic system. Legitimate sovereignty belongs to God, via his apostles, Imams and jurists (*fuqaha'*), being the deputies of the occulted Mahdi.[75] He takes the idea further, claiming that selecting the *faqih* for leadership and sovereignty implies the sovereignty of Islam, because the '*faqih* is acquainted with the whole of Islam, thus he would be able to implement it fully and justly'. The logic behind this view is that, since religion is from God, the sovereignty of the *faqih* implies the sovereignty (*hakimiyya*) of God over humanity.[76]

Although Mawdudi distinguishes the rights of Muslims from those of non-Muslims (*dhimmi*s) in that the latter are excluded from high sovereign posts (e.g. head of state, head of the legislature, head of the judiciary, supreme leader of an army), he regards them as citizens of his Islamic state.[77] Al-Mudarresi, on the other hand, argues that non-Muslims are not classified as 'citizens' of the Islamic state, on the grounds that 'an Islamic government would only accept those who believe in its principles; non-Muslims are regarded, from an Islamic perspective, as alien to it'. By this criterion of citizenship, non-Muslims are entitled neither to elect nor to be elected.[78] Furthermore, Muslim women, although regarded as citizens of the Islamic state, are not eligible for leadership, on the basis of psychological factors and traditional accounts.[79]

While Mawdudi's thesis of the Islamic state incorporates a human element, in the sense that it permits individual Muslims the right to govern, al-Mudarresi, by contrast, argues that the Islamic state should be entrusted to a certain class, namely the *fuqaha'*.[80]

Based on the notion of popular *khilafa*, that is, the succession of humans to God on earth, Mawdudi argues that in an Islamic democracy, though subject to Allah's sovereignty, the people are His caliphs in the realm of political power. In his view, the difference between Western democracy and Islamic democracy is that the laws in the former are made by the people through the power of the legislature, while in the theo-democratic state, the people must follow and obey the dictates of the *shari'a*, as given by Allah. Conversely, al-Mudarresi rejects the separation of powers, on the grounds that the three powers fall into the realm of God's sovereignty and should be bestowed, according to the Shi'i and Islamic traditions, on the *fuqaha'*, who are the heirs of the prophets and Imams and thus the deputies of God on earth.

Like Qutb, al-Mudarresi argues that government in Islam is based on the Qur'anic verse: 'We inspired all the apostles whom we sent before you, saying, "There is no god but Me. Therefore serve Me."'.[81] The words 'There is no god but Me', he argues, bear witness to the fact that there is no god but God in the doctrinal sphere, while 'serve Me' points to legislation. According to this interpretation, when one confesses that divinity belongs to God alone, he thereby confesses that sovereignty (*hakimiyya*) in human life belongs to God alone. Thus it is impermissible for man to subjugate himself to any sovereignty other than that of God, or to follow any law other than God's law, or to obey a system that is not bound by His *shari'a*.[82] This view corresponds to that of Qutb, who claims that government in Islam is based, after acceptance of the sole divinity and sovereignty of God, on justice on the part of the rulers, obedience on the part of the ruled and consultation between rulers and ruled.[83] Yet one subtle difference between Qutb and al-Mudarresi relates to consultation (*shura*). From al-Mudarresi's point of view, this principle should not be fused into the characteristics of the Islamic state.

Al-Mudarresi argues that the government in the period of occultation should be based on God's sovereignty, which manifests itself in the application of His *shari'a* law and justice on the part of the ruler/*faqih*. Note that justice ('*adl*) and jurisprudence (*fiqh*) on the part of the ruler/*faqih* are equivalent to infallibility ('*isma*) and revelation (*wahy*) on the part of the prophets and Imams: both are necessary for prophecy as well as rule in the name of God's sovereignty. As such, the *fuqaha*', like the Imams, 'possess equal authority thanks to their divinely ordained position'.[84] This shows clearly that al-Mudarresi is among the first Shi'is Islamic revivalists to herald the concept of jurists' absolute guardianship, or *wilayat al-faqih al-mutlaqa*. Although Khomeini's lectures on *al-hukuma al-Islamiyya* concluded in February 1970, shortly after al-Mudarresi had written his book *Al-Qiyada al-Islamiyya* (Islamic Leadership), the purport of both works was identical, though their approaches to the topic were different.

In a series of lectures on Islamic government, Khomeini was not attempting to formulate an Islamic political theory or a deep and detailed plan for the institution of an Islamic state. Indeed, he strove to critically study and refute the prevailing views within Shi'is religious circles and, more specifically, the *fuqaha*', in terms of their distorted understanding of the principles of waiting (*intizar*) and dissimulation (*taqiyya*). He emphasized the need for government to implement the *shari'a*. Al-Mudarresi seems to have been more concerned with the theoretical aspects of Islamic government, aiming to formulate a Shi'i version of Islamic political theory vis-à-vis other versions, both Sunni and secularist. While al-Mudarresi confined his thesis to an intellectual purpose, Khomeini's objectives in his thesis were straightforward and directed mainly at creating an Islamic state. His main concern was to encourage the *fuqaha'* to take on the task of establishing an Islamic government, so that Islamic laws, goals and criteria could be implemented.[85]

Like the majority of those Islamic fundamentalists who claim that Islam possesses an intact state theory, al-Mudarresi was also faced with the existing political reality, namely, the modern state model. Although al-Mudarresi's doctrine of government evolves from the vocabulary of Shi'i discourse and authorities, it also builds on the modern nation-state, in particular the notion of the state as it appears in the Western world. Though he made every possible effort to eschew modern political terms, he, like many Muslim scholars, appears to have felt impelled to borrow Western notions such as the three powers of government, i.e., legislature, executive and judiciary. Furthermore, he acknowledges the paramount importance of these powers for realizing justice among all people. In addition, he uses terms such as Islamic state, constitution, civil rights, freedoms, law (*qanun*) and people (*sha'ab*),[86] which are often considered alien to Islamic thought.

The last point, but not the least, is that while Mawdudi accepts the incorporation of modern political notions into his Islamic political theory, both Qutb and al-Mudarresi try to avoid Western notions. Their theories reflect the ideological confrontation in their respective countries. Thus, the radical tendency colouring their religious-political theorization may be regarded as a response to the totalitarianism of the state both in Egypt and Iraq, and is, perhaps, an attempt to arrest the de-Islamization process in these regions under the patronage of secularist states.

According to the internal literature of the MVM, the Movement emerged, first in Iraq in the late 1960s and then elsewhere in the Gulf states, because of the failure of the secularization process in Iraq, the defective religious learning system in Najaf's *hawza* and internal political and socio-economic causes.

Secular ideologies, particularly communism, Ba'th socialism and secularly oriented nationalism, allegedly failed to attain the dreams of the Arabs, i.e.

comprehensive unity, economic prosperity and political pluralism, along with the disengagement of the Najaf *hawza* from the political and socio-economic crisis in Iraq. The exposure of the latter to a wide spectrum of works written by Islamist thinkers, scholars and activists enabled the MVM to formulate socio-religious visions and strategies for the pursuit of its goals, namely a message-bearing, human, faithful vanguard and an Islamic civilization.

Despite the significant differences between the MVM and other Sunni Islamist groups on many basic issues, the impact of, for instance, Sayyid Qutb is very clear. The notion of *jahiliyya*, which represents a cornerstone of Qutb's school of thought, gained wide currency amongst Shi'is Islamist activists, and hence served as a tool with which the MVM analyses the existing Muslim society, particularly in Iraq. The literature of the MVM in the given period reveals a posture towards society clearly identical to that of Qutb, in that *jahiliyya* is seen to permeate all facets of Muslim society. In response to this perceived crisis, the MVM asserts the notion of a comprehensive Islam, with the aim of eliminating the roots of *jahiliyya* and reinforcing a modern-oriented Islam, so as to appeal to a wider segment of people who have been subjected to secular orientations.

The MVM, being aware of the huge support for and dominant role of the traditional *'ulama* in Najaf among the Arab Shi'is, strove to set up its own *marji'iyyat*, religious *hawza*s, social clubs and political movements, in the hope of attracting a significant proportion of Shi'is supporters in those regions where the traditional *'ulama* had a marginal presence, such as Kuwait, the Eastern Province of Saudi Arabia, Bahrain and Oman.

The ideologists of the MVM endeavoured to put right the alleged defects of the Shi'i religious learning curricula. The major alteration that the MVM attempted was to inject the traditional *hawza* curricula with modern disciplines, such as literature, historical studies and politics, in addition to introducing Qur'anic ponderance (*tadabur*), which is not included in the curricula of the traditional Shi'i *hawza*s.

The MVM attached great importance to the religious learning system prevalent in the *hawza*, which emphasized the negative social, political and religious impact of alien (mainly Greek) philosophies. However, with the passage of time, students of the MVM's religious schools opted for the traditional *hawza*, since the courses and teachers in the former were deemed insufficient for higher studies, or what is best known as *bahth al-kharij*.

A more crucial aspect of the MVM's activities relates to Shi'i thought. Stimulated by the revolutionary thought of 'Ali Shari'ati, the ideologues of the MVM succeeded in propagating a type of Shi'ism that appealed to large segments of the Arab Shi'is in Iraq and the Gulf region as a whole. The adoption of a more progressive interpretation of Shi'i central doctrines (*intizar*, *taqiyya*, *ghayba*, *'Ashura* and so on), created potential supporters who, for a long time, had been religiously alienated, because of the domination of passive Shi'ism, or who had been recruited by communist parties. Given the fundamental economic, social and political problems in the Shi'i regions, the revolutionary ideology of the MVM attracted the attention of those who had formerly viewed religion as the 'opiate of the masses'. The erosion of the influence of the traditional *'ulama* and secularly oriented parties in Iraq and other parts of the Gulf contributed to the enhancement of the MVM's popular presence, as well as the expansion of its activities, as we shall see in the following chapter.

FOUR

The Revolutionary Decade (1979–89)

Islamic Revolution is the Only Solution.[1]

For half a century after the suppression of the *ikhwan* revolt in 1928–30, Saudi Arabia did not experience a religiously motivated opposition movement. The seizure of the holy mosque in 1979 challenged the legitimacy of the Saudi rule, which was largely justified by the commitment of al-Sa'ud to Wahhabi religious norms and tenets and its protection of the holy places. The Juhayman revolt represented the first sign of a cleavage within the religious establishment, a cleavage that led to further divisions, such as among the neo-Salafis, notably during the Gulf crisis in 1991. The most dangerous aspect of the Juhayman Movement was that the same Islamic rhetoric was used to devalue the religious allegations of the regime.

The Shi'i religious opposition, though classified as external, has added more suspicions surrounding the religious allegations upon which al-Sa'ud base their rule. Between 1980 and 1993, the Islamic Revolution Organization (IRO) became the voice of the Shi'is as well as some other political groupings from different persuasions (notably communist, liberal, nationalist and pan-Arab) who failed to continue their oppositional activities in the national and international domains. This chapter highlights the factors that contributed to the uprising of the Shi'is in November 1979. It also focuses on the political ideology, strategy and aims of the IRO in the period 1980–90.

Background

In the course of the 1970s, a group of activists subscribing to the MVM, led by Shaikh Hassan al-Saffar and Shaikh Tawfiq al-Saif, became active in al-Qatif region. Those of their activities that were directed at the young centred on intellectual and organizational aspects; anyone who was fully prepared to join the Movement was sent to Kuwait.

Series of intellectual and organizational courses were held during summer holidays at the School of *al-Rasoul al-Azam* sponsored by Ayatullah al-Shirazi and headed by Muhammad Taqi al-Mudarresi, the leader of the MVM in Kuwait, and attended by a large number of Shi'i youngsters, mostly high school and university students. The courses, which lasted for two weeks, were designed to indoctrinate the participants and edify those Islamic tenets, political awareness of the crisis of the Islamic *umma* and the underground organizational activities.

In combination with the courses held in Kuwait, small and secret sessions were also held in private houses in al-Qatif and al-Hasa. The sessions used to concentrate on the political situation of the Islamic *umma*, the critique of the traditional religious trend (*al-ittijah al-taqlidi*) among the Shi'is and the importance of intellectual change in the Islamic world.

To prop up the new progressive Islamic ideas, the taped sermons, pamphlets and books of Sayyid Muhammad al-Shirazi were widely circulated among Shi'is youngsters. The al-Shirazi school of thought was increasingly concerned with providing a new interpretation of Islamic tenets, jurisprudence and history. Together with Sayyid Muhammad, Taqi Mudarresi formulated a dynamic and vibrant picture of the history of Shi'ism with particular focus on the experience of Imam Hussain, Imam Musssa b. Ja'far (best known as al-Imam al-Kazim). In short, they strove to revitalize and emphasize the aspect of resistance in Shi'ism in an effort to mobilize the present Shi'is to protest against the traditional and predominantly quietist Shi'ism.

In addition, huge religious ceremonies were held in al-Qatif region, such as the *al-Ghadir* feast on the 17th of *Dhi al-Hijjah*, the last month of the Islamic calendar. In this ceremony, the Shi'is celebrate what they believe to be the day on which the Prophet assigned his cousin and son-in-law, 'Ali, as his successor. Another ceremony is held on the 15th of the month of Sha'ban in which the twelfth Imam, Mahdi, is believed to have been born.

Such ceremonies were attended by notable and religious figures as well as quite a large number of laymen Shi'is. The sermons delivered during these occasions used to deal with social and intellectual issues of the time. The impact of these ceremonies on the Shi'is community was remarkable.

The IRO capitalized on the religious tenor of Ramadan by promulgating its ideas for the purpose of social mobilization and awareness. Moreover, certain activities were designed to bring the attention of the Shi'is to their socio-economic and religious conditions, and encourage them to challenge their inherited passivity in both religion and politics. Among other preachers, Shaikh Hassan al-Saffar delivered numerous speeches during religious ceremonies attended by a large number of Shi'is commoners. For instance, in 1976 Shaikh al-Saffar presented an organized series of sermons about the companions of Imam 'Ali, such as Hijr b. 'Audi, Maitham al-Tammar and Malik al-Ashtar, with particular emphasis on their resistance to Ummayad rule and its repressive policies to extinguish political protest.

As the images of these figures were revived, Shi'is laymen became inspired to follow the path of the ancestors in the hope of re-establishing themselves in the line of active figures in Islamic history, especially those who were close to the Imams. The aim of emphasizing the role of those figures was to politicize the Shi'is community.

The activities created an environment in which the seeds of an organized movement began to grow. The members of the Movement were organized in cells to pursue certain tasks, which were usually dictated by the leaders of IRO, whose personalities were veiled for security reasons.

Such activities were condemned by the conservatives within the Shi'is in the Eastern Province. The conservative faction was behind a series of religious decrees (*fatawa*) issued by Sayyid Abu al-Qasim al-Khoui, the supreme religious authority in Najaf and the symbol of conservatism in contemporary Shi'ism. The *fatawa* discredited Shaikh al-Saffar and religiously delegitimized his activities. They also drew a thin line of distinction between two trends among the Shi'is: a progressive and revolutionary trend exemplified by the school of Karbala and the imitators of Ayatullah Sayyid Muhammad al-Shirazi; and a traditional and conservative trend, *al-ittijah al-taqlidi,* exemplified by the Najaf *hawza* and the religious authority of Sayyid al-Khoui.

Another distinction between the conservatives and revolutionaries is the involvement of women in the latter's activities. Women had previously been confined to the household and were denied the right to have a say in personal matters, let alone in social and political ones. The women who joined the Movement wanted to reclaim their rights in the light of new interpretations of Islamic teachings and the historical and intellectual legacy of Islam.

During the 1970s, a group of renowned and influential preachers subscribing to the school of Ayatullah al-Shirazi came to the Eastern Province and delivered a series of sermons at the *hussainiyas* in different parts of al-Qatif and al-Hasa. Among those preachers was Sayyid Murartad al-Qazwini, a famous and skilful preacher and respectful religious figure in Karbala. He fled Iraq following the arrest of his father and took up residence in Kuwait. He was invited by Shi'is notables to deliver sermons during 'Ashura. In 1978, al-Qazwini delivered sermons whose spiritual tenor aroused the emotions of his audience.

Another talented and skilful preacher was Sayyid Hadi al-Mudarresi, the second man in MVM, whose revolutionary sermons stirred large numbers of people with the manner of his address and the courageous ideas he presented. He came to the Eastern Province with the aim of fortifying the new formation of MVM in al-Qatif and al-Hasa. Similarly, Shaikh Sahib al-Sadiq, the headmaster of the school of al-Rasoul al-Azam in Kuwait, came to al-Qatif and presented several speeches about progressive Islamic thought. He also met selected persons who were responsible for constructing a new base of the MVM in the Eastern Province.

Renowned preachers from the region of al-Qatif include, among many others, Shaikh Hassan al-Saffar, Shaikh Tawfiq al-Saif, Shaikh Fawzi al-Saif, Shaikh Mahmoud al-Saif, Shaikh Mansour al-Saif, Shaikh Yousif al-Mahdi and Shaikh Hassan Khawildi. They were based in Kuwait and studied at the School of al-Rasoul al-Azam. They had regular religious missions in the Eastern Province and actively participated in religious ceremonies, in addition to their social and organizational commitments.

In the course of less than five years, therefore, the Shirazi trend succeeded in establishing an active movement, with distinguished leaders, religious bodies and a distinct body of thought. This Movement was initially founded as a response to the stagnation of the religious authority (*marji'iyyat*) in Najaf and the dominance of conservative and quietist Shi'ism and then transformed into a political movement following the Iranian revolution in 1979.

Motives for the Uprising

Understanding the dynamics, motifs and circumstances that contributed to the Shiʻi upheaval in November 1979 requires careful investigation. Under conditions of economic deprivation and cultural, economic and political marginalization, large numbers of the Shiʻis began to resort to religious discourse as a way to project authenticity and to deal with their problems. Gradually many Shiʻis came to believe that the regime was endeavouring to undermine their cultural peculiarities and their religious identity. They were thus spurred to move beyond their material needs in order to protect their social unity and cultural continuity. According to a Saudi Shiʻi, 'Shiʻis suffer not so much from an empty stomach as from a sense of injured dignity'.[2] This is evident in the slogans chanted by Shiʻi demonstrators during the *intifada* in November 1979, such as, 'NO Sunna no Shiʻis ... Just Islamic Unity' and 'We are Jaʻfari Shiʻis, what we want is freedom'.[3]

The unrest in the Eastern Province was not rooted solely in economic deprivation or social injustice but also in a deep sense of collective crisis and the growing fear of the loss of social and religious identity and unity.

Throughout the preceding century, the Shiʻis in the Eastern Province employed two different strategies to attain their rights: the first was a legal strategy, adopted by the Shiʻis notables (*wujahaʼ*) subscribing to the renowned scholarly and wealthy families such as al-Khunaizi, al-Jishi, al-ʻAwami and al-Mubarak. They used the existing channels of communication designated by the state. The notables were convinced of the effectiveness of the methods of petitioning and maintaining an amicable relationship with the rulers through the so-called 'Open Councils' (*al-majalis al-maftuha*) in which the Shiʻis might voice their grievances and attain their demands. As Shiʻis expectations grew, however, the method became ineffective.

The second strategy was extralegal. It was embodied in a popular revolt in 1979 and thereafter embedded in an organized political movement, namely the IRO. It was a reaction to the state's refusal to negotiate, let alone to realize, the Shiʻis' fundamental demands.

To understand the process of extralegal options, two variables must be taken into account:

1. The increased expectations of the Shiʻis. The Shiʻis' demands have

increased throughout the last century and fall into three major categories: economic, i.e. lifting or reducing heavy fiscal burdens imposed on the Shi'is from the time of the occupation of al-Hasa in 1913 up until the death of King Abdulaziz in 1953; socio-economic reforms, i.e. building schools and hospitals, sewage systems and water drains, paving roads, and so on, fuelled by nationalistic fervour during the reigns of King Sa'ud and King Faisal, 1954–74; and finally a broad range of religious, political, economic and social demands following the ascension of King Khalid to the throne, from 1975 to the present.[4]

2. The ideologization of the state. Although Islam represents the legitimating ideology of the state, in that the Saudi rule was anchored in Wahhabi tenets that were of 'pure concrete', according to an ex-British ambassador in Saudi Arabia in 1955,[5] the cultural and social impact of secular and national ideologies on the local community is vividly apparent. However, subsequent developments show that the rift between Nasser's regime and al-Saud prompted the latter to begin wide Islamic mobilization in order to resist the exportation of Nasserism to Saudi Arabia. Islamic rhetoric was increasingly employed with the success of the Iranian revolution, where the Saudi regime used all possible efforts to defend its religious legitimacy by recourse to the *'ulama*. The Saudi government was afraid that revolutionary Islam in Iran would be transformed into a paradigm for all Muslims. The Wahhabi *'ulama* were therefore enlisted to become involved in the confrontations between the regime and its adversaries.

The religious establishment classed the Shi'i opposition as 'associationists' (*mushrikun*), which made it impossible for them to operate from within the country. The IRO was concerned with the sectarian barrier that made it difficult for the Shi'is opposition to confront the Saudi regime. Al-Saffar argues that an Islamic movement opposing an anti-Islamic regime, whether it be communist, Ba'thist, nationalist or secularist, has no need to justify revolution and *jihad*, whereas an Islamic movement facing a hypocritical regime that pretends to be Islamic, as is the case in Saudi Arabia, is obliged to provide solid justifications for *jihad* to those who are deceived by the hypocrisy of the regime. According to the leader of the IRO, 'this is what we are facing in our struggle against the Saudi regime which clothed itself with Islamic garb'.[6]

On such a pretext, the IRO made strenuous efforts to denounce the Saudi regime's religious allegations. For example, the IRO issued a communiqué in October 1981 to pilgrims on the *hajj*, in the hope of provoking suspicion of Saudi Arabia's Islamic claims. It posed such challenges as:

> Is hereditary rule the formula sanctioned by Islam?
>
> Are despotism and lack of political participation permissible in Islam?
>
> Is the abandonment of intellectual, political and social freedoms legally permissible?
>
> Do the coalition with the infidel tyrant America and the opening of the country for its forces and surveillance air planes (AWACS) conform with Islamic criteria?
>
> Is the depletion of national wealth in favour of foreign factories acceptable in Islam?[7]

The Changing Forms of Protest

Shi'is resistance to Saudi coercive policies has taken three different forms: limited protest, exemplified in the popular movement led by Shaikh Muhammad al-Nimer in 1928; an elitist movement, which consisted of nationalists and socialists, in the 1950s and 1960s; and finally populist religious movements in the late 1970s. These three types have exerted varying degrees of pressure on the Saudi regime; the effectiveness of each can be examined by looking at governmental reactions to Shi'is demands, considering whether the reactions translated into the fulfilment or acknowledgment of the demands and assessing whether the demands were accepted or denied. Ultimately the test lies in the extent to which the government opted for change to improve the lives of the Shi'is. The answers are not so easy to come to, as each type has achieved some gains, although the change of form of protest indicates that previous types were not sufficiently effective.

The Impact of Modernization

The rapid urbanization process, along with educational, economic and technological development, transformed the Saudi population. The urban population increased from 30 per cent in 1960 to 82 per cent in 2000. The Saudi government spent around 776 billion dollars in the course of four five-year plans from 1970 to 1990. During the first five-year plan, 1970-75, the government was the prime client of 67 per cent of total construction activities such as roads, railways, seaports, airports, military sites, hospitals, schools, universities, fast housing projects and government buildings.[8]

In recalling the past social, economic and political conditions in the Eastern Province and the Gulf region as a whole, we need to refer to the description by L. S. Amery in 1928 in his foreword to Arnold Wilson's book *The Persian Gulf*. Amery refers to the Gulf as '... an area of bleak coasts, torrid winds, and pitiless sunshine, where ... nature is in her fiercest humor and man has done little to improve on its handiwork.'[9]

However, the conditions of this region gradually improved, because oil provided the region with unprecedented wealth which led to developing the communities in the Gulf in a matter of decades:

> The Eastern Province developed more rapidly than the rest of Saudi Arabia. Villages became large cities in the span of a generation and entirely new cities were established. The general population continues to be urbanized. A completely new environment is in creation. The shifts offer opportunities to meet the educational, health and housing needs of the inhabitants.[10]

Significant changes occurred in socio-economic, cultural and political spheres affected by the economic development. The country hosted legions of skilled expatriates in the Eastern Province to help promote oilfields from the time of the exploration of the first oil well in 1938 on the basis of a concession granted to Aramco in 1933.

In an effort to meet the pressing need for American expertise because of the expansion of oil installations, Aramco invited hundreds of expatriates to help develop the oil industry through training programmes for Aramco Saudi workers.

How important was the Arabian American Oil Company (Aramco) in building the country's infrastructure? The role of Aramco was not confined to oil extraction and shipment to overseas markets, but extended also to wholesale construction. Apart from paving roads and installing pipelines, ports and airports in the oil regions and elsewhere, Aramco provided schools, hospitals and quasi-state administration. Aramco filled a gap left by public services, education and health facilities that were barely developed and in some parts of the country virtually non-existent. It provided vital services and 'water and health provisions'.[11]

In 1941 Aramco launched a massive campaign to fight malaria, which threatened the population in the Eastern Province. A medical centre was founded in 1942 to treat those affected by the disease.

From the company's point of view, malaria was a particularly difficult problem for almost 98 per cent of the people suffered from it in oases like Qatif. The company has carried on an extensive campaign with insecticides in the coastal towns, and the incidence of malaria among its employees has been reduced to negligible proportions.[12]

As the government failed to stem an epidemic of trachoma, Aramco launched a comprehensive campaign against the disease, aided by research carried out by the Harvard School of General Health. By 1983, Aramco health services included thirteen general clinics and a number of dentistry clinics, in addition to two sophisticated, modern hospitals in Ras Tanoura and Dhahran.

From the 1940s and 1950s, Aramco was in effect the kingdom's public works agency and oil ministry and America's private diplomatic and intelligence operation rolled into one.[13] During this period not many Saudis came into contact with the company or its American managers and their families, partly because high-ranking officials lived a secluded life in the so-called 'American Camp', where race and caste segregation was practised. Indeed, there were crudely racist institutions and norms that perpetuated separation and inequality of rights and privileges.[14] American employees recruited by Aramco had special privileges and status.

> All Americans on the twenty-four-month tour of duty receive fourteen days' regional leave with full pay, which they may take in Cairo, Beirut, Tehran, Asmara, or some other Near Eastern city. In addition, they earn two months' paid vacation in the United States every two years. Wages range from $250 a month for file clerks to over $800 a month for executives and a high percentage of income can be saved because there is little to spend it on in Saudi Arabia.[15]

In contrast, the starting wage rate for local labour was half a riyal or 12 cents a day, and in 1954 became 3 riyals a day. Monthly rates of pay ranged from 90 to 1,500 riyals.[16]

The cruelty inflicted on those who resided in 'Saudi Camp' is still veiled in secrecy, probably because its victims died or lacked the opportunity or the will, for security reasons, to speak of it. As there were neither paved roads nor means of transport, those who survived had to walk on foot for tens of kilometres to Dhahran. Most came from Qatif and Hasa. They were allowed to leave the camp and see their families once a month.

Until 1933, the year that Standard Oil of California started its operations on Saudi soil, there were no local workers in the company. By 1950, there were 20,400 Aramco workers, of whom there were 400 Americans and 13,400 Saudis; the remainder were of other nationalities (African, Arabian and Mediterranean).[17] Almost all of the Saudi employees held low-level, unskilled positions, whereas the managers who made up the top 5 per cent were expatriates.[18] Saudis, recruited from among the indigenous Shi'is population of the oases of Hasa, in 1954 constituted 60 per cent of the Aramco Saudi workforce.[19] In 2004 the number of Saudi workers reached 43,226 out of the total workforce of 54,000.[20]

While the Shi'is in Eastern Province were almost isolated from the outside world until the early 1950s, with Aramco starting to explore oil in commercial quantities thousands of local and foreign workers were recruited. As a result, Shi'is workers were able to travel abroad. Some were sent to Lebanon, Egypt, Europe and the United States to attend training courses and some distinguished workers went into higher education, as the need for skilled workers and technicians intensified. Those who returned after relatively long absences brought back new values, ideas and customs, despite the attempts by the government to neutralize the foreign cultural and political influence on the Saudis studying abroad.

In the early 1950s, only a limited number of Saudis in al-Hasa began to benefit from public health work in hospitals and schools. Conditions improved following a series of labour strikes in 1953 and 1956 led by the Saudi dissident Nasir al-Sa'id.

The strikes continued for three weeks and succeeded in securing a relative improvement in the conditions of the workers. The 1956 strike was a protest against King Sa'ud's visit to Dhahran Air Base in the Eastern Province, which led to the intervention of the Saudi Army and American troops.

Later, protest by Saudi workers in Aramco took a political form. Influenced by Nasir's ideology, the Popular Union for the Liberation of Arabian Peninsula emerged in 1966. The Union appealed to nearly all workers from different persuasions who aimed to realize an Arab national state.

Despite the defeat of Nasirism after the 1967 war, Aramco workers played a very important role in supporting the movement of Lieutenant Dawood al-Rumaihi, the commander of Dhahran Air Base, and the military commander Sa'id al-'Amri in 1969. The movement, which aimed to overthrow the Saudi regime, failed and its leaders were imprisoned or killed, among them Muhammad al-Rabi', who died in the 'Abeed Jail in Jeddah.

The local workers were ordered not to leave their camps in Dhahran, under the pretext that cholera was spreading in Qatif region, but in fact to prevent them from organizing strikes. Aramco workers were confined within an area designated by Aramco, from Dammam Radio Station, on the highway between Dammam and Saihat.

Nevertheless, the attitude of Aramco towards Saudi workers gradually improved as the company's need grew for a skilled and expert local workforce to run its major operations. Rudimentary training schemes and literacy classes were introduced. In 1953 Aramco built the first elementary school in the Eastern Province and in 1959 it started to build intermediate schools. In 1960 girls' schools were opened in the Eastern Province. By 1979, there were fifty-eight boys' and girls' schools with 25,000 students, financed by Aramco.[21] And by 2004, there were more than 150 schools for Saudi citizens and foreign expatriates.[22]

In addition to numerous privileges such as access to health services, housing, transport and a respectable salary, Aramco workers enjoyed respect and social standing and had no difficulty finding a wife, as some Shi'is families even preferred to marry their daughter to a *Kouli*, as Aramco employees were called.

In its annual report for 1968 Aramco stated that, 'for most of Aramco Saudi employees, life in all aspects is similar to the life in the West; they go to their jobs by modern means of transport and buy houses with mortgages and watch television at night'.[23]

Nevertheless, the fact remains that the Shi'is workers who were once the backbone of Aramco's workforce feel that their region and community have lagged behind others.

The Eastern Province's oil resources continue to be drained by the rulers of the Kingdom's dominant central region, Najd. The east's large (40 per cent) Shi'i minority, whom American officials describe as 'second class citizens' in Saudi Arabia, pay the combined price of the weak oil market, tense relations with Iraq and Iran, and a dictatorship that is brutally crude and direct about exacting compliance.[24]

The Saudi regime has repeatedly argued that it gave compensatory incentives to the Shi'is by recruiting a relatively high number of them into Aramco.[25] However, the fact is that the government needed a large local labour force to start up the oil industry. Its policy towards the Shi'is in Eastern Province evolved in accordance with the requirements of the state and not as a result of the government's change of heart towards the Shi'is.

However, development plans had a profound political impact on the Saudi population. The process of urbanization produced massive social changes. Saudi rulers view city-dwellers as a dangerous element, which, over time, became politically active as a result of their exposure to the influences of modernization such as education, communication and industrialization. The first manifestation of this was during the reign of King Sa'ud, when a nucleus of urban technocrats was formed. King Sa'ud once said that, 'the real source of trouble was the cities because of their educated people'.[26]

In Saudi Arabia, wherever people are exposed to modernization and have experienced modern education, many automatically become involved in politics. Despite intense efforts by the government to the contrary, such individuals became dislocated and ripe for religious and political mobilization. Aware of the economic boom in the country, they began to compare their position with that of other groups. They noticed the widening gulf between rich and poor, the ruling class and its wealthy allies and the ruled majority, the Sunnis and the Shi'is, their country and the outside world, notably America and the West at large.

The Shi'is in the oil-rich Eastern Province have been exposed to various political and intellectual influences, notably from migrants to the region from different parts of the world. Official (but conservative) figures for 1975 claimed that 314,000 non-Saudis were working in the kingdom;[27] by the end of 2000 the number had risen to more than 7 million.[28]

Modern education has also had an influence on the Shi'is and encouraged them to strive to realize what they admire in other, particularly more advanced, societies. A shortage of teachers opened the gates for an influx of large numbers of teachers from various Arab countries, mainly Egypt, Palestine, Jordan, Syria, Iraq and Sudan, some of whom were members of political organizations (e.g. PLO, the Muslim Brotherhood). The literature of these organizations became available in Saudi markets, which contributed to an increase in religious consciousness, leading to 'the general air of dissatisfaction bordering on hostility that existed among many circles in Saudi Arabia'.[29] The writings of Sayyid Qutb, Hasan al-Banna, Fathi Yakun and Zeinab al-Ghazali undoubtedly contributed to the increase of religious and political awareness among the Shi'is in the Eastern Province.

The Impact of Iran's Revolution

Some observers argue that the Shi'is in the Eastern Province were receptive to Khomeini's provocative call for an uprising to topple their tyrants (the Shahs).[30] There is no doubt that the Islamic revolution had an impact upon the whole of the Islamic world, but it had particular significance for the Shi'is. The outbreak of demonstrations throughout Iran in 1978 invigorated the shattered spirit of the Shi'is in Saudi Arabia as well as the Shi'is elsewhere in the Muslim world. It provided them with a sense of power and self-confidence they had previously lacked and gave them the courage to stand up to their Saudi masters and publicly voice their grievances and demands.[31] Indeed, the Iranian revolution 'produced a new consciousness among the Shi'is and served as a model for their future conduct',[32] as well as creating a new atmosphere and hastening the political manifestation of the Shi'is' opposition.[33]

The Intifada of 1979

Before the uprising in November 1979, the social and organizational status of the MVM was powerful and deeply established. It had enjoyed a wide popular base and a strong following among the Shi'is and thus had succeeded in overcoming the difficulties posed by the conservative trend, which vehemently opposed any form of political involvement by the Shi'is.

And, since political parties are officially banned in the country,[34] political demands may arise in sectors that are not directly concerned with politics.

As David Easton has it, 'Demands bridge the gap between political and non-political sectors of life'.[35] Thus political activities take place in *masjid* and *hussainiya*, which are not political institutions, but which are platforms where many people gather at specific times and for specific purposes. These institutions are not controlled by the state, since they are traditionally funded by the Shi'is, which makes control and monitoring by the state difficult.

It was in the mosques and *hussainiya*s that Shi'is political ideologies and visions were transmitted. Thus it is not surprising that the Shi'is opposition began to mobilize in areas that could not be directed by the religious establishment or controlled by the state without trespassing on a sphere that the Shi'is have, from the start, sacrificed themselves to secure.

Until the outbreak of the Iranian revolution, the Shi'is mosques and *hussainiya*s had no political role. For many Shi'is, these traditional institutions are considered the embodiments of Shi'is social solidarity. After 1979, though traditional mosques and *hussainiya*s still existed, the role of these institutions changed dramatically: they became outlets for various religious and political movements within the Shi'is. Moreover, Shi'is *marji'iyyat*s have become identified with their political attitude and the extent to which they are involved in politics.

Throughout the procession of *'Ashura*, the *hussainiya*s turned into gathering centres for the Shi'is, where demonstrations were prompted by rousing sermons by Shaikh Hassan al-Saffar and other preachers subscribing to the MVM, such as Shaikh Fawzi al-Saif. During the first ten days of Muharram in November 1979, the leader of the IRO, Shaikh Hassan al-Saffar, presented a new, revolutionary Shi'i Islam that the Shi'is in the Eastern Province were not aware of. Al-Saffar, being an adept and audacious social psychologist, knew how to whip up his audience. He devoted his speeches to tackling the psychological obstacles impeding Shi'i activism. He emphasized fear as the prime cause of Shi'is stagnation.

The 'excessive fear which handicaps the mind, exhausts the body, impedes the progression and the explosion of energies is the illness from which the overwhelming majority of our society suffers', he said. In his view, the Shi'is are excessively afraid of everything – failure, tiredness, pain, government, centres of power, the future and death. 'This critical phenomenon dominating our society allows tyrants to continue suppressing and making them stupid (*estehmar*).'[36]

Although he recognized that fear is an inherent feature of the human temperament, he thought it could be dealt with if it was redirected to the fear of God, which implies a programme of commitment to God's laws and injunctions, avoidance of prohibitions and vices and motivation towards good deeds. It also means implementing divine values and ridiculing any temporal and false values. Missionaries (*risaliyun*) are those who 'embody the true fear of God so they bear divine responsibility and function for [implementing] right, freedom and progress'.[37] People who are suppressed by despotic or puppet governments should act promptly to rid themselves of the government, which constitutes a source of fear. 'Waiting for the danger to occur is worse than the danger itself, and thus it is better to attack the danger'.[38] Al-Saffar also criticized the educational system within the Shi'is community in the Eastern Province, which he believed was the cause of the subjection of the Shi'is. Fear of the government 'made our people humble and vulnerable'.[39]

With respect to death, al-Saffar asked, if death is unavoidable, 'why do we let death attack us?'. It is the human, argued al-Saffar, who should take the initiative to attack death as 'he holds paramount goals, a holy banner and a great task, so he throws himself into dangers and immerses himself in adventures to defend the cause of faith for the sake of God'.[40] With his invocation of a transcendental rhetoric, al-Saffar aims at asserting the paramount power of religion upon Shi'is laymen, who are supposed to follow what religion dictates through its alleged representatives and ultimately to rise up and politically protest.

On the eve of 6 Muharram 1400 (25 November 1979), the Shi'is in various parts of Qatif and al-Hasa took to the streets right after the end of recitation of *'Ashura* presented by Shaikh Hassan al-Saffar and other preachers. The Shi'is mourners decided to perform *'Ashura* processions in public, which took political forms as the National Guard intervened. As the episode of Muharram reached its peak, the Shi'is determined publicly to observe the martyrdom of Abbas b. Ali, the brother of Hussain, Ali al-Akbar, and son of Hussain and Hussain b. Ali. At this point religious fervour reached its climax.

The preachers affiliated with the MVM used the *hussainiya*s to mobilize the Shi'is in the region and thus challenged the official ban on the public procession, signifying their determination to defy the government prohibition. On the eve of 7 Muharram (26 November), the Shi'is held the traditional mourning procession, leading to demonstrations by around seventy thousand

Shi'is in various parts of the region, which quickly turned into violent clashes with the security forces stationed in the area. As the police and troops from the National Guard intervened to disperse the crowds who participated in the 'Ashura procession in Qatif on 28 November, the Shi'is decided to resist and went on the rampage, and eventually the trouble spread to various parts of Qatif and Hasa.

The Saudi authorities, having been intimidated by the Juhayman Movement in Mecca, were anxious about events in the Eastern Province. Consequently, 20,000 soldiers from the National Guard were deployed to the region to extinguish the *intifada*. The demonstrations continued for five days, despite the attempts by Shi'is notables and police forces to stop them. As the National Guard opened fire on the crowds in Qatif town, the Shi'is in other regions rallied into the streets, determined to show their anger and to voice their demands. On 9 and 10 Muharram, the Qatif region was sealed off and news began to spread that a number of people had been killed. The Shi'is demonstrators chanted slogans demanding rights equal to those of their Sunni counterparts – 'No Sunnis, no Shi'is, but Islamic unity' – and affirming their religious-ethnic identity – 'We are Shi'is and Ja'fariyya ... What we want is freedom' and 'The Prophet's religion is one without discrimination'.[41]

The National Guard killed twenty people and injured over a hundred more. Four of these were aged between seventeen and nineteen; seven between twenty and thirty; three between thirty and forty and one was sixty. Eight were high-school students; eight were self-employed; two, one a teacher and one a woman, and two were Aramco workers.[42]

In an attempt to tame the resentment prevailing in the Shi'is regions, the regime promptly allocated massive investment to the development of the economic structure, education system and other local services. Remarkable changes occurred during a very short period from 1980 to 1985. Roads were paved, schools and hospitals were built, land was distributed, loans were granted, a sewage system was constructed, and shopping centres were opened.

However, the regime merely intended to restore control in a region that lay in the vicinity of the oil wells. Discrimination against the Shi'is did not cease, but took different forms. In an attempt to re-consolidate its control over the region, the regime took very harsh measures against Shi'is activists. The expenditure of billions of dollars by the Saudi regime in the years following the *intifada* had a significant impact on the Shi'is' attitude towards the regime. However, to say that the Shi'is became 'immune to the Iranian influence'[43] is far from true, since while the economic conditions of the Shi'is were improved, religious discrimination, political alienation and cultural marginalization continued to fuel their resentment.

The spontaneous upheaval of the *intifada,* which was, according to Sheikh al-Saffar, 'beyond anyone's expectations', is regarded as a milestone in the history of Saudi Shi'is. The general resentment was 'so tense'. The Saudi government, shocked by the rampage of the Shi'is, promptly tried to contain the critical situation in the Eastern Province. It summoned the preachers and ordered them to renounce provocative statements that could incite listeners to rebellion and violence. However, the situation was dramatically changed by Tehran Radio (Arabic Section), which was controlled by members of the MVM, devoting hours of its broadcasting schedule to the *intifada* in the Eastern Province. It also called upon the Shi'is to continue their protest against the Saudi regime and to demand religious liberties and the foundation of an Islamic republic modelled on the Iranian one.

Generally, the *intifada* was 'a symbol of the repression to which the community had historically been subjected'.[44] It appears to have transformed the Shi'is perception of themselves as an underprivileged group into a community that challenged the regime's discriminatory policy.

In November 1980, the Shi'is notables submitted a petition to the crown prince at the time, Fahad b. Abdulaziz, the former king, condemning the government's discriminatory policies against the Shi'is. 'We complain about atrocities that must not be continued as have been articulated and clarified. We have not obtained a positive result and these demands represent the minimum level of our demands.' They added, 'We have not originated in a vacuum and are not morally bankrupt to the extent that no one among us is liable to be trustworthy in the state.' The petition emphasizes two major issues: the first is religious discrimination such as the denying of religious rights to the Shi'is religious rights; the second part relates to the socio-economic conditions of the Shi'is which 'have long been raised but no positive result has been achieved'.[45]

The most significant development that followed the *intifada* was the IRO's emergence in December 1979, which marked a new chapter in the relationship between the Shi'is and the government. The IRO formed the political outlet of the Shi'is.

In a country that officially bans political parties, free assembly, public discussions or criticism of the political status quo, the Shi'is opposition was compelled to voice its discontent from abroad by setting up opposition offices, media centres and human rights organizations in Iran, Lebanon, London and Washington. The Saudi regime forced the Shi'is opposition to develop political alternatives and other means to make it impossible for its members to operate from home.

The Social Breakdown of the IRO Membership

The *intifada* helped reconstruct the community from within, and emphasized the cultural identity of the Shi'is community. It brought a group of cadres and leaders from the periphery to the centre of society. They were exposed to a variety of religious and political activities both inside and outside the country, which helped them learn the techniques of opposition.

In general, the IRO is urban-based, drawing its membership mainly from the lower middle and middle classes. While the leading members of the IRO earned academic degrees from Saudi and American universities, IRO has gained particular support among high school and university students, young professionals and semi-skilled Aramco workers. The organization recruits from the mosques from where so much of its strength is derived.

Oriented towards Islam and committed to social and political activism, the members of the IRO continued to believe that their ultimate task was to bring about a more Islamic society. This aim is reflected in their writings and activities. Following the migration of the leader and leading committee of the IRO, a large number of individuals were recruited in the 1980s. According to the spokesman of the IRO, 3,000 left their homeland and joined the organization in Tehran and Damascus.[46]

The IRO's Political Ideology (1980–90)

Before the *intifada*, the branch of MVM in the Eastern Province did not adopt a clear and specific political ideology and strategy, though its declared intellectual discourse emphasized the political Shi'i uprisings throughout Islamic history, including present experiences such as the movement of Imam Musa al-Sadr in Lebanon, and the revolutionaries in Iran. It was, indeed, aimed at encouraging the community to participate in social and cultural activities and abandon the influence of the conservative trend.

Overall the MVM prepared the ground for the uprising of November 1979. In response to the victory of the Islamic revolution in Iran in February 1979, the political, psychological and social climate in the region changed dramatically, for the revolution generated political zeal among the Shi'is in the region and elsewhere in the Islamic world.

The leaders of MVM strove to capitalize on the Iranian event in an effort to reinforce their influence in the Gulf region as a whole. Indeed, the victory of the Islamic revolution in Iran was a golden opportunity for MVM to strengthen its popular base and to prop up its revolutionary leanings. It also provided MVM with an effective ideological weapon to fight its rival, namely the conservative and quietist trend. In short, MVM was the luckiest party to exploit the Iranian revolution for its own purposes.

The political ideology of the IRO can be illustrated by considering two main issues: the Islamic revolution; and cosmopolitanism (*umamiyya*).

Islamic Revolution: A Vehicle of Change
Throughout the decade 1980–90, Shi'ism became more active and increasingly appealed to young people who, for decades, had remained receptive to secular ideologies. Their return to religion via Shi'ism points to its inspirational quality. The new version of Shi'ism allowed many of its adherents to articulate their dissatisfaction in religious-political terms. Furthermore, in the new version of Shi'ism, the Shi'is found an ideology of salvation in this life and in the hereafter. This is evident in their invocation of Shi'is traditions about justice, equity and even the notion of the occultation of Imam Mahdi, who is interpreted as a symbol of the ideal life for humanity. With regard to life after death, martyrdom is an inherent feature of Shi'ism; for some Shi'is activists 'Shi'ism is, in essence, a form of martyrdom', and for others it is a highway to paradise.

It is true that Shi'i Islam cannot be said to be the cause of revolution, since Shi'i themes that have been reinterpreted by the MVM have legitimized their political goals. According to Marvin Zonis and Daniel Brumberg, 'Shi'ism can be read by its adherents to accord legitimacy both to passive submission and explosive activism.'[47] What made revolutionary Shi'ism marketable, then, is that it was exploited to explain the socio-economic conditions that plagued the Shi'is and the attitude they should adopt to deal with these conditions.

The use of Shi'i terms to explain and devise solutions for the current problems of the Shi'is put special emphasis on Shi'is activists, marking a significant departure from their passive counterparts who continued to persuade the Shi'is to cling to their alienated status.

The diminished popularity of Shi'i traditionalists led to the rise of a revolutionary trend that, from the early 1980s, began to overwhelm the Shi'i spectrum. Faced with harsh criticism from the IRO, the quietist-traditionalist faction within the Shi'is, who opposed any form of political involvement, were compelled to retreat, while the IRO attacked those who appeared in religious guise, describing them as a 'backward force'. This force, according to al-Saffar, aimed 'to rescue its social influence and interests as they observed the success of the revolutionary forces in gaining a wide following among the masses'.[48]

In the Arab world (e.g. Lebanon, Iraq and the Gulf region), Shi'is leaders' adoption of revolutionary change provided them with popular support. This is not to say that Shi'i movements had gained their support simply thanks to their popular appeal; grass-roots organizations had also embraced its principles and political slogans. Almost all Shi'i political groups had, since the success of the Iranian revolution, been bent on achieving their central goal of establishing a state based on the principles and teachings of Islam, relying on those organizations whose prime function was to pave the way for the victory of the revolution.

In practice, the Iranian revolution of 1978–9 proved the continuing power of religion in the contemporary world. Experts and scholars of modernization and development theory reassessed the assumptions and the predicted outcomes of modernization, concluding that industrialization, urbanization and advancement in education did not lead to a decline in the importance of religion, as many had predicted. On the contrary, the rapid transformation of society led to a renewed interest in traditional religious values in some parts of the world. According to Olivier Roy, modernization has produced both secularization and Islamic revival.[49]

The establishment of the IRO by the end of the first development plan in 1975 represented a significant shift in Shi'is political awareness, indicating that an umbrella organization is crucial for Shi'is political mobilization and the voicing of demands. Indeed, the emergence of the IRO made a distinction between two trends within the Shi'is community of the Eastern Province: the conservative/traditional and the revolutionary.

The MVM, being influenced by the Palestinian and Iranian revolutionary experiments and literatures, expounds revolutionary change. Unlike Marx, the ideologues of the MVM argue that turning points in human history are due to revolutionary movements led not by a certain social class (i.e. the exploited workers, the proletariat) but arising out of the whole of society. They also argue that revolution does not have the sole goal of changing the mode of production, but that it is a precursor of a reformation based on a new value system, mode of thinking, social order and government. The prime objective of revolution is to 'restore humanity to the human being. It restores confidence to the human being; it tells him that he is capable of moving forward. ' The tyrant *'taghut'* endeavours to 'make you [i.e. the human] vulnerable and weak through his manipulative devices, coercion and intimidation'.[50] Therefore revolution in Islam is directed towards eliminating all sources of weakness,[51] with the ultimate goal of overtaking modern civilization by faith and science, though with recourse to the same means as modern civilization, meaning the scientific rules.[52]

The MVM seems to have espoused the famed Marxist phrase that revolutions are the 'locomotive of history'. 'Revolution is everywhere' is the rallying cry that was adopted by the MVM during the 1980s, which appeared in the writings, sermons and activities of different sections of the Movement. According to Shaikh Hassan al-Saffar 'Islamic revolution is a religious duty on all Muslims;'[53] it is, 'in essence, a revolution against backwardness, oppression and tyranny'.[54] Every conscious believer should bear religious responsibility and have a legal duty to protest against corrupt reality.[55] To handle this task properly, al-Saffar argued, the Shi'is should build a sophisticated organization consisting of leadership, a clear strategy and central channels suitable for a more effective revolutionary formula: a revolutionary organization is the only effective vehicle to counter the repressive measures of tyrannical regimes.[56] In a nutshell, Islamic teachings argue that Muslims should fight against oppression and corruption. Apparently, al-Saffar aims to wipe out Shi'is popular misconceptions in order to bolster his new version of Shi'ism, that it is an ideology of revolution. But the important question is, when did the MVM begin to adopt a revolutionary option?

Generally, observers and scholars have argued that Islamist movements in the second half of the twentieth century have formulated an intention and a strategy to acquire political power by overthrowing governments and replacing them with Islamic ones. In this sense, Olivier Roy argues, Islamists are, as a whole, revolutionary.[57] However, this view is a later projection based mainly on political developments in Iran and Egypt, and is not necessarily derived from the genuine agendas and strategies of these movements.

Indeed, many Islamist movements believe that the re-Islamization process should come from the bottom up and not the reverse.[58] Nearly all Islamist movements that originated before the Iranian revolution in 1978–9 adopted a strategy of *marhaliyya*, or gradualism. This includes the Muslim Brotherhood (*al-ikhwan al-muslimun*), the Islamic Liberation Party (*hizb al-tahrir*), the Islamic Call Party (*hizb al-da'wa al-Islamiyya*) and the MVM. With the exception of *hizb al-tahrir*, which is alleged to have been in a position, as early as 1965, to seize power in Jordan and Iraq, among other places,[59] the rest have confined their activities to disseminating the Islamic message with limited political and social involvement.[60]

The literature of these movements shows that the general aim was that the Islamic *umma* would not arise until every member of the community had completely submitted to Allah's laws. This would entail a long-term strategy beginning from the grass-roots and eventually reaching the acme of society, the political apparatus.

Although the majority of Islamist movements in the 1960s and 1970s believed that the states in which they lived were anti-Islamic, in the sense that they were not anchored in the *shari'a* by which they were supposed to abide, they shunned any attempt to unseat the rulers. In the three decades up to the Iranian revolution, mainstream Islamist movements believed that the establishment of personal and social transformation was a prerequisite for true Islamic government.[61] However, with the success of the Iranian revolution, a significant shift occurred in the discourse of Shi'i Islamist movements towards adopting a revolutionary option.

MVM literature that appeared in its formative years applied the term 'revolutionary' to the leftist radical movements that resorted to violence as a tool of change. With the passage of time, and as the movement was exposed to various schools of thought and political experiments in Iran, Egypt and Palestine, the term has become less sensitive, and gradually, particularly with the victory of the Iranian revolution, has been integrated into Islamist religious-political terminology and literature. Indeed, the strategy of the MVM was drastically modified in that gradualism was no longer a preferred option. A distinction was made between the *da'wa* party and the MVM: the former advocated gradualism while the latter espoused abrupt revolution, in which all stages would be fused in one.

Muhammad Taqi al-Mudarresi is considered the mastermind of a revolutionary ideology that aimed at establishing an Islamic state, not only in Iraq, but also throughout the Islamic world. The role the MVM had played in the Shi'i community in Iraq and the Gulf at large and its efforts to counter the political realities in these regions led to a period of great turmoil in the region. The MVM had a significant impact on the Gulf populations in general, affecting political systems and the social fabric.

The literature of the MVM and of the IRO identifies two forms of socio-political change: evolutionary and revolutionary. Evolutionary change means a gradual and peaceful process of social transformation, which ultimately leads to a change of government. This change is to be achieved with the use of existing institutions such as syndicates, parliaments, press and so forth. Revolutionary change means comprehensive alterations starting from changes in personnel and extending to social values, social structures and political institutions. Such alterations are to be achieved by recourse to every possible means; they may entail the use of peaceful tools or violence, depending on how effective these tools are in attaining such revolutionary change.[62]

The MVM–IRO has vehemently rejected the evolutionary method. In a crucial pamphlet, a distinction is made between the five types of Islamic movements on the basis of the strategy adopted by each one. These strategies are: politically motivated (e.g. Jamal al-Din al-Afghani); intellectually motivated (e.g. Shaikh Muhammad Abduh, Muhammad Iqbal and *Nadwat al-'Ulama*); militarily oriented (e.g. *Fidaiyn Islam* in Iran and Algeria, *al-Ikhwan al-Muslimeen*, or the Military Wing); distorted *risaliyya*-oriented (e.g. *Ikhwan al-Muslimeen* and *Jama't Islami*); and finally faithful *risaliyya*-oriented (e.g. MVM).

The MVM's is a comprehensive strategy geared towards the change of intellectual, military, political and civilizational aspects of society. This is based on the apprehension of Islam as a 'message', that is, a universally valid form of 'revolution'.[63] According to al-Saffar, 'revolution is a comprehensive civilizational project, and confrontation with government is the tangible facet of this project'.[64]

The MVM has also made a distinction between reform and revolution. While reform is a perpetual process in both material and moral human life, revolution is an unrepeated human phenomenon.[65] According to an internal pamphlet, the IRO rejects partial reform, since the advocates of such an option ignore the comprehensiveness of the predicament of the *umma*, which needs deep and multi-faceted alterations of society.[66]

If this is the case, then what are the conditions and circumstances that could lead to another revolution in Iraq and elsewhere in the world? Mudarresi argues that revolutions require four main conditions:

1. A clear deviation in society from Islam
2. A deep awareness of the deviation
3. A solid determination for change
4. A strategy for translating this determination into deeds.[67]

In Mudarresi's view, these four conditions are present, although the success of revolution depends on four main factors: financial support, message-oriented thought (fikr risali), a committed vanguard and supportive masses.[68] Therefore he concludes that 'as for us – the Muslim – this is the most suitable time in our history for revolution'.[69]

The IRO believes that revolution originates in religious institutions, Islamic schools and universities, mosques and religious centres and that the 'ulama, being the vanguard of society, assume a leading role in revolution and change in the society.[70] Therefore revolution is not always associated with violence, but it is a multi-faceted process. 'The danger of deviation and falsification in the path of the masses is possible unless countered by intellectual and cultural Jihad which enlightens the masses.'[71]

It seems that this view, however, contradicts a basic principle of the MVM's revolutionary ideology, that is, the principle of violence. According to a pamphlet, 'revolution is an abrupt uprooting of a false construction, with reliance on violence and vigour'.[72] It also contradicts a clearly stated belief of the IRO, that 'violence is the sole means for changing the defective reality'.[73]

In practice, the ideologues of the MVM do not take this definition at face value. In the final analysis, revolution carries manifold meanings and implications, depending on what region, society and groups it is applied to. According to al-Saffar, revolution is directed against the prevailing traditions, customs and defective social realities.[74] In this respect, a prominent aspect of revolution is cultural. In al-Saffar's view, there is what he calls a 'cultural empty quarter' that the Islamic movement should try to fill. The willingness to implement Islam involves profound personal commitment to detailed studies about various aspects of Islam that have been ignored by Muslim intellectuals for centuries.[75]

Nevertheless, revolution, as presented in the literature of the MVM, in effect means the overthrow of a regime. The adoption of a revolutionary ideology by the IRO has meant, at least in theory, the commitment to dismantling the Saudi regime and replacing it with an Islamic state modelled on the Islamic Republic of Iran.

Although revolutionary ideology was an effective mobilizing force in the 1980s, the leader of the IRO argues that:

> the revolutionary ideas propagated by the IRO were employed to serve a peaceful oppositional agenda, meaning political and journalistic activities in the form of demonstrations, rallies, printing books, magazines, pamphlets and flyers, in addition to writing anti-Saudi slogans on walls.[76]

This view does not, however, reflect the fundamental strategy of the MVM, which continued to advocate a revolutionary option. What might be called opportunism lies in revolutionary rhetoric, which is meant to be a force for mobilization, since such rhetoric has been the most effective tool in the Shi'i cause. Yet, it should be noted that the IRO has shunned violence against the Saudi regime on the pretext that the Shi'is 'are not prepared for such a stage.'[77] However, revolutionary violence remained the preferred option for the MVM after the Iranian revolution emboldened Shi'is and Islamist activists everywhere, and reinforced the belief that Islam could come to power through revolution.

The adoption of revolutionary ideology corresponds with Geertz's argument in interest theory, in which ideology becomes a mask and a weapon.[78] Revolutionary ideology, for the IRO, is not based on conviction and belief but, rather, it is a means of mobilization and pursuing power. As is overtly stated, 'The contradiction between people and government could not be eliminated without the removal of the infidel government.'[79] This is a clear attempt by the IRO to justify its call for revolutionary change leading to the overthrow of the illegitimate rulers, the al-Sa'ud.

Although the ideology of the MVM touches upon every aspect of Muslim life, there is great diversity within and among the branches of the Movement, reflecting local, national, cultural and political realities. However, this diversity could not have surfaced before the end of the 1980s, since up until then the IRO lacked an independent role among the Saudi Shi'is members in the MVM.

Martyrdom: A Revolutionary Weapon

Central to the revolutionary ideological formulation of the IRO is the doctrine of martyrdom. The philosophy of martyrdom is predicated upon two elements: a cause; and a willingness on the part of worthy men to shed their blood and sacrifice themselves to secure the cause. Sacrifice in the pursuit of a cause incurs suffering and pain. According to Dr Shari'ati, sacrifice becomes the motor of life, as a cause cannot be pursued and secured without those men who cherish pain for its own sake. It is not only Khomeini who placed emphasis on martyrdom, but the Shi'i activists as a whole use the mantra of 'Ashura to inspire discontented individuals and 'to justify the deliberate sacrificing of one's life for Islam'.[80] The success of the Iranian revolution tempted Islamists of all kinds to think of further attempts to employ revolutionary violence that would bring them to power.

Although martyrdom is ever present in the consciousness of Muslims, in Shi'ism the concept has been more thoroughly elaborated as a main component of the Islamic faith. Hence the Shi'i maxim: 'Every day is 'Ashura and every place is Karbala' – referring to the martyrdom of the Imam Hussain.

The martyrdom of Imam Hussain has become a prominent feature of Shi'i activism. The call for self-sacrifice is always conveyed in *hussainiya*s or during Muharram, and the validation of martyrdom continues to be linked to the episode of Karbala, the symbol of confrontation between the oppressed and the oppressor.

Inspired by the success of Khomeini's movement and moved by the teachings of the ideologues of the MVM, the IRO won mass support and directed Shi'is rage and discontent against the Saudi regime. Al-Saffar insists on using martyrdom as a vital weapon in the political struggle against the Saudi regime. He states, 'Martyrdom is, in itself, a critical weapon the rebels raise in the face of tyrannical regimes. Martyrdom contains immense potential to destroy the crowns of oppressors.'[81] In other words, 'we still possess an effective weapon, that is, the weapon of martyrdom.'[82]

The Revolutionary Masses

The literature of the MVM lays particular emphasis on the role of the masses in revolution. Mudarresi claims that the failure of *ikhwan al-muslimfn* and of the Mashumi party in Indonesia can be attributed to the absence of the masses, that is, to the fact that these movements failed to transform into populist movements but relied solely on organizational cells. The Islamic movement needs 'to multiply its efforts to organize the masses, so revolution may be possible'.[83]

The IRO paid a great deal of attention to young people, believing that they are liable to embrace any tempting idea, regardless of its source,[84] and that if they are granted a social role and religious responsibility, they will be more concerned with the needs of their community and more committed to religion. Therefore, it is important that they get involved in social activities that shape their role.[85] Taped sermons, pamphlets, leaflets and religious festivals were aimed at attracting Shi'is youth in the Eastern Province. They were heavily engaged in the *intifada*, and became increasingly involved in political activities of the IRO both inside and outside the country.

The aversion of the young to Islam is due, according to al-Saffar, to the absence of true Islam. He argues, 'the majority of our youth do not know the principles and decrees of Islam. What is apprehended from Islam is limited to the precepts of worship, while the intellectual, economic, political and social aspects of Islam are neglected.'[86]

Women were also to play a crucial role in revolution. The IRO generally rejected two conflicting models of women. The first was the conservative, backward and quietist woman, who 'in the name of chastity and veil ... became embedded in domestic affairs while remaining ignorant', and whom society disdained, reducing her status on the basis of her ostensible inferiority to man. The second was the emancipated woman influenced by Western civilization, 'who rid herself of familial commitment and an education-oriented role and became increasingly involved in public services and entertainment activities'.[87]

The alternative model the IRO espouses is what it calls 'the *risaliyya* woman', who is acquainted with true Islamic culture and takes part in social activities. The ideologues of the IRO assign to women a crucial role in social and political life, which is not voluntarily assigned but is a religious duty. Women are called upon to incite and mobilize the masses, in addition to performing certain secret tasks that they can safely do, because they cover their faces, but men cannot.[88] The social change envisaged by the IRO could thus be attained by the use of revolutionary violence perpetrated by the masses of believers.

Umamiyya *(Cosmopolitism)*

The notion of the *umma* is undoubtedly a historical product that is closely associated with the advent and expansion of Islam. Thus *ummamiyya* is a tendency towards reconstituting a universal nation based on religious grounds and motivated and inspired by Islamic teachings. Since the collapse of the Ottoman Empire in 1924, the *umma* as a religious-political reality no longer exists, prompting Islamist movements to revive and struggle to restore it.

The universalist tendency of the leaders of the MVM echoes Khomeini's slogan of the 'downtrodden people in the world'. It also resembles Marx's universal appeal, when he calls upon the crushed masses all over the world to revolt. Although the universal message of the MVM has been, from the outset, deeply embedded, the Iranian revolution undoubtedly gave added urgency to this message. Needless to say, a universalist tendency is pregnant with implications, since it suggests that the community of Muslims should be united. Indeed, the literature of the MVM during the 1980s shows that the ideologues of the Movement claim that the Iranian revolution needs to be universalized. The leader of the IRO believes that, 'the success of the Iranian revolution hinges on its transformation into a universal revolution with the collaboration of anti-imperialist liberation movements and its concern with the issues of oppressed peoples around the world'.[89]

Echoing the rhetoric of Khomeini, al-Saffar claims that:

> ... we are genuinely part of the realm of the downtrodden [*mustad'afun*] while the despots of 'Al-Sa'ud [*tawaghit*] are genuinely part of the realm of oppressors [*mustakbirun*] and colonizers, the ongoing battle is now between these two realms ... our struggle against the tyrannical rule [e.g. Saudi] is a cycle of a long chain of a universal revolution which will, inevitably, lead to the collapse of imperialistic superpowers and the rise of the world of *mustad'afun*.[90]

The fusion of the idea of Islamic unity with revolutionary violence echoes the eschatological element in Shi'ism as articulated in the concept of the occulted Imam, who will eradicate the roots of oppression throughout the world by revolution.

In contrast to the traditional Shi'i categorization of the world, the ideologues of the MVM, like Shari'ati, present their view of the duality in terms of the majority oppressed (*mustad'affn*) and the minority oppressors (*mustakbirun*) rather than in terms of the realm of Islam (*dar al-Islam*) and the realm of war (*dar al-harb*).[91] The MVM takes this duality to its extreme, viewing all things in binary terms, which means that everything can be either oppressive or just. This division of the world into two camps entails humanizing world conflicts and resolutions. Though the ideologues of the MVM, like nearly all Shi'is activists, contend that the only way to avoid the oppressors' world is to adhere to Islam as embodied in its law, the invocation of terms such as 'the oppressed', which assemble Muslims and non-Muslims in one unified category, indicates a shift from a religious to a human sphere.

In this respect, the success of the Iranian revolution stimulated those who found themselves victims of the coercive modern nation-state to cling to the legacy of Islamic civilization. Many tended to support universalism, expressed in the Islamic *umma*, an ideology that has risen to challenge the *de facto* reality. Thus the universalistic tendency of the MVM is an implicit rejection of the nation-state.

In opposition to the status quo, Mudarresi portrays nationalism, which distinguishes between Muslims, and patriotism, which is not based on Islam, faith and piety, as false values and idols that must be destroyed.[92] For this reason, Mudarresi opposes the Islamic movements that confine their activities to Iran or to any other particular region or community and instead calls for a universal Islamic movement.[93]

To justify adopting the idea of a broader religious-political entity, the IRO has articulated its opposition to the nation-state. It claims that the Saudi regime tries to deepen the sectarian divisions among Muslim people in order to crush unity, which could lead to the overthrow of the regime; to fragment the Islamic *umma*, as the prevailing status of the *umma* has always been a colonial target; to divert the attention of people from more important issues; and to create an illusory enemy so that every sect perceives all other sects as its main enemy.[94]

The IRO has sought solace in the Iranian revolution, embracing it as '[o]ur revolution ... it is the revolution of Islam in Iran and not the Iranians' revolution'.[95] Moreover, the leader of the MVM argues that the Islamic revolution in Iran defends not the soil of Iran but the dignity of every Muslim.[96] This is because, according to Mudarresi, revolution is not owned by a person, region or group of people.[97]

In Mudarresi's understanding, the exportation of revolution should call for collective efforts that encompass all Muslims in order to arrest the Westernization process and Muslims' total dependence on the West.[98] The realization of this principal goal, explains Mudarresi, entails Islamic authenticity, political independence and technological advancement.[99]

Mudarresi argues that revolution must be rooted in the soil of the society: 'Revolution which has grown outside its soil is liable to failure when exposed to storms'.[100] This view points to a paradox. While the MVM insists on following the path of Islam in order to rebuild the fragmented *umma*, at the same time it recognizes existing political realities, namely the state, in which revolution must occur. The paradox of this debate can be understood on the basis of what universalism and localism would achieve. Championing the notion of the *umma* would secure the legitimacy of the MVM, while recognizing the existing political realities would pave the way for it to gain power.

Closely associated with the universalistic tendency of the MVM is the political context in which this tendency is manifested. The MVM, being based in Iran, strove to distance itself from any sort of influence from the Iranian leadership. It therefore persistently rejected the chance to enter into a coalition with the Iranian regime or a coalition based on mutual planning, coordination and collaboration and called instead for a broader-based coalition of a universal Islamic revolutionary front encompassing liberation movements around the Islamic world. In the eyes of the MVM, reliance on people would enhance its independence and cause, as 'people would provide it with a shield, weapon, and resource'.[101]

The concept of cosmopolitism was more appealing to Saudi Shi'is than to Iraqi or Bahraini Shi'is. The Saudi Shi'is participated in nearly all activities of the MVM in various parts of the world. In addition, a significant number of those involved in the failed coup attempt in Bahrain in December 1982 were Saudi Shi'is. Some others were involved in smuggling explosives, books, secret letters and so on to Iraq and Bahrain. On the other hand, the IRO drew its membership from the Saudis alone, while the Islamic Action Organization (IAO) and the Islamic Liberation Organization (ILO) had a following among the Saudi Shi'is. The reason for the divergence between the different branches of the MVM is to be found, at least in part, in their socio-political backgrounds, particularly in their sense of being a minority. The Saudi Shi'is seem to have favoured a broader identity that would offer them a sort of psychological compensation, while the Bahraini and Iraqi Shi'is, who constitute majorities in their respective countries, would rather exploit all resources to serve their cause as a majority.

However, on the higher level, the IRO leadership was realistic enough to embrace a popular ideology that is cosmopolitan, aside from its immediate objective of countering Saudi discriminatory policy. In their public leaflets and announcements, they called for a cosmopolitan *umma* throughout the Islamic world, while refraining from cultivating such an option in their homeland. This does not mean that the IRO had its own agenda separate from the MVM, where cosmopolitism is a central feature of its discourse.

Crystallization of Internal Political Opposition

Shortly after the end of the uprising in November 1979, the leadership of the IRO, including Shaikh Hassan al-Saffar and Shaikh Tawfiq al-Saif, fled the country and sought refuge in Iran, where the IRO based itself. Other leaders remained inside the country to administer the activities of the IRO and foster an organizational network in an effort to recruit new members and carry out important tasks. Following a wave of arrests in December 1979, the organizational network of the IRO had to be dismantled. This was a serious challenge for the leaders of the IRO in light of severe security measures inflicted on the Shi'is towns and villages.

In the years following the *intifada* the internal leaders of the IRO were most vitally concerned with the distribution of books, pamphlets, magazines and taped sermons, which were smuggled from Iran to Saudi Arabia via other Gulf states. Another activity carried out by the IRO inside the Shi'is towns and villages was the sporadic writing of revolutionary slogans on walls and public buildings, demanding the release of the Shi'is prisoners and expressing loathing for the Saudi rulers. In addition, the internal leaders engaged in logistical activities such as raising funds to support the IRO's activities outside the country.

All prisoners were released, and the socio-economic conditions of the Shi'is in the Eastern Province were significantly ameliorated following the appointment in 1984 of Prince Muhammad b. Fahad as the governor of the Eastern Province, replacing Prince 'Abdulmuhsin b. Jilwui. The government allocated billions of dollars for a comprehensive development programme in al-Qatif region.

However, the tense security situation in the Eastern Province since 1982 had compelled a large number of members of the IRO to leave the country, as external oppositional activities broadened, whereas the internal organizational network of the IRO, reconstructed in 1982, fell apart following harsh campaigns and crackdowns on a large number of suspected members. The wave of 1982 arrests also included a significant proportion of the Communist Party and Socialist Action Party in Saudi Arabia, most of whom were Shi'is. Following the *intifada*, both parties mustered all efforts to reconstitute their cells and resume their activities.

While in prison, members of the IRO were subject to harsh torture at the hands of the *'mabahith'*. As a result, some prisoners died, such as Sa'ud al-Hamad (aged twenty-two years) from the village of al-'Awamiyya, and others suffered permanent disabilities. Members of the IRO were held for three to five years under the pretext of possessing banned books, taped sermons or photos of Shi'is leaders. The wave of arrests continued for two and a half years; however, nearly all prisoners were released in the middle of 1984 on the basis of a general amnesty issued by King Fahad.

In retrospect it can be seen that the arrests contributed to entrenching the political and organizational experiment of the IRO. It enhanced their determination to develop new tactics to face the challenges imposed by the security forces. In addition, external oppositional activities created a feeling of reassurance for those who were inside by publicizing their grievances.

Social Entrenchment and Political Contention

Throughout the years 1980–85, the IRO succeeded in deepening its social presence and widening its socio-religious and intellectual influence within the Shi'is community. The roles of local religious leaders who were associated with the IRO played an important part in consolidating the existence of the IRO. They also helped gain more support among a wide segment of the Shi'is. Shaikh Yousif Salman al-Mahdi became a renowned religious figure, respected for his moral and spiritual qualities, who founded numerous social and intellectual institutions and played a pivotal role in the internal activities of the IRO. Another renowned figure was Shaikh Hassan al-Khwuaildi, who was arrested several times in Saudi Arabia between 1983 and 1987. An influential and popular preacher, he overtly condemned the religious campaigns and socio-economic discrimination against the Shi'is.

Other activists who have contributed to strengthening the political and social status of the IRO include 'Abdulmehsin 'Al Kidar, 'Abduljabbar Salat and members of al-Quraish family in Safwa city, such as Muhammad 'Abdulrahim al-Quraish and Muhammad Hussain al-Quraish. All belonged to the IRO, though without an explicit form of membership.

Nevertheless, in response to the successive waves of arrests among the followers of the IRO, some members detached themselves from the Movement and preferred to keep aloof from politics. Others rethought the political strategy of the IRO and came to the conclusion that intellectual change is the prelude to change in all spheres. This group also assigned an added urgency to rethinking the religious discourse of the Movement.

A Dual Challenge

Faced with the danger of internal fracture, following the withdrawal of a group of members and growing concerns about security, the IRO turned its attention to recruiting new elements and promoting organizational forms. It allotted tasks and teams using new organizational tactics, for security reasons, relying on known separate 'islands' where cells operated independently. Each cell pursued a certain task, and in the event of its discovery by the security police, other cells would not be implicated and would remain intact. Numerous cells were formed not only in the Eastern Province but all over the kingdom, to facilitate the tasks of the Movement and neutralize security dangers.

As the activities of the IRO rapidly grew and widened, the security authorities decided to use an iron fist. In 1985 the security authorities started to crack down on the adherents of the IRO. It was one of the most organized and carefully planned waves of arrests against the Movement. A great number of the core figures of the IRO, including religious learned men, social notables and senior organizers, were taken into custody and their confessions enabled the security authorities to trace the internal organizational lines of the IRO.

In response to these harsh measures and to growing support for Iran among the Shi'is all over the world, a group of members of the IRO called for the adoption of the theory of *Wilayat al-Faqih* and the religious authority of Ayatullah Khomeini. The proposal confused many in the Shi'is community in the Eastern Province and elsewhere in the Gulf.

For the first time, the IRO was facing a challenge to its legitimacy and credibility as a revolutionary movement. Doubts were cast on the leaders of the IRO who did not comply with the authority of Ayatullah Khomeini. Conversely, the IRO and MVM as a whole were overseen by Sayyid Muhammad al-Shirazi, who did not conform to the Iranian leadership and strategy.

The internal leaders of the IRO reacted by striving to fortify the bases of the Movement and its independence, with special emphasis on its local characteristics, and thanks to their effectiveness and solid unity succeeded in meeting this severe challenge. The leaders of the IRO outside the country also played a primary role in containing new threats to the Movement. This is because the leaders of the IRO were connected with various Shi'i religious groups, including traditional ones, which they could discredit as backward and outdated, and because of their relationship with the Shi'is religious authorities in Qumm.

What lends the IRO its unique character is the involvement of women in political, organizational and social activities. A large number of young women travelled to Iran for religious education, and many of them engaged in socio-religious and intellectual activities following their return home. For the first time in the history of the Shi'is in the Eastern Province, women stand before crowds and preach. The Movement has paid the price of its forward thinking and openness in the arrest by the government of women activists, among them 'Aliya Maki Farid, who was arrested in 1985. After her release, Mrs Farid documented her experiences in prison in a book entitled *Youmiyat 'Emra' fi al-Soujoun al-Sa'udiyya* (Daily Diary of a Woman in a Saudi Jail).

The emergence of the IRO is considered a turning point in the history of the Shi'is in the Eastern Province and also in the story of the Shi'is opposition in Saudi Arabia. Three major points of interest are reiterated here.

First, Shi'i religious conservatism, which advocates aloofness from politics, found itself challenged by a revolutionary trend emanating from religious circles, which advocated involvement. This trend denounced religious conservatism as reactionary and an obstacle to the progress of the people.

Second, the MVM–IRO made every possible effort to recruit individuals from among the Gulf Shi'is, with the aim of seizing power and establishing an Islamic state. To that end, it devised a rigorous strategy to indoctrinate revolutionaries and fight corrupt regimes. It then planned to implement Islamic laws and export the Islamic revolution to the rest of the world.

One major consequence of the *intifada* was that fear of the government was shattered. The Shi'is, who had previously been preoccupied with a fear of government oppression, noew became more capable of overtly voicing their demands regardless of the consequences. Indeed, the more people were involved in the political struggle, the more they overcame their fear of the regime.

This, of course, could not have happened if the leaders of the IRO had not stimulated the crowds to challenge the armed National Guards. In this respect, the leaders altered the popular conception of Shi'ism, changing it from passivism to activism. Thus Shi'ism has become an ideology of social protest. Reinterpreting Shi'i tradition and history has helped to invigorate the spirit of resistance among the grass-roots Shi'is and political activism has become an essential feature of the religious activities of the Shi'i community. Shi'is individuals aligned themselves with those Imams who were politically active, even though they were not well acquainted with traditional Shi'i disciplines. Since the success of the Iranian revolution, therefore, political activism has become an integral part of Shi'is leadership.

At the same time, collective sentiment among the Shi'is has been enhanced. Before the *intifada*, Shi'i individuals were more concerned with the situation inside their own village, which represented the limit of their geographical and cultural space. They had little knowledge about other villages. Moreover, intermarriage within the Shi'is community between people from other villages and towns was rare, because of weak ties among the Shi'is. With the outbreak of the *intifada*, the links between the Shi'is strengthened considerably and intermarriage became much more common. The individualistic tendency within the Shi'is dwindled in favour of a collective spirit, evident in the petitions signed by a large number of Shi'is individuals from different parts and of different ages concerning Shi'i fundamental demands.

Although classified as part of a revolutionary movement, the IRO confined its activities to cultural and socio-religious matters, avoiding provocative activities, such as military operations that might jeopardize its status, on the pretext that the Shi'is were not ready for revolutionary violence. However, the IRO did not cease to advocate the revolutionary option, at least to appease the dominant tendency, both within the MVM and Shi'i contexts.

FIVE

—

From Revolutionary Option
to Reformative Alternative (1989–93)

The IRO underwent a dramatic change at the end of the 1980s. It moved away from an extreme and confrontational position towards a more moderate and modern one, thereby entering a new phase, which might be called the 'reformative phase'. The movement accepted the status quo as well as subsequent efforts by various national forces to stabilize the Saudi political situation. Emphasis was placed on a participatory model, which embraced all factions in Saudi Arabia's political system at the expense of the early revolutionary Iranian model. The Movement concentrated on a peaceful transformation of the political system and avoided military confrontation. The aim of this new approach was to encourage the toleration of debate and pluralism. Although the Reform Movement had, through the 1980s, become increasingly radicalized, driven by a revolutionary ideology that was formulated by the MVM, redirection towards moderation became possible. The main reason was that many Saudi Shi'is became convinced that the revolutionary option had been unsuccessful in their region.

The new tendency must be seen in the context of a pragmatic approach to the Saudi Shi'i issue, transcending the ideologized cosmic Islam of the MVM, and thus returning to a more realistic hope for survival and an attempt to work out the immediate goals of the Shi'is in the Eastern Province.

This chapter discusses the Reform Movement's new political outlook and its changing role in Saudi politics. It examines the tactical changes in the

Movement and the historical and political context in which they occurred. I will also analyse the implications these changes had upon internal and external developments. More important, I will examine the major issues associated with reformative discourse.

A Political Shift

The seeds of reform were planted around 1985. However, this applied only to a tiny circle of leading members whose ideas were never widely communicated to ordinary members. According to the Chief Editor of *al-Jazira al-'Arabiyya*, Hamza al-Hassan, Shaikh Hassan al-Saffar proposed at the annual meeting of the Central Committee in Damascus in August 1985 that the name of the organization and the magazine be replaced with a new moderate one, following reports that attached the organization to Iran. Despite general agreement among the Central Committee, the debate over the proposal ended without a firm decision, on the grounds that a decision would provoke both the leadership of MVM and the organizational base inside the country.[1] At the end of the 1980s, however, the validity and rationality of revolutionary change began to be widely debated.

In the wake of the massacre of the Iranian pilgrims in Mecca in 1987, when several hundred lost their lives, a great deal of disruption occurred and internal and regional circumstances were destined to bring about serious new challenges to the Saudi regime. This must be combined with the effective political and journalistic roles that the IRO has played in different parts of the world, including Europe and United States.

In a bid to reduce tension inside the country, King Fahad issued a general amnesty in favour of the Shi'i prisoners in the Eastern Province, most of whom were members of the IRO. The IRO described the step as a big achievement. At this time, the IRO entered a new stage of rethinking its political strategy, taking into account regional developments, notably the ceasefire between Iran and Iraq in 1988.

One of the most important issues to both inside and outside leaders of the IRO was the reorganization of the internal structure of the Movement. They also agreed that emphasizing the fundamental demands of the Shi'is was a first priority of the Movement. This change was a reflection of the nature of struggle with the government. The situation in the Shi'i region became calmer, and compromise and reform were the order of the day.

The Movement concentrated on its cultural and social roles. The most distinct feature of the new phase was that the IRO established a strategic connection with various social forces, including conservative ones, who were antagonistic to Shi'i political ends. Another development was that a number of the cadres of the IRO were encouraged to return to the country following the general amnesty. Many of them contributed to reinforcement of the new reformative orientation and to the proliferation of publications by the IRO, in addition to assembling information and documents about the legacy of the Shi'is in the Eastern Province.

Impact of hizbullah

Relations between Iran and Saudi Arabia had been disrupted since the advent of Ayatullah Khomeini and the foundation of an Islamic state in Iran in 1979. In the aftermath of the massacre of the Iranian pilgrims in 1987, these relations worsened and accordingly the political climate in the Eastern Province became tense. Many supporters of the Islamic republic among the Shi'is were willing to pursue military means to retaliate against the Saudi regime. Small explosions occurred in oil installations in Jubail and Ju'aima in the Eastern Province in the early 1988. A new group called *hizbullah* claimed responsibility. As a result, the security authorities arrested a group of suspected members of the *hizbullah*, as well as a few members of IRO and leftist groups.

A military confrontation between four elements of *hizbullah* and Saudi security forces took place in a building in Qatif in the summer of 1988. The four individuals were arrested and then executed in a public area in the town of Qarif.

These tragic incidents, which affected all the Shi'is in the Eastern Province, created a clear distinction between extreme, moderate and traditional trends within the Shi'is. The IRO fell into a line between quietist and radical trends. Although this categorization indicates a division within the Shi'is community and also the diversification of orientations and allegiances, the IRO remained the most popular and widely recognized political force in the Eastern Province. This continued to be so until the announcement of the initiative of dialogue between the Reform Movement and the Saudi government, which culminated in the meeting between King Fahad and leaders of the Movement in October 1993.

In 1987 a decision was made by the Central Committee of the Movement to soften gradually the tension with the Saudi regime following the general amnesty decreed by the king. The organizational cells operating inside the kingdom were instructed to avoid provocative acts, among which was the distribution of anti-Saudi flyers.

In 1990 interest in reform gained wide momentum among segments of the Saudi Shi'is in the MVM as the revolutionary ideology failed to attain its declared goals.

An ideological shift at the end of the 1990s led in turn to a shift in the centres of political activity. The transformation from revolutionary to reform movement reduced the importance of Tehran, where the Movement's headquarters and activities were based. After the bulk of the Movement had moved from Iran to Damascus in 1989, London and Washington had gained in importance as the centres of political, journalistic and human rights activities, although Damascus remained a centre of intellectual, socio-religious and organizational accomplishments.

However, the roles of London and Washington (or, more accurately, the USA) can be traced back to the early 1980s and to understand the context in which the shift of the centre of gravity took place we need to examine these roles.

London Office (1983–94)

Following intense discussion held in Damascus in March 1983, the Central Committee of the IRO agreed to select London as a site of political and journalistic activities. The concentration of the IRO in Iran had made it liable to unforeseen risks as a result of the changing political circumstances in Iran. In 1983, rumours circulated widely that a new chapter of relations was due to begin between Tehran and Riyadh, following the Saudi Foreign Minister Prince Sa'ud al-Faisal's visit to Tehran. The leadership of the IRO was prompted to transfer some of its weight to other sites in order not to be affected by such relations.

The IRO considered three sites for relocation: Cyprus, France and the UK. Cyprus was chosen as a location for organizational communications, while London was selected to be a primary site for journalistic and publishing activities.

Since the early 1980s, London had become a centre of Arab media, as civil war plagued Beirut, leading to the emigration of Lebanese media pundits to London. Until the early 1990s there were thirteen daily newspapers published in London in addition to dozens of weekly and monthly magazines. Moreover, the Arab and Muslim community in London, the largest in Europe, made London a familiar and safe place to live and work. The presence of the MVM there could even be traced back to the late 1970s.[2] In addition, frequent visits by Gulf families to London made communications very easy and safe by comparison to Syria and Iran. Communications with Shi'is visitors to Iran and Syria have sometimes led to their arrest and interrogation on their return to the country. Finally, IRO members felt no inhibitions about coming to London because, having learnt English in their own country, they were at ease with the language.

One of the most important activities of the IRO between 1983 and 1987 was the publication of a magazine called *al-Thawra al-Islamiyya*, or The Islamic Revolution. A publishing house called Dar al-Safa was founded in this period, where a collection of books criticizing the Saudi regime were published, as well as communications with the internal leaders of the IRO.

Following the ceasefire between Iran and Iraq in August 1988 and the emigration of the leaders and the majority of the members of the IRO from Iran to Syria, London became still more important as a site of journalistic and political activity. This coincided with the ambition of the Iranian political leadership, particularly Hashimi Rafsanjani and Ali Khamanei, to re-establish Iran in world politics and reintegrate it into the international scene.

In this context, there was the intriguing episode of Robert McFarlane, the former National Security Adviser during Reagan's reign, who arrived in Tehran in September 1986. McFarlane took 23 tons of weapons to Iran, in addition to a cake in the form of a key, as a gesture of the willingness of the American administration to resume relations with Tehran.

On 3 November 1986 the Lebanese magazine *al-Shira'* reported that the US had sold arms to Iran. Moreover, the magazine published a provocative article about the dramatic transformation in Iran from revolutionary mode, exemplified by the former deputy of Khomeini, Shaikh Hussain Ali al-Muntazari, to what the revolutionaries called statism, exemplified by the so-called trinity of Sayyid Ali al-Khamanaei, Hashimi Rafsanjani and Sayyid Ahmad al-Khomeini (the son of Ayatullah Khomeini).

The transformation in Iran could be traced back to the struggle between the right and left wings, which escalated in January 1986 following the dissolution of *sazman mujahidi enqilab Islami*, the Organization of the Warriors of Islamic Revolution, which represented the left wing in the Islamic revolution. Afterwards, the pragmatic trend led by Shaikh Rafsanjani began to prevail as he and Sayyid Ali al-Khamanaei, the former leaders of *hizb Jemhouri Islami*, the Islamic Republic Party, became the dominant rulers of Iran. The dissolution of both *sazman mujahidi enqilab Islami* and *hizb Jemhouri Islami* undoubtedly boosted the pragmatic trend, which was becoming more liberated and hoped to rebuild relations with the West. They capitalized on the US presidential elections to end the war with Iraq, which allowed communications between Tehran and Washington to start.

Consequently, the revolutionary trend in Iran began to wane, inclining its leaders to reveal the details of McFarlane's visit to Tehran. This took place in a meeting between Sayyid Mahdi Hashimi, the chairman of the Office of Liberation Movements, and a leader of the MVM. In an attempt to spoil the secret arrangement between the Reagan administration and the pragmatists, members of the MVM travelled to Beirut and sent the story to a number of newspapers and magazines. However, only *Al-Shira‘* magazine agreed to publish the story, which led to a serious dilemma in the United States. William Casey, the CIA Chairman, committed suicide and McFarlane was admitted to hospital following a suicide attempt, while now ex-President Reagan and high officials in his administration were questioned before a special commission.

The responses in Iran were quite different. The influence of the revolutionaries diminished and its leaders lost their positions, like Shaikh al-Muntazari, or were executed, like Mahdi Hashimi, or were repressed and marginalized, like the former members of *sazman mujahidi enqilab Islami* and the former commander of the Revolutionary Guards, Abu Sharif, who escaped to Afghanistan and joined the Ghulbal-Din Hukmatiar Movement.

Consequently, the MVM lost a strong ally in Iran, leading to the emigration of the leaders of the IRO to Syria, where they established a new base, though with limitations, because of sensitivity to the relations between Riyadh and

Damascus. Damascus became the centre of the intellectual and organizational activities of the IRO, whereas London and Washington continued to host political, journalistic and human rights activities.

From the end of the 1980s onwards, London took a central role in the strategy of the IRO and by the end of 1993 a number of leading members of the IRO, including the general secretary, his deputy and members of the Central Committee, resided in London. They were engaged in various activities such as the publication of the magazine *al-Jazira al-'Arabiyya*, the organ of the Reform Movement, as well as critiques of Saudi Arabia. The London office also fostered a broad network of relations with journalists, human rights activists and politicians, be they inside the UK or elsewhere in Europe or the Middle East. This network helped the *islahiyya* Movement to convey its political message and demands through respectable and legitimate avenues in the West, namely media, human rights organizations and independent political institutions, even including the British Parliament.

Interestingly enough, London hosted the negotiations between the Saudi government and the *islahiyya* Movement in which all major decisions on both sides were made, including the abandonment of all oppositional activities and the announcement of a general amnesty for members of the Movement.

The Islahiyya *in the United States (1975–94)*

Prior to the *intifada* in 1979, there was a group of advocates of the so-called Shirazi trend among Shi'is students in the United States. What linked them to the leaders of this trend inside the country was that they all subscribed to the same religious authority or *marj' taqlid*, namely Ayatullah Sayyid Muhammad al-Shirazi. However, the activity of the group in United States was solely limited to distributing the books and taped sermons of the preachers and clerics belonging to the Shirazi school of thought.

With the outbreak of the *intifada* in November 1979, those students intensified their activities and began regularly to communicate with the leaders of the Shirazi trend in the Eastern Province. They were encouraged to establish what subsequently became known as the Islamic Union of Students of the Arabian Peninsula, which coincided with the launch of the Islamic Revolution Organization (IRO).

The Islamic Union was virtually the political arm of the students' activities in the United States. Its first political activity was a student demonstration near the White House on the first anniversary of the *intifada* in November 1980. Dozens of Saudi Shi'is students came from all over the States and assembled in Washington. Some other Shi'is students from other GCC and Arab states also joined the demonstration, which had a significant impact in the American media, receiving coverage in most of the newspapers both in Washington and elsewhere.

Afterwards, members of the Union issued a magazine entitled *al-Ettihad*, which was distributed by post to many students all over the States. The magazine was devoted to covering the activities of the IRO inside Saudi Arabia as well as among the Saudi Shi'is students in the States. It also provided political analysis of the issues of moment in the Gulf region, with the aim of encouraging students to engage in political activity in the US, so as to put pressure on the Saudi government to meet the demands of the people.

Meanwhile, Shi'is students who subscribed to the IRO started to recruit new members through the Islamic Union. They also participated in the Islamic conferences held in some states during the Christmas holidays, among them the annual conference organized by *Hizb al-Da'wa* under the umbrella of the Muslim Group (*al-Jama'a al-Islamiyya*), which was founded in the early 1980s by supporters of *al-Da'wa* party from Kuwait, Iraq and Lebanon, particularly those who were affiliated with the Lebanese *Amal* Movement. The members of the IRO took advantage of such gatherings to communicate with students from both Saudi Arabia and the Gulf as a whole. Hitherto, the focus of *al-Jama'a al-Islamiyya* had been confined to religious matters and it had distanced itself from politics. This group did not therefore appeal to many Shi'is students, who had until then taken their cue from the Iranian revolution. Some students joined the Union and became active members, handling important roles and responsibilities.

In summer 1981 a preliminary survey was carried out by the leaders of the Union on the Shi'is students in the United States, with particular emphasis on those who were receptive to the ideology of the IRO. The survey aimed to examine the willingness of the students to engage in public activities. Afterwards, a leading member of the IRO, 'Isa al-Miz'el, who was sent by the IRO to recruit new members and organize political and intellectual activities in the States, strove to assemble as many as possible of the Saudi Shi'is students to form a broader student framework inside the US. Thus, he invited the leader of IRO, Shaikh Hassan al-Saffar, to meet a group of new members and cadres. The meeting, held in Texas in September 1981, discussed the options available to formulate such a framework in which students could operate unrestricted. Interestingly enough, in the summer of that year, members of the MVM, led by a chief member of the IRO, Ja'far al-Shayeb, had succeeded in organizing student conferences with the cooperation of *al-Jama'a al-Islamiyya*.

During his visit to the United States, Shaikh al-Saffar met several groups of students and always al-Saffar emphasized the need for the students to be active and responsive to Muslim issues all over the world. This led to a wider meeting in Texas, at which a decision was made to establish the *Markaz al-Shabab al-Muslim* (Muslim Youth Centre, MYC), which was founded in September 1981 in Denver, Colorado. Ja'far al-Shayeb and Ahmad al-Nasir, both leading members of the IRO, who lived in that city, were in charge of organizing the first student conference in December of that year.

The first conference organized by the MYC was held in Colorado Springs, Colorado, and attended by about 200 students of both sexes. The organizers and the lecturers, who came from the United States, Iran and Pakistan, together fomented a heated debate about the differences in views about revolution between the sources of Shi'is religious authority (*maraj' taqlid*).

This conference gave new impetus to the Shirazi trend and proved its capability to become an active player in Islamic and political domains in the United States. From there on, MYC became an influential body, under the supervision of the IRO and the administration of Shaikh Hussain al-Jadar, who had previously been studying in Iran. From his residence in Denver, Shaikh Jadar began to communicate with students all over the States by mail, telephone and the distribution of taped sermons and books of the leaders of the MVM.

The significance of the MYC stemmed from the fact that, through this framework, a large number of enthusiastic students, many of whom engaged in the intellectual and political activities of the MVM, were recruited to the IRO. The MYC became one of the most widely recognized and effective student centres in United States and thereafter organized a series of annual conferences. It had opened nine branches in the largest states and issued two monthly magazines, one for male students, entitled *al-shabab al-Muslim* (The Young Muslim), and the other for females, entitled *mariam* (Mary).

In addition, each branch published booklets and organized meetings and seminars for its members.

It was imperative to form an executive committee to manage the activities of the MYC and serve its broader purpose. A general assembly was established, comprising active elements from the nine branches. The members of the assembly arranged a rolling programme in the branches of meetings to discuss the general concerns, plans and objectives of the MYC. The organization's annual conferences became important to Shi'is students from different countries, partly because they were well prepared and offered quality services to the students and their families, and partly because of the interesting topics covered by well-known Islamic lecturers, both Sunni and Shi'is. The last conference was held in Atlanta, Georgia, in December 1990.

Political Activities in the US

The activities of the MYC prepared fertile ground for political activities. The experience of organizing conferences and conducting sophisticated relationships with various groups and institutions helped the members of the IRO to engage in more profound activities, particularly political ones. This coincided with the new orientation towards political and journalistic actions by the IRO in the late 1980s. A group of leading members of the IRO, led by Ja'far al-Shayeb, moved to Tennessee, where they embarked on political and human rights activities. In 1987, the group, with the cooperation of their colleagues in the IRO in Syria, established the International Committee for Human Rights in the Gulf and Arabian Peninsula (ICHR–GAP). The committee was concerned with monitoring human rights conditions in Saudi Arabia and GCC states in general. A series of communiqués, urgent actions and reports were issued in this respect.

During their activity in Tennessee in 1987–90, the group's main focus was on creating a wide range of relations with different groups and institutions, particularly academics and human rights activists. Most importantly, the group endeavoured to build bridges between those who were interested in Saudi affairs, especially researchers, journalists and human rights organizations. As a result, the group helped significantly to make the human rights and political reforms in Saudi Arabia objects of interest for academics, human rights organizations and media in the United States. For instance, the Minnesota

Lawyers Human Rights Committee issued in May 1992 a detailed report entitled *Shame in the House of Sa'ud* condemning the attitude of the Saudi regime towards the Shi'is, women and foreign labourers. The ICHR–GAP had considerably helped in providing the necessary data.

Likewise, the ICHR–GAP had regular contacts and reciprocal meetings with Human Rights Watch, providing it with information and documents about human rights violations in Saudi Arabia. The reports issued by human rights organizations in the US clearly reflect the amount of information provided by the Committee.

In addition, numerous IRO demonstrations and sit-ins were organized in Washington, Atlanta, Dallas, Los Angeles and New York and elsewhere in the United States in front of exhibitions under the name 'Saudi Arabia between Yesterday and Today'. Demonstrators managed to reverse the tide in their favour by inviting visitors of the exhibitions to read the reports on human rights in Saudi Arabia and then sign communiqués and letters to US officials to urge the Saudi government to respect human rights conventions. The protesters received wide coverage by the US media, while the organizers of the Saudi exhibitions, by contrast, refused to comment on the protests. Conversely, members of the *islahiyya* exploited the heavy presence of the US press to voice their demands.

Furthermore, the cadres of *islahiyya* were able to communicate with other Saudi opposition forces (most of them were leftists); many of its members were not willing to get involved in overt political activities. The on-stage activities of the *islahiyya* in the US press stimulated segments of these forces to collaborate with the *islahiyya*. Also, leading members initiated relations with various eminent Saudi Sunni figures who used regularly to visit the United States and participate in conferences sponsored and attended by Saudis, such as *rabitat al-shabab al-Muslim al-'Arabi*, the Muslim Arab Youth Association (MAYA). At these gatherings, members of the *islahiyya* distributed various oppositional publications.

The Move to Washington

At the end of 1990, the political team of the *islahiyya* moved from Tennessee to Washington, for its political and journalistic advantage. They rented an office in the famous National Press Building and set up under the title

International Committee for Human Rights in the Gulf and Arabian Peninsula (ICHR–GAP). The committee was registered in Washington as a non-profit organization.

The first activity of the Committee was to issue a monthly newsletter entitled *Arabia Monitor* in English, on human rights conditions and political developments in the Gulf region and in Saudi Arabia in particular. It was also concerned with the amendment of the rules and regulations in the country, as well as any significant developments, be they political, economic or intellectual. Though not publicly circulated, hundreds of copies of the newsletter were sent by post regularly to academics, study centres, journalists, politicians and experts in the issues of the region.

Moreover, regular communiqués were issued by the Committee in the event of the arrest or release of political activists from the *islahiyya* and other political groups, regardless of their ideological backgrounds. The communiqués and statements issued by ICHR–GAP were sent by fax to human rights organizations, the US press and politicians as well as to Saudi officials inside the kingdom. The activities of ICHR–GAP were covered by local newspapers, particularly in Washington. Human rights campaigns were also organized by the ICHR–GAP with the cooperation of human rights organizations, some local, such as branches of Amnesty International, which launched regular campaigns in defence of prisoners of conscience.

The Committee held public conferences about Saudi Arabia at the National Press Building, focusing on political reforms and human rights conditions in Saudi Arabia. Academics, news reporters, law experts and human rights activists attended. The conferences attracted the attention of a wide range of media and academic institutions. Several US newspapers, TV channels and radio stations interviewed members of the Committee, among them Voice of America (VOA) and Public Broadcasting Service (PBS) television channels.

The ICHR–GAP strove to strengthen its relations with various political and human rights institutions inside United States, such as members of the Human Rights Committee in the US Congress and the Human Rights Division at the State Department. It provided information about human rights violations in Saudi Arabia to both institutions, with the aim of lobbying the Saudi government to mend its ways.

The Committee also communicated with officials in the Saudi Embassy in Washington. Though they had reservations about the activities of ICHR–

GAP, Saudi officials maintained a relationship with the Committee as a means of reducing its influence. In October 1990, a meeting was held at the Saudi Embassy between the Saudi Ambassador in Washington, Prince Bandar b. Sultan, and members of the *islahiyya* including Ja'far al-Shayeb, 'Isa al-Miz'il and Ali Shwaikhat. The meeting centred on the delicate situation in the region following the invasion of Kuwait on 2 August 1990 and the emergence of reformist forces from both religious and liberal backgrounds inside the kingdom. They also stressed the need to promote the Saudi political system. According to J. al-Shayeb, the ambassador expounded the principle of elections for *al-Shura* council, asserting the need to upgrade the Saudi political system. The members of *islahiyya* Movement also raised the issue of discrimination against the Shi'is in Saudi Arabia. The ambassador tried to make light of the Shi'is problem, putting the blame on religious extremism in Saudi Arabia.

Interestingly, members of ICHR–GAP were regularly invited to the Embassy on national occasions and to meet Saudi officials who visited Washington between 1991 and 1993. Another consequence of the meetings was that ICHR–GAP had good relations with Saudi institutions in the United States, such as the Institute of Arabic and Islamic Sciences, World Islamic League, and International Conference for Muslim Youth. Despite sectarian and political divisions, the relations between ICHR–GAP and these institutions were somewhat good.

On the other hand, with the emergence of the Committee for the Defence of Legitimate Rights (CDLR) as a political outlet of the neo-Salafi trend that came into being during the Gulf crisis, ICHR–GAP made a significant gesture. In a telephone call to the general secretary of CDLR, Muhammad al-Mas'ari, the chairman of the ICHR–GAP, Ja'far al-Shayeb, offered his support to the nascent committee and any possible assistance to prop up the CDLR. In the aftermath of the detention of al-Mas'ari and members of the CDLR, the chairman of ICHR–GAP made phone calls to al-Mas'ari's father, Shaikh 'Abdullah, offering cooperation and coordination in order to pressurize the Saudi government to release the founders of CDLR.

Communication between the Shi'is opposition and the Salafi opposition was unprecedented and even unimaginable to the Saudi authorities, who worried about the extent of relations between the Shi'is opposition and the moderate Wahhabis and what such collaboration might lead to.

There seems to be a clear, if unprovable, connection between the potential risks of the relations between the *islahiyya* and the CDLR and the king's initiative to reach an accord with the *islahiyya*. However, as negotiations took place in both London and Beirut leading to a meeting between the *islahiyya* delegation and King Fahad in October 1993, things began to change dramatically. The ICHR–GAP completely abandoned its activities, and the Saudi Embassy in Washington issued travel documents for the members of *islahiyya* to return home.

The Cost and Context of Shift

The *islahiyya*'s crucial decision to withdraw from the MVM was significant, since religious legitimacy could be gained only by the MVM's adherence to the *marji'iyyat* (see Chapter Four) and the spiritual umbrella of Sayyid Muhammad al-Shiirazi. But the negative consequences of such a step were tackled by the leaders of the Reform Movement from 1991 onwards. The leaders of the Reform Movement were looking to forge a new framework aimed at reducing the political impact of *marji'iyyat* activities by relying on their openness towards other Shi'is leaders and movements, as well as to moderate Sunnis and liberal groupings.

Although the Reform Movement experienced set-backs and underwent harsh criticism following its separation from the MVM, it became a distinct movement among the Shi'is groupings in the Gulf region. To understand the factors behind the Reform Movement's moderation we need to focus on three unusual factors. First, there was the announcement of a ceasefire between Iran and Iraq in July 1988. This dramatic decision, initially made by Iran, meant that hopes for the success of a revolution in Iraq were dashed, and it was in this hope that the Movement had invested most of its resources. As a result, the MVM became fractured, leading to disputes among the leading class about the strategy that should be adopted to face the new dramatic phase.

Second, there was the fall of the Soviet Union in 1989 and Mikail Gorbachev's policy of *perestroika*, which embraced two central notions: reconstruction/restructuring and transparency. A number of members of the Reform Movement who had lived in Syria following the ceasefire between Iraq and Iran in 1988 were exposed to the vast literature on Gorbachev's reforms that quickly accumulated in Syria and Lebanon. The impact of these reforms was evident in the reconstruction process of the IRO and in its position towards transparency and openness, both with regard to the relationships within the Movement and the Movement's relationship with other political groups. The decision of members to abandon fake names reflected this transparency, as did internal literature, in which an agenda and ideology were clearly stated. In fact, the impact of Gorbachev's reform programmes affected nearly all political movements in Syria and Lebanon, encompassing a wide range of ideological trends, both secular and Islamic. The exposure of the IRO to intellectual activities and literatures in a socialist state like Syria coincided with its departure from Iran, and hence the transformation towards moderation. Consequently, Gorbachev's reform notions enhanced the IRO's determination and influenced its direction.

Third, the invasion of Kuwait in August 1990 and the crucial transition period during the Gulf crisis in 1991 marked what ex-American President George Bush called a 'New World Order'. The region was due to witness an aggressive process of reform.

Shortly after the invasion of Kuwait and the arrival of foreign troops in Saudi Arabia, discontent among a large segment of the population steadily rose. From the outset, the royal family was criticized for its ineptitude at defending the country and for its reliance on non-Muslims, despite massive military spending over the two previous decades. The criticism of the royal family was transformed into open political activity by nationalist and neo-Salafi trends, who pressed the government to introduce essential changes into the state institutions.

The changes that took place within the IRO reflected a reorientation in policy and strategic emphasis. Political reform, social work, community development and the propagation of Islamic values and religious and cultural practice in Shi'i life were emphasized at the expense of revolutionary/military ideology. These changes also represented a struggle to define and implement norms and values in the public as well as in the private domain, and an attempt to reconstruct the collective within both an Islamic, i.e. authentic, and modern framework. The strategic shift from confrontation to moderation was accompanied by a redefinition of the Saudi Shi'is' crisis, insofar as the Reform Movement ceased to place Saudi Shi'i society in the cosmic context in which the Saudi regime represented the greatest threat to the rise of Islamic umma. This view made the eradication of the regime a strategic option for the Movement. The Reform Movement contended that redress of Shi'i socio-economic conditions and Shi'i religious and human rights were the prime objectives of the Movement and should be won in exchange for recognition of the Saudi status quo.

The IRO renamed itself *al-haraka al-islahiyya* in early 1991 in order to remove its revolutionary and religious overtones. It decided to occupy a place in the political game in the Saudi realm. The new strategy required a more straightforward agenda, peaceful tools and a clear structure. Until late 1989, the Reform Movement relied on a considerable invisible organizational structure. With its new political shift, a visible organizational structure was required to regularize relations with the public.

In contrast to the MVM, the Reform Movement is led by a collective leadership rather than by one charismatic personality, though the emphasis on the role of the *'ulama* in society is a central feature of Shi'i Islam and thus of the Reform Movement's structure. Indeed, even before the separation of the MVM, the IRO had a Central Committee of eight members who ran the day-to-day activities.

Structurally, the first body that was established following the separation of the IRO from the MVM was the Consultative Council (*majlis al-shura*) comprising 40 members. The Council, although not the highest decision-making apparatus of the Movement, has played a pivotal role in coordinating the work of the Movement's committees. The Council used to be convened annually to discuss the general long-term strategy of the Movement. The *shura* Council is charged with the overall administration of the Movement and with calling meetings when necessary. Decisions made by the Council are reached either unanimously or by majority vote. The Council also has the right to call for the election of a general secretary for the Movement. In the 1991 election the members of the Council elected Shaikh Tawfiq al-Saif as the second general secretary of the Reform Movement. Al-Saif, who is considered as one of the founding fathers of the IRO, held the post after wide criticism of Shaikh al-Saffar's leadership. While al-Saffar focused on regulating relationships with the Shi'is notables, al-Saif and other leading members of the Movement, notably in London and Washington, devoted themselves to political issues. The reason for this duality was that the tactical political shift and the Reform Movement's new leaning towards moderation gave rise to peaceful political and journalistic activities, for which London and Washington were the main bases, whereas Syria and, to a lesser extent, Iran became more and more confined to socio-religious activities. Many Saudi Shi'is travel to the holy shrines of Syria because they have been prevented from travelling to Iraq since the outbreak of the war against Iran in 1981. Its effective political activities enabled the Reform Movement to gain momentum among a large segment of both the Shi'is and other political groupings in the kingdom, notably liberals, nationalists and socialists.

As a result, clearance from the Jurist Guardian (*wali faqih*) for legitimate decisions reached by the *shura* Council was not needed, since the Movement opted for localism. A crucial role was thus entrusted to the *shura* Council and other decision-making bodies in the Movement such as the Central Committee.

Al-islahiyya's transformation into a moderate movement had major implications. First, there was reconciliation between religious and modern discourses. Generally speaking, the political and intellectual literature of the Reform Movement projected a dual image of its purpose and function. The first image anchored the Movement in the domain of political parties; the second placed it in Islam, identified as the framework for all its actions and motivations. Despite its emphasis on Islam as a source of inspiration and legitimacy, frequent reference is made to Western political notions and human rights perceptions. This attitude, expressed with varying degrees of subtlety, implies reconciliation between religious commitment and temporal realities.

According to the new orientation of the Reform Movement, the sacred texts do not change, but interpretation of them does, because understanding is subjected to the changing conditions in which Muslims live. So no interpretation is absolute or fixed for all time and all places. If Islam is the religion designed for the end of time, then it must be adaptable to changing conditions, such as characterize this crucial stage of history.[3] Still, it should be emphasized that Islam, in the eyes of the Reform Movement, is an instrument for gathering political support and that mobilization behind Islam can win support and legitimacy.

Second, the Reform Movement, by adopting the option of reform, implicitly recognized the status quo in Saudi Arabia and the Saudi regime. This is evident in *islahiyya* leadership's call to defend the Saudi borders from the military threats of the Iraqi regime during the Gulf crisis in 1991.

Saddam issued an appeal for support couched in Islamic terms, and called for *jihad* against the forces gathering to confront his troops in Saudi Arabia.

The Reform Movement responded negatively, because of the Iraqi leader's total lack of legitimate Islamic credentials and his record of repression of his people, notably the Shi'is. Rather, the leadership of *islahiyya* 'urged the Shi'is citizens to join military service for the purpose of defending the country. We are ready to defend the nation and the independence of the nation,' said the spokesman of *islahiyya* Movement.[4]

A statement issued by the Reform Movement is symptomatic of the dramatic shift in its ideological and political discourse: 'The royal family is playing a crucial and necessary role in stabilizing the situation in the kingdom and developing the political system, allowing the people to participate in bearing responsibility in that system, which does not contradict such a role.'[5]

Third, the Movement abandoned revolutionary violence as a tool of change and adopted a peaceful pro-democratic stance. *Islahiyya*'s reformative agenda has been described as rather moderate, perhaps because about 60 per cent of the members of the Central Committtee of *islahiyya* were studying and/or living in the West and they were inclined to use peaceful tools such as journalism and humanitarian organizations to voice their political discontent and demands. The leaders were neither prone to violence nor had they launched military operations against Saudi or Western interests internally or externally. Moreover, nearly all members, including the leadership of the Movement, were exposed to modern culture via Arab secular and liberal intellectuals, among them Muhammad 'Abid al-Jabiri, Hisham Sharabi and Burhan Ghalioun. This could be taken as an indicator of the political opening of *islahiyya* towards Western political institutions, such as the US Congress and State Department, the UK Parliament and Foreign Office and the European Parliament. Leading members of *islahiyya* had regular meetings and discussions with officials in these institutions, in the hope of encouraging them to influence the Saudi regime to introduce political reforms and to redress human rights conditions.

Thus, it is inappropriate to imply that the *islahiyya* Movement originally advocated violence and military confrontation, as Madawi al-Rasheed assumes,[6] although the sparse literature about the Movement in the early 1980s may have given a different impression.

The Movement's moderation manifested itself, first, in *islahiyya*'s decision in 1989 to distance itself from the MVM, a revolutionary movement that clung to the military option, and, second, in its adoption of a reformative agenda in the early 1990s.

The Movement's goal, at least in the short term, was not so much the creation of an Islamic society as the building of a moral consensus and Islamic value system as the basis for growth, progress and national reconstruction. Al-Saffar's writings from 1989 onwards exhibit a new moderate rhetoric that emphasizes religious pluralism, intellectual freedoms and civil institutions.[7] Thus, the struggle is no longer to gain political power *per se*, but to define, without violence, new social arrangements and appropriate cultural and institutional models that meet social needs.

Al-islahiyya Movement therefore took note of the importance of increasing people's awareness; using the media as a peaceful and effective means of disseminating ideas; cooperating with human rights organizations such as Amnesty International, Human Rights Watch, Article 19, Minnesota Lawyers International Committee for Human Rights and so forth. The Movement also recognized the significant role that Western political institutions and diplomats could play in influencing the Saudi regime.

Fourth, the Movement abandoned its *umami*, or cosmopolitan tendency, in favour of *al-mahaliyya*, or localism. There were two overlapping but profoundly separate orientations in the IRO: the universalist and local. These were both initially embodied in the IRO's ideology, which advocated adherence to the cosmic view exemplified in the Islamic *umma*, which the MVM expounded and endeavoured to revive; at the same time there were the Saudi Shi'is in the Eastern Province who suffered from various forms of discrimination and needed to muster all efforts to urge the Saudi regime to cease to discriminate against them.

With the end of the first Gulf crisis in 1988 and the dashed hopes of change in Iraq, these two different orientations separated. However, the new local orientation encompassed a universal dimension, since the consensus among the leaders of the Reform Movement was that a sustainable balance between local and cosmopolitan tendencies had to be maintained in order to gain legitimacy and support from the Shi'i hierarchy and movements outside its homeland.

Apart from this, the local tendency began to surface at the end of the 1980s, when Iraq invaded Kuwait, and it became clear that the geopolitics of the whole region was about to undergo drastic change. Although the majority of the Reform Movement's members had been indoctrinated over several years with the vision of a universal Islamic *umma*, the leaders of the

Movement publicly de-emphasized this. Thus the notion of the Islamic *umma* remained within the Movement's rank and file, but was not stated publicly as an immediate goal, because this would conflict with the new localist leaning.

While the Reform Movement had previously rejected the notion of the nation-state and instead had called for the integration of a greater Islamic *umma*, an ideology formulated by al-Mudarresi and derived from the religious-political writings of Ayatullah Muhammad al-Shirazi, the Reform Movement now appeared to have shifted to localism. Although MVM's ideologues preferred the cosmic overview, Shaikh al-Saffar's stance was rooted in his homeland and particularly in the Eastern Province, and then applied to other Muslim societies. He was also heavily influenced by Arab nationalism and the views of Sunni Islamist intellectuals in the Gulf region, particularly those subscribing to the *ikhwan* Movement, who saw their region as locked in a struggle against 'nationalism'. As a consequence, the IRO ceased its plans to invite individuals to leave their homelands and join the Movement, and instead decided to dedicate its activities to local issues. To understand such a decision, we need to refer to the literature of the MVM, in which the concept of immigration (*hijra*) is firmly associated with the concept of the universal Islamic *umma* and to some extent with Islamic revolution and *jiha*d. As such, the abandonment of immigration implies that the Islamic *umma* is not an immediate goal of the Reform Movement, although it remains the model of which its members dream.

Although the Reform Movement was numerically very small, since a relatively large number of the members adhered to the MVM, resumed religious schooling or returned to the country, a large proportion of the members based in London and the United States have played a pivotal role in voicing resentment inside the country. Closely aligning itself with local activities and political forces, the Reform Movement became an outlet for opposition groups in the country and the Gulf in general. This is particularly evident in the voice of the Reform Movement, *al-Jazira al-'Arabiyya*, where various views were reflected. Among the writers of the magazine were leading members of the Communist Party in Saudi Arabia, the Popular Front and *'Ahrar* Movement in Bahrain and political activists in Qatar, UAE and Kuwait. In addition, with the announcement of the Committee for the Defence of Legitimate Rights on 3 May 1993, *al-Jazira al-'Arabiyya* gave exclusive coverage of the CDLR.[8]

The new inclination of the *islahiyya* was the subject of harsh criticism by some Shi'is extremists, especially in regard to the particular attention paid to Salafi activities, which are reflected in the magazine.[9] The new inclination also reignited the dispute with the leadership of the MVM, who attempted to undermine *al-islahiyya*'s growing support among the Shi‘is in the Eastern Province, who welcomed its separation from the mother movement. Despite this, *al-islahiyya* followers and sympathizers ranged from Shi‘is notables and young clerics to regime opponents, intellectuals, political independents and government technocrats. Although the government banned its publication inside the country, the Reform Movement succeeded in smuggling its publications in, and many were reproduced and distributed in Shi‘is regions and elsewhere in the country.

At this juncture, it may be appropriate to have an overview of *al-islahiyya*'s writings on human rights, political reform and Shi‘i authenticization.

Human Rights Discourse

The subject of human rights took a different form in the 1990s. Unlike in the 1980s, when the issue of political prisoners captured the attention of the IRO, *al-islahiyya*'s human rights activists began to broaden the issue of human rights to include cultural, political, social and minority rights.

Al-islahiyya reformers contend that Islam is flexible and that Islamic tenets can be interpreted to accommodate and even encourage tolerance, reconciliation and pluralism. These elements are preconditions for coexistence among various groups in one state.

The Reform Movement adopted the human rights document, the 'Universal Document of Muslim Human Rights', which was ratified and signed by celebrated Muslim scholars and intellectuals in September 1981. Among the central rights included in it are: individual freedom, equality, freedom of belief and expression, justice, the right to a fair trial and protection from government repression, torture or invasion of privacy.[10]

The leader of the Reform Movement equates the Saudi Wahhabi government with the former Communist regime, insofar as they both failed to undermine other faiths despite frequent attempts, particularly in the case of Muslims living in the Soviet Union. Thus, al-Saffar contends, the Saudis will reach a similar stage that will require the recognition of other faiths.[11] Al-Saffar's acceptance of pluralism is a response to what might be described as the Wahhabi absolutist tendency. He contends that religious freedom is the first fundamental right that human beings enjoy.[12]

Taking a number of Qur'anic verses as his reference point, al-Saffar argues that diversity and pluralism of peoples and cultures are perpetual facts of human life and he thus calls for mutual recognition and coexistence. He also contends that Islam opposes the use of force to impose belief. Al-Saffar recalls what the Shi'is in the Eastern Province experienced following the issuance of the 1927 *fatwa*, when they were forced to 'renew their Islam' (see Chapter One).

However, while al-Saffar admits that Islam recognizes religious and intellectual freedoms, he also argues that Islam calls upon humanity to embrace the right path; therefore Islam makes its followers responsible for guiding others to Islam through dialogue in an atmosphere of freedom and mutual respect. The teachings of Islam, al-Saffar argues, call for openness towards other religions and ideologies, and for dialogue with them on the basis of reason and logic.

Apparently, al-Saffar expanded his thinking in the years following the separation from the MVM in 1989. However, his understanding of pluralism was merely theoretical. He used to say that, as an Islamist, he was not afraid of ideas and wanted a free dialogue with believers from different faiths and political systems. From the beginning of his exile in 1980, he came into contact with a wide range of Muslim activists and leaders from various persuasions. However, it appears that al-Saffar's acceptence of pluralism is limited to the Islamic world only. He asserts, for example, that the only unity that Islam recognizes is the unity of true believers, though they may be diverse. On the other hand, outside Islam, the unity of infidels and polytheists (e.g. Christians and Jews) is not in the interests of humankind, since their unity empowers and this power will inevitably threaten the security and freeedom of all people.

Shaikh Tawfiq al-Saif, the spokesman of the Reform Movement, has, however, built a firm link with the Arab leftist movements that struggle to attain Arab unity, regardless of their ideological persuasions and faiths. Al-Saif has attended a number of conferences held in Syria, Lebanon and Libya, sponsored by socialists, who are traditionally classified as non-believers. In al-Saif's understanding, the Reform Movement is not a doctrinal movement but a social liberation force that aims to mobilize all forces to reform the existing Saudi regime.[13] This implies that there is a conflict between what appears to be a religious and political stance regarding pluralism, meaning the religious stance that advocates pluralism within the Islamic framework but excludes non-Muslims, and the political stance that advocates pluralism within the political game and power struggle, which allows all forces from different faiths and ideologies.

From various issues of *al-Jazira al-'Arabiyya*, the organ of *al-islahiyya* Movement, it is clear that there was a particular emphasis on the human rights reports issued by human rights organizations such as Amnesty International, Human Rights Watch, the US State Department, the Arab Forum for Human Rights, the Lawyers International Committee for Human Rights – Minnesota and the Article 19 organization.

Preoccupied with the Saudi government's brutal record of repression towards the Shi'is community, the leaders of *al-islahiyya* focus on freedom of expression in both religious (including non-Muslim) and political spheres. Affiliated with the *al-islahiyya* Movement, the International Committee for Human Rights in the Gulf and Arabian Peninsula (ICHR-GAP), founded in 1983, has played a significant role in uncovering human rights violations in the country. With the collaboration of human rights organizations based in Europe and the United States, the Committee has provided substantial information on violations relating to freedom of expression. In October 1991, a detailed report entitled *Kingdom of Silence* was sponsored and published by the Article 19 organization, based in London.[14] It concentrates on the regulations sanctioned by the Saudi government that allegedly impeded freedom of expression in the country.[15] According to the laws of the country, freedom of speech, of the press and of assembly and the right to strike and to conduct demonstrations are banned on both political and religious grounds.[16]

Pressure for Democracy

With the arrival of foreign troops in the country during the second Gulf war in 1991, 'the Saudi regime, being hostile to democracy, [was] facing a real challenge from inside'.[17] As early as 1991, the Reform Movement urged Saudi policymakers to put a higher priority on introducing essential changes in the state institutions and to declare war against corruption.

A dramatic change in the Saudi political climate occurred in 1991–3. The political and religious groups, both mainstream and extremist, in most regions of the country, tried to take advantage of the general political disarray of the region in the aftermath of the Iraqi invasion of Kuwait by mobilizing their activities on political and religious fronts.

Numerous groups emerged in this period as a response, partly to the deception of Saddam's regime, which was heavily backed by the Saudi government in the war against Iran, but largely also to the local issues as clearly stated in the petitions, sermons and pamphlets that proliferated during these years.

A petition to the king, signed by forty-three national figures, was circulated in December 1990, urging that the proposed *majlis al-shura* (consultative assembly) must have, among its responsibilities, the authority to monitor the performance of the executive. According to the petitioners, the *majlis al-shura* should have the power to adopt 'laws and rules related to all economic, political, educational and other issues and should exercise effective scrutiny of all executive agencies'. The petitioners also called for a more independent and open media, equality among all citizens and reform of the agency that preaches virtue and prohibits vice.[18]

In February 1991, scores of religious leaders and university academics signed a petition addressed to King Fahad calling for a series of governmental reforms. They supported the idea of the establishment of an elected *majlis al-shura*, emphasizing that it 'must be totally independent and not subject to any pressure that may affect the authority of the council. It must also be endowed with the power of legislation'. The petition also called for strengthening the system of accountability for all government officials, and 'government agencies must be cleansed of anyone whose corruption or dereliction is proven regardless of any other consideration'.[19]

In a country where organized political activity is banned and the circulation of petitions limited, Salafi activists began to voice their criticism of aspects of political life in the kingdom from the pulpits of mosques and in cassette tapes circulated through Islamic bookstores and religious institutions. The Saudi government decided to contain the radical Wahhabi trend in the central province by calling on religious leaders to rein in the radicals, and by taking fundamentalist leaders in for questioning.[20] The government even deprived them of their pulpits in mosques and imprisoned key Salafi activists.[21]

Al-Saffar's article on 'National Unity' in Saudi Arabia clearly recognizes Saudi rule within the existing borders and considers the Islamic *umma* less applicable in the foreseeable future, although it is still an ideal model. Instead, he asserts the need for a national framework and strategy embracing all groups from various religious, regional and tribal backgrounds.[22] Moreover, the Reform Movement identifies itself as a 'national force' since it advocates national demands, i.e. a constitution, an elected parliament, decentralized government and a free press.[23] However, the national tendency of the Reform Movement has gained a lukewarm reception from both the Shiʿis and the Salafi trends, because the country lacks a national culture, as is evidenced by the fragmented opposition. Nevertheless, the Reform Movement was among the most active promoters of national demands such as democracy and human rights.

From the outset, *al-Jazira al-ʿArabiyya* magazine became a national forum for displaying the political demands of various groups and exposing human rights violations in the country, thereby 'undercutting the monopoly on information about the country that the regime has long sought to maintain'.[24] Furthermore, the magazine became a locus of national mobilization as different views were reflected in the petitions, reports and articles of groups ranging from the so-called liberals/secularists to the Salafi Sunnis.

The spokesman of the Reform Movement praised the critical memo entitled '*mudhakirat al-nasiha*', or Memorandum of Advice, signed by 108 Salafi activists in November 1992 as a response to the Three Royal Orders announced by King Fahad in March 1992. In an article entitled '"The Memorandum of Advice" Represents the Whole People', al-Saif says that, 'the remedies presented in the memorandum are identical to those of the main organized political opposition ... we express our full support of the contents of the memorandum; in this sense it reflects our standpoint in regard to the reforms required in our country'.[25]

Members of *al-islahiyya* Movement made contact with Dr Muhammad al-Masari following the announcement of the Committee for the Defence of Legitimate Rights (CDLR) in May 1993.[26] The members expressed their willingness to cooperate with the Committee in defending human rights in the country. When al-Masari was jailed, the author and members of ICHR contacted his father, Shaikh Abdullah al-Masari, a former chairman of the Council of Grievances (*diwan al-mazalim*), and pledged that they would exert their utmost efforts to force the government to release his son.

'Isa Ahmed, a representative of the ICHR, expressed his reservations about the criticisms contained in a statement issued by the State Department in Washington against the CDLR based on Shaikh Abdullah Ibn Jibrin's attitude towards the Shiʿis and women. Ibn Jabrin, a former member of the CDLR and a member of the Senior *'ulama* Council, issued a *fatwa* excommunicating the Shi'is, labelling them 'apostates' and calling for their death.[27] Advocating the establishment of the CDLR, Ahmed argued that, 'If [the] State Department aims to criticize those reducing the status of women and denying the rights of the Shi'is, then it should direct its attention to the Saudi government, which should be blamed for this problem.'43[28]

On the whole, the political groups, namely the Shi'is, nationalists, liberals and, to a certain extent, moderate Salafis (e.g. Dr Muhammad al-Masari and Dr Sa'ad al-Faqih), not to mention the Salafi extremists, tend to exaggerate their following in a bid for popular credibility. As such, these groups need to exercise careful political calculation. Mancur Olson's *The Logic of Collective Action* asserts that participation in collective action stems from a deliberate calculation of cost and benefits.[29] Olson emphasizes that:

> Size is one of the determining factors in deciding whether or not it is possible that the voluntary rational pursuit of individual interest will bring forth group-oriented behaviour. Small groups will further their common interests better than large groups.[30]

In other words, as powerless groups, they are required to compromise their principles in order to gain some political acheivement, though the leaders of these groups can not afford to ignore the sentiments of their members, nor the realities of political competition at home and abroad, and thus gradually find the means to assert their ideologies. At a time when the Shi'is, Salafis and liberals tried not to reveal their ideological stances towards each other, in an attempt to direct all their efforts towards political struggle with the Saudi regime, their literatures and their ordinary followers tended explicitly to articulate their ideological views, though they conflicted with their political tactics.

Overall, the Reform Movement capitalized on popular political discontent to take the political initiative. It advocated rapprochement with other fundamentalist and non-fundamentalist groups and so favoured the insinuation of the Movement into the mainstream of Saudi politics. For the Reform Movement's leaders, protracted involvement with political activities all over the country, as occurred in the years after the Gulf crisis when the tempo of political reforms accelerated among many segments of the population, would elicit concessions from the ruling order in the form of new laws and the redistribution of political and economic power.

In this atmosphere, the Reform Movement focused on the absence of a constitution and democratic system in Saudi Arabia. It called for a broader political participation of citizens, limiting the power of the royal family, political pluralism and curtailing the power of security services in public affairs.[31]

The *islahiyya* advocates a political system that features free elections, free press, protection of minorities, equality of all citizens and the right of women to vote. Islam's role is to provide the system with moral values. As such, the *islahiyya* sees no contradiction between Islam and the freedoms inherent in democracy. Their advocacy of democracy for Saudi Arabia rests on two pillars: freedom of expression and religious pluralism.

It could be argued that *al-islahiyya*'s advocacy of democracy was meant to be used as a means by which they hoped to pursue their private demands and not the basic principle of the political system in an Islamic state. Despite the common reservations of the West towards the advocacy of democracy by Islamist movements, on the pretext that the latter use democracy to seize power and make changes in the political system only to eventually undermine democracy, there is an inconsistency in the literature of the Reform Movement. The adoption of democracy by *al-islahiyya* seems to be a necessity rather than a free choice, since democracy would benefit the Shi'is minority and thus secure their political and religious rights. The *islahiyya* was influenced by the Shi'is and Sunni moderates such as Shaikh Muhammad Mahdi Shams al-Din, Shaikh Rashid al-Ghanoushi, Shaikh Hassan al-Turabi and others who advocated democracy and the alternation of power through the ballot box.

Islahiyya's *Response to King Fahad's Orders*

In March 1992, King Fahad issued a royal decree consisting of three orders: Basic order, Consultative Council order and Regional Council order. The decree came after a wave of demands from all over the country calling for the introduction of some essential changes to the political system and state institutions at large. The orders did not accord with the people's expectations and thus provoked widespread criticism.

According to al-Saffar,

the opposition has received the three new orders with dissatisfaction, since the orders do not correspond to the international developments such as the collapse of the Eastern Bloc and the liberation of its peoples from the shackles of dictatorship and despotism and the rise of democracy and human rights on a wider level, as well as with the regional developments in neighbouring countries such as Yemen, Iran and Kuwait; and, finally, the orders do not correspond to the internal developments where numerous petitions have been raised to the king demanding political reforms.[32]

The orders therefore, created a shock among the people.

On 28 March 1993, in an interview with a Kuwaiti newspaper (*al-siyasa*), King Fahad made it clear that his reforms were not going to lead to a democratic system in the country. 'Western democracy is in total opposition to the Saudi pecularity ... the system of free elections is not part of Islamic ideology,' he stated. 'Democracies in the West might be good in those countries, but this [does not] suit our country.'[33]

Shaikh al-Saffar disagreed:

> What the king has said about democracy and elections is very strange and irrelevant since Islamic history shows that the first election held was in accordance with the commandment and guidance of the Prophet, namely the allegiance of the Second 'Aqaba, where some 70 people from Medina sneaked into Mecca and pledged allegiance to the Prophet and henceforth 12 people were selected to represent the tribes in Medina.[34]

Like many Islamists, al-Saffar equates *shura* with democracy, without considering the profound meaning, implications and conditions of democracy. He confines democracy to the electoral aspect, namely, choosing members of parliament, with little regard to the whole package of democracy, particularly the secular element that implies that it is the right of the people to legislate.

In a series of articles, the leading members of the Reform Movement have criticized the three orders. For example, in comparison to the constitutions of Arab and Western states, the articles of the Saudi Basic Orders relating to the rights of citizens are general, vague and short.[35] With regard to the relationship between the three powers, article 44 of the Basic Order states that 'the king is the source of all powers', bestowing an absolute authority on the head of the state. Later articles clearly state that the king has the right to monitor the implementation of the *shari'a* and the state laws (article 55), abort the right of the Consultative Council to monitor and investigate the performance of the executive power, lead the armed forces, declare war, declare a state of emergency and issue laws that may exist for an indefinite prolonged time. He also has the right to appoint and dismiss members of the Consultative Council, dissolve and replace it, and issue rules, treaties and international contracts, without recourse to the Consultative Council.[36] These orders indicate a complete absence of any democratic system.

The leadership of the Reform Movement argued that the absence of constitutional government was a greater danger to the state than the opposition and urged the government to reform the political structures that rule the state. Yet, like many governments in the Middle East, the Saudi regime remains fearful of opening up the political system of the country too far, thereby eroding the royal family's power and prerogatives. The government's strategies of inclusion are always constrained by the alleged historical right of the royal family to rule the country on the grounds that it was occupied and unified by the family of al-Sa'ud.

In fact, countries in which political forces are not allowed to engage openly in the political process are liable to be exposed to unseen and radical activities that the state is not able to monitor. There is some evidence that this happened during the Gulf crisis in 1991, where radical new forms emerged as a response to a long-term policy of marginalizing political and religious groups in various regions of the kingdom. For this reason, memories of the Iranian revolution have led many Saudi activists, notably liberals, nationalists and moderate Islamists, to believe that it is better for the Saudi regime to adopt an open political system than to risk the consequences of maintaining authoritarian rule.

However, there is a long way for Saudi Arabia to go before it becomes a democratic state. It lacks a democratic infrastructure in terms of civil society institutions. Local social bodies such as women's clubs and charities play a limited role in confronting the issues affecting people's lives. However, there is a consensus that the democratic option is vital for solving internal problems, particularly political tensions, between the government and large segments of the population. Participation in the political process has become the common demand of all political forces of different backgrounds, articulated by peaceful means such as petitions, pulpits and the media.

Needless to say, in the absence of traditions of democracy, its practice by any group, regardless of its ideological persuasion, will be precarious. The political culture of each country has a direct impact on the conduct of groups. In this respect, the Reform Movement does not really differ from other political players in the country. It is unclear whether the democratic discourse adopted by the Reform Movement also cuts across ideological boundaries to include communists and Christians (though there are no Christians in Saudi Arabia) or women.

This issue has not been widely discussed by the leaders of the Reform Movement, but certain indications could help clarify the issue. The great dilemma in the political strategy of the Reform Movement is that it was not entirely ready to collaborate with individuals or currents that were not avowedly Islamist. Collaboration with secular forces would make them targets for extremist opponents from both Shi'is and Sunna sides.

The ideological turmoil in which the Reform Movement found itself was partly due to its lack of readiness to recognize the legal rights of non-religious forces to participation in political assemblies, to political expression and to power. Although al-Saffar urges opposition forces to collaborate to challenge despotism and to pressurize the government to recognize political freedom, participation and human rights, this position is based not so much on political grounds as on religious ones.[37] Al-Saffar elswhere admits that the antagonism prior to the 1990s between Islamic movements and secular and leftist movements has now diminished and has called for 'collaboration and constructive dialogue'.[38]

Shi'i Cultural Authenticization

The search for cultural authenticity is essentially an attempt to reconstruct and re-root the Shi'i identity within the Saudi context, a context that remains strongly under Wahhabi religious-cultural influence.

The leaders of the Reform Movement have had to contend with the power of the state and the impact of Wahhabism on local society while also striving hard to advance their interests, namely, protecting and treating their own religious legacy and practices with the utmost respect and dignity.

The techniques of resistance of subordinate groups vary but they all exclude any reliance on the military option. In case of the Shi'is opposition, there has been a radical shift from open, collective protest against the Saudi regime, aiming to secure the immediate needs of the Shi'is minority in the Eastern province, such as physical safety, adequate living conditions and the right to practise religious rites, to what James Scott calls 'everyday forms of expression'.[39] Scott's thesis on the arts of resistance shows that people draw on the symbols, postulates and rhetoric of a particular framework to fight for survival and advancement. He stresses that 'whatever form the individual assumes – offstage parody, dreams of violent revenge, millennial visions of a world turned upside down – this collective hidden transcript is essential to any dynamic view of power relations'.[40] The masks worn in public may convince powerholders of compliance, but reflect only what Scott calls 'false consciousness'.

Although Scott's approach to 'hidden transcripts' is widely criticized by anthropologists, the importance of this approach is that it emphasizes how subordinate groups express everyday forms of resistance. He distinguishes between four types of political discourse available to subordinate groups: the *public transcript* (the discourse of the dominant power structure); the *hidden transcript* of dominated peoples; *infrapolitics* (or the 'politics of disguise' that takes place in public view but is designed to have a double meaning); and the *public displays* of resistance that are the focus of mainstream analysis.[41] For Scott, all but the first of these discourses are contentious, in the sense that the public transcript represents the 'open interaction between subordinates and those who dominate'.[42] The public transcript represents 'onstage' discourse – a discourse that represents a performance by the powerful as well as the subordinates. The public transcript is thereby coded by both groups to obscure the full meaning behind the rhetoric. That underlying meaning is produced in hidden transcripts, which provide the keys to unlock the secrets coded into the public discourse.

Additionally, hidden transcripts are constructed by members of the subordinate group as they congregate 'offstage' to speak and act outside the purview of the dominant group. Their hidden transcript allows them covertly to express their antagonism toward the dominant, while overtly appearing to comply with them. This form of infrapolitics is the only form of resistance possible in situations in which powerless groups dare not demonstrate open confrontation.

Gradually the 'hidden transcripts' erupt in the public sphere, where they are transformed into public transcripts, generating political electricity for powerless groups, whose acts, attitudes and pretensions are directed by the discourse emanating from the public transcripts.[43] According to Mamoun Fandy, Scott's concept of 'hidden transcripts' helps us to understand the shift of the Reform Movement's resistance from confrontation to 'constructive opposition'.[44]

The emphasis on cultural and historical authenticity and on the religious identity of the Shi'is in the Eastern Province is thus an open declaration of a previously hidden transcript that is shared by the collectivity, but has not been clearly articulated in the public sphere.

This section focuses on the efforts of the Reform Movement to re-establish its cultural authenticity by examining the publications of two affiliated associations, the Establishment of al-Baqi' for the Revival of Legacy (*mu'sasat al-baqi' li ihiya' al-turath*) and the Pan-Shi'i Association in Saudi Arabia (*rabitat 'umum al-Shi'a fi al-Sa'udiyya*).

Although the Baqi' Establishment was founded in 1987, it was inactive until 1990. It was primarily concerned with gathering documents, manuscripts and data relating to the Saudi Shi'is, dating from both past and present. Its stated objectives are: to emphasize the importance of the legacy of the *ahl al-bayt* and the Shi'is in the Arabian Peninsula by collecting and providing documents and information relating to the political, social and cultural history of the Shi'is, both past and present; to study and compile a comprehensive encyclopedia on the lives of prominent Shi'i figures in the Arabian Peninsula; and to preserve Shi'is books and manuscripts and annotate preparatory to publication.

The Baqi' establishment has published a number of books about prominent figures in the Eastern Province, as well as on Shi'is historiography. Here I will focus on three major sources: *Shaikh Ali al-Biladi al-Qudaihi* (d. 1853) by Shaikh Hassan al-Saffar; *Shaikh Hassan Ali al-Badr al-Qatifi* (1878–1914) by this author;[45] and *Al-Shi'a fi al-mamlak al-'Arabiyya al-Sa'udiyya* (The Shi'is in the Kingdom of Saudi Arabia) by Hamza al-Hassan, a leading member of the Reform Movement and the editor of *al-Jazira al-'Arabiyya*.

Shaikh al-Saffar's book on Shaikh al-Biladi bears a clear message for the Shi'is that they should revive, preserve and publish their historical and cultural legacy.[46] Stimulated by al-Biladi's biographical work on the clerics of the Eastern Province and Bahrain, al-Saffar argues that al-Biladi was perhaps the first Shi'i scholar perpetuating the Shi'i legacy in these regions.

In the book al-Saffar has incorporated a large number of figures, symbols and activities that had a direct or indirect link to al-Biladi, probably in an attempt to draw a picture that is both appealing and rich in information about the Shi'is in the Eastern Province, a region that is increasingly neglected by its own inhabitants, let alone the government. Al-Biladi's *'Anwar al-badrain fi tarajim 'ulama' al-Qatif wa al-ahsa wa al-Bahrain'* (The Lights of the Two Moons in the Biographies of the Scholars of Qatif, Ahsa and Bahrain) is considered a landmark source for the modern history of the Shi'is in the Eastern Province, containing valuable information, reports and documents about the Shi'is over the last three hundred years. This undoubtedly explains the importance al-Saffar attaches to al-Biladi, an exemplary Shi'i scholar who devoted his life to recording and maintaining the legacy of the Shi'is in the region.[47] Al-Saffar focuses too on the significant role played by Shi'i religious schools and scholars during al-Biladi's life in protecting the Shi'i religious legacy.[48]

On the other hand, al-Saffar also discusses the political circumstances in which Shaikh al-Biladi lived, both in Bahrain and the Eastern Province, demonstrating how the Shi'is men of religion resisted the hardships that were inflicted on them by the rulers, notably the Saudi ones.[49]

The main objective of *Shaikh Hassan Ali al-Badr al-Qatifi* is to provide a narrative that serves the new orientation of the Reform Movement, notably including proof of the authenticity of the Shi'is in the region, contrary to Saudi Wahhabi propaganda, which portrays them as Persian immigrants. The author's research shows that Shi'ism in the Eastern Province can be traced back to the migration of Abdulqais, an ancient tribe from the centre of Arabia, to the Eastern Province. Segments of the tribe moved to Basra in the south of Iraq during the reign of the Caliph Uthman and sided with Ali against his rivals. Some leaders of Ali's army during the battles of the Camel, Siffin and Nahrawan were from the tribe.[50] The work also focuses on aspects of the life of Shaikh Ali al-Badr, such as his political activism, his devotion to serving the cause of his own people and that of Muslim people elsewhere in the Muslim world (Libya, Iraq, Iran and the Indian subcontinent) and finally his reformative tendency as a *mujtahid*. These points are made as implicit criticism of the passive, stagnant and backward Shi'is scholars in the Eastern Province.[51]

The life of Shaikh al-Badr is significant mainly because of his association with the leaders of the constitutional movement in Iran based in Najaf, notably Sayyid Kadim al-Khurasani. Inspired by the political climate in Iraq, in 1909 al-Badr wrote a pamphlet entitled *Da'wat al-Muwahidin ila Himayat al-Din* (The Call for Unitarians to Defend the Cause of Religion), denouncing the Italian invasion of Libya and declaring *jihad* with reference to the four sources of the *shari'a*, according to the Shi'i school of jurisprudence.[52]

The third book was written by Hamza al-Hassan, a Saudi Shi'i activist, primarily to 'defend the Shi'is citizens in the kingdom since they are the most deprived and oppressed community in the country'.[53] In essence, the book fully describes the history, culture and identity of the Saudi Shi'is and sheds light on the ordeal of the Shi'is on sectarian grounds.[54]

Al-Hassan too presents a historical narrative that seeks to underline the authenticity of the Shi'is in the Eastern Province.[55] He contends that Shi'ism here can be dated back to the time of the Prophet Muhammad, when a dispute erupted between Abu Bakr and Ali. The appointed deputies in the historical Bahrain were loyal to Ali and advocated his right to the succession of the Prophet and it was they, al-Hassan argues, who implanted the seeds of Shi'ism in the region.[56] Moreover, al-Hassan draws a genealogical map of the Shi'is families, providing firm evidence of their 'Arabness'.

What this research shows is the concern the Saudi Shi'is have about their Arabness and therefore their identify.[57] In the late 1950s, a prominent religious cleric, Shaikh Faraj al-Umran, recorded day-to-day events in Qatif region, which later appeared in fourteen volumes entitled *Al-azhar al-arajiyya fi al-'athar al-farajiyya* (The Aroma Blossoms of the Faraji Legacy). It held little appeal among the Shi'is, although it stimulated certain of their writers and religious clerics to register, preserve and revive the cultural and historical heritage of the Shi'is in the Eastern Province. In the 1960s, a Shi'i, Muhammad Said al-Musalim, wrote a book entitled *Sahil al-dhahab al-aswad* (The Coast of Black Gold), focusing on the social, economic, cultural and literary legacy of the Shi'is in the Eastern Province. Although the book was initially banned in Saudi Arabia and its author interrogated, it has gained wide currency among the Saudi Shi'is. The book is well organized and rich in information and many writers refer to it as the main source on the Shi'is in the Eastern Province.

In his discussion of the national sentiment of the Shi'is opposition, al-Hassan emphasizes the importance of a national front that encompasses various groups from different regional, social and intellectual backgrounds.

Obviously, the message of the book is to urge the Saudi government to introduce essential changes in the state institutions based on the full meaning of citizenship.[58]

The second organization associated with the task of asserting the authenticity and identity of the Shi'is is the Pan-Shi'i Association, established in 1989. The stated demands of the association are as follows:

> The Saudi government is to publicly announce its respect of the Shi'is sect as one of the Islamic sects, and to recognize the right of Shi'is citizens to practise their religious rituals.
>
> Religious freedom of the Shi'is should be recognized, in terms of permitting the construction of mosques, *hussainiya*s and religious schools (*hawza*s). Sectarian practices should be allowed.
>
> The religious materials of the government education system in Shi'is regions should be in accordance with the Shi'i doctrine.
>
> The intellectual freedom of the Shi'is should be respected and the ban on printing and the import of Shi'is religious literature lifted. Moreover, Shi'is have the right to issue magazines and newspapers in compliance with state laws.
>
> Propaganda campaigns against the Shi'is should be banned and the Shi'is should be given the right to defend their sect.
>
> Full authority should be bestowed on the Shi'i courts as on other courts in the kingdom.
>
> Sectarian discrimination against the Shi'is in education, employ-ment, and government, military and security institutions should be abandoned.
>
> The living conditions of the Shi'is should be improved and the urbanization of the Shi'i regions redressed.[59]

These demands are reflected in the publications of the Pan-Shi'is Association. They show that the Reform Movement attempted to re-establish itself in the Saudi social and political fabric by drawing attention to the way in which the Saudi regime perceives the Saudi Shi'is as enemies. Al-Saffar wrote an article entitled 'The Shi'is Are not Enemies', in which he asserts that the Shi'is were subject to unfair measures, despite the fact that, 'the history of the Shi'is in Saudi Arabia and their loyalty to their land proves their sincerity and love of their country and their consistent stance toward the government'. They did not, he notes, militarily protest against the regime but sought a dialogue with the Saudi rulers in an attempt to secure their rights and freedom. Their good faith is evident too, according to al-Saffar, in the fact that they favoured the Saudi rulership over the British mandate.[60]

Resituating the Shi'is opposition in a different context, al-Saffar explains the causes of Shi'is protest, namely, sectarian discrimination and hostile policies by the government, which 'made a grave error' in equating friends with enemies.[61]

The Reform Movement endeavoured to develop a discourse for the reconstruction of Shi'is identity, which was neither weakened nor distracted by the enormous power of the state and its religious establishment. At the same time, it was necessary for such an identity to be developed in a positive, creative and constructive way so that it would not lead to secession or hamper national unity. While the Reform Movement insisted on reviving the legacy of the Shi'is in the Eastern Province, it eschewed the polemical issues of the Sunna and Shi'is.

What the writers of these books endeavoured to convey is that all identities pertaining to Saudi Arabia could live together despite their diversity. The enormous power of Wahhabism should not give them the right to consider themselves superior to other religious identities or to exercise religious hegemony.

Needless to say, the emphasis on the Shi'is' identity and its historical and cultural authenticity is, to a great extent, a response to the state's tendency to impose its own favoured religious identity and cultural and historical legacy on the Shi'is and other groups in the country as a whole. Within such a context, it is to be expected that the Shi'is from different political and ideological backgrounds would continue to resist subversion of their identity and to maintain their legacy, and indeed the literature of the political opposition among the Shi'is in the Eastern Province bears this out.

The historical and religious-cultural narratives of the Reform Movement are what Scott called the 'cooked declarations', as 'they arise under circumstances in which there is a good deal of offstage freedom among subordinate groups, allowing them to share a rich and deep hidden transcript [that is] a product of mutual communication that already has a quasi-public existence'.[62]

The Reform Movement, being an external-based opposition, enjoyed greater freedom in which the 'cooked declarations' of the Shi'is could be produced and members of the Movement could share and articulate their concerns and demands without fear of the government.

A number of factors have shaped the political dynamics of the Reform Movement. Its orientation was tied largely to a shift within Iran following the ceasefire with Iraq in July 1988. Consequently, after its separation from the MVM, the Reform Movement began to chart a more pragmatic course in politics.

The Reform Movement proved to be a dynamic and energetic force within less than four years, from 1989 to 1993, and increasingly important in Saudi politics. Its shift to moderation signified that it had entered a process of political and intellectual maturation, triggered by various conditions and circumstances that beset the Gulf region in the late 1980s and the world at large, particularly with the collapse of the Soviet Union and the wave of democratic reforms that pervaded the entire bloc.

Armed with a more sophisticated awareness, the Reform Movement was able to acknowledge and assimilate modern notions and to deal effectively with new problems as they arose in its country, particularly as the tempo of popular demand for reforms accelerated. The Reform Movement attached particular important to human rights, democratization in Saudi Arabia and Shi'is cultural authenticization.

The Reform Movement broadened its understanding and activities in the area of human rights in the 1990s. Whereas the issue of political prisoners captured the attention of the IRO in the 1980s, *al-islahiyya* human rights activists tended to give particular attention to cultural, political, social and minority rights and individual liberties, freedom of expression, free press and freedom of assembly. The adoption of universally recognized human rights is connected with the shift in the Movement's political discourse, as the latter decided to dissociate itself from its revolutionary past and involve itself in the political game within the Saudi realm.

The Reform Movement also called for a number of political reforms in the kingdom. Spurred on by the ideological shift in the political climate that followed the Gulf crisis in 1991, as many segments in the country voiced their demand for essential changes in the Saudi political system, the Reform Movement focused on the lack of a constitution and a national assembly and called for the broader political participation of citizens, limiting the power of the royal family, political pluralism, and curtailing the power of the security services in public affairs.

The Reform Movement's advocacy of a democratic political system arose from its commitment to freedom of expression and religious pluralism. However, it appears that the *islahiyya*'s adoption of the democratic option was to be used to pursue private demands and not necessarily to be the basic principle of the political system in an Islamic state. In other words, democracy for the *islahiyya* Movement seemed to be a necessity rather than an option, since democracy would benefit the Shi'is minority and thus secure their political and religious rights.

The Reform Movement was also committed to the cultural authenticization of the Shi'is in the Eastern Province. Its attempt to reconstruct and re-root Shi'is identity within the Saudi context, which itself is under the influence of Wahhabism, is aimed at shifting the struggle with the regime towards attaining Shi'is political, socio-economic and religious rights.

The *islahiyya*'s techniques of resistance were transformed from open collective protest against the Saudi regime to what James Scott calls 'everyday forms of expression'. However, changing its oppositional techniques does not mean that the *islahiyya* had previously resorted to violence, rather, that it discarded the revolutionary option as a means of change.

The Movement's emphasis on Shi'i identity and on its historical and cultural authenticity is, to a great extent, a response to the state's tendency to impose its own favoured religious identity and cultural and historical legacy on the Shi'is and other groups in the country as a whole. Reactions to the state's attempts to subvert the construction of Shi'i identity continue as a form of resistance, and declarations of the Shi'i legacy are a major concern of Shi'is all opposition groups. Such a tendency will possibly grow stronger in the future and perhaps even come to be the dominant orientation, thanks to local factors, modernization and the vulnerability of national unity.

SIX

The Accord (1993)

In October 1993, the Saudi government reached an agreement with the *islahiyya* Movement to shut down its publications abroad that were critical of the regime's repression of the Shi'is' political and human rights, in particular *al-Jazira al-'Arabiyya* magazine. It was announced in September 1993 that the magazine would cease publication for two months and re-publication would then be considered, after preliminary talks with the Saudi authorities. In return, members of the Shi'is opposition, including those of *hizbullah al-hijaz*, an offshoot of the Iranian *hizbullah* network, were to be allowed to return home in safety, some prisoners (most of whom were members of *hizbullah*) would be released, and passports would be issued to members of the Shi'is in the Eastern Province.[1]

In this chapter we shall explore the ideological and political standpoints of both the opposition and the Saudi government in regard to the agreement and the extent to which both sides were ready to proceed with it. We shall also examine the circumstances in which the accord took place by discussing the problems and the issues that beset the accord.

Information on the accord is sparse and superficial, and no detailed study has been published so far. The dialogue has also been steeped in secrecy and the following review takes into account the sensitivity required in mentioning the names of the mediators in the dialogue.

Background

In the ten years before the accord between the Reform Movement and the Saudi government, the government had made successive attempts to reach an agreement in response to Shiʿis demands, in return for the closure of all opposition activities, both inside and outside the country. These attempts failed for a number of reasons, in particular the lack of determination by both sides. Both the government and the Movement charged low-ranking members with the task of participating in the dialogue but without giving them real authority to act on behalf of their side. Moreover, the political circumstances of the 1980s were not favourable for such a dialogue. Antagonism rather than compromise between the Shiʿis opposition and the Saudi government was the order of the day. Further, the Movement, which was affiliated with a broad-based movement, namely the MVM, was not in a position to take the initiative without reference to the leadership of the MVM, which was immersed in revolutionary activities in Iraq, Iran and, to a lesser extent, Bahrain.

A number of people, ranging from Shiʿis notables to Arab journalists and diplomats, attempted to open channels of communication between the government and the Reform Movement. Some acted on personal initiative and not in coordination with or with the consent of either side. Others arose out of the amicable relationship that the mediators had with both sides.

Indeed, the leaders of the Reform Movement used these channels to convey their views and demands to the Saudi authorities, and not necessarily to reach an agreement with the government. This was because it was not the time for the Reform Movement to undertake the kinds of structural and ideological changes that would be required to make possible a peaceful alternative, such as dialogue with the Saudi regime. In other words, the Shiʿis opposition was, at that time, committed to the revolutionary ideology. A spokesman of the Movement stated that:

> Our movement is founded on the premise that the Saudi royal regime is contradictory to the Islamic *shariʿa*, and is unqualified, from a legal perspective, to govern the country; thus we refuse to negotiate with it. What we demand is not partial reforms, but rather giving the people the opportunity to choose the form of government that they aspire to;

liberating the country from the shackles of economic dependency on the capitalist market; eliminating the Western cultural hegemony.[2]

However, attempts at dialogue between *islahiyya* and the Saudi government, based on initiatives adopted by the Shi'is notables in the Eastern Province, can be traced back to the mid-1980s. For example, a dialogue took place in Syria in August 1986 between three Saudi Shi'is notables, Abdulhamid al-Mutawu', Salman al-Nasir and 'Abdulkarim b. Humoud, and the spokesman of the IRO, Shaikh Tawfiq al-Saif. They conveyed an offer of general amnesty for members of the IRO from Prince Muhammad b. Fahad, the governor of Eastern Province, in exchange for a complete shutdown of oppositional activities by the IRO. The offer was rejected as it neglected the religious and socio-economic demands of the Shi'is.

Another meeting was held in Washington with Prince Bandar b. Sultan, the Saudi Ambassador in the United States. The meeting took place at the Saudi embassy in Washington in September 1990 and was attended by Ja'far al-Shayeb, a leading member of the Reform Movement and Chairman of the International Committee for Human Rights in the Gulf and Arabian Peninsula (ICHR–GAP), 'Isa al-Miz'il, and Ali al-Shuaikhat, leading members of the political committee of the Reform Movement. Although no agreement whatsover was reached in regard to the demands of the Shi'is, such meetings helped facilitate subsequent arrangements and dialogue in 1993.

1993 Dialogue: The Context

The Movement's transformation into a reformist movement and its inclination towards peaceful and universally recognized institutions in its oppositional activities enabled it to acquire a respected position among political and human rights organizations, as can be seen in the reliance of both human rights organizations and Western political institutions on information provided by the Movement, notably in respect of human rights abuses.

The Gulf crisis in 1990 created a context that encouraged the Shi'is opposition to convey its views and demands to the international media, which became concerned with the events that occurred in the region as a consequence of the Gulf crisis. Indeed, the Saudi government became the centre of media attention and hence an object of criticism because of its violations of human rights, the absence of democracy and political corruption.

The government eventually entered into dialogue with the Shi'is opposition for a number of reasons:

Growing internal dissatisfaction

According to a prominent member of the royal family, 'the move [the accord with the Reform Movement] was part of a wider effort to neutralize young militants rising in the ranks of the Sunni clergy. These Sunnis object to such policies as ties with the West and the presence of foreign troops.'[3] The emergence of loosely organized groups from different political and ideological persuasions calling for political reforms, along with the departure of foreign troops, urged the Saudi regime to act promptly, in order to silence the growing clamour for change.

Declining legitimacy

In his comment on the agreement between the Saudi government and the articulate Shi'is opposition group, Hudson states that,

> [with] its intensively Islamic legitimacy formula, its virtually unlimited financial resources and its demonstrated American security umbrella, the Saudi dynasty finds itself on the defensive against the new murmurings of Islamist protest and its struggling to pre-empt the challenges.[4]

It is quite true that:

> In search of a more robust legitimacy formula than that provided by tradition and oil money, the Saudi ruling elite is cautiously examining the benefits – and costs – of a more participatory system. A coalition – unlikely as it may seem – between relative secularists and Islamists now excluded from power may render the pre-emption strategy inadequate to preserve the royal family's absolutism.[5]

The ideological transformation of the Reform Movement

The reconciliatory tendency of the Shi'is opposition encouraged the regime to reassess its attitude towards the Shi'is opposition and to take a step forward, leading to a direct dialogue.

The transformation from revolutionary ideology to an evolutionary one was clearly rationalized by the leadership of the Movement and based on six considerations. First, the announcement of the ceasefire between Iran and Iraq in July 1988, put an end to the revolutionary option, since Iran decided to cease its support of the liberation movements. Second, the Shi'is in the Eastern Province, being an isolated minority, was not able, in the circumstances that followed the ceasefire, to tolerate the costs of the revolutionary option, as the Movement admitted. Third, the apparent increased flexibility of the Saudi government was interpreted by the Shi'i opposition as an encouraging sign that the regime may be ready for dialogue. It was thought that realization of some of the demands of the Shi'is might extend the Movement's margin to add more pressure for national demands. Fourth, as the Movement purported to lead the Shi'is community, it was compelled to adapt to the Shi'is mainstream, which was anti-revolutionary and inclined towards more limited and realistic demands. Fifth, as the Movement decided to exchange evolution for revolution, it was necessary to tone down its opposition to the regime, so as to conform with sentiment among the Shi'is engaged in oppositional activity. Sixth, the massacre of the Iranian pilgrims in 1987 and the subsequent attempts of Iran to retaliate culminated in the emergence of *hizbullah al-hijaz*, which resulted in a harsh campaign against the Shi'is in the Eastern Province and the exercise of discriminatory measures against them in nearly all spheres. The Shi'i community held the Shi'is opposition primarily responsible for leading the government to impose such measures.[6]

The government also undertook dialogue with the Shi'is because of the impact that opposition activities were having on it, particularly the Reform Movement. According to *The Economist*,

> A number of Saudi Shi'is have been vocal in opposition to the regime since Iran's 1979 revolution: they are important both for themselves and for the influence on the ultra-religious Sunni Muslims who condemn the corrupt ways and malpractices of many in the ruling family.[7]

One remarkable example is the students' protest that took place in front of a Saudi propagandist exhibition called 'Saudi Arabia between Yesterday and Today' in Washington, Atlanta, Dallas, Los Angeles and New York in 1990. This protest had an enormous impact on the Saudi regime, as groups of the

Reform Movement took advantage of the event to distribute leaflets about human rights abuses in Saudi Arabia. The protesters chanted slogans about 'freedom, constitution, human rights, justice and equality', which appealed to their Western audience. Numerous articles were published in widely distributed US newspapers such as the *Washington Post* and the *New York Times* and cited on TV channels such as CBS and NBC. The published materials reversed the trend of the propagandist campaign.

The economic condition of the country

The *New York Times* argued in summer 1993 that Saudi Arabia's economic troubles would lead to political ones, since previously, political dissatisfaction had been silenced by recourse to generous bounty. As such, the Saudi economic setback led to a concession, namely 'an agreement with the Shi'is Muslim opponents in exile'.[8]

The Shi'is' attitude towards the Gulf war was of particular importance. The governor of the Eastern Province assembled the Shi'is notables in his palace in Dammam to inform them that the leadership of the Reform Movement acknowledged the delicate situation the country was in and called the Shi'is to join the military camps to defend the country's borders. Shaikh Hassan al-Saffar thus called on the Shi'is in the Eastern Province to mobilize. The Reform Movement's attitude favourably impressed the regime at a time when the Iraqi regime was bringing heavy weight to bear on the Shi'is to rise against their rulers. A call was issued on Baghdad Radio to the Shi'is in the Eastern Province to rise in the name of Islam against both the government and the American military presence. As a consequence, a Saudi official declared to *Time* magazine, 'We think we can gradually bring the Shi'is into the system and it will be OK'.[9]

In a letter sent on 28 September 1990 to the Saudi ambassador in Washington, Prince Bandar Bin Sultan, a leading member of the Reform Movement wrote, 'The Shi'is' main demand is to obtain no more than treatment equal to the rest of the population, as a precondition for the Shi'is' loyalty to the government.' Loyalty, he said, 'is based on a mutual interest; loyalty and doctrinal affiliations are separable, otherwise, *hizbullah* and *amal* in Lebanon and Ba'th in Iraq and Syria would not be enemies, and thus the Islamic Republic of Iran and the Ba'thi regime in Syria would not be allies'.

Prince Bandar replied that, 'many Shi'is, both men and women, joined the voluntary centres to defend the nation, a move that is considered a slap in the face to those who have doubts'. He added that, 'our enemies tried [to seek] and still seek gaps in our Arab Muslim society by discriminating between Sunna and Shi'is or by saying that the Shi'i is not a citizen, or is a second-class citizen, or alienated, or has no rights, and so on'.[10]

Apparently, the ambassador recalled the common criticisms against the Saudi regime for its discriminatory attitude towards the Shi'is; he also recalled the provocative messages transmitted on Baghdad radio. His aim was thus evidently to defuse those criticisms and defend the regime.

The improvement in Iranian-Saudi relations
This must have had its part in the Saudi attitude towards the Shi'is, although it is somewhat difficult to measure. In November 1988, King Fahad announced that the propaganda campaign against Iran should stop, a decision that was considered a clear sign of the improvement in the relationship between the two countries. King Fahad declared that, 'I directed the Minister of Information to abandon the propaganda campaign against Iran.' In return, an internal directive was issued in Iran to the local press to stop criticisms against the Saudi government.

The growing international pressure from both human rights organizations and Western governments
The latter advised the Saudi government to settle the Shi'is case. The annual country reports on human rights conditions in Saudi Arabia released by the Bureau of Democracy, Human Rights and Labour of the US State Department focused, particularly in the period 1991–93, on three major issues: women's rights, foreign labour and the Shi'is minority in the Eastern Province.

Islahiyya's *Demands*

The central challenge to the Reform Movement throughout its experience was to promote an understanding and appreciation of Shi'is' fundamental demands by the Saudi government and the outside world in general. These demands were either neglected by the government or overshadowed by the perceived security and political threats posed by the Shiʿis following the Iranian revolution. Dialogue with the Saudi government was aimed at showing the other face of the Shiʿis, as flexible, pragmatic and negotiable. The leaders of the Reform Movement hoped dialogue would help the government understand the causes, motives and demands of the opposition.

According to a draft letter sent by Tawfiq al-Saif, the spokesman of the Reform Movement, to King Fahad in September 1991, the main cause of the opposition was doctrinal persecution compounded by various forms of cultural and economic persecution. 'What lies between the Shiʿis and the government is this sectarian persecution,' he wrote. More provocatively, al-Saif insisted that, 'the Shiʿis do not respect a regime which persecutes them'. Al-Saif rejected the government's alleged view that, 'the oppressed should give up opposition and seek forgiveness from the oppressor'. Instead, he countered that, 'the ruler is obliged to assure the rights of citizens, rather than that the latter assure the right of the ruler', and went on to claim that, 'The general sense [among the Shiʿis] is that the government has no objective but to humiliate and persecute the Shiʿis'.

The objectives of the Movement can be found in an article published in the internal magazine some time before the dialogue began. The article specified two main categories of demands:

1. The religious rights of the Shiʿis, which include freedom of religious practices; freedom and maintenance of worship sites (e.g. mosques, *hussainiya*s); religious texts in government-funded schools in the Shiʿis areas to be in accordance with their tenets; freedom of intellect and sectarian culture, including allowing the Shiʿis to print their religious books inside the country; the right to build religious schools (*hawza*s); the abandonment of the propaganda campaign against the Shiʿis and investing them with the right to defend themselves against accusations, particularly from the Wahhabi side; and independence of the Shiʿis legal code.

2. Equality in terms of employment opportunities, distribution of wealth and services, and education.[11]

Shiʿis notables had raised a number of these demands to the king on various occasions. According to al-Saif, the present demands were nearly the same as those submitted in a petition to King Faisal some thirty years ago. 'The ten demands included in the notables' petition revolve around religious freedom in terms of building mosques and *hussainiya*s.'

In another letter to King Fahad in December 1990, Tawfiq al-Saif emphasizes national and local demands. On the national level, he pleaded with the king to 'realize the promises [in regard to political reforms] which he said are imminent, according to his speech on 19 November [1990], including sanctioning a basic order for the state, Consultative Council and Regional authorities' orders'. Expressing a collective desire for political reform in the country, al-Saif said, 'I hope that the Custodian of the Two Holy Mosques selects a group of those who entertain wisdom and intellect so as to pave the way for attaining such a goal'.

On the local level, al-Saif called for 'abandoning discrimination against the Shi'is community, both in the Eastern Province and elsewhere in the kingdom, and equating them with citizens from other sects, and ceasing the sectarian discrimination inflicted on them on nearly all grounds throughout prolonged decades'. He added that, 'we do not assume that the king is not aware of what his sons [the Shi'is] are facing and suffering'. He reminds the king of the Shi'is' attitude during the Gulf war, and how they expressed their readiness to counter Iraqi military threats and defend their homeland. This attitude was surely reason enough to abandon discriminatory policies by the government against the Shi'is in the military. 'The Shi'is are still denied access to join the army and the military forces in general.'

Highlighting the Shi'is' grievances about employment in Aramco, the building of mosques and *hussainiya*s, the practice of religious rites, arbitrary arrests, discrimination in education and all other state establishments, al-Saif claimed that, 'it seems to some people that the government is determined to regard the Shi'is as second-class citizens, an attitude that has become commonplace both inside and outside the country'. He asserted that, 'the Shi'is are part of the people and their land is part of their precious country'. Consequently, he called for the opening of a new chapter to assure those who were inside and outside the country that a new epoch had begun based on justice and equality. This could not be realized unless good intentions were put into practice.

Oppositional activities could be abandoned and the Reform Movement could return to the country, al-Saif indicated, once these demands were met. 'We believe that resolving these issues would reassure many people, build confidence and convince many that reform is possible from inside, which ultimately could encourage them to return [to their homeland] and practise a social role,' he said. He explicitly stated that:

> all brothers in our organization, notables, religious scholars and the youth whom I consulted regarding the contents of this letter, along with previous discussions, expressed their full willingness to cooperate in a positive way [...] they are all waiting for an initiative from your great government.

In a letter sent to the special adviser of Crown Prince Abdullah (the present king) and the deputy of the National Guards, Shaikh Abdul Aziz al-Tuwaijri, in September 1991, the leadership of the Reform Movement emphasized a number of fundamental rights, described as 'the minimum level of the Shi'is demands'.

1. Religious demands. This included recognizing the Shi'is as Muslims and their sect as an Islamic sect; prevention of any abuse whatsoever against the Shi'is and their sect; and vesting the Shi'is with the right to refute all accusations against them. It also included giving the Shi'is the right to build and legalize mosques and *hussainiya*s, to teach their children the Shi'i doctrines, to practise their religious rites without intervention from the authorities; and reassigning full and equal authority to the Shi'i courts. On a cultural level, Shi'i books were to be permitted, particularly those books that did not touch on or threaten national unity or provoke any form of sectarian division.

2. Socio-economic demands. The Shi'is must not be regarded as second-class citizens; sectarian discrimination in universities and government establishments should be abandoned; all rules that prevent the Shi'is from participating in the security and the military and in building their nation should be abandoned. The Shi'is should have equal opportunities to reach high positions in the government. In addition, the economic policy that excluded the Shi'is from working in Aramco should be outlawed. Shi'is citizens should be able to continue their higher education on the basis of their grades and marks and not on the basis of sectarian affiliation.

3. Political demands, leading to the elimination of tension in the Eastern Province. This included freeing all political prisoners, re-granting passports to hundreds of Shiʿis citizens so that they could travel peacefully and freely; ceasing all arbitrary arrests and respecting the dignity of Shiʿi citizens, so as not to intervene in their privacy or assault their religious and social values. Shiʿis detainees should also be given the opportunities to defend themselves and have a just trial in compliance with universally defined human rights. All forms of physical and psychological torture should be stopped and all confessions taken under repression and force must be discredited.[12]

These demands have been repeated in letters by the leaders of the Reform Movement to Crown Prince Abdullah (the present king), who was thought to be best able to resolve the Shiʿi issues. In a letter sent to Shaikh Abdul Aziz al-Tuwaijri on 21 May 1992, the spokesman of the Reform Movement asserted that the Movement was considering him and the crown prince as a 'hope'. While assuring him that the Movement was ready for dialogue, he reminded al-Tuwaijri that he intended to succeed in achieving the Shiʿis demands.

Although the spokesman criticized the Basic Order issued by the king, al-Saif regarded it as 'a good base for initiating the process of development and awaited change'. Al-Saif admitted that:

though the government was somewhat annoyed as we have not expressed our full support of the new orders, yet, in general, we have not rejected them and we did not overtly criticize them. However, we consider these orders a starting point, and we look forward to transforming them into a framework for resituating the conditions of our country, leading to compromise and an accord between adversaries. [...] Our constant aim is the rule of law and equality among all citizens, a motive behind our instant demand for reform, and as the initial bases have been established, then many of our demands are liable to be achieved. Therefore, we will be more flexible in discussing these demands and more understanding of the [long] process [needed] in dealing with these demands.[13]

In another letter, al-Saif pleaded with the crown prince that either he or the king should take the initiative to resolve the Shiʿis problem. The initiative proposed by al-Saif included a government acknowledgment of the Shiʿis' religious rights;

the abandonment of all forms of discrimination; allowing the opposition members to return home; and the elimination of the causes of tensions such as the sanctions imposed on the study of the Shi'i doctrines and cultural and social activities.

However, comparison of numerous letters and petitions presented by the leadership of the Reform Movement to the Saudi government on different occasions shows that the political demands were eventually downgraded, if not neglected by the Movement. Either the Movement was not sure that such demands could be realized or it lacked very few cards to play during the dialogue; or the Saudi government insisted on confining the dialogue to religious and socio-economic issues and firmly declined to negotiate political demands.

The Saudi Response

The regime's initiative was admittedly unprecedented, in that for the first time in modern Middle Eastern history, a regime called upon its opponents for dialogue to discuss the demands of the opposition. What is more striking is that the Saudi regime, in the light of previous experience, was perceived to be extremely intolerant towards its adversaries, and it would be a rare exception for the regime to enter into dialogue with Shi'is opposition.

As noted, the series of attempts made by Prince Muhammad b. Fahad, the governor of the Eastern Province, some Shi'is notables, Arab journalists and diplomats failed to bring both parties to the negotiation table. What made the 1993 dialogue effective was the personal involvement of the king. He dispatched his personal envoy to the UK to contact opposition leaders, and he issued the general amnesty and received the delegation of the Reform Movement at his palace in Jeddah.

Unlike the dialogue with the Reform Movement, the general amnesties issued following the death of King Faisal in 1975 that allowed leftist opponents to return to the country were neither part of a dialogue nor did they encompass political and religious issues.

Based on numerous meetings with some high-ranking officials in the Ministry of Interior, a member of the *islahiyya* Central Committee claimed that the government intended that the demands of the Shi'is should be promptly realized in order to abort the attempts of those who opposed the dialogue, such as the Salafi extremists in the religious establishment and some elements within the security services.

The Accord

During the dialogue between the leadership of the Movement and government representatives, a telegraphic royal decree was sent on 10 August 1993 to Saudi embassies throughout the world. It stated:'We inform you that generous royal directives have been issued to the Minister of Interior to pardon all those from the Shi'is denomination who have conducted oppositional acts of all kinds, and allowing those who are outside the kingdom to return if they wish.'

As the royal directive took effect, arrangements were made for some selected leading members of the Reform Movement to travel to Jeddah to meet King Fahad. On Monday 20 September 1993, a delegation of the Reform Movement, consisting of Tawfiq al-Saif, Ja'far al-Shayeb, Sadiq al-Jabran and 'Isa al-Mizze'l, arrived in Jeddah. Prior to the meeting, the delegation met Major General Muhammad al-Huwairini and Major Khalid al-Hamdan (both from the public relations department in the Ministry of Interior). Al-Huwairini claimed the Shi'is' grievances were minor and resolvable, indicating that he had good intentions. He blamed the Shi'is for isolating themselves and not communicating with others, and for failing to capitalize on the opportunities available in other areas, particularly in terms of employment.

On Wednesday 22 September 1993, a delegation of the Reform Movement met King Fahad in his Al-Salam Palace and was attended by Prince Muhammad b. Fahad, the governor of the Eastern Province. The spokesman of the Reform Movement thanked the King for his efforts and for receiving the delegation. He also thanked him for deciding to release the political prisoners. He then focused on the new aims of the Movement in the wake of the Gulf crisis, saying, 'We have reached these new convictions in dealing with the situation differently in terms of our contribution to building our country, and we hope to find the opportunity to handle this role'.

The delegation raised with the king their demands, such as employment of the Shi'is in local companies, religious rights and permission for foreign wives of the members of the Reform Movement to enter the country and join their husbands and children.

A number of meetings were also held between the delegation and some high-ranking officials, such as Prince Naif, the Minister of Interior, and Prince Muhammad b. Fahad, the governor of the Eastern Province.

On 25 September 1993, the mediator claimed that he met the king and spoke to him about the issues that the delegation had wanted to discuss with him, namely, discrimination against the Shi'is in employment, education, judiciary and religious practices. The king requested a list of the names of the sacked Shi'is employees so that they could be re-employed. He also requested a list of those who were excluded from travel and promised to resolve the issue. He also promised that a meeting would be arranged with the Minister of Justice and the Minister of Islamic Affairs in order to settle the issue of Shi'is mosques and *hussainiya*s.

The Minister of Interior, Prince Naif b. Abdulaziz, told the delegation on 18 October 1993 that national security was the first priority and that it was not debatable. The prince affirmed amicably that, 'the Shi'is are part of this country and we preserve documents known to both of us and the Shi'is notables since the foundation of the state by King Abdulaziz'.[14]

Analysis of Islahiyya's *Debate*

There was growing concern among the members of the Movement that the dialogue would fail. According to a report sent by a member of the Central Committee (December 1993), 'the situation is very delicate and nothing important has been achieved so far, apart from issuing passports'. There was a fear among the leaders of the *islahiyya* that the Movement might be impacted by the socio-political climate inside the country, and that their personal affairs may become the issue at the expense of the cause for which they struggled.

These assessments were revealed to only a very few within the Central Committee since there was some difficulty in communicating between the returnees and the members who remained abroad awaiting the outcome of the dialogue.

There were a number of attempts within nearly all levels of the Reform Movement to formulate possible responses to the tactics and techniques of the government. The debates within the Movement exhibit different views and stances. Some believed that a peaceful return to the country was the principal aim, since the return would provide the Movement with the opportunity to communicate directly with the community and put pressure on the government from inside in order to attain its demands. Tawfiq al-Saif seems to have been influenced by a number of Islamists who considered such an aim crucial for Islamic movements, such as Shaikh Rashid al-Ghanushi.[15] Al-Saif also assimilated certain ideas that have been debated among groups such as Bahraini leftist parties, and some Iraqi activists such as Dr Muaffaq al-Rabi'i, a former member of *da'wa* party and then a member of the American-based Governing Council in Iraq.[16]

The majority of the members of the Central Committee of the Movement argued that the return to the country was, in itself, insufficient, since the Movement represented a community that had suffered from sectarianism and the Movement had deserted the country only in order to pressure the government to accede to the fundamental demands of the Shi'is community.

Two members of the Central Committee wrote to the spokesman of the Movement:

> We disagree with the offer [of a] peaceful return unless it goes along with realizing the minimum demands such as releasing prisoners, giving back passports to those who are inside, providing opportunities for employment in all companies, particularly in Aramco, and allowing [the Shi'is] to build mosques and *hussainiya*s.

Return without tangible gains 'would result in negative consequences',[17] the most important of which was harm to the reputation and credibility of the Reform Movement.

Some few members contended that the Shi'i issue was a part of a national crisis and that resolving the Shi'is' problems could thus only be possible if there was a resolution to the issues relating to the whole nation. According to this view, there were many problems in the country that were not limited to the Shi'is but also encompassed the vast majority of the population, such as unemployment, lack of individual freedoms, freedom of expression, free press and so on. However, this view seems to have appealed to a small number of the members, such as Hamza al-Hassan, the Movement's representative in the dialogue held in London between 1993 and 1994.

Amid the debates within the Movement regarding the possible scenarios for dealing with the government's attitude, a Royal Decree of a general amnesty was issued on 28 July 1993, resulting in the release of some forty Shi'is political prisoners. The Reform Movement warmly welcomed this step. According to a communiqué issued by the International Committee for Human Rights in the Gulf and Arabian Peninsula (ICHR–GAP), 'The committee intends that such a move should lead to a broader transformation which corresponds with the international changes towards respecting human rights and implementing general freedoms'.[18]

In response to the Royal Decree, the Reform Movement suspended the publication of its most provocative magazine (*al-Jazira al-'Arabiyya*). The present author, as managing editor of the magazine, sent a letter to subscribers on 27 September 1993 informing them that, 'the magazine will be suspended during the period between September and October'. This decision was justified in vague terms, such that it gave a general indication of the political situation in Saudi Arabia that 'needs to be carefully observed and thus reacted to positively'.

What is striking is an article written by Tawfiq al-Saif praising the *shura* Council; the article was published in a daily newspaper, *al-Riyadh Daily*. Al-Saif expressed his support for the political wisdom of King Fahad in emphasizing the importance of the *shura* Council. This article caused shock among the members of the Movement, and its leader, al-Saffar, wrote a letter denouncing the content of the article:

> The article was a clear mistake in terms of its content, approach and timing. As we are still in the process of negotiation, every action we make should be carefully counted. This article is not based on careful calculation and collective thinking [... It] caused critical harm to our credibility.[19]

Al-Saif's justification was that, since the Movement opted for a gradual political transformation of the country, and the *shura* Council was the means by which this political transformation could be achieved, then support for it was necessary. And as the Council had, at the time, just commenced its sessions, he espoused its role and emphasized its importance.[20] However, such a justification conflicted with articles that al-Saif had written in *al-Jazira al-*

ʻArabiyya magazine, in which he argued the three orders issued by the King were far short of the people's expectations.[21]

Responses

The dialogue between the Reform Movement and the Saudi government generated different responses among various groups, whether on religious, political or ideological grounds. An important thread throughout, however, is that dialogue between the Shiʻi opposition and the Saudi regime was unprecedented. Historically, the Shiʻis are always perceived as an opposition while the Sunnis are perceived as rulers; this perception was fortified following the eruption of the Iranian revolution and the breeding of Shiʻis opposition groups in many regions, notably Iraq and Gulf states. These groups followed the Iranian style of change and rejected compromise with governments, which they regarded as corrupt and oppressive. Until the beginning of the dialogue between the Reform Movement and the Saudi regime, there was no a tradition or example among the contemporary Shiʻis of compromise and reconciliation with the Sunni regime.

The Saudi Shiʻis

During the early days of the dialogue between the Reform Movement and the Saudi regime, 'there [was] consensus among the Shiʻis about the demands,'[22] according to a Lebanese newsletter. The Shiʻis in the Eastern Province looked upon the dialogue as a triumph that would mean an end to their misery. They showed full support for the Reform Movement, as reflected in the crowds gathering at the returnees' houses and at the *hussainiyas,* where they delivered public speeches.

However, the Shiʻis' support for the dialogue began to wane. Their aims were not achieved and thus their hopes were gradually dashed. As a member of the Central Committee observed, 'the majority [of the Shiʻis] welcomed the return of the brothers [...] but now the return is not welcomed any more', since many people, who had waited so long to see the realization of their demands, were ultimately disappointed.[23]

Although they did not suppose that the dialogue would lead to a new epoch for the Shiʻis, the wave of rumours created expectations that were illusionary;

many Shi'i individuals thought that the government would bow down to the Shi'i opposition and agree to their demands. But, in time, the Shi'is became more and more sceptical about the government's policies. One might conclude that the response began as an optimistic one, just as was their expectation, and ended in a sharp decline, reflecting their frustration.

Hizbullah

The emergence of Iranian-based *hizbullah* in 1987, following the massacre of the Iranian pilgrims during the *Hajj* in Mecca, could be described as strong evidence of the disconnection between the Iranian government and the Reform Movement. In their response to the massacre, the Iranians searched for a Shi'is opposition group in Saudi Arabia to take vengeance. Until the day of the announcement of *hizbullah*, the Reform Movement was the only Shi'i opposition group in Saudi Arabia:

> Iranian attempts to convince the leadership of the Reform Movement of its cause, grievances and political agenda have failed, so an opposition party has been formed, which is loyal to the Iranian leadership and imbued with its slogans and ambitions. *Hizbullah al-hijaz* and now works according to the Iranian political agenda.

Following the Iranian line of thinking, *hizbullah al-hijaz* showed very strong opposition to the dialogue. According to an editorial of the monthly magazine, *risalat al-haramain*, the mouthpiece of *hizbullah*:

> Past experience exposed the Saudi regime and unveiled its secrets; thus it is impossible to acknowledge any change in the foreseeable future; so the entirety of the dialogue has nothing to do with our strategy and activity [...] We have repeatedly said that the new changes in the regime's policy aim at absorbing the opposition in order to focus on suppressing the new Salafi opposition [...] if there is sincerity, then the regime should officially recognize the Shi'i sect [...] a formal recognition is not sufficient but it should be translated into practical steps.

The *hizbullah* reaffirmed the basic beliefs of the party, firstly that the Saudi regime does not represent the whole population and does not enjoy an absolute support from the various segments; secondly, that the regime is not qualified to rule the country; thirdly, that the Saudi regime is corrupt and untrustworthy; and fourthly, the whole population, particularly the Shi'is, should cooperate and strengthen their ties and cautiously observe the regime's plans.[24]

In aggressive language, *hizbullah* called upon the opposition forces to multiply their efforts to confront the treason of the Reform Movement and the resignation of its members, whom they described as cowards. 'Let the cowards leave and let the people choose and pave the way, which will lead to the emergence of sincere and committed men.'[25] *Hizbullah* also ridiculed the Reform Movement for its intellectual foundations:

> If the possibility of treason is ruled out then the intellectual defects of the ideology of the movement are still valid, meaning that the group either has abandoned its cause in favour of a reactionary version of Islam, limiting their roles to ritual individual practices, or they are politically shallow and immature, as they believe that the accord with the regime would serve the Islamic movement.[26]

However, *hizbullah*'s attitude was inconsistent. A source in *hizbullah* commented on the accord between the Reform Movement and the regime, saying, 'if we do not support the accord, we simultaneously do not oppose it, awaiting its outcomes'.[27]

In *hizbullah*'s view, the accord came at a time when the regime could exploit the Islamic movement's abandonment of its revolutionary option. The regime's move aimed at 'whipping out the sources of violence' and at 'ending a chapter of security tension that the region has witnessed for decades'. With the emergence of the Jihadi movements in Algeria and Egypt, the Salafi movement in Najd was liable to lean towards the new revolutionary trend in Sunni Islam.[28]

Hizbullah's criticism centred upon the Reform Movement's increasing moderation, which it described as 'surrender'.[29] However, the overwhelming majority of *hizbullah*'s members had benefited from the dialogue, since, under a general amnesty issued by the king as part of the accord, they were able to return home, and all their prisoners were released.

Iran

Although, *hizbullah*'s views and attitude reflected the Iranian stance towards the dialogue, the background needs to be considered. In general, the Iranian response was provocative, since the Iranians had not been informed of the dialogue towards the end. Ties between the Reform Movement and the Iranian authorities were very weak, especially after the exodus of the group from Iran in 1988–9 to Syria, Lebanon, India and Pakistan.

In an attempt to derive some gain from the release of the *hizbullah* political prisoners, the Iranian authorities tried to link this event to the rapprochement between Iran and Saudi Arabia.[30] Indeed, the revolutionary wing in the Iranian government, particularly the wing responsible for *hizbullah*'s network outside Iran, tried to persuade its ally, *hizbullah al-hijaz*, that it had played a part in the release of *hizbullah* prisoners, who were accused of being involved in violent acts inside Saudi Arabia. However, the Iranian attempt failed to affect *hizbullah*'s determination to benefit from the general amnesty issued by the king during the dialogue between the Reform Movement and the Saudi regime.

Wahhabi 'Ulama

One striking response to the accord was a *fatwa* issued by Shaikh Abdullah b. Jibrin, a member of the Senior *'ulama* Council on 30 January 1994, in which he retrieved a previous religious jurisdiction that he had issued on 1 October 1991. He classified the Shi'is as polytheists who deserved to be killed.

The *fatwa* was interpreted by many Shi'is as a sign of the neo-Salafi activists' opposition to the accord between the Reform Movement and the government. These activists included Shaikh Salman al-'Awda, Shaikh Safar al-Hawali, Shaikh Nasir al-'Omar and others who opposed any form of reconciliation with the Shi'is. These activists described the Shi'is as associationists with whom rapprochement was impossible.

On the other hand, Shaikh Abdulaziz bin Baz, the former grand *mufti* of Saudi Arabia, amicably received the leader of the Reform Movement, Shaikh Hassan al-Saffar, at his house in October 1995. According to Tawfiq al-Saif, who participated in the visit, Shaikh Ibn Baz seems to have been keen to learn more about the religious ideas adopted by the Movement, affirming that this visit had persuaded him of the value of the dialogue, though he repeated the commonplace accusations against the Shi'is in regard to the veneration of saints, the cursing of some of the wives and companions of the prophet, and exaggeration (*ghuluw'*). According to al-Saif, Shaikh Ibn Baz was very polite throughout the visit, which lasted for an hour.[31]

Islamists Outside Saudi Arabia

The responses of Islamists elsewhere in the Gulf were disparate, depending on religious and political persuasions. According to a Bahraini Sunni Islamist, the accord was 'a step in the right direction', although he was sceptical about the hidden objectives of the regime. 'It is perhaps easy to interpret [the compromise] in the light of the regime's desire to focus on the other problems arising in other Islamic trends within the country [...] However, such accords and settlements deserve to be welcomed, encouraged and propagated'.[32]

Islamists in Kuwait, such as Isma'il al-Shati, Mubarak al-Dwuailah, Yousif al-Sani' (Sunnis) and 'Adnan Abdulsamad (Shi'i), former members of the Kuwaiti parliament (*majlis al-umma*), who had amicable relations with the leaders of the *islahiyya*, supported the dialogue, on the grounds that opposition forces should base themselves in their homelands in order to understand the needs of their communities and also to invoke tools that are effective and appropriate to internal conditions. Shaikh Rashid al-Ghanoushi welcomed the step taken by *islahiyya* on the same grounds, saying that émigré Islamic movements should all strive to return to their natural cradles, their peoples. Opposition forces were like fish taken from the sea, which would die once removed from their homelands.

The leaders of the MVM, however, firmly opposed the accord and the new orientation of the Reform Movement, recognizing the *marji'iyyat*'s role in such issues and thus acknowledging that the Reform Movement had failed to gain Ayatullah Shirazi's permission to conduct such a dialogue with the Saudi regime. However, although Ayatullah Shirazi had had reservations regarding the accord, he emphasized the importance of the role of the Consultative Council of the Movement and at the same time warned the Movement's leadership of the regime's tricks.[33]

Harakat al-ahrar, the Free Men Movement in Bahrain, which is pro-Iranian, acknowledged that the Reform Movement had played a part in pressing the

Saudi regime to enter into dialogue, but at the same time emphasized the importance of other factors such as the Gulf crisis, the emergence of the Salafi trend and the activities of lobby groups throughout the Western world.[34]

Assessment

The dialogue between the Reform Movement and the Saudi government was an unprecedented occurrence, not only in the history of the relationship between the Shi'is and the government but also in Saudi history as a whole. It was evidence that transformation had occurred in both the dominant group, the Saudi government, and the subordinate group, the Shi'is opposition. Both sides had reached a point where they were ready to engage in dialogue to settle deeply rooted problems. In the past, both had relied stubbornly on force and confrontation, thereby excluding the possibility of reciprocal concessions and mutual understanding. According to Jane Mansbridge, 'members of groups embedded in a tradition of domination and subordination often experience faulty communication: [t]he dominant group has not learned to listen and the subordinate group has learned to distrust'.[35]

Yet, because of the lack of democratic infrastructures and traditions of dialogue, both inside Saudi Arabia and in neighbouring countries, the leaders of the Reform Movement pursued this new and complicated enterprise with undeveloped scenarios and plans.

It is interesting to note that the leaders of the Reform Movement did not at any level question or even discuss the legality of dialogue with a regime they had formerly described as *taghut*, or tyrannical. One may conclude that the Movement had become more pragmatic, in an effort to achieve political gains, and given up its idealistic objectives. In fact, with the exception of its Shi'i rival, *hizbullah al-hijaz*, the Reform Movement encountered no dispute on the legality of its stance during the whole of the dialogue, either from the side of their former ally, the MVM, or from the *marji'iyyat*, Sayyid Mohammad al-Shirazi.

Nevertheless, two years before the accord, a member of the *islahiyya* Movement had asked the General Secretary of the Reform Movement, Tawfiq al-Saif, whether, as a religious movement, he considered accommodation with the Saudi regime to be legitimate. Al-Saif had replied by saying that the Reform was a religious movement in terms of social belonging, and it was indeed difficult to say that this disqualified it from coexisting with a regime that was not in complete conformity with religion. The crucial and ultimate verdict on such a matter was left to the jurists, he said, and we would be bound by their judgement, even though the jurists themselves were not in total agreement about the legality of the relationship between an opposition group and a government.

He added:

> [If] we consider this government is religiously excommunicated (*kafira*), then the position is different, and this is not the case with regard to the Saudi regime. Our standpoint is that this government has lagged behind in the implementation of religious precepts, the most important of which is the rule of consultation (*shura*). Once it has realized this objective, then it will have re-established itself on religious ground, and this is what we aim to achieve.[36]

On the other hand, King Fahad is said to have sought legal opinion from Shaikh 'Abdullah al-Ghadiyan,[37] a member of the Senior *'Ulama* Committee, prior to the initiative in September 1993, about the legality of entering into a dialogue with the *islahiyya*. Al-Ghadiyan was believed to be among the more moderate and loyalist Wahhabi scholars on the Senior *'Ulama* Committee.[38]

However, it was easy for the Saudi government to deal with opposition groups, as it had faced many opponents from different backgrounds who eventually were bought off or pardoned on the basis of a royal decree. Some former opponents expressed their fear that the dialogue with the government would end with the same result, that is, the unconditional return of the dissidents, leading gradually either to the erosion or to the isolation of the opposition, as was the case with the leftists and nationalists in the 1960s and 1970s.

Though aware of this previous experience, the leadership of the Reform Movement had a different outcome in mind. Some members of the Movement exaggerated the results of the dialogue, which in turn inflated the Shi'is' expectations. In time, the Shi'is became disappointed. The leaders of the Reform Movement used apologetic language, referring to the local authorities' obstructive attitude to implementing the demands. According to a member of the Central Committee, 'we have informed the people [the Shi'is] that the issue of passports will be resolved soon, but as time passed we started to use diplomatic language in order to defend our position, but henceforth people started to lose confidence in us, and the question of where the demands were was frequently posed.'[39]

Six months after the return to the country of a group of *islahiyya*'s members, a member of the Central Committee addressed the leadership of the Movement, stating, 'The time is not suitable for the return of the rest of the Movement, as none of the major demands have been realized. [...] The Shiʿi notables believe that your return is not useful unless these demands are attained.'[40]

Members of the first group, who returned to the country three months after the dialogue, agreed that those who remained outside should not be pressed to come home, as the government appeared to be inconsistent about defining the terms and conditions of the dialogue. The government could do little to exert pressure upon those outside the country and the return of the whole Movement would weaken its position vis-à-vis the regime. In addition, no promising sign had appeared on the horizon in relation to the opposition's demands.

According to a letter sent to the Central Committee by the spokesman of the Movement, Tawfiq al-Saif, from Riyadh,

> on the official level, there is no defined mechanism with regard to the relationship with the government, and we do not know exactly what would happen in the near future, despite the positive signs, such as the directives issued to prayer Imams to avoid provoking sectarian matters, in addition to the notable improvement in officials' attitudes towards the Shiʿis.

The central question to be answered is why the demands were not met. Some members argued that, since the demands had accumulated over decades, it would simply take a long time for them to be resolved. Others argued that the real impediment to the resolution of the Shiʿis problem was the local government in the Eastern Province, led by Prince Muhammad b. Fahad, whose previous attempts in setting up a dialogue with the opposition had ended in failure. Some members of the Movement even alleged that he had used every means to impede the success of the accord. The failure, according to those members, was attributed to the obstacles the members faced as they endeavoured to obtain decisions from local authorities regarding religious rights such as the building of mosques and employment of the Shiʿis in Aramco.

However, a member of the Central Committee involved in the meeting with Prince Muhammad b. Fahad disagreed, stating, 'Prince Muhammad wants to resolve the regional turmoil, but he mentioned that this issue needs some time, and the situation does not tolerate sharp changes that may lead to unforeseen consequences.'

Fearing that Prince Muhammad would undermine the accord, the leadership of the Reform Movement opted for partial disclosure of the details of the dialogue, at least to certain groups and journalists. They argued that the demands were discussed with the king, who himself took the initiative in participating in the dialogue with the opposition.[41] Prince Muhammad claimed that the royal family were still committed to their promise of 'dignity and passports',[42] implying that the Shi'is' fundamental demands were not part of the dialogue.

Another group among the Reform Movement alleged that the government was the main impediment to the success of the Movement. In a centralized government like that of Saudi Arabia, where the king holds absolute power, it is difficult to exonerate him from the failure of the dialogue.

Nevertheless, the dialogue itself was considered a significant step. This was reflected in the Shi'is' attitude, private and public talks, and even in stories and legends. Some Shi'is believed that an accord would bring solutions to their entire problem. Others, more pessimistic, focused on the details of the dialogue to try to prove that it was an unforgivable mistake.

It would appear that one notable effect of the dialogue on the religious views, attitudes and thinking of the Shi'is was a reduction in the differences between the Shi'is in terms of their *marji'iyyat* affiliations, which had been a major factor of disruption since the rise of the Islamic Republic of Iran in 1979.

Another consequence was a decline in the Shi'is' fear of the government, to the extent that individuals began to voice their demands, to involve themselves in their community's issues and to sign up to collective petitions. Most importantly, the dialogue created a more open and encouraging atmosphere. The Shi'is became confident enough to articulate their demands without fear of arrest or interrogation.

The spokesman of the Reform Movement, having had numerous meetings with officials in the Ministry of Interior, claimed that the government's image of the Shi'is was distorted during the periods of confrontation. The common view among government circles was that the Shi'is complained but did not know what they wanted, and when they were given what they wanted, they did not feel satisfied. Their loyalty to the government was perceived to be precarious, since they had their own legitimacy, which was based on religious grounds exemplified in the *marji'iyyat*. According to a member of the Central Committee, Prince Faisal b. Salman, a son of the governor of Riyadh, 'the voice of the Shi'is is so weak that many people are against them because of the unclear image that is reflected of them; the repeated complaint is that they do not interact with the situation in their country; such weakness sends a wrong message to the officials in the government.'[43]

A member of the Central Committee argued that the discussions held with Shi'is scholars and notables in the Eastern Province showed that, although it was true that the Shi'is' loyalty was rooted in religion, the religious discrimination and the use of violence against the Shi'is had made them consider the state as oppressor and usurper since, by virtue of its sectarian ideology, it deprived them of their basic rights.[44]

The assessment of the Reform Movement's leader, Shaikh Hassan al-Saffar, is somewhat different from that of the majority of the Central Committee's members. He was optimistic that Shi'i demands could be met, but believed that there were two factors involved in the slow progress towards this end: first, the bureaucratic traditions of the government, and second, the unfair attitude of the local government towards the Shi'is, particularly Prince Muhammad b. Fahad and the security service (*al-mabahith*). Consequently, there should be intensified and consistent efforts to press the government to accelerate its procedures in regard to the Shi'is demands.[45]

A radical assessment came from a member of the Central Committee, who argued that the Movement achieved many political gains in comparison to its real size. He stated that, 'the popular momentum the Movement gained in the early days of its return made us plant a mistaken impression in people's heads that we are a powerful force that could threaten the regime.' The aim had been 'to gain personal credit rather than resolve the Shi'is problems, and the consequence was the decline of the people's confidence in us.'[46]

Since few positive signs appeared from inside with regard to the realization of Shi'is demands, the group abroad started to question the whole dialogue and whether it was useful to continue. In a meeting held in Damascus on 8 April 1994, the members asked whether the Movement should give more time to the Saudi government to implement their demands. Although the majority of the Central Committee's members had not given up hope, the Movement seemed to have been faced with pressures from inside, namely from the Shi'is community in the Eastern Province, and other Shi'is forces abroad, mainly the MVM and *hizbullah*. Popular momentum had started to erode as a result of the government's slow response to the opposition's demands.

What is more striking is the positive and rosy picture drawn by the spokesman and some other members of the Central Committee concerning the progress of the dialogue, probably so as to reinforce the decision that the Movement had made or to prove that they were capable of managing the dialogue.

However, the report sent by a member of the delegation to the Central Committee abroad reversed all of these expectations, since the meeting with King Fahad had not led to an agreement with the government on the demands that had been raised in the letter to him prior to the meeting.

As among the Shi'is in the Eastern Province, the expectations of the members of the Reform Movement fluctuated sharply in accordance with the conditions associated with the dialogue and the degree of their acquaintance with the details of it. This included ordinary members along with leaders of the Movement, such as its spokesman, Shaikh Tawfiq al-Saif, and, to a lesser extent, the spiritual leader, Shaikh Hassan al-Saffar. The spokesman, who had been more hopeful at his first meeting with the king, commented publicly on the dialogue with the government that, 'success is not guaranteed in this regard [...] it is just an attempt to approach our aim, that is, improving the conditions of the Shi'i community'.

The possible explanation is the lack of a detailed, far-reaching plan prior to the return of the Movement, which led to inconsistencies and then to schism among the returnees and between the Movement's insiders and outsiders or, more accurately, between the co-opted and non-co-opted. It is worth noting that no plan whatsoever had been formulated by the leadership of the Movement or the Central Committee, neither for inside nor for abroad, apart from the division of the Movement into two groups. One group was to return to the country and the other was to stay outside awaiting the developments of the dialogue with the government. However, those who were outside started to return home, despite the fact that nothing of significance had occurred. In fact, the psychological atmosphere following the return of a segment of the *islahiyya* created massive pressure on those living abroad, particularly on the wives of *islahiyya* members, who wanted stable and decent living conditions.

As the leaders of the Movement realized that the government had no serious intention of resolving the Shiʻi problem, they started to shift their focus to the future and the transformations that might occur with the death of King Fahad and a new balance of power, with increasing public awareness of the deterioration in political and economic conditions, and with regional and international political changes.

There was agreement among the leaders of the Movement that Shiʻis individuals should be encouraged to handle their cases directly and to exercise pressure on the government to resolve their problems. However, they were aware that promoting a 'culture of complaint'[47] could have a negative impact, such as their resignation and isolation, so in a meeting on 8 April 1994, the Central Committee decided that the Shiʻis should be encouraged to become involved in the political struggle, in order to exert more pressure on the government.

Generally, the dialogue between the Shiʻis opposition and the Saudi regime revealed conflicting views, standpoints and ideologies. However, the dialogue was significant in that it represented the physical recognition of the Saudi government by the Shiʻis opposition and an acknowledgement that such recognition was the only way to assure Shiʻis rights. According to al-Saif, 'we are not calling for toppling the regime or changing the order. Our aim, precisely, is to bring about remedies to the causes of social tension, which, if not treated, may lead to political tensions.' A conventional view, often repeated and expressed by Fuller and Francke, is, 'The position of the Shiʻis in the states and societies in which they live is the historical legacy of their rejection of the legitimacy of government.'[48] However, such a view has been rejected and had little currency among students of Shiʻi political thought. There are ample examples of present Shiʻis communities who live in harmony with their governments, such as in Kuwait and Oman. Besides, the Shiʻis' rejection of the legitimacy of a government is not necessarily on religious grounds; rather, it has much to do with the political and socio-economic conditions in which the Shiʻis live. So, whereas the government was ready to honour the fundamental rights of the Shiʻis, in response the Shiʻis were ready to be loyal to the government. Conversely, the failure of the government to assure the Shiʻis of their rights would inevitably lead to their rejecting the government's legitimacy. Indeed, the Saudi authorities' obstruction of the dialogue had a negative consequence, affecting not only the Shi'is but also nearly all religious and political groups of different backgrounds in the country. On various occasions, former opponents of the government, mainly from the Sunni side, criticized the Reform Movement for its return, on the grounds that the government was devious and untrustworthy.

However, the dialogue with the Reform Movement did not necessarily entail recognition of the opposition. Indeed, the dialogue revealed that the regime perceived the whole state as its 'private property', and those who opposed the regime were overtly and blatantly considered not only illegitimate but intruders. In response to a query in November 1990 from a UN committee specializing in discrimination on religious grounds, a Saudi official stated:

Nobody is compulsorily forced to live or work in Saudi Arabia. He who supposedly opposes its rules and regulations should choose another place to live. But once he has opted for living in this county, he should respect and literally accept all its rules and limitations; if he violates them, then he is liable to the designated current punishments.

The statement is striking not only for its uncompromising hard line but also because it casts doubt on the origin of the Shi'is, implying that they are immigrants from Iran or other neighbouring countries.

The statement echoes one made by King Khalid in response to a petition submitted by Shi'i notables on 24 December 1979, following provocative measures taken by security forces during the *intifada*, such as using live bullets, arrests, curfew and shooting from helicopters. The king rejected claims about the death of a number of demonstrators and the injury of others, saying that, 'whoever wants to stay in this country should do so and if not, he should leave'.

The notables were shocked by this reply and promptly wrote another petition (28 January 1980) to the Crown Prince Fahad (former king), in which they implicitly condemned the king's statement, saying, 'we will stay in our homeland, the cradle of our forefathers and sons, despite what the plotters aim to achieve; we will not leave even if force is brought to bear on us to do so'.

Controversy over the Security Solution

Members of the Movement were greatly concerned that the government would deal with the Shi'is issue from a security perspective, while they insisted on a political solution. Indeed, the sort of solution worked out (either political or security) would inevitably affect all that was going on between the government and the opposition. The question arises: what was the government's perception of the arrangements with the Reform Movement?

According to a prominent member of the royal family, 'you have always got to leave a door open that says you can still become a member of the mainstream, which is what we have done.' He added, 'there are no deals as such, but those who issued these publications will stop them and they can come back home where they are welcome.'[49]

Such a statement epitomizes the ideology of the ruling class, as well as reflecting its attitude towards its opponents. The general amnesty ('afu') and Royal Bounty (makrama malakiyya), the common terms used by the Saudi government, reflect the royal family's perception of the state and its inhabitants. The Shi'is file was considered as a security issue and not a political one, and the members of the Reform Movement were classed as a security hazard.

On the other hand, an obsession with individual safety seems to have led the members of the Reform Movement to focus on the security issue and to assert it repeatedly as a central part of the dialogue with the government. Al-Saif blamed the role of the security forces, stating, 'the attitude of the security men [al-mabahith] made the people suffer much pain [...] because of their violations of universal human rights, their attitude is roundly decried by those with dignity and a national sense.' He added, 'the security men are not maintaining security, rather they contribute to undermining it [...] they pushed groups of people to oppose the government as a response to their bad attitude.'[50] He cited examples of the attitude of the security men, saying that he himself was chased by a security vehicle from early morning to midnight[51] and that another member of the Central Committee was under continuous surveillance, being tailed by security vehicles wherever he went, and he believed that his telephone and his house were monitored.[52]

Obviously, the government and the opposition differed sharply in defining what had happened between the two parties in 1993. While the opposition claimed that there was an 'accord' based on a 'dialogue' held in London and Beirut, the Saudi regime denied this and described it as a 'general amnesty'. However, the meetings, talks, letters and arrangements, including the meeting between a delegation of the Reform Movement and the king, could be considered as a deal, if not an accord.

The letters, reports and notes of the members of the Reform Movement on the government's slow response to the Shi'is issues show that differences among the members was not affecting the consensus about return to the country. Though the overwhelming majority of *islahiyya*'s members endeavoured to carry some gains back home to present to the people they defended, the priority was simply to go home in safety, as nearly all members did. By July 1994, the Movement had no presence outside the country's borders.

It is clear that the dialogue was a turning point in Saudi history in terms of the relationship between the opposition forces and the regime. For the first time, the king and his opponents were gathered at one table and under one roof. Furthermore, the dialogue was a significant step in the context of the relationship between the Shi'is and the Saudi government, and it ushered in a new epoch in which the two sides could reach an accommodation.

Yet, the dialogue was not a success in that it did not eliminate the Shi'is grievances, even if it reduced their intensity. The government's attitude towards the Shi'is underwent minor changes, particularly in religious matters, but on socio-economic and political issues, which entailed comprehensive solutions, it was intransigent.

SEVEN

Accommodation and Evolving Attitudes (1993 – the Present)

Following a decade and a half of open conflict between the Shiʻi opposition and the Saudi regime, a new era began in September 1993. For the Reform Movement, the return of its members to the country marked the beginning of a period of accommodation in which the Shiʻi community might eventually be integrated into mainstream Saudi society. The return was seen by many observers as a turning point in the relationship between the Shiʻis community and both central government and local authorities in the Eastern Province.

Generally speaking, in the course of the last four decades, the Saudi state witnessed various forms of opposition: secularist, nationalist, leftist and eventually religious. The conventional wisdom of the Saudi ruling class is that opposition must be curbed in one way or another, be it through force, containment, exclusion, marginalization, pre-emption or very limited accommodation. Some of those who participated in anti-government activities in the 1960s were appeased by the amnesty or 'were reconciled to the gradual improvement in their position'.[1]

This chapter will examine the political and intellectual stance of the *islahiyya* following its return to the country. It will also examine Saudi strategies towards political opposition in general and the Reform Movement in particular, exploring whether they were geared towards excluding, marginalizing and containing the opposition or including, accommodating and collaborating with it. We shall ask whether there was perhaps a third strategy that contained elements of both the others. The chapter will also consider the challenges facing the process of accommodation.

Although the themes debated in this chapter are consistent with and overlap with some themes of the reformative period, they are more specific than the latter, as they clearly and directly deal with the urgent problems between the Shi'is and the government and focus more precisely on what should be done to overcome them. These themes are discussed within the context of the strategy of accommodation adopted by the Reform Movement, which posed a challenge for the Movement as it strove to become a local-based movement and to reconstitute itself through social and intellectual activities, while avoiding being embedded in a defined political form.

After the Return of Islahiyya (1993–2004)

The meeting in October 1993 between the leaders of *islahiyya* and King Fahad, Prince Naif, the Minister of Interior, Prince Muhammad b. Fahad, the governor of the Eastern Province, and his deputy, Prince Sa'ud b. Naif, marked a turning point in relations between the Shi'is and the Saudi regime. Following this meeting, the leaders of *islahiyya* organized a series of public meetings in the Eastern Province, in which they explained the motives and circumstances that had led them to negotiate with the government and hence to abandon its activities and return its members to the country.

The meetings, held at public halls and *hussainiyas*, were attended by large numbers of people. Some eagerly raised questions about the nature of the accord with the government and the demands of the *islahiyya*, while others were obsessed with the new orientation of the Movement following its decision to re-establish itself inside the country.

The release of Shi'i political prisoners and the granting of passports to a couple of thousand people who had been banned from travelling outside the country created an optimistic climate in the Shi'is region and inevitably brought credit to the leaders of the *islahiyya*, who were received like heroes. However, the leaders were faced also with legions of queries about the imperative problems of the Shi'is concerning employment, education, public services and religious freedom, and found themselves unable to offer convincing answers, particularly to the most deprived among the Shi'is. Within six months, the hopes of the Shi'is dwindled nearly to nothing, as the leaders of the *islahiyya* battled with a slow and complicated system of bureaucracy.

The Stage of Uncertainty (1993–4)

After the return of the bulk of the *islahiyya* to the country by the end of 1993, three pivotal issues acquired a great deal of urgency. First was the need to reassure the security agencies that the *islahiyya* as an organized movement was officially and practically dissolved and hence that it had entered a new phase of open and partly legally recognized activities. Second, the returnees needed to sort out their finances and legal status and to re-establish themselves in their local communities. Third, the Shi'is' problems had to be revived and all necessary steps taken to press the government to resolve them.

Among the first priorities were the security restrictions on a large number of Shi'is individuals and religious freedom. The leaders of the *islahiyya* were almost entirely immersed in dealing with these two issues, at the expense of both the national objectives, as stated in *al-Jazira al-'Arabiyya*, and the political aims of the Movement.

The circumstances in which the returnees lived were delicate, as the security agencies had not been engaged in arrangements between the *islahiyya* Movement and the government from the outset. The returnees were subjected to security measures, particularly at the borders, where they were asked to provide detailed information about where they lived. Their telephones were bugged and their cars were followed by security vehicles from the moment they left their houses until the moment they returned. Furthermore, the sermons, writings and communications of the leaders of the Movement were closely monitored. On certain occasions, prominent Shi'i preachers subscribing to the *islahiyya* Movement, such as Shaikh Hassan al-Saffar and Shaikh Fawzi al-Saif, were interrogated by security authorities in the Eastern Province, specifically to verify the Movement's claim that it had been dissolved.

Throughout the first two years, the political status of the *islahiyya* Movement was, to a great extent, volatile and confused. Members became more involved in their personal affairs and many sought jobs, although the leaders strove to offer financial assistance to the returnees. The returnees also found the social situation very tense, as the expectations of the Shi'is in regard to the accord with the government were too high; many members thus felt embarrassed and frustrated at being unable to fulfil these expectations and became detached from their community.

It seemed to the leaders of the *islahiyya* that the government wanted to undercut and discredit the Movement by repeated futile promises, which would lead first to increased resentment among the returnees and then to the fission of the Movement. A quite large number of the members chose to see to their own lives and futures, investing very little energy and time in public concerns; others opted to leave and go back to the country where they had lived previously. To this day, there remain groups who fell foul of security monitoring and are living in Syria, the UK or the USA, some from the upper levels of the Movement, such as Shaikh Tawfiq al-Saif, the former general secretary, Hamza al-Hassan, a member of the Central Committee and the editor of *al-Jazira al-'Arabiyya*, and others.

Meanwhile, the remaining leaders of *islahiyya* endeavoured to reformulate a new cultural discourse for propagation among the Shi'is. The new discourse centred primarily on justifying the dialogue with the government and hence bolstering the new political orientation of the *islahiyya* Movement. This discourse embraces a variety of themes, such as social and cultural openness, religious tolerance, political pluralism and civil liberties, though with limitations.

Such a dramatic transformation must have faced wide criticism from other Shi'is religious forces, as well as revolutionary groups such as the leftist ones. However, such criticisms were gradually damped down thanks to the determination of the leaders of the *islahiyya* to become heavily involved in social and political activities at both local and national level. Moreover, it formed alliances with various groups from different ideological backgrounds.

The Stage of Self-Reconstitution (1995–7)

When it became clear to the leaders of the *islahiyya* Movement that their demands would not be formally met, the next step was to engage in the political game countrywide, specifically forging a broad alliance with sections of the royal family.

A stage of self-reinvention therefore took place at the end of 1995, starting with detachment from the political legacy of the past (e.g. the MVM) and eventually re-establishing the *islahiyya* Movement, though with different structures and agenda. The central message was that the *islahiyya* Movement was now resolved to be entirely a local political force, with no external commitments whatsoever, either towards the *marji' taqlid*, Ayatollah Sayyid Muhammad al-Shirazi, or the leaders of the MVM, who hitherto had a following among the Shi'is in the Eastern Province. The leadership of the *islahiyya* Movement also mustered all efforts to bridge the gap with other active local political and social forces, including the traditional ones. The collaboration between the *islahiyya* Movement and those groups took the form of a mutual understanding about the urgency of Shi'is problems and the best options available to resolve them.

Furthermore, the leaders of the *islahiyya* Movement insisted on preserving and promoting relations with the Saudi authorities at various levels. They remained wary at this stage, trying to balance the demands of the Shi'is with a show of loyalty to the state. Teams were constituted to communicate with Saudi officials, particularly those in the Ministry of the Interior, including Prince Naif and his son and deputy, Prince Muhammad b. Naid, and senior members of the royal family, such as the crown prince Abdullah (present king) and Prince Talal. Undoubtedly, such relations were reassuring to the leaders of *islahiyya* as well as providing a security and political umbrella. At the same time, this arrangement offered Saudi officialdom an opportunity thoroughly to understand the Shi'is grievances and demands.

However, such ambitions were not readily realized, since the new strategy and orientation were not based on consensus – leaders of the Movement enjoyed a monopoly of decision-making – and the divide within the *islahiyya* was so deep. The disruption of the Movement at this stage could be attributed to the frustration of some leading members at the failure of the Saudi government to fulfil its promises to them in October 1993.

One of the main complicated issues that emerged at this stage was the organizational structure of the *islahiyya* Movement. Discussion centred on whether to maintain the old organizational structure or to forge a new one encompassing internal leaders. Another burning issue was the series of controversial articles written by the leaders of the *islahiyya* Movement in local newspapers. For instance, Tawfiq al-Saif wrote two articles endorsing the Consultative Council and the Taliban regime in Afghanistan, which were published in the Riyadh daily newspaper in December 1993 and in *Okaz* daily newspaper, based in Jeddah, in January 1999. These articles triggered very heated debates within both the *islahiyya* Movement and the Shiʿi community as a whole. The Movement was criticized for supporting an anti-Shiʿis regime (the Taliban), and al-Saif was personally excoriated for making such an indefensible personal judgement.

A group of active leading members of the *islahiyya* Movement left the country at this point and went to live abroad, many in the UK and the USA. The members of this group are not united on a certain set of actions and goals, but they maintain a minimum level of coordination. While some members in the US got involved in human rights activities, such as those of the Saudi Institute in Washington, led by ʿAli al-ʿAhmad, other members in London, such as Hamza al-Hassan and the author, published a semi-academic magazine called *Saudi Affairs*, espousing political reforms in Saudi Arabia. It conveys and amplifies the demands of the national reformist trend that emerged inside the country in January 2003. The *islahiyya* members in Syria are engaged in merely religious and intellectual activities.

The Stage of Re-activism (1998–2002)

From 1998, activism and interaction on internal and social levels prepared the ground for the *islahiyya* Movement to become involved in internal politics with confidence. The relationship with the state institutions significantly improved, on the basis of mutual respect, and security restrictions were softened in all but a few cases. Moreover, the Shiʿis problems were overtly and widely debated.

Since then, the *islahiyya* Movement has opted for partial solutions to the Shiʿis problems. In order to establish a certain acceptable status for the *islahiyya*, its leaders have consciously broadened their relations to include lower-ranking state officials and moderate Wahhabi clerics and judges in the Eastern Province and elsewhere in the country. Such relations have helped resolve problems such as the building of licensed mosques and the improvement of public services in the Shiʿis towns and villages. Another remarkable development in this period has been the collaboration with a wide spectrum of social and political forces and intellectual elites throughout the kingdom, achieved partly by reciprocal visits between the leaders of the *islahiyya* Movement and the leaders of these forces. Coordination and mutual political activity have resulted. Interestingly enough, leading members of the Movement have permitted wide press coverage of their activities, notably Shaikh al-Saffar, who became the focus of some local newspapers such as *al-Yaum*, based in Dammam, *Okaz*, based in Jeddah, and *al-Madina*, based in Medina. He and other members regularly write articles for the most widely circulated newspapers in the kingdom.

Shaikh al-Saffar strove during *'Ashura* ceremonies to present a message of moderation and religious tolerance, in the hope of eliminating the then prevalent negative impressions about the Shi'is. His taped sermons were widely circulated and mainly targeted the Wahhabi community. Although al-Saffar implicitly criticized Wahhabi religious extremism, he insisted on inviting Wahhabi clerics to Shi'is religious festivals. He has a weekly open salon, which is attended by notables and political activists from different backgrounds.

Another striking feature of this stage of development is the spread of widely accessible Shi'is Internet sites such as *Qateefiat* Intellectual Website (qateefiat. com), *Hajr* Intellectual Network (hajr.org), *al-Sahel* Electronic Encyclopaedia (alsahel.org) and *Saihat* Oases Forum (saihat.net). These websites, which were sponsored by either members or sympathizers of the *islahiyya* Movement, played a crucial role in drawing Shi'i public attention to the main issues and objectives adopted by the *islahiyya* Movement.

Impact of the War in Iraq

The atrocities of 9/11 marked a turning point in the political and intellectual conditions of the *islahiyya* Movement, the Shi'is in the Eastern Province, the Kingdom of Saudi Arabia and finally the whole world.

These tragic events caused wide criticism of the Wahhabi religious discourse, and for once attention shifted away from the Shi'is.

Without doubt, the dramatic political change in Iraq and the fall of the Saddam regime gave prominence to the grievances of the Shi'is in Iraq. This extended also to the Shi'is in Saudi Arabia, first, as an oppressed minority and second, as they were expected by some American circles to play a divisive role in their country. A plethora of articles were published in the American press encouraging the US government to fuel separatist tendencies in Saudi Arabia; in practice this was undoubtedly directed towards the Shi'is in the Eastern Province, being the most deprived of all communities in the country.

However, the separatist calls received a lukewarm welcome by the Shi'is in the Eastern Province. The leaders of the *islahiyya* Movement clearly and strongly condemned such calls and instead recommended nationalist-motivated activities. They played a pivotal role in the petition entitled '*shurka' fi al-watan*' (Partners in One Nation), submitted to the crown prince 'Abdullah (present king) and signed by 450 Shi'i clerics, notables and political activists. They capitalized on the new political circumstances to enhance relations with Saudi officialdom.

The Saudi government endeavoured to pacify the leaders of the *islahiyya* and the Shi'is in the Eastern Province as a whole. Shi'is grievances were openly discussed at both formal and informal levels. Some princes and ministers were also engaged in such discussions, and expressed their readiness to help resolve Shi'is problems.

In this period the Eastern Province was exposed to Western reporters, researchers and journalists, who made a series of interviews with Shi'i political activists, among them leading members of the *islahiyya* Movement, such as Ja'far al-Shayeb, Muhammad al-Mahfouz, Zaki al-Milad, Muhammad Baqer al-Nimr and 'Aliya Maki.

The *islahiyya* Movement also came to occupy more column space in the press in this period. Dozens of Shi'is writers and journalists wrote for the local press, and daily newspapers have given coverage to Shi'is clerics, publishing pictures of them in their traditional religious dress. For the first time ever, several Shi'is books were printed and distributed inside the country.

The most important feature of this period was the participation of Shaikh Hassan al-Saffar in the two meetings of the National Forum for Intellectual Dialogue. Leaders of the *islahiyya* Movement described this as an implicit recognition of the Shi'is as a community that needed to be integrated and respected, and of his personal status as representative of the leadership of the Shi'is in the Eastern Province. Others thought differently, echoing the official view that the participation of al-Saffar in the National Dialogue merely reinforced the Saudi narrative.

A few words are also necessary to highlight the importance of the Tuesday Intellectual Salon sponsored by Ja'far al-Shayeb, a leading member of the *islahiyya* Movement. The Salon, which started its activities in summer 2001, hosted a group of intellectuals from different ideological persuasions. The events at the Salon ranged from social and charitable activities (e.g. provision of financial and moral support to patients) and purely intellectual ones (e.g. discussion of the socio-cultural shackles that bound social development or of the trend towards violence in Saudi society), to debates on very sensitive political issues, such as political reform and the mechanisms of change.[2]

The Salon acquired a significant reputation at national level; nearly a majority of the most prominent Saudi thinkers and political activists took part in the activities of the Salon. The papers delivered there were circulated and published on the website, where they were enthusiastically received by a wider audience.

In 2003, the Salon organized twenty-seven lectures about, among other topics, the trend of reforms in Saudi Arabia, projects of development in the Eastern Province, the promotion of religious institutions, the petitions of the Saudi intellectuals, the impact of the change in Iraq on the region, the consequences of the National Dialogue and human rights in the Gulf. The Salon helped prepare a common ground for different political groupings.

Two other salons also exist in Shi'i towns. One is in Qatif, sponsored by Najeeb al-Khunaizi, a leftist activist, and the other in Dammam, sponsored by Shaikh Hassan al-Nimr, a former leading member of Hizbullah.

Islahiyya's Accommodative Policies

Donald Horowitz argues that, 'many accommodative policies result from genuine efforts to reduce conflict'.[3] At first glance, the tendency towards accommodation among the Reform Movement can be clearly noted in its intellectual shift resulting from its transformation from a revolutionary movement to a reformative one, a shift that began to crystallize during and after the dialogue with the government and the subsequent return of the *islahiyya* members to the country. Since then, a new intellectual class has begun to burgeon within the Movement, devoting its efforts to the formulation of a new discourse aimed at fortifiying and legitimating the accommodative strategy of the Reform Movement.

Pluralistic discourse and the promotion of the principles of civil society, democracy and individual liberties, and finally the emphasis on religious tolerance, dialogue and difference, a set of salient ideas and values, have coloured the agenda of the *islahiyya* Movement since its transformation into a reformative movement. The writings, sermons and stated demands of the *islahiyya* leaders were dedicated almost entirely to promoting and propagating these ideas.

However, the themes that attracted most attention among the new intellectual class during this period were: pluralism, abolishing the causes of confrontation, propagating a culture of tolerance and reconciliation; and proposing a framework for cooperation among diversified groups.[4] Of these, pluralism seems to have been a priority. To Shaikh al-Saffar, for example, pluralism is a source of enrichment, as can be seen in civilized societies, whereas in backward societies, pluralism becomes a pretext for oppression and a prelude to discrimination.[5] This understanding of pluralism is in the context of the Saudi realm, where the Wahhabi religious tendency tries to impose a certain interpretation of Islam.

New ideas and notions such as coexistence, pluralism, freedom of expression, dialogue and finally accommodation are always encountered with suspicion and fear, since the Shi'is are accused of using *taqiyya*, which casts doubts on al-Saffar's statements.

The *islahiyya*'s strategy of accommodation may be divided into two major aspects: socio-religious and political.

Religious and Social Issues

There seems to be an emphasis upon the role of religion in societies, upon rites, upon the relationship between Shi'is laymen and *mujtahid*s, and so on. Simultaneously, the *islahiyya* leadership stresses the need to renew Islamic concepts, which will fit into the new orientation of the movement. Al-Saffar, for example, argues that religious renewal is imperative if society is to meet the demands of the time.[6]

Furthermore, the *islahiyya*'s leaning towards accommodation spurred its leaders to provide new interpretations of Shi'is traditions in addition to new interpretations of the ideas they used to hold, during the period of confrontation, in order to bolster the revolutionary discourse for the purpose of mass mobilization. At this stage, the leaders of the Reform Movement seem to have exploited their intellectual and political capabilities to provide the necessary ideological foundations, religious interpretations and political agenda for the movement. Two key issues that have been debated and reinterpreted by the leadership of the Reform Movement are the *marji'ite* and *'Ashura*.

The Marji'ite

The role of the *marji'ite* always evokes questions about the loyalty of the Saudi Shi'is to their government. The Saudi Shi'is are repeatedly accused of offering their loyalty to their religious leaders, who live beyond the borders and for whom the Shi'is are willing to fight their government. This question arose in the aftermath of the Iranian revolution in 1979 as a response to the advent of the *marji' taqlid*, namely Ayatollah Khomeini's leadership of a religious state.

Inspired by his charisma, many Shi'is individuals opted to follow his jurisdictions (*fatawa*); this came at a controversial time, when Saudi-Iranian relations rapidly deteriorated following the Shi'is revolt in 1979. The growing number of Khomeini's followers among the Saudi Shi'is seems to have aroused qualms among the Saudi ruling class, which regarded such a development as evidence of the Shi'is' disloyalty to their homeland and government.

However, later developments helped change the situation and relations between Iran and Saudi Arabia began to improve significantly following the announcement of a ceasefire between Iran and Iraq in July 1988. Furthermore, as the Saudi Shi'is became more and more politicized, and as many Saudi Shi'is clerics and activists became primarily involved in internal Shi'is affairs, the authority of the *marji'ite* over the Shi'is gradually declined. The Shi'is' new orientation corresponds to Benedict Anderson's notion of the reinvention of the self. The Saudi Shi'is' adherence to their immediate concerns and interests could be interpreted as an attempt to reinvent themselves in the local context, from which they have been excluded for so long.

Furthermore, the death of the most prominent and dominant *marji' taqlid*s (e.g. Khoei, Khomeini and Shirazi) led to a reduction in the influence of the *marji'* in general, for the new *marji'*s failed to match their spiritual influence and social hegemony. Moreover, the deep divisions due to the differences between Shi'is *marji'*s (revolutionary versus conservative), which prevailed throughout the 1980s, induced the Shi'is to distance themselves from the sources of this division, which made them vulnerable.

Indeed, a number of leading members of the Reform Movement argue that the role of the *marji'* expanded at the expense of religion itself. Now that the old competitors are gone, Shi'i laymen should restore their legitimate right to conduct their temporal affairs independently.[7]

'Ashura

The political interpretation and understanding of *'Ashura* is that it is an episode of revolution by the oppressed against the oppressors. While *hussainiya*s were regarded as a means of political mobilization, as was the case throughout the revolutionary phase (1979–90), the role of *'Ashura* and *hussainiya*s was, since the accord in 1993, reduced and exploited to enhance national and Islamic unity.[8] By the same token, Imam Hussain is perceived, in the phase of accommodation, not as a revolutionary icon, but as a symbol of the unity of 'the Islamic *umma*' for which he sacrificed himself.

There seems to have been a tendency among Shi'i preachers to 'de-revolutionize' the ritual of *'Ashura*. They emphasize the social and moral issues of the ceremony, while shunning the political aspect of the event or interpreting it differently. Indeed, the *islahiyya* Movement resorted to the conventional interpretation of *'Ashura* prevalent among the Arab Shi'is before the Iranian revolution in 1979.

Towards Resocialization

The leaders of the Reform Movement regard social alienation, isolation and estrangement as major obstacles that hinder the process of accommodation. Thus, they believe, the Shi'is should transform their culture of complaint[9] into a culture of activism,[10] on the grounds that the Shi'is could change their status if they become more active and armed with knowledge.[11]

The sense of vulnerability among the Shi'is minority in the Eastern Province makes issues such as national unity, social integration and openness very sensitive, particularly when they are placed in a context like Saudi Arabia, where the dominant religious community leaves those who embrace different sects with no choice but to abjure their beliefs. Therefore the leaders of the Reform Movement have been compelled to adopt ideas that reflect their sense of weakness and their fear of fusion. According to Muhammad Mahfoud, a leading member of the Reform Movement, unity does not mean conformity of opinion, thinking systems and standpoints between citizens of a nation; rather, unity means respect for diversity.[12] This view recalls Robert Melson's argument that, 'the stability of culturally plural societies is threatened not only by communalism per se, but by the failure of national institutions explicitly to recognize and accommodate existing communal divisions and interests'.[13]

As a minority, the Shi'is have always faced threats to their social cohesion; this is vividly clear in the issue of intermarriage between the Shi'is and the Sunna. As the Reform Movement opted to establish itself in the Saudi socio-political context, the leaders of the movement sought a solution that was feasible and had little negative impact on the distinctiveness of the Shi'is as a 'group for themselves'. Shaikh al-Saffar's sermon entitled 'Does Sectarian Difference Prevent Intermarriage?' is a courageous attempt to broach a very sensitive social issue. Against the ethno-religious background of the Shi'is and the political background of the Reform Movement, Shaikh al-Saffar argues that, in the past, 'intermarriage and familial interaction were a manifestation of the unity and integration of Muslims, as differences did not impede intermarriage'. Because of divisive factors, al-Saffar believes that, 'reciprocal hatred and sectarian antagonism encourage [both the Sunna and the Shi'is] towards alienation and separation, resulting in the issuance of *fatwas* that excommunicate (*takfir*) each other and prevent intermarriage between Muslims [the Sunna and the Shi'is].[14]

The possible implication of such a view is that intermarriage between the Shi'is and the Sunna could be regarded as an indication of Shi'is readiness for reconciliation with the Wahhabis, although such a view has not been tested; al-Saffar argues that, 'the question [of intermarriage] is mainly related to an atmosphere of peaceful coexistence and mutual respect'.[15]

M. Mahfoud stresses that social peace cannot be achieved by those who classify and divide, but only by those who unite and seek commonalities.[16] In his sermons, al-Saffar argues that justice and equality are the basis for social peace: 'the society in which individuals enjoy equal rights before the law becomes immune to antagonism and hostility'.[17]

The social approach here serves the new orientation and political goals of the Reform Movement, while eschewing the essence of social alienation, particularly the theological factor, which dominates the attitude of the Shi'is. Alienation is not necessarily a response to the repression of the state, but may be attributed to the ethnic and cultural backgrounds of groups.

Political Issues

The leaders of the Reform Movement maintained a nationalist approach as a prelude to attaining their religious and political objectives. They regard notions such as nation, national unity, citizenship and national integration as tools of accommodation, though these notions are at odds with their Wahhabi religious interpretation, as noted in Chapter Two. In addition, they are not neutral when seen in the light of the religious background of the Reform Movement, particularly the notion of the Islamic *umma* and its related issues.

The *islahiyya* leaders' devotion to promoting individual freedoms for the purpose of accommodation encouraged them to incorporate the ideas of Western intellectuals in the accommodative period. Inspired by Jeremy Bentham's and John Stuart Mill's advocacy of unlimited individual freedoms, the *islahiyya* leadership triggered debates within Saudi society about the severe restrictions imposed on individual freedoms.

Following the same line of argument, M. Mahfoud emphasized the importance of openness as a step towards mutual respect. He argued that openness is the right option for establishing grounds for progressive social dialogue, which enriches the social sphere and fortifies the principles of national unity.[18] Furthermore, he argues that reconciliation between government and society entails opening up the political domain to all groups, such that no group is excluded or marginalized.[19]

The purpose of espousing openness is to facilitate direct contact between different groups so they can listen to each other without a third party. It is also to allow the groups to know each other in reality, in order to provide a catalyst for dialogue between them on controversial issues.[20]

Mamoun Fandy suggests that al-Saffar's vigorous plea for the openness of the Shi'is is based upon a response to official Saudi advice that Shi'is conditions could be improved only if they were to liberate themselves from the shackles of apathy. This explains, Fandy argues, why al-Saffar encourages his audience to participate in Saudi life.[21] This view, though correct, needs to be placed in a context, since al-Saffar is determined to search for a political position within the Saudi context, both for him and for his followers. Such a quest goes along with the ideological transformation within the Movement as it moved towards moderation.

Al-Saffar has striven, since his return, to formulate a discourse based on religious grounds, and a new political orientation, which is open and accommodating and appealing to both the Shi'is and the Sunna. Unlike in the revolutionary period, al-Saffar repeatedly refers to the experience of Imam Hassan, who is portrayed in the Shi'is literature as a passive Imam, who relinquished power to his rival, Mu'awiya. By implying a parallel between Mu'awiya and al-Sa'ud, al-Saffar aims to persuade his audience that he is following the path of Imam Hassan, since he has opted for a peaceful option and dialogue with the regime. Indeed, the version of Shi'ism devised by al-Saffar does not lean towards passivism but rather towards pragmatism and compromise.

In his well-received book *al-Watan wa al-Wuwatana* (Homeland and Citizenship), first published in 1996, al-Saffar transcends ethnic, regional, tribal and sectarian affiliations, in order to promote national sentiment, mainly among the Shi'is. His new understanding is that the love of the homeland is a reflection of faith.[22] In another sermon, al-Saffar refers to a number of religious traditions in order to encourage his audience to offer their respect and love to their homeland. He argues that loving one's homeland does not conflict with belief; rather, it is an expression of belief.[23]

Inspired by the religious-political literature of the theorists of constitutional movements, Tawfiq al-Saif, the former spokesman of the Reform Movement, asserts that the relationship between people and government should be based on the bond of citizenship, which entails equality between Muslims and non-Muslims before the law.[24] In Shaikh al-Na'ini's work on constitutional government, al-Saif seems to have found what might be the guiding framework for crucial minority issues. Al-Na'ini affirms that non-Muslim minorities should be equally and fairly represented in parliament, since their absence from the representative council would make it imperfect.[25]

In contrast to their previous views, the leaders of the *islahiyya* appreciate the value of citizenship for the people living within the borders of Saudi Arabia, as a resolution to sectarian, regional or tribal conflict. Indeed, al-Saffar's book attempts to address a deeply rooted problem related to the ideological basis of the Saudi state, a state that upholds private components of identity, namely the Wahhabi sect, Najdi region and the al-Sa'ud family.

Considerable attention has been paid to rights and obligations in the light of the modern concept of citizenship, a type of citizenship that contrasts with the interpretation of the royal family, which associates citizenship with loyalty. Al-Saffar highlights three main citizenship rights: dignity, security and decent living conditions.[26] Poverty, he argues, makes citizens lose their sense of belonging.[27]

Along the same lines, the leaders of the Reform Movement view civil society as a medium for fostering a balanced relationship within society as a whole and as a platform for equal collective actions that help create an atmosphere of tolerance, openness and responsibility. For M. Mahfoud, civil society provides the necessary power to challenge the repression and cruelty of the state. He argues that civil society is an institutional framework for bearing and fulfilling national and religious responsibilities. Likewise, maintaining order and security can be possible only if civil society institutions operate parallel to the state.[28]

Al-Saffar praises the American model of civil society, where 'there is an abundance of civil organizations, institutions, and so on, which help settle societal problems and ills'.[29] In this topic, as in many other topics, al-Saffar attempts to delineate boundaries between state and society, emphasizing the role of the latter as a constraining force in the face of the coercive power of the former. He believes tolerance and openness should begin from society and then be backed by the state, as these values cannot be imposed from above. Al-Saffar's message is that unless tolerance and openness become part of the culture of society, no force whatsoever, including that of the state, can prevent violence.

Neverthless, the main issue concerning the accommodative agenda of the *islahiyya* writers and intellectuals is intellectual freedom, which is a means of aborting possible compulsion imposed by the Wahhabi religious establishment. Inspired by the theorists of the Iranian constitutional movement, Tawfiq al-Saif argues that freedoms assured by the constitution are all geared towards liberating citizens from the repression of government: 'these freedoms are sanctioned to prevent anybody from repressing others or forcing them to act against their will by recourse to coercion'.[30]

Another argues that freedom and democracy are tools for regulating intellectual and political differences. Therefore, the value of freedom should be enhanced in order to create a climate of dialogue between different groups, as dialogue is impossible without freedom.[31] Likewise, unity cannot be realized without the acknowledgment of diversity.[32]

The intellectual class of the Reform Movement endeavoured to approach all imperative Shi'is issues (religious practices, freedom of expression, participation, political representation, unemployment and so on) by using moderate language aimed at expressing their demands and views from within. However, the remedies suggested for these problems are somewhat vague and open to disparate interpretations.

Challenges to Accommodation

The Shi'i-Wahhabi Divide

Although the Shi'i–Sunni divide dates back to the early history of Islam on the basis of the succession to the Prophet, it could be argued that Shaikh al-Islam Ibn Taimiyya (b.1263, d.1328) appeared to be the pioneer of Sunni polemicists who launched a systematic and harsh criticism of Shi'i beliefs.

After the collapse of the Abbasid Caliphate in 1258, Ibn Taimiyya blamed Mu'aid al-Din Muhammad b. Ahmad al-'Alqami (d. 1258), an influential Shi'i minister under 'Abbasid Caliphs al-Mustansir (r. 1226–42) and al-Musta'sim (r. 1242–58), for the tragic end of the caliphate, in favour of the Mogul. The accusation of treason against the Shi'is acquired more currency with the conversion of the Mogul rulers to Shi'ism at the hands of a renowned Shi'i scholar, Shaikh Ibn Mutahar al-Hilli.

Ibn Taimiyya's *Minhaj al-sunna fi naqd kalam al-Shi'ia wa al-Qadariyya* (The Sunni Method in the Critique of the Theology of the Shi'is and the Qadariyah – a Predestination-oriented sect – is devoted to refuting the famous Shi'i theologian Ibn Mutahar al-Hilli's *Minhaj al-karama fi ma'rifat al-imama*. Ibn Taimiyya's *Minhaj al-sunna*, which was hugely influential among the Wahhabi scholars and polemicists, makes a comparison between Judaism and Shi'ism. Ibn Taimiyya claims that there are similarities between the two in terms of ethos, extremism, ignorance and so on.[33] Indeed, Ibn Taimiyya has devoted a considerable amount of his writing to the similarity between Jews and the Shi'is, though many of the examples he has used are not based on a profound analysis of Shi'is or Jewish sources.

Influenced by Ibn Taimiyya's works, the Wahhabi *'ulama* followed his footsteps in scorning the Shi'is. Indeed, the adoption of Ibn Taimiyya's polemical legacy by the Wahhabiyya fuelled and deepened the divisions

between Saudi citizens, as also within Muslim society as a whole. The Shiʻi–Wahhabi divide has a particular reflection on the status of both the Shiʻis and the Saudi government.

While the divisions within Muslim society were tamed by serious efforts of renowned and respectful scholars of both the Sunna and the Shiʻis in the 1950s and 1960s, culminating in a series of meetings held in Cairo, the Wahhabi *ulama* launched vigorous attacks on attempts at reconciliation between the Sunna and the Shiʻis.

Some scholars argue that Wahhabism represents the kernel of division within Muslim society. Others say it is the ultimate threat, not only to national unity, but also to Islamic unity. The prominent Sunni thinker Dr Muhammad al-Bahi argues that, 'Wahhabism has widened the gap of difference between the Sunna and the Shiʻis, reflecting the negative impact of the Wahhabi call'.[34] Following the same line of argument, Yann Richard talks of Wahhabism as the main impediment to Sunna–Shiʻis coexistence.[35] By the same token, Hamid Enayat argues that Wahhabism represents the 'greatest challenge to Shiʻism since the beginning of Islam'.[36]

These Wahhabi polemical writings have contributed to the formulation of images, attitudes and political stances towards the Shiʻis, which have led to the deepening division within the Saudi population.

A book entitled *Tabdid al-zalam wa Tanbih al-Niyam ela Khatar al-Shiʻia wa al-Tashiuʻ ʻala al-Muslimeen wa al-Islam* (Diffusing Darkness and Awakening those who are Asleep to the Danger of Shiʻis and Shiʻism to Muslims and Islam), by an eminent Wahhabi polemicist called Ibrahim al-Jabhan and sponsored by the Religious Establishment, is evidence of such provocative writings. The book appeared in the mid-1970s and, following the Iranian revolution of 1979, was widely circulated both inside and outside Saudi Arabia. The author possesses few academic credentials; he did not graduate from a religious university, nor has he written any other books. However, his book was well received by the Wahhabi community, as is evident from the fact that the book was republished nine times between 1976 and 1988. The author's central aim is clearly to decry the Shiʻis.

He claims that, 'Shiʻism was founded by Jews to serve Jewish ends'. Against the conventional definition of the *rafida*, al-Jabhan refers to the *rafida* as those who 'reject Islam as a whole'. He describes Shiʻism as a 'foreign and absurd doctrine, with rotten traditions, decayed intellectual foci. It is a new religion derived from Magian, Christianity and Judaism, a despotic religion, a canon stemming from Masonic centres and Jewish aeries, trash, jugglery, dotage, cancer and so on'. Furthermore, he says, those 'who are sceptical about labelling the Shi'is infidels are Magians like the Shi'is'.[37] Indeed, these labels are no more than repetitions of the accusations of the prominent anti-Shi'is scholar, Shaikh Ibn Taimiyya.

Inspired by Ibn Taimiyya's legacy, Sunni and particularly Wahhabi polemicists levelled the same accusations against the Shi'is.[38] The Egyptian Muhib al-Din al-Khatib and the Pakistani Ehsan 'Elahi Zahir were among other polemicists responsible for promulgating Wahhabi polemical literature. Al-Khatib's *Al-khutut al-'arida* was prompted by the disagreement with the efforts of Sunna and Shi'is *'ulama* in the mid-1950s to pave the way for reconciliation between the two sects, and seeks to prove the incompatibility of Sunni Islam with Shi'i Islam, since the latter, he claims, is an entirely different religion. The Wahhabi *'ulama* also rejected any attempt at reconciliation and rapprochement between the Sunnis and the Shi'is. Al-Khatib argues that:

> The fact is that the impossibility of reconciliation between the Sunni sects on one side and Shi'is on the other is due to the latter's disagreement with and contradiction of the rest of the Muslims in the very fundamentals of faith, as we have seen from the declarations of the Shi'is scholars, and as can be seen from the beliefs and practices of every Shi'is. This was the state of affairs in the past, and it is the state of affairs at the present time.[39]

He goes on to identify views and traditions that could be used as evidence against Shi'i claims for possible reconciliation with the Sunnis. One such is a book called *al-zahra'*, written by a number of Shi'is *'ulama*, in which they cite traditions defaming the second Caliph Omar. They claim that, 'he was suffering from a disease, which was treated by male orgasm'. This tradition can also be found in the famous voluminous Shi'is corpus *Bihar al-anwar* (The Oceans of Light) by Shaikh Muhammad Baqer al-Majlisi, a theologian of the Safavid era (d. 1699).

Influenced by al-Khatib, Shaikh bin Jibrin, a senior Wahhabi Saudi scholar and one of the most influential hardliners, suggests 'those who still have doubt about the *rafida* should read the refutations of their beliefs, written by Qafari, al-Khatib's *al-khutft al-'Arida* and Ehsan 'Elahi Zahir's books'.[40]

The former grand Mufti, Shaikh bin Baz, also insists that the Shi'is belong to a different religion and thus, 'As it is impossible to effect a reconciliation between Jews, Christians, Idolists and the Sunnis, then, by the same token, reconciliation is impossible between the *rafida* and the Sunnis'.[41]

In his refutation of Muhammad Bahi's critique of Wahhabism, Muhammad Kahalil al-Harras, a teacher at the Islamic University in Medina, dismissed the accusation that Wahhabism is opposed to the principle of reconciliation, affirming that, 'The Wahhabi movement did not get embroiled in reconciliation with the Shi'is [...] because this reconciliation is groundless as the difference is deeply rooted in the basics and principles of religion'.[42]

Despite Wahhabi insistence on the fundamental differences between the Sunnis and the Shi'is, Wahhabi anti-Shi'is writings show that the two practices that are most provocative to the Wahhabis and perhaps to the Sunnis in general are: *sabb*, public vilification of the first three Caliphs, the Companions, and the Prophet's wives, specifically 'Aisha, the daughter of Abu Bakr and Hafsa, the daughter of Omar; and *rafd*, the repudiation of the legitimacy of the caliphate of the first three Caliphs.

Yet, whether the Wahhabi *'ulama* represent a unified front against Shi'i Islam, and whether there is a distinction between moderate and extremist Wahhabi *'ulama* in the view of the Shi'is remain unanswered questions. It is generally agreed that the divisive tendency within Wahhabism is internal, that is, its teachings draw a clear distinction between true and false Muslims, because the Wahhabis allege that they represent the true followers of the Prophet and his Companions, while other Sunni sects, particularly the Shi'i ones, are beset by innovations and heresies.[43] For the Wahhabi *'ulama*, the universe is divided into two camps: those who are Unitarians (*'ahl al-tawhid*) and those who are *mushrikin*, the people of innovations (*'ahl al bida'*). This rigid categorization shows that it is nearly impossible for the Wahhabis to tolerate other factions within Islam. It appears from various books, *fatwas* and taped sermons that those who do not commit to the guiding framework of Wahhabism are classified, at best, as religiously misguided (*dal*) and, at worst, as infidels.[44]

Nevertheless, until recently, it was difficult to differentiate between moderate and extremist Wahhabi *'ulama* inside Saudi Arabia. We can, however, distinguish between different lines within the Wahhabi religious school. First, there are a number of extremists, such as Shaikh bin Jibrin, Shaikh Abdul Muhsin al-'Ubaikan, Shaikh Nasir al-'Omar and Shaikh al-Hudhaifi, among many other Wahhabi popular *'ulama*. This group draws support from young men who have become prone to violence in order to achieve their aims and who, simultaneously, view the Saudi royal family as corrupt and incompetent. This group believes that the Saudi authorities should not have let the Shi'is perform their innovative practice: the Shi'is should be silenced, forced to revert, killed or expelled from the country.

One Wahhabi individual working for the oil company Aramco asked Shaikh bin Jibrin whether it would be permissible for him to sit with Shi'i workers at the same dining table. Shaikh bin Jibrin replied, 'you should attempt to move to a place where they [i.e. the Shi'i workers] are not; otherwise, you should show them your abomination, disrespect and sarcasm.' He adds, 'you should try to debunk their defective belief, and then you should convince them of the rightness of yours, so they give up their charade; otherwise, they have to face their fate [namely, to be killed].' Bin Jibrin was also asked about the legal validity of paying the *zakat* to Shi'i poor families. He replied, 'In their juristic books, the *'ulama* stipulate that *zakat* should be paid neither to the infidel nor to the innovator; and the *rafida* are undoubtedly infidels.'[45]

Shaikh Nasir al-'Omar, an eminent member of the Salafi extremist trend, harshly opposes the concept of reconciliation with the Shi'is, on the basis of the incompatibility between the Sunni Islam and Shi'ism. He states, 'Our differences with the *rafida* are not merely sectarian ones. We differ with them in principles and fundamentals and not parts of religion [...] In fact, we never agree with them at any point.' In response to the inter-sectarian dialogue that took place in June 2003 in Riyadh, al-'Omar calls, instead, 'for inviting the *rafida* to revert to the true Islam [...] and commit to the method of the people of *Sunna* and *Jama'*.'[46]

Under the heading 'Expel the Jews, Christians and *Rafida* from the Arabian Peninsula', the famous Wahhabi Internet websites published the Friday sermon delivered by the former Prayer Imam of the Prophet's Mosque in Medina, Shaikh Al-Hudhaifi, on 3 March 1998, in the presence of the former Iranian president Hashimi Rafsanjani.[47] Shaikh al-Hudhaifi decried those who advocate reconciliation between the Sunnis and Shi'is, asking:

How could there be reconciliation between the Sunnis, who bear the

Qur'an and the Prophet's tradition, so religion was maintained and glorified, and the *rafida*, who publicly scorn the Companions and thus destroy Islam [...] Unless the Shi'is abjure their beliefs and enter Islam, we, the people of the Sunna and Jama', will not move a step towards them; they are more dangerous to Islam than Jews and Christians and can never be trustworthy; thus Muslims should be extremely cautious towards them.[48]

Second, within the Wahhabi school there are the traditional Wahhabi *ulama*, including members of the old generation such as Shaikh bin Baz and Shaikh Muhammad bin 'Uthimein and some members of the neo-Salafi trend, like Shaikh Safar al-Hawali. Although they adhere to the polemical legacy, from which they derive their views and their antagonistic stance towards the Shi'is, traditional *ulama* do not believe that the Shi'is are to be killed, expelled or forcibly reverted to Wahhabi Islam, as this might lead to anarchy and disorder. They prefer instead to advise the Shi'is to abjure their innovative practices.[49]

The third group, which includes Wahhabi intellectuals such as Abdullah al-Hamid, Abdullah al-Subaih, Abdulaziz al-Qasim and Abdulaziz al-Khudr, began to develop progressive and reconciliatory ideas. Although the trend has not yet crystallized in a socio-religious form, there are many indications that it is rapidly growing within the Wahhabi community.

Al-Hamid, for instance, has devoted a great deal of attention to the promotion of human rights concepts, based upon a different understanding and interpretation of Islamic history and traditions. He asserts that Islam is built upon justice and freedom, two pillars that have supported the spread of Islam. He believes that the Umayyads and the Abbasids did not bring justice and freedom to the regions they invaded; rather they deprived the People of the Book of their rights, and imposed a form of Islam that is not derived from revelation and the experience of the Prophet. Al-Hamid concludes that, 'the Arabian governments and contemporary Salafi movements inherited the legacy [of the Umayyads and the Abbasids], which they advocate, allegedly, in the name of Islam and authenticity'. He warns that '[Arab] rulers forgot that every state that represses freedom will die out, as this repression goes against human temperament [...] and the Salafi movements forgot that every sect that does not fully understand the close relationship between Islam and justice and freedom is distortion of divine revelation'.

As such, civil society institutions cannot be constituted unless freedom of opinion and expression and justice are guaranteed. According to al-Hamid:

> The nullification of ideas that led to the abandonment of the basic freedom of individuals, such as the idea of repression of the people of innovations, [led] to a shattering of the peace among Muslims, and [paved] the way for the emergence of sectarian state.[50]

Al-Hamid throws the blame on some Salafi ancestors who have over-zealously excommunicated Muslims from other sects without profound investigation.[51]

A Salafi activist and a lecturer at Imam Muhammad b. Sa'ud Islamic University emphasizes the importance of commonalities between different groups living in one country. Using psychological theory as a basis, Abdullah al-Subaih argues that the land in which different groups dwell creates amicable feeling, positive emotion and compassion among individuals, which can lead to coexistence and cooperation. He says that, 'maintaining commonalities is a collective responsibility, which requires a high degree of social interaction, permitting plurality and different viewpoints'.[52]

Shaikh Salman al-'Awda, a Wahhabi populist hardliner, has come to the fore since neo-Salafi murmurings began to be heard, shortly after Iraq's invasion of Kuwait in August 1990. In a series of critical lectures, he harshly disdained the Shi'is, whom he equated with infidels.[53] However, since al-'Awda was released from prison in 1998, his thoughts have become significantly more inclined towards moderation and openness. Although he firmly believes that Islamic unity is not realizable, because of deep contradictions, the stances of different groups could be unified: 'There are so many and such significant points of agreement that could be employed and developed instead of highlighting the issues of difference [...] The areas of agreement between many segments of this *Umma* are broad, just like the breadth of this religion, which has unified the divided.'[54] Although this view could be applied solely to the Sunni Muslims, the language used to formulate it is clearly different from the typical Salafi language in such a matter, which was to a great extent pejorative.

I have questioned the leader of the *islah* movement in London, Sa'ad al-Faqih,[55] about the new inclination of Shaikh Salman al-'Awda. He explains that al-'Awda entered into profound discussions with other moderate Salafis such as Shaikh Abdulaziz al-Qasim, 'who helped widen the horizon of his thinking and interest'. He added that, 'al-'Awda is now leaning towards moderation, openness and dialogue'.[56]

Shaikh al-'Awda became an active player in the inter-sectarian dialogue in June 2003, which aimed to facilitate progress towards national reconciliation. In a reversal of his previous stance, Shaikh al-'Awda appealed to the crown prince to bolster moderate Islamic discourse, which is antithetical to extremism and exaggeration. He called for the discourse to be promulgated throughout the country by the use of the media and education.[57]

A Saudi journalist quoted Shaikh al-Saffar during the National Dialogue meeting in Riyadh as saying that, 'he is pleased with the generosity of Shaikh Salman al-'Awda, who asked him for a prolonged meeting to become acquainted and exchange views'. Al-Saffar added, 'Shaikh Salman kindly offered him a ride in his private car to the National Conference' in King Fahad National Library in Riyadh.[58]

However, for many, al-Saffar's compromising attitude seems to have fortified the Saudi political discourse, since he has lost his credentials of being a protester against injustice, corruption and despotism in his country. In the eyes of many, particularly in the West, the Saudis can now claim that their discrimination against the Shi'is is a thing of the past, as they have integrated the leaders of the Shi'is opposition into the political process.

On 17 September 2004, Shaikh al-Saffar denounced the State Department's report on religious freedom in Saudi Arabia. He stated that, 'The Shi'is citizens in the Kingdom of Saudi Arabia reject foreign intervention in the affairs of their state.'[59] Al-Saffar repeatedly rejects any role that the Americans might play in protecting minority rights or promoting democracy in the region. He assumes that the Americans are exploiting minorities' rights in the cause of their project of dominance in the region. Thus he warns 'all Muslims, Arabs and the community in the Eastern Province not to be deceived by the American illusion', namely, promoting democracy and protecting human rights and minorities. Yet he calls for consolidating national unity and eliminating the effects of sectarian discrimination.[60]

In an interview on 20 September 2004 with *alarbiya* website, which is affiliated with the Saudi-owned satellite television channel *alarbiya*, Shaikh al-Saffar claims that the general conditions of the Shi'is have improved remarkably. 'Notable changes have occurred in general conditions since 1994.

Though some problems are not yet resolved, mutual efforts are continuing to resolve them.' He also praised the National Dialogue sponsored by the state, claiming that it had led to interaction between different groups.[61]

The Shi'is' Response

Although the Shi'is legacy is filled with anti-Sunni articles that need to be carefully scrutinized, the leaders of the Reform Movement assigned particular importance to the issue of reconciliation between the Sunnis and the Shi'is. Nearly all the eminent writers of the Movement have published books or articles in both *al-waha* and *al-kalima*, or participated in meetings, conferences or activities in connection with this. Some of the activities are referred to in this chapter.

The writings show that there is consensus among the *islahiyya* leaders on the idea of 'unity within diversity'. Advocating Islamic unity does not entail the elimination of diversity or the melting of different groups into a single one; rather, it means the acknowledgement of difference within the Islamic *umma* on the basis of the principle of *ijtihad*, since no one group can arrogate to itself the exclusive right to speak on behalf of Islam.[62]

The recognition of *ijtihad* as a method of deducing religious stipulations should be the basis for regulating differences among Muslims. If Muslims believe in *ijtihad*, then they should also believe in difference, as *ijtihad* would inevitably bring about disparate jurisdictions. Moreover, the acceptance of *ijtihad* would transform differences from the religious domain to what might be called the secular domain, so they would not be subject to religious criteria for judgement such as *halal* (religiously legal) and *haram* (religiously forbidden), but would be measured by rational criteria such as 'correct' and 'incorrect'. This view corresponds to Shaikh Hassan al-Banna's approach to the issue of the Sunni–Shi'is difference,[63] which seeks to prevent all parties from garbing the result of their *ijtihad* in a religious cloth. In other words, the de-sacralization of the process of *ijtihad* should prevent any sect from monopolizing religion. Freedom of opinion is accepted as a religious value, in the sense that belief and worship would not be valid without freedom. 'The freedom of belief entails continuous coexistence between different sects and schools of thought.'[64]

Therefore, there are three options available for those who subscribe to different sects but live in one state. First, the dominant group can use force to impose its beliefs on other groups; second, each group can alienate itself from other groups and mobilize its followers against them; third, the groups can coexist, which entails reciprocal acknowledgement of each other's rights, including the right to belief.

Endorsing Fuller and Francke's views in their book *The Forgotten Muslims: the Arab Shi'as*, the *islahiyya* Movement espouses the new approach to the Saudi Shi'is, drawing attention to their painful experience, having been victimized by the political conflict between Iran and Saudi Arabia following the Islamic revolution in 1979, and the distortion of their image by both local and international media. The new reading of the Shi'is would, according to *al-waha*, repair their image and provide a catalyst for building national unity.[65]

The leaders of the Reform Movement insist that sectarianism is a constraining force that plagues national unity and the future of the country.[66] Therefore, religious difference should not lead to confrontation and conflict.[67] In an indirect message to the Wahhabi *'ulama*, the *al-waha* editorial warns that, 'the collection of *fatawa*, articles, sectarian books and pamphlets in their present inflammatory form represents explosive materials that are directed against [...] national unity'.[68]

Of the religious culture prevailing in Saudi Arabia, al-Saffar holds it 'responsible for propagating hatred and enmity among people and exaggerating the points of difference, while ignoring the points of agreement'.[69] He calls on Wahhabi clerics to take a courageous initiative to start dialogue and to cope with potential challenges and dangers facing the people.[70] In the 1980s, al-Saffar argues, a climate of hostility prevailed, but the circumstances changed in the 1990s, such that different groups were able to rethink the past and enter into a serious dialogue aimed at resolving disputes.[71]

Al-Saffar asserts that neither the Shi'is nor the Sunna should be judged on the basis of legacy of their ancestors. Instead, they should 'neglect the dark and negative aspect of this legacy and focus on the bright and positive one, which helps both of us to reform our situations and resolve our problems and solidify our unity'. Indeed, such a view, though it appeals to a wide segment of both the Sunna and the Shi'is, is difficult to defend, since neglecting a part of this legacy does not imply it is rejected or abandoned, nor does it change the fact that what is neglected remains a part of the belief system of both sects. In fact, al-Saffar opted for negligence rather than rejection, for fear of provoking the Shi'i traditionalist and stirring up polemical differences between the sects.[72]

The essence of the new orientation of the Reform Movement is the principle of religious plurality. In a long article published in *al-waha* magazine, attention was paid to differences within the Muslim community in the first three centuries of Islam over the fundamental pillars and sources of Islam: the unity of God, the Qur'an, the Sunna, Reason and the Imamate.[73] The article provides a historical review of the different schools of thought and jurisprudence that appeared throughout Islamic history. It argues that during the first three centuries of Islamic history there was a wide spectrum of schools of thought and jurisprudence, but, with the passage of time, creative Islam began to be overshadowed by an imitative and rigid form of Islam. The whole article indicates that Wahhabi attempts to impose its own interpretation of Islam are contradictory to the pluralistic and creative spirit and legacy of Islam.[74]

There is a tiny, yet effective, circle within the Central Committee of the Reform Movement that believes that the prelude to reconciliation between the Wahhabis and the Saudi Shi'is should be self-criticism, since involvement in polemical issues has led each sect to concentrate on the defects of the other, while ignoring or justifying the defects of the self. According to this group, this method has proved unsuccessful in defusing sectarian disputes, a view echoed by Hamid Enayat in his discussion of Shi'i-Sunna polemical debates. He notes that the themes that were debated in the thirteenth century by Ibn Taimiyya and Ibn Mutahar al-Hilli remain unsettled today and, in the last hundred years, Sunna and Shi'is polemicists have resumed the debates based on the same old themes.[75] He also notes that the Sunna–Shi'is polemics do not relate to the essence of Islam or its fundamentals; rather, they are concerned with 'the concrete details of Islamic history, theology, rituals and law'.[76]

The image of Wahhabism in Shi'is writings is equally important, since it reflects the degree to which the Shi'is in Saudi Arabia are willing to be reconciled with Wahhabism. Shi'is writings label Wahhabis as the enemies (*nawasib*) of the household of the Prophet.[77] According to Shi'i jurisprudence, the *nasibi* is tantamount to an infidel.[78]

Although in 1979, Iran, under the leadership of Khomeini, imposed an unofficial ban on any form of abusive anti-Sunni statements in the official political and religious discourse in sermons, books, newspapers, radio or television programmes,[79] an Iranian-based magazine enumerates 200 books and pamphlets on the refutation of Wahhabism, a large number of which were written by Shi'is polemicists.[80] According to some Shi'is publishers, the Eastern Province of Saudi Arabia represents the biggest market for polemical books printed in Lebanon.[81]

The *islahiyya* leaders' advocacy of a reconciliation between the Shi'is and the Wahhabis is not formulated in a comprehensive vision that reflects their conviction. I asked a leading member of the Movement whether he was willing to denounce some Shi'is practices that the Wahhabis see as provocative, such as cursing the three Caliphs and the Companions, in the same way that the Shi'is ask the Wahhabi *'ulama* to denounce their provocative practices. He replied, 'I personally disagree with these practices but my task is not to denounce them but rather to teach the people what their rights are.'[82]

Like the majority of Shi'is intellectuals and activists, the leaders of the Reform Movement assert that sectarian polemical issues should not be debated, as this is a source of provocation for both the Shi'is and the Wahhabis. The latter acknowledged that, 'It is difficult nowadays to find a *rafidi* scholar who curses the Companions.'[83]

Central to the perpetuation of the dispute between the Sunnis and the Shi'is is the impact upon *'ulama* of both sides. Whereas the Sunni *'ulama* are highly influenced by governments, the Shi'is *'ulama* are influenced by the *khums* payers, particularly those Shi'is merchants who finance the activities of the *'ulama*. The Shi'is *'ulama*, being financially supported by the laymen (*muqalidin*), particularly the Shi'is merchants, eschew what might provoke their followers in order to maintain their financial sources and popular support. According to the Iranian thinker Shaikh Murtada Mutahari, since Ayatollah Shaikh 'Abdulkarim al-Ha'iri (d. 1936), the founding father of the Qum *hawza*, considered introducing foreign languages and other modern disciplines to the *hawza* curriculum in order to be able to disseminate Islam among modern educated groups and also in foreign countries, groups of Shi'is came from Tehran to Qum to protest. They claimed that the money paid under the title of Imam's share, which is nearly half of the fifth (*khums*), should not be exploited in learning infidels' languages. They warned that they would take every possible measure to abolish such a plan. Shaikh Hai'ri therefore gave in, in the interests of maintaining the *hawza* intact and stable. The protest against any attempt to change the *hawza* curriculum extended even to minor points relating to issues of moment. Likewise, in Najaf, the senior *'ulama* held a meeting during the reign of Sayyid Abu al-Hassan al-Asfahani (d. 1946) and all agreed upon the need to revise the curriculum in the Najaf *hawza* and inject it with new and modern disciplines. However, this ambitious project ended in failure, as al-Asfahani recalled the experience of al-Hai'ri and chose to avoid the protest of the Shi'is commoners. He wrote to the *'ulama* that the status of the *hawza* should remain unchanged during his lifetime, adding that the Imam's share should be distributed on condition that students adhere to classical Shi'i disciplines such as jurisprudence (*fiqh*) and principles of jurisprudence (*usul al-fiqh*).[84]

According to an article in *al-waha*, Shi'is commoners have an impact upon the *'ulama*, which impedes the process of religious renewal, self-criticism and reconciliation. Elaborating on the idea of the 'authority of the common people', devised by Murtada Mutahari, the article argues that 'the *'ulama* are sometimes misguided by the common people, who provide them with false information about other groups, or ask questions that compel the *'ulama* to reveal their hidden, yet provocative stances towards others'. However, the common people in both sects could play a destructive role in the context of the relationship between the Sunnis and the Shi'is.[85]

Asked about the proliferation of anti-Sunni materials outside the *hussainiya* in which he performs the recitation of *'Ashura*, an eminent Shi'is preacher claims to disagree with such materials, but refuses to declare his position publicly.[86]

It is thus of signal importance to the position of religious leaders on both the Shi'i and the Wahhabi sides that reconciliation emerges within the matrix of their communities, which are still dominated by religious traditions. Should they resolve or regulate disputes, the Shi'is and the Wahhabi leaders might need to break the vicious cycle, namely, the social taboos that restrain them from articulating their real (i.e. more conciliatory) convictions, lest they endanger their popularity.

Shi'is' Dual Loyalty and Identity

The common accusation levelled by the Saudi authorities against the Shi'is is that they are disloyal to the status quo. Indeed, it is commonplace, since the rise of nation-states, for the issue of disloyalty to become associated with minorities who survive discrimination and persecution, particularly in heterogeneous states. Among many factors involved in generating feelings of loyalty, however, is the government's general attitude to the perceived needs and interests of its citizens; loyalty is also related to grievances and the government's integration of individuals into state structures.

A questionnaire conducted during the course of the Hajj in 2000 among a group of randomly selected Shi'is asked them to organize their 'identity choices' in order of importance. Out of some 500 questionnaires distributed among different Hajj groups (*hamalat al-Hajj*), 186 were returned, a response rate of around 30 per cent[87] – not bad in a place where such activities are not permitted without the consent of the Ministry of Information and security devices.

The results obtained give an insight into the general tendency among the Shi'is. Empirical evidence shows that national sentiments rarely manifest themselves among the Shi'is and indeed in this survey a sense of Saudi identity was found to be minimal in comparison to other choices. Identity associations came out as follows: Muslim (69%), Shi'is (22%), Arab (6%), Saudi (2%), Qatifi-Hasawi (1%).

The first conclusion to be drawn from the above is that the accommodative policies that the government has followed have not been effective or, more accurately, have not persuaded the Shi'is to offer their loyalty to the Saudi regime. Indeed, it is conceivable, particularly in a country like Saudi Arabia in which national sentiments and traits are untenable, that loyalty would be offered only for something that is worthwhile, valuable and sound.

It is worth recalling that, in the aftermath of the occupation of al-Hasa in 1913, Shi'is citizens ceased to associate themselves with any foreign forces in seeking protection or securing their culture and legacy. Rather, they forged traditions, practices and mechanisms that were not necessarily guided by religious precepts, but were motivated by the sectarian divisions and the harsh measures inflicted on them by the *ikhwan*. The central objective behind all that was to enhance the sectarian identity of the Shi'is. The sectarian legacy of the Shi'is debarred later generations from interacting with the local community in changed circumstances. Indeed, the Shi'is sectarian legacy made the new generation either reluctant to get rid of the past or lukewarm about the invitation to play a part in the present political arena, equal to other parties, including the government and the Salafis.

The isolation of the Shi'is is not only due to repression but is also an effect of Shi'i teachings, which call upon believers to wait for the reappearance of the occulted Imam and to dissociate themselves from the usurping rulers, namely, all temporal rulers, since just rule would be possible only under the Imam Mahdi.

The focus on the sectarian component of their identity has harmed the reputation of the Shi'is, who are seen as disloyal to their homeland and government. This causes a problem, insofar as their interaction with internal issues is marginal, reflecting their alienation and isolation.

However, in order to foster a common sense of belonging among the cultural communities that make up a multicultural society, four conditions are said to be necessary: constitutional accommodation of diversity; justice; a multiculturally constituted common culture; and a shared sense of loyalty to the political community.[88] So, are these conditions available for the Shi'is to develop a sense of belonging in Saudi Arabia?

The answer can be found in a petition signed by 450 Shi'is figures and submitted to the the then crown prince on 29 April 2003.[89] The petition has a number of very important implications.

First, it is signed by Imami Shi'is from different parts of Saudi Arabia, particularly Qatif, Hasa and Medina. The fact that the Shi'is of Medina were among the signatories is unprecedented and could indicate the revival of a religious alliance between the Shi'is throughout the country, which subscribers to any sect may find effective and reassuring.[90]

Second, it emphasizes the local and national framework and motives of those who signed the petition, as is apparent in the linkage made with a previous petition submitted by a group of liberal and Islamist activists. As the petition coincided with dramatic changes in the region following the fall of Saddam's regime, the signatories strove to dismiss the accusation levelled against the Shi'is that they are affected by external factors and forces. Therefore, while the Shi'is petitioners voice their private demands, they also confirm their commitment to a national framework for the realization of those demands.

Third, the petition went beyond the traditional Shi'is demands and asked for the recognition of Shi'ism as an Islamic sect, equal to other Sunni Islamic sects, and for the participation of the Shi'is in the religious establishments sponsored by the Saudi government, such as the Muslim World League (*rabitat al-'alam al-Islami*), the World Association for Muslim Youth (WAMY), the Higher Council for Mosques, the World Muslim Charity Association and other organizations. In addition, the petitioners appeal to the government to pave the way for reconciliation between Islamic sects in the light of the Islamic Unity Convention issued by the Islamic Jurisprudence Assembly.

Fourth, although the signatories assert their loyalty to the Saudi state, they simultaneously emphasize the principle of citizenship, with all of its political and legalistic implications. 'The Shi'i citizens in the Kingdom of Saudi Arabia are an original integrated part of the entity of this beloved nation, it is their final homeland, they do not have any other alternative and they do not have any loyalty except to it'.

The emphasis on the Shi'is' status as citizens of the Saudi state inevitably highlights the question of inferiority, which was – and still is – a major grievance of the Shi'is. In response to that, there remains the concept of citizenship as a mechanism to assimilate all groups into the state. From the Shi'is' perspective, citizenship is the best source of protection. This source is also central to the stability of the state and to the formation of national identity and unity.

The petition reveals that the status of the Shi'is, since the dialogue between the government and the leaders of the Reform Movement in September 1993, has remained unchanged, in that there are still discriminatory policies against them in terms of education and job allocation, particularly in the military, security and diplomatic spheres. The petition also recalls traditional complaints about restrictions on building mosques and *hussainiya*s, importing or printing religious books and the diminished power of the Shi'is courts.

Fifth, unlike previous petitions raised by the Shi'is scholars and notables, this petition includes political representation and power-sharing among the list of demands. The signatories demand fair representation in the executive power and *shura* Council.

To conclude, the contents of the petition seem to show that the Shi'is demands remained unmet a decade after the dialogue took place. This is not to suggest that the government had completely failed to meet the basic demands of the Shi'is. The truth is that the expectations of the signatories were higher than they had been a decade before. Even their perception and explanation of discrimination were different, since the official restrictions on the building of mosques and *hussainiya*s had been significantly loosened, according to al-Saffar.[91]

Economic Instability

The stereotypical image of Saudi Arabia as a prosperous and stable country is no longer accurate, since the Saudi economy is not as healthy today as it once was. The chronic high budget deficits, which began in 1983 and continued up until 2003, indicate potential problems in the future. The Saudi Minister of Finance announced that the public debt reached 168 billion dollars and was expected to rise to 180 billion by the end of 2002, while the accumulated deficit in the period 1983–99 was 200 billion dollars.[92]

I am not suggesting that the Saudi economy is on the verge of collapse, but certainly that its weakening has social implications that are likely adversely to affect primarily public services. Further, the link between people's socio-economic and political expectations and the government's reduced ability to deliver has impacts on the relationship between the state and society and may lead to irreversible confrontation, particularly if the sluggish efforts to counter economic problems are not stepped up and coupled with vigorous efforts to offer essential social benefits.

The fact that Saudi Arabia is a rentier state, with a poorly performing economy and rising level of unemployment (about 32 per cent), could create serious challenges to accommodating the Shi'is and the population as a whole, especially since the political development permitted by the absolute monarchy lags far behind the expectations of the people and behind the political changes that have already taken place in neighbouring countries, notably Bahrain and Qatar.

Assessment of the Saudi Response

Reconciliation with the Shi'is has led to a significant degree of tranquillity in the Eastern Province, if not in other regions, since the Shi'is always represent a focal point for oppositional activities in the country and thus its potential source of instability. According to Madawi al-Rasheed, reconciliation can 'be interpreted as a pre-emptive strike by the government to prevent the possibility of the Shi'is opposition joining forces with the Wahhabi dissidents'.[93]

The state policy of discrimination towards the Shi'is softened as a response to internal, regional and international political changes, particularly following the 9/11 attacks, the fall of Saddam's regime and the rise of the Shi'is in

Iraq, the growing national reformist trend inside the country that emerged in January 2003, and the escalation of violent acts carried out by the *jihadi* groups allegedly affiliated with al-Qaeda.

A number of licences were granted for the building of Shi'is mosques, the restrictions imposed on ceremonial activities during *'Ashura* were loosened and discrimination against Shi'is applicants to universities, as well as to employment in Aramco, was reduced. In the 2003–4 College Preparatory Program (CPP), Aramco recruited 120 high school graduates, among them 60 Shi'is, some of whom were granted scholarships in the UK, the USA, Canada, Lebanon and Egypt.

Moreover, members of the Reform Movement started to move away from their oppositional stance and engage in activities that could be regarded as reconstruction of the image of the Saudi regime. Three of the editorial team of *al-Jazira al-'Arabiyya* worked for local newspapers (Tawfiq al-Saif for *okaz* based in Jedda, Merza al-Khuwaildi for *al-sharq al-awsat* and Faiq Hani for *al-youm* based in Dammam), while Shaikh al-Saffar writes a weekly article for *al-youm*. Indeed, nearly all *islahiyya* writers and journalists wrote regularly or occasionally for the local newspapers.

Nevertheless, of the twenty journalists and writers of the Reform Movement who returned to the country, only five were officially recruited by local newspapers. The majority of Shi'i writers were either excluded from writing in local newspapers on the basis of official directives issued by the Minister of the Interior or *al-mabahith*, while some of them were allowed to publish their articles but without written contracts.

However, reconciliation is not something that can be attained at once, but requires a series of steps from both sides. Since September 1993, the door has been open for new thinking about the reciprocal demands and objectives of both the Shi'is and the government.

One of the most potent grievances of the Shi'is is that the political system in the country is exclusive. Shi'is opposition groups directly attacked the al-Sa'ud family's domination of the state. The Saudi Shi'is are not fairly represented in the ministerial body, nor in the consultative or regional councils. Based on the most modest estimate of their percentage of the total population (about 10 per cent), the Shi'is' representation would be: three ministers, twelve *shura* members and nearly one third of the regional council in the Eastern Province (where the Shi'is represent, according to some sources, 33 per cent of inhabitants). Currently, the Shi'is are represented by two *shura* members and three regional consultative members, while there are no Shi'is in the ministerial body.

Other realities must be recognized. The Saudi regime is particularly restrictive of the religious practices of the Shi'is, and has banned the import of Shi'is religious literature, while their children are taught the ultra-conservative Wahhabi religious doctrine, which brands their school of Islam as heretical. Moreover, the Shi'is are socially stigmatized; both the government and the Wahhabis consider them apostates. The Saudi royal family has favoured containment but at the same time political exclusion, which has resulted in their marginalization.

This has consequences from the Shi'is side. They are unlikely to hasten to accommodate themselves to a state that stigmatizes them and fails to recognize their religious distinctiveness or their religious rights and freedoms. They are also unlikely to accept the seriousness of a government that has failed to offer the leaders of the Reform Movement a strong sign of commitment to its promises.

The Saudi strategies for dealing with the opposition have ranged from strong security control, co-opting potential dissidents, divide and rule, and ideological flexibility to pseudo-participation. These strategies cannot be described as accommodative and the relationship between the Shi'is and the Saudi regime remains that of subordinate–superordinate. The gains that the Shi'is have made through the alleged process of accommodation have not been enough to induce them to offer the regime loyalty and submission. Unless the Shi'is are represented in the governmental body, the process of accommodation will remain uncertain, as political representation is always a reflection of actual integration. Furthermore, the Shi'is, like any patriarchal community, can be politically integrated only if those at the top of the religious and social hierarchy are included in the government. According to Claude Ake, the ultimate objective of political integration is a considerable degree of stability, which is achievable only if the government is in the hands of what is called an 'elite coalition', that is, a coalition of leaders of all the major social, religious, professional and ethnic groups. This view is based on a belief that consensus can be sought at the leadership level and not at grass-roots level.[94]

Outcomes

Since their return to the homeland in 1993, the leaders of the Reform Movement have successfully used a range of means to encourage Saudi official circles to adopt a different attitude towards the Shi'is. However, the steps taken by the Saudi government to redress the socio-economic and religious conditions of the Shi'is were insufficient to motivate the Reform Movement to accelerate the pace of accommodation. Rather, the pace began to slacken as economic conditions as a whole deteriorated in the country.

The literature of the Wahhabis and the Shi'is clearly shows that both are equally culpable in advancing their interests and failing to resolve their polemical issues. Hence, there is a stand-off. Religious accommodation will remain unattainable unless some compromise is reached.

Indeed, both the Shi'is and the Wahhabi *'ulama* are being challenged to make essential concessions. They must confront misconceptions and hostile attitudes prevalent among their followers if the potential causes of a sectarian rift are to be eliminated. Such ideas turn into combustible compounds when mixed with religious, tribal and regional factors.

The Saudi government could, in its own interests, play a crucial role in calling adversaries of both sides to meet and to suspend their differences for the political good and to avoid endangering the stability and continuity of Saudi rule. No more incentive should be required than the synchronized suicide bombings in Riyadh on 12 May 2003.

The occupation of al-Hasa and Qatif in 1913 and hence the foundation of the Saudi state in 1932 has determined the religious, economic and political status of the Shi'is in the Eastern Province. Although the Shi'is favoured peaceful submission to Saudi rule as a means of obtaining their religious and socio-economic rights, the Saudi rulers persisted in inflicting severe discriminatory measures against their Shi'is subjects, in order to consolidate their rule.

Inevitably, the Eastern Province became liable to unrest, particularly during big religious occasions, notably *'Ashura* days, which called for a strong police presence. The discriminatory policies of the al-Sa'ud towards Shi'is subjects led many discontented Shi'is individuals to protest against the regime and to join resistance groups to lobby the government.

The regime's uncompromising attitude created among the Shi'is a sense of distinctiveness but also of powerlessness and danger, as well as growing concern about the unfair treatment and discriminatory treatment meted out to them by the Saudi rulers in social, economic and political spheres.

The sense of danger among the Shi'is has been intensified by the growing tendency among the Wahhabi religious community and the Saudi royal family to insist that private identity contains two essential components: Wahhabi Islam and loyalty to the royal family. These components may have appealed to those who joined Ibn Sa'ud's troops and contributed to the realization of his political ends, but to other regions and groups they seem to imply the abandonment of their own identity. The policy has had two opposite consequences for the Shi'is: one has been to enhance their unity and solidarity, the other to isolate them, along with many other groups, from the state.

The conventional assumption that Islam must have played a central role in the unification of the country and continued to do so after the foundation of the state seems mistaken and dismissive of the country's religious heterogeneity. The dominant group's failure to promote national identity based on the political, economic and cultural integration of different groups into the state structure has only alienated these groups and encouraged them to cling to their traditional identities.

The emergence of the IRO in 1979 is considered a turning point in the history of the Shi'is in the Eastern Province and also in that of the Shi'is' opposition in Saudi Arabia. As an offspring of an Islamic movement founded in Karbala in 1968, the IRO represented the universal Islamic socio-religious vision formulated by the leaders of the MVM for the pursuit of its goals, namely, the formation of a faithful human vanguard that would establish an Islamic civilization.

In response to the perceived crisis of the Islamic *umma*, the IRO asserted the notion of a comprehensive Islam, in the hope of eradicating the roots of *jahiliyya* and strengthening a modern Islam and so appealing to wider segments of people who had been subjected to secular orientations.

The adoption of a more progressive and revolutionary interpretation of the central doctrines of Shi'ism (*intizar, taqiyya, ghayba, 'Ashura* and so on) created potential supporters who, for a long time, had been religiously alienated because of the dominance of passive Shi'ism. After the *intifada* in 1979, Shi'is religious conservatism, which advocates withdrawal from politics, was challenged by a revolutionary trend emanating from religious circles. This trend denounced religious conservatism as reactionary and an obstacle to the progress of Shi'is communities. There emerged a new climate in which recruitment of individuals from all over the Gulf's Shi'is was possible with the goal of seizing power and establishing an Islamic state.

The *intifada* was a turning point in the relationship between the Shi'is and the government; naturally this could not have happened if the leaders of the IRO had not played a major role in stimulating a large proportion of the Shi'is to challenge the government's repressive measures. In this respect, the leaders of the *intifada* have altered the popular image of Shi'ism, from passive to active, and therefore Shi'ism has become an ideology of social protest.

With the decline of revolutionary impetus in 1989 (following the ceasefire between Iran and Iraq); the internal disputes within the leadership of the MVM; and the proliferation of new ideas, such as transparency, *glasnost*, human rights and democratic reforms, the political ideology of the Reform Movement began charting a more pragmatic course in politics after its separation from the MVM. Its shift to moderation implied that it was able to acknowledge and assimilate modern notions and so effectively deal with new problems as they arose in the country.

Although the *islahiyya*'s adoption of the democratic option was meant to serve its private demands and not necessarily to be the basic principle of the political system in an Islamic state, the new orientation would benefit the whole population and thus secure their political and religious rights. Indeed, the advocacy of democracy and human rights formed common ground for both the *islahiyya* Movement and a wide range of groups in Saudi Arabia, especially the liberal and nationalist ones. As the *islahiyya* Movement succeeded in affirming the national dimension of its activities, rhetoric and goals, it was also able to share common concerns, interests and roles with groups from different ideological persuasions. This has become clear with the sharp decline of political, socio-economic and security conditions and the erosion of the welfare state since 2001, as the sense of deprivation has engulfed many groups. The inclination of the *islahiyya* Movement to establish itself as a national mainstream movement has helped to strengthen its options in national and local politics. As a result, it has succeeded in creating links with other national political groups, fostered a different outlook towards the Shi'is within Saudi official circles and national political groups, and contributed to improved relations between the Shi'is and some groups and regions.

As already noted, however, the conflict between the Shi'is and the Wahhabis persists, since the resolution of disputes between them would require a complex combination of efforts. Both sides seem unable either to advance their interests or to tone down their sectarian polemics. Fear of the price of compromise has made the leaders of both sects reluctant to touch upon issues that are deeply rooted in the thinking, attitude and vision of their followers. For example, the Shi'is distinguish themselves by their belief in Imam Ali's right to the succession to Muhammad, which accordingly leads to their belief in the usurpation of the first three Caliphs. The Wahhabis, for their part, still believe that the Shi'is are associationists and *rafida*, as they resist acknowledging Sunni Islam, including the succession of the first three Caliphs and the status of the Prophet's wives, 'Aisha and Hafsa, as mothers of the believers, and show disrespect for a number of Companions. Failure to resolve these issues inevitably leaves the dispute between the Shi'is and the Wahhabis unresolved. Religious figures from both sides have made serious efforts, yet compromise entails self-criticism and a reassessment of the sectarian legacy that is responsible for sectarian disputes, and tensions cannot be eliminated by mere intellectual dialogues like the one held in Riyadh in June 2003. The Saudi government itself could and should take the lead in trying to resolve this problem.

The Saudi state was threatened with disintegration and chaos by internal economic, political and security crises, in addition to a dramatic change in the geopolitics of the Gulf region following the occupation of Iraq in May 2003. National and Islamist forces from various regions strove to form a united front to urge the government to introduce essential reforms. Although collaboration between the liberals, the moderate Salafis and the Shi'is was motivated by political considerations, there are many indications that the Shi'is have become a main player in the Saudi national sphere. They were the real architects of the petitions that were submitted to the then crown prince Abdullah (the present king) throughout 2003 and signed by a group of reformists, notably 'A Vision for the Nation's Present and Future' and 'for Defending the Nation', in January and September 2003, respectively. Both petitions have gained unprecedented support from a large number of Saudis, mainly because their content reflects their aims and expectations.

R. Dekmejian suggests that Shi'is participation in the so-called *wathiqat al-ru'ia*, or 'the petition of vision', is 'a dramatic indicator of the changes in

Saudi society in the last decade, which included greater tolerance of the Shi‘is minority.[95] It is also an indicator that the Shi‘is are exploiting the new political climate to participate in national activities as a means of achieving their goals.

So far, it is clear that the Saudi government has made remarkable progress in political reform. Throughout 2003, a series of events occurred that resulted in the emergence of three non-governmental organizations (NGOs), the announcement of local elections and the establishment of the King Abdulaziz Centre for National Dialogue. Freedom of expression has improved since; Shi‘is religious ceremonies and festivals received unprecedented media coverage during Muharram 2004. Many foreign reporters visited the Eastern Province during the days of *'Ashura* and interviewed Shi‘is mourners who were pleased at the religious freedom they were able to enjoy. Censorship of critical articles in the local press about internal issues has been partly lifted. The reporters and writers on quality daily newspapaers such as *al-Watan* and *Riyadh* have commented on the tangible change in their freedom of expression and the contribution of the press to creating a culture of reform.[96]

On the other hand, steps taken by the Saudi government to redress the socio-economic and political conditions of the Shi‘is have been meagre and, indeed, not motivating. This may be, as noted above, because of the decline in state revenue, but that is no consolation to the Shi‘is, who, having been deprived for decades, fear that discrimination against them at this stage would make them suffer more.

We must remember that political, religious and socio-economic changes are always liable to be reversed. In a country like Saudi Arabia, where the king and the royal family as a whole have a paramount role in national politics, reforms of any sort cannot be guaranteed. The empirical evidence of the sudden set-back in March 2004 suggests that the movement towards political inclusion, freedom of expression and human rights was on the point of collapse. Many Saudis viewed the arrest of a number of prominent reformers on 15 March as a disappointing indicator that the hope of reforms had been dashed. Moreover, a series of press conferences given by high-ranking princes confirmed that the royal family had determined to reverse the current of reforms.[97] Crown Prince Sultan, the Minister of Defence and Aviation, repeatedly announced that, 'No election will be held in regard to the *shura* Council ... we will appoint whoever is good for the people.'[98]

At a private meeting on 23 March 2004, Prince Naif, the Minister of the Interior, was provocative and outrageous. He began by praising the history of the royal family and its right to rule the country. He emphasized the role of his father in eradicating the dissidents, namely the *ikhwan*, in 1928. He threatened those present (about fourteen people) that he and his family would not tolerate any more acts by that group. 'This state,' he declared, 'was unified by the sword, and whoever opposes the state, let him show himself if he owns a sword.'[99]

By arresting widely respected, moderate figures, the government has, according to Mai Yamani, 'made a mockery of its claims about moving the political process forward, its promises of a more open society and its desire to play a full part in global bodies such as the World Trade Organization'. As a result of such arrests, Yamani suggests, Saudi Arabia's high-profile public relations operation to sell its vision of political reform to a sceptical West has collapsed.[100]

It is also worth noting that the crown prince, who was described as the initiator of reforms in the Saudi Kingdom, has become a falling star, according to a Hijazi political group,[101] and has failed even to comment on the arrest of the reformers, though he supported their demands and promised to meet them. Indeed, with the arrest of the reformers, many Saudis have become convinced that the crown prince's capacity to act was overestimated, as he failed to follow through on his promises of reform that he had announced on various public occasions.

The focus on the crown prince's role has been misleading. A number of Saudi political activists have seen him as the symbol of liberalization in the royal family. Although he has shown nominal support for political reforms in the country, he has not taken the expected initiative. In addition, his call for reform should be read in the context of the internal tensions that the country saw following the 9/11 atrocities.[102] The rising level of violence and international pressure imposed on the royal family, in addition to the growing popular demand for reforms, forced the government to loosen its grip on the media and local press in order to contain the storm. With its success in the fight against violent groups, the hard-line princes, namely the Seven Sudairies (King Fahad and his six full brothers), were encouraged to continue trying to eliminate the dangers facing their rule from other groups, such as moderate liberal reformers.

Any analysis of the Saudi state must examine the mechanisms and institutions by which individuals and groups have access to state apparatus. Both the increase in the people's expectations and the search for a degree of autonomy by many groups (e.g. Hijazis, the Imami Shi'is in the Eastern Province and the Ismailis in the South), on the one hand, along with the state's persistence in confining the running of the state to the royal family and a very small group of its allies, on the other, keep the options for all excluded groups open. This could lead to a future marked by new forms of coalition, social protest and, eventually, unexpected changes. It is clear now that the Saudi state is without a nation, and this could result in disintegration. Thus, how each group perceives the state, how it thinks for the future and what options these groups will follow remain vitally important. It may be that the covert ambition for the Shi'is, like other deprived and underprivileged communities, would be secession if the structures of the Saudi state begin to disband.

Indeed, with the Saudi government failing to offer essential political and socio-economic reforms to pacify the majority of its people, the country is destined to witness a rise in violent acts, organized political groups and even, in some parts of the country, political protest that could lead to the decline of order as a preliminary form of separation, as the riots of Juof in the northeast of Saudi Arabia may indicate.[103]

Thus, I suggest that future research should deal with questions relating to the future of the state, rather than its past and present, as many uncertainties will accumulate, starting with the relationship between state and society, socio-economic conditions, political participation and representation, national identity and, finally, the fate of the Saudi state itself.

New King: A Challenge of Reform

The accesssion of Abdullah to the throne on 1 August 2005, immediately after the death of his brother Fahad, who had been ill since suffering a stroke in 1996, signalled a new era for the country. This came after a decade in which power had been concentrated in the hands of an ailing king, leading to political stagnation and socio-economic hardship. The shift of power potentially diffused the monopoly held by the so-called 'Seven Sudairies', the full brothers of the dead king, Fahad.

Two significant events occurred in the early period of King Abdullah's reign. The first was the increase in oil prices, leading to a significant economic improvement, which has been reflected in the rise of state revenues[1] and the abundance of money in local markets and stocks.[2] The second was the notable progress in the war on terror achieved by recourse both to force and persuasion. At that time, the legitimacy of the Saudi regime was in question since the eruption of violence on a large scale by Salafi groups, linked with the al-Qa'ida network, which were logistically sponsored and ideologically supported by prominent religious figures who are part of the traditional and state-supervised religious establishment.

As a result, the government restored much of its image, tarnished since the 9/11 attacks, by using harsh measures against political activists in March 2004, as well as by choking off the sources of violence and encouraging members of al-Qa'ida to transfer their *jihad* operations to Iraq. These developments coincided with a significant economic improvement stemming from an increase in oil prices, but they also had a direct impact on the role, policy and agenda of the new king, who seemed to be the only reformer in the Saudi royal family. However, the portrayal of King Abdullah as a reformer was based on an obsequious acceptance of his promises, not on actual moves towards reform.

Ultimately, the recent political stability has been anchored not in a comprehensive strategy combining security measures with social, political and institutional reform but rather in economic factors, specifically the rise of oil prices, which boosted the power and credibility of the royal family, following a decade of turbulence. Whereas the local and, to some extent, the outside media paid a great deal of attention to the smooth transfer of power to the new king, little if any was directed to the recurrent issues that King Abdullah must urgently tackle, including the distribution of power within the royal family and social and political reforms.

Before coming to the throne, Abdullah took a significant initiative by sponsoring the newly established King Abdul Aziz Center for National Dialogue, which carried out a series of conferences on reforms, women, youth and attitudes towards non-Muslims, which were held in different cities and attended by many intellectuals from all over the country. At the end of each conference, Abdullah invited all participants to give him recommendations. This was described as 'an opportunity for open discussion on what used to be considered crucial and sensitive issues, such as national identity, pluralism, social and political reform, and women's rights.'[3]

However, the government has not yet adopted any of the recommendations drafted by the conferences. The direct involvement of King Abdullah in the arrangements for power has given the impression that political reform is not an imperative, as it requires changes in the political and economic constructs. By contrast, some might argue that the question of political reform will not be resolved unless the disputes within the royal family are settled.

Central questions about the future direction and success of King Abdullah's reign remain. Fahad's era had a long history of socio-economic and political problems. Prof. Madawi al-Rasheed argues that King Abdullah will not be able to play a heroic role, as he will be overshadowed by the dominance of the previous regime and its sweeping impact on state structures.[4]

Similarly, some perceive Abdullah as a figurehead without real power.[5] According to al-Hijaz magazine, 'Abdullah lacks will and competence to initiate serious and effective political reforms; he is an elderly person with no time left for reforms.'[6]

Pessimists argue that Abdullah is not a reformer and never was, and that, even if he had the will, there is little time for him to instigate a fundamental transformation in the country. Instead, he will remain wedded to the hereditary traditions and proceed towards change with the utmost calculated caution lest there be any unexpected consequences. By contrast, Khalil al-Khalil, a senior adviser to King Abdullah, claims that the system of government and executive order will be essentially renewed. He states that, 'during the reign of King Abdullah, Saudi Arabia will transform into a state of law'.[7]

As for the Shi'is in the Eastern Province, King Abdullah represents a not-to-be repeated opportunity and hope for redressing their socio-economic and political conditions. A delegation of prominent Shi'i scholars met with King Abdullah in Jeddah in September 2005 to pledge allegiance and plead for the release of prisoners. However, the Shi'i prisoners were still in jail, whereas a large number of Salafi prisoners involved in violent acts were released in accordance with the recommendation of the so-called Advice Committee (*lajnat al-munasaha*) set up by the Ministry of the Interior and led by senior Wahhabi scholars. The grievances of the Shi'is in the country are publicly expressed in the websites and foreign press.[8]

It seems that expectations of King Abdullah, in terms of political reforms, were too high. It was the king himself and his entourage who created this image of the ruler as reformist. He is the first Saudi king to have used the word *islah* (reform) in the official political context, and he is also the only member of the royal family to have adopted a reformative initiative during the Arab Summit held in Beirut in March 2002. He has also notably fought against profligacy and corruption within the royal family.

Abroad, the US administration showed timid support for democratic change in Saudi Arabia. Indeed, the American democratic rhetoric sharply reduced after talks between the leaders of the two countries in Dallas in April 2005. The agreement between Abdullah and Bush revealed Saudi willingness to pump oil at Washington's behest, to increase Saudi investments in the United States and to collaborate closely with the US in its efforts to fight terror.[9] According to some observers, King Abdullah's generous offers to President Bush had an immediate impact on the rhetoric of American officials, who, for several weeks before the meeting, had repeatedly blamed themselves for supporting despotic regimes in the Middle East and promised remorse and penitence. However, the atonement did not occur and the Saudi offers were sufficient to silence the demands for reforms within the Bush administration. Abdullah stated in an interview with *Le Monde* on 12 April 2005 that he aimed to transform Saudi Arabia into a democratic state within twenty years, and reforms could not be imposed from the outside![10]

Similarly, Crown Prince Sultan dashed the hopes of many in the country by denying ministerial change and reforms. He stated on 25 December 2005 that, 'we are not against elections, and we are not less advanced than those countries with elections, yet public interest entails that people support their wise leadership for the interest of the people now and hereafter.'[11] Evidently Sultan holds that reforms are in contrast with public interest, that is to say, he supports the king.

The evidence is that King Abdullah is a minor and reluctant reformer. Apart from allowing the release of three leading reformers on 8 August 2005, he has shown no firm determination to commit himself to a reforming agenda. According to the Salafi reformer Shaik Muhsen al-Awaji, 'the amnesty decree does not imply that King Abdullah will take more serious steps in the path of reforms.'[12] This accords with the view of a former deputy minister of finance and member of a consultative council, Abdulaziz 'Urai'r, who does not 'expect significant changes' during the reign of Abdullah.[13]

One serious indication of the trend of Abdullah's rule is the disappearance of prominent reformers from the Saudi political scene since the arrest of 12 leading reformers on 16 March 2004. It could be that their disappearance relates to their disappointment in the national reformist trend and distrust of King Abdullah, who once told a delegation of reformers that, 'your vision is my project'. However, his project seems to have made a sharp turn in another direction. King Abdullah may be concentrating his efforts on economic issues, as this could hinder the tempo of political demands.

It is widely believed that the revival of a rentier state would inevitably delay the process of reforms, if not nullify them for some time. Immediately after assuming power, King Abdullah decreed a 20 per cent rise in the salaries of civil servants, followed by 5,000 scholarship grants to US universities, many of them given to Shi'is, in addition to an increase in allocations to families on social security. Also, the ban on the participation of Saudi women in the socio-economic sphere was partially lifted, though they have a long way to go to attain their full political and social rights. Abdullah's speech to the nation following his accesssion focused on 'enforcing the right, implementing justice and serving citizens without discrimination'.[14]

There seems to be widespread agreement that Abdullah intends to tackle the major problems, yet many still doubt that he has the power to turn the words into deeds and the dreams into realities.

The Saudi experience shows that economic welfare was used as an alternative to political reforms. With the rise of oil prices and tangible economic improvement, which will give new life to the rentier state, King Abdullah seems set to devote his efforts to improving the living conditions of the people, albeit at a slow pace and in conformity with the traditions of the royal family.

Ultimately, the challenges facing the Saudi kingdom are not easy to tackle, and King Abdullah's keenness needs to be translated into a profound reformative agenda in order to rebuild the state on a truly national basis.

Appendix

A petition was submitted to the Crown Prince Abdullah (the present king), on 29 April 2003 and signed by 450 Shi'is, among whom were 151 businessmen, 42 academics, 50 religious scholars, 24 women and 31 journalists and writers.

Partners in One Nation

His Royal Highness Prince Abdullah bin Abdelaziz al-Saud
The Crown Prince, Deputy Prime Minister and Head of the National Guards
Peace and the mercy of Allah upon you

Deriving from religious and national responsibilities, and from the duty of solidarity and advice, particularly at this crucial time, and because of our belief in the Kingdom's dignity and that the protection of its unity is a shared responsibility between the leadership and the people, therefore, we present to Your Highness some of the nation's concerns and the hopes of its citizens. We fully trust your good understanding and eagerness to discover the sincere and true way of thinking, which intends to promote goodwill and reforms. We would like to take this opportunity to declare solidarity with our nation and its noble leadership in the face of threats and challenges.

We declare our appreciation of your generous gesture of meeting some of the intellectuals and informed elites from among the citizens of our country. We also consider that your welcome to their project, 'Focus for the Present and Future of the Nation', which includes the views and seeks to promote the well-being of the citizens, is a good sign, which makes hearts full of hope for a better future.

In this initial reading, we rely on deep and wide national awareness, which considers the treatment of the sectarian situation in our homeland as a significant sign in the path of reform and development. We look to solving this problem as a national and collective responsibility in which all the citizens of the country must participate.

First: The Enhancement of the Nation's (Umma) Unity

At this stage, our Arab and Islamic nation faces the most dangerous challenges. There is a massive global hostile campaign intended to give a false image of Islam and Muslims. Additionally, the Zionist crimes were unleashed in the Palestinian Occupied Territories, at the time when the American and British forces started their intensive attack against Iraq, with no consideration given to the Security Council and the United Nations and world opinion, and they are raising their threats to other Arab and Islamic countries.

The nation (*Umma*) is targeted in its being, interests and its holy aspects; the threat surrounds all of us, no matter how different are the sects and directions. This requires that we stand collectively, shoulder to shoulder, before these severe challenges.

However, religious and sectarian conflict remains a tool to destroy the nation's unity. It will hinder national solidarity and cooperation. Additionally, it will keep major segments of the people involved in this conflict and divert their attention from the real issues.

The Kingdom of Saudi Arabia, with its distinguished role of leadership in the Arab and Islamic world, resulting from having and serving the two holy mosques and enjoying a leadership that is concerned about Islamic solidarity, is expected to play a major role in eliminating sectarian conflicts and in bridging the differences between religious sects.

Failure to achieve this task and allowing such unpleasant and fanatical tendencies to flourish make our country liable to earn a bad reputation and to look like a partner in this conflict.

Therefore, a moment of thought is required to erase the confusion and to enhance the shining face of our country, as a centre for the whole Muslim world and as a force for Islamic solidarity. That will prevent the followers of different religious sects from making a hostile stand against the country.

According to our views, the following actions will help in attaining this objective:

Issuing a clear declaration indicating the Kingdom's respect for all Islamic sects, including the Shi'i.

Opening up to all the various Islamic sects access and representation in all Islamic institutions supervised by the Kingdom, including the Muslim World League (*Rabitat al-'Alam al-Islami*), the World Association for Muslim Youth (WAMY), Higher Council for Mosques, World Muslim Charity Association and other organizations that are concerned with general Islamic and human affairs.

Encouraging communications between the Saudi religious bodies and the Muslim religious leaders from other sects, in order to achieve convergence and acquaintance between Islamic sects. This can be guided by the Islamic Union Covenant issued by the Islamic Jurisprudence Council – Resolution No. 98 (1/11) dated 25 Rajab, 1419

AH, and by the Strategy of Approximation between the Islamic Sects founded by experts in the Islamic Organization for Education, Sciences and Culture (ISESCO).

Second: National Unity

The dramatic changes taking place in the region and the world today are intensifying the pressure from world superpowers, which talk in no uncertain terms about changing the political map in the region, disassociation of entities and disintegration of countries. To face this pressure, it is necessary to ensure national unity and solidarity, to enhance and activate it practically with what may ensure protection and solidarity on the internal front, prevent enemies' penetration and frustrate their efforts to stimulate any misguided separatist tendencies.

Your Royal Highness,

The Shi'i citizens in the Kingdom of Saudi Arabia are an original integrated part of the entity of this beloved nation. It is their final homeland; they have no alternative and they have no loyalty except to it. They have taken the initiative to join it without any hesitation or objection, since King Abulaziz, may Allah rest him in peace, founded this country and they put all their abilities and fortunes toward the building of the nation. They are looking forward to justice, security, equality and stability.

In these difficult circumstances, they give assurance of their loyalty to their nation. Out of their adherence to national unity and their concern for the development and future of their homeland arises their belief that these issues require quick treatment, and such issues have been repeatedly and frequently submitted to Your Highness and all the honourable officials.

1. The Shi'i citizens look forward to being equal with the rest of the citizens and to having the opportunity to serve their homeland in all fields. Some levels and a number of governmental agencies and departments exclude Shi'i citizens, such as the military, security and diplomatic arenas. Women are excluded from any administrative positions, even the Girls' Section of the Ministry of Education. This is a kind of sectarian discrimination that is admitted neither by Islamic *shari'a* (Islamic Laws) nor by international convention. It deprives the Shi'i citizens of a natural right as well as depriving the homeland of the opportunity to benefit from their abilities and capabilities.

    Educational programmes provided by the government have developed the abilities and capabilities of their sons as all citizens. What leads to frustration and pain is that the Shi'is' capabilities are not recognized equally and they have fewer opportunities than other nationals, who are advancing in different locations and positions in the government agencies. The Shi'is are disregarded and marginalized because of sectarian policies.

To deal with this issue, we propose the following:

A. The efforts of the officials to clearly ensure equality between all citizens regardless of their sects or areas.
B. The urgent formation of an authorized national committee, including qualified Shi'is, to study the problem of sectarian discrimination and treat it by allowing Shi'i representation in higher government positions, such as the Council of Ministers, ministerial deputies, diplomatic posts, military and security fields, and by elevating their participation in the Consultative Council (*Majlis al-Shura*).
C. Incrimination and condemnation of the practice of sectarian discrimination that may be committed by the prejudiced and the privileged anywhere in the country, and making all necessary laws relevant to this measure, in addition to the cancellation of all previous circulars and discriminatory administrative procedures.
D. Stopping all unlawful security procedures such as arrest, pursuance, interrogation, deprivation of travel, detention at the borders and intrusive personal frisking, and endeavouring to relieve the effects of previous arrests.

2. Our country is suffering from the existence of sectarian fanatical tendencies stimulating hatred and aversion against other Islamic sects and followers, particularly the Shi'is. The religious educational curricula at schools and universities repeatedly describe the other Islamic sects and their opinions – Shi'is and others – as disbelievers, polytheists, deviants and heretics.

Religious programming and the official media are exclusive to one sect, propagating a culture of non-acceptance of the other Islamic sects and insulting their followers. This policy is applied in most of the religious bodies in the country such as the legal courts and in the institution of public morality and centres of mission and guidance.

Many instigative *fatwas* (legal opinions) have been issued by some of these bodies against Shi'i citizens. In addition, a large number of books of similar tendency have been – and still are being – printed and distributed, as well as numerous sermons and lectures.

This continuous instigation has educated generations in fanaticism and spite, and created an atmosphere of hatred and animosity between the citizens of the one nation, which creates anxiety for the future of national unity, social peace and security. External powers may benefit from feeding this atmosphere and utilize it against our country's interests. What happened in some other Muslim countries, which suffered civil wars and severe sectarian conflicts, must not happen here.

To confront this serious situation, we hope that the government will adopt the following measures:

A. Put an end to these fanatical tendencies and practices, starting with the educational curricula, the media and official religious bodies.
B. Adopt a cultural national policy announcing toleration, recognition and acknowledgment of the sectarian variety in the county, ensuring respect for human rights and the citizen's dignity and his religious and intellectual freedom.
C. Confirm deterrent procedures to incriminate and condemn any form of instigation to hatred between citizens or to insult different Islamic sects.
D. The leaders to make an official announcement assuring the Shi'is' rights in the Kingdom and equality with other citizens.

3. When the government recognizes the citizenship of its people, regardless of their different sects and areas, and bears the responsibility of taking care of them and protecting their interests, this means that they practise under state laws their right to worship according to their own teachings and to perform their religious rituals. Shi'i citizens in the Kingdom are still suffering from restrictions in performing their religious rites, they find difficulty in building mosques and *hussainiyas* (community halls) and they have no cultural freedom, as they are not allowed to print their books or bring them from outside or found any religious centre.

The powers and authorities of the judges of the two courts of endowments and inheritance in Qatif and al-Ahsa are greatly diminished by the interference of the *shari'a* Great Courts (the official government Sunni courts).

In some areas such as Medina, Shi'i citizens are suffering severe restrictions, which are not acceptable or justified.

These pressures and constraints contribute enormously to the infuriation and irritation Shi'i citizens feel and to decreasing their human, religious and citizenship rights. This also gives the opportunity to our enemies to defame the image and reputation of our country.

For the treatment of these problems, we propose the following:

A. Establishing an official body subordinated to the Ministry of Endowments and Islamic Affairs, similar to the Court of Religious Endowments and Inheritances subordinated to the Ministry of Justice, under the supervision of Shi'i scholars, to organize their religious and cultural affairs under the care of the government.
B. Cancellation of all restrictions on religious rites, and giving the freedom to print or publish Shi'i books and printed matter, and admitting their freedom of opinion.

C. Allowing Shi'i citizens to exercise their right to religious education and to establish their institutions and colleges for religious education according to their sect.

D. Application of the royal decrees calling for the Shi'is' freedom to refer to their *shari'a* courts and to give these courts suitable legal executive power.

May God protect you and keep our country away from any adversity and perpetuate God, Grace of Security and Belief, under the shade of the Custodian of the Two Holy Mosques' care and Your Excellency Crown Prince and venerable Government.

Peace be upon you.

Copy with special regards to His Excellency Prince Sultan bin Abdelaziz al-Saud, Second Deputy of the Council of Ministers, the Minister of Defence and Aviation and General Inspector.

Copy with special regards to His Excellency Prince Talal bin Abdelaziz al-Saud, President of AGFAND.

Copy with special regards to His Excellency Prince Nawaf bin Abdelaziz al-Saud, President of General Intelligence.

Copy with special regards to His Excellency Prince Naif bin Abdelaziz al-Saud, Minister of the Interior.

Copy with special regards to His Excellency Prince Salman bin Abdelaziz al-Saud, Governor of Riyadh.

Copy with special regards to His Excellency Prince Ahmed bin Abdelaziz al-Saud, Deputy Minister of the Interior.

Copy with special regards to His Excellency Prince Moqrin bin Abdelaziz al-Saud, Governor of Medina.

Copy with special regards to His Excellency Prince Saud al-Faisal bin Abdelaziz al-Saud, Minister of Foreign Affairs.

Copy with special regards to His Excellency Prince Mohammad bin Fahd bin Abdelaziz al-Saud, Governor of the Eastern Province.

Copy with special regards to His Excellency Prince Abdelaziz bin Fahd al-Saud, State Minister, Member of the Council of Ministers and Head of Council of Ministers' Office.

Note: A leading signatory to the petition made this translation from Arabic to English.

Notes

Introduction
  1. *Taqiyya* means, in essence, concealment of belief.

Chapter 1
  1. Saudi Arabia possesses a quarter of the world's proven oil reserves, and oil revenues make up around 90–95% of the total Saudi export earnings (and around 35–40% of the country's gross domestic product GDP). See: www.eia.doe.gov/emeu/cabs/saudi.html
  2. R. K. Ramazani, 'Shi'ism in the Persian Gulf', in Juan R. I. Cole and Nikki Keddie (eds), *Shi'ism and Social Protest* (New York, 1986), p. 45.
  3. Uzi Rabi and Joseph Kostiner, 'The Shi'is in Bahrain: Class and Religious Protest', in Ofra Bengio and Gabriel Ben-Dor (eds), *Minorities and the State in the Arab World* (London, 1999), p. 172; Introduction, in Cole and Keddie (eds), *Shi'ism and Social Protest*, p. 3.
  4. See Jacob Goldberg, 'The Shi'i Minority in Saudi Arabia', in Cole and Keddie, *Shi'ism and Social Protest*, p. 230.
  5. *Saudi Country File 1992–93*, The Economist Intelligence Unit, p. 9.
  6. http://islamicweb.com/beliefs/shia_population.htm 22/01/1421–2000, p. 2; *2000 Annual Report on Religious Freedom: Saudi Arabia*, issued by Bureau of Democracy, Human Rights and Labor, US Department of State, 5 September 2000. http://www.state. gov/www/global/human_right/index., accessed on 23 March 2001
  7. Ibid.
  8. According to estimates of 1998 in *Shi'i in Saudi Arabia,* published in June 1999, the Shi'is number 3,118,000, 15% of the total population of 20,786,600. http://www.bsos.umd. edu/cidcm/mar/saudishii.htm.
  9. Angelo M. Codevilla, 'Heresy and History', *The American Spectator*, 14 May 2004.
  10. According to a member of the Permanent Committee of Proselytizing, Religious Jurisdiction and Guidance, Shaikh Saleh al-Fawzan, the great majority of humanity is embroiled in *kufr* and *shirk*. See: Shaikh Saleh b. Fawzan al-Fawzan, *Kitab al-Tawhid* (The Book of Theology; Riyadh, 2003), financed by the Saudi Minister of Defence and Aviation, Prince Sultan b. Abdulaziz, pp. 9, 24, 32, 34, 58–59, 93–95.
  11. It should be pointed out that, with the exception of Wahhabi traditionalists, contemporary Muslim scholars discounted the conventional interpretation of certain Qur'anic verses in regard to staging war against Jews and Christians.
  12. Ali al-Wardi, *Lamahat 'Ejtima'iyya min Tarikh al-'Iraq al-Hadith* (Social Aspects of Modern Iraqi History; London, 1991), p. 182.
  13. Ibn Ghanam, *Rawdat al-Afkar wa al-Afham* (Riyadh, 1947), vol.1, p. 244.

14. Sulaiman Ibn Sahman, *Minhaj Ahl al-Haq wa al-'Etiba' fi Mukhalafat Ahl al-Jahl wa al-'Ebtida* (The Method of Rightly Guided People in Opposing the People of Ignorance and Innovation; Riyadh, n.d.), p. 90.

15. *al-Durrar al-Saniyya fi al-Ajweba al-Najdiyya* (The Bright Gems in the Najdi Answers), compiled by 'Abdulrahman b. Muhammad b. Qasim al-'Asimi al-Najdi (Riyadh, 2004), vol. 8, p. 455.

16. *al-Durrar al-Saniyya*, vol. 8, pp. 475, 478.

17. *al-Durrar al-Saniyya*, vol. 8, p. 238.

18. Faisal b. Mish'al 'al-Sa'ud, *Rasail A'emat Da'wat al-Tauhid* (Letters of the Imams of the Monotheist Call; Riyadh, 2001), pp. 55–79.

19. *Majmou'at al-Rasail wa al-Masail al-Najdiyya* (The Collection of Najdi Letters and Jurisdictions, sponsored by Imam 'Abdulaziz al-Sa'ud; Egypt, 1928), vol. 1, pp. 742–6.

20. Christine Moss Helms, *The Cohesion of Saudi Arabia: Evolution of Political Identity* (London, 1981), p. 98.

21. Ibid.

22. Shaikh Ahmad b. Hajar al-Tami, *Shaikh Muhammad b. 'Abd al-Wahhab, 'Aqidatahu al-Salafiyya wa Dawatahu al-islahiyya wa Thana' al-'Ulama' 'Alaihi* (Shaikh Muhammad b. Abdulawahab. His Fundamental Belief and Reformist Call and the Ulama Praise on him; Riyadh, 1999), p. 79.

23. Ibid., pp. 51, 72–3.

24. Abd al-Kareem al-Gharaibah, *Qiyam al-Dawala al-Arabiyya al-Saudiyya* (The Rise of the Saudi Arabian State; Cairo, 1974), p. 75.

25. al-Shaikh al-Imam Hussain b. Ghannam, *Tarikh Najd* (The History of Najd, annotated by Nasir al-Din al-As'ad; Beirut, 1985), p. 179.

26. Goldberg, 'The Shi'i Minority in Saudi Arabia', p. 232; also see: Ibn Ghannam, *Tarikh Najd*, p. 182.

27. Ibn Bishr, *'Enwan al-Mjd fi Tarikh Najd* (The Landmark of Glorification in the History of Najd; Riyadh, 1982), vol. 1, pp. 121–2.

28. Goldberg, 'The Shi'i Minority in Saudi Arabia', p. 233.

29. Muhammad 'Urabi Nakhlah, *Tarikh al-'Ahsa al-Siyasi* (The Political History of al-Hasal; Kuwait, 1980), p. 54.

30. Palgrave, *Narrative of a Year's Journey*,(London, 1865), vol. 2, pp. 84–6.

31. *al-Durrar al-Saniyya fi al-Ajweba al-Najdiyya*, vol. 14, pp. 66–7.

32. Quoted from a letter sent by the Shaikh of Saihat Hussain Bin Neser on 8 May 1913 to a notable from Bahrain, Shaikh Yusuf Ahmad Kano; *IOR-R\15\2\31*.

33. *IOR-R15\5\27*; based on a report sent by Captain W. H. I. Shakespear, the Political Agent in Kuwait, to the Political Resident in the Persian Gulf, Bushire, 20 May 1913.

34. Shaikh Ali abu al-Hassan b. Ali al-Khunaizi was born in Qatif in 1874 into an eminent family. He went to Najaf for religious schooling and subsequently became a disciple of the leader of the constitutional revoution in Iran, Akhund Khurasani, who accredited al-Khunaizi as a *mujtahid*. He returned to Qatif in 1911 and became the judge of the Qatif region following the death of his nephew, Shaikh Ali Abu Abdulkarim al-Khunaizi. He authored a number of books on Shi'i theology and jurisprudence, the most eminent being *al-Da'wa al-Islamiyya ela Wehdat Ahl al-Sunna wa al-Imamiyya* (The Islamic Call for the Unity of the Sunnis and the Imamis). The books is a refutation of Abdullah al-Qasimi's *al-Sira' bin al-Islam wa al-Wathanyya* (The Conflict between Islam and Atheism). Fouad al-Ahmad, *al-Shaikh Hassan Ali Albadr al-Qatifi* (Beirut, 1991), pp. 102–4.

35. Shaikh Ali Abu al-Hassan al-Khunaizi, *al-Da'wa al-Islamiyya 'ela Wehdat 'Ahlu al-Sunna wa al-Imamiyya* (Beirut, 1958), vol. 1, p. 223.

36. *IOR-R\15\5\27*, dated 7 June 1913.

37. Hamza al-Hassan, *al-Shi'a fi al-Mamlaka al-'Arabiyya al-Saudiyya* (The Shi'ites in the Kingdom of Saudi Arabia; Beirut, 1993), vol. 2, p. 12.

38. H. R. B. Dickson, *Kuwait and her Neighbours* (London, 1956), p. 281.

39. *IOR-R\15\2\74*, dated 1 March 1923.

40. *IOR-R\15\2\74*, dated 18 February 1924.

41. Dickson, *Kuwait and her Neighbours*, p. 302.

42. Hafiz Wahbah, *Jazirat al'Arab fi al-Qarn al-'Eshrin* (The Arabian Peninsula in the Twentieth Century; Egypt, 1935), p. 318.

43. Ibid, p. 320.

44. Goldberg, 'The Shi'i Minority in Saudi Arabia', p. 236.

45. *IOR-R/15/2/74*, dated 10 August 1929.

46. Although these men were originally from Bahrain and resided in Qatif owing to 'the tyrannies practised by Shaikh 'Isa 'al-Khalifah', the petition alluded to the indirect role of the Shi'is in Qatif and Tarut who 'have undoubted cause for complaint'. This meant that the government of Bahrain could not officially move in this matter if all or some of the petitioners were not his subjects. *IOR-R15\2\74*.

47. *IOR-R\15\2\74*, dated 10 August 1929. The claims mentioned in the petition were confirmed by a British official source on 22 November 1927. According to this source, 'In about March 1927, I first heard that the Shi'is were being compelled to conform to Wahabi rules as to praying in mosques behind Wahabi Imam. This man is evidently the "boy" to whom the petitioners allude.'

48. John S. Habib, *Ibn Sa'ud's Warriors of Islam* (Leiden, 1978), pp. 123, 129.

49. Juhaiman b. Muhammad b. Saif al-'Utaibi, *al-Emara wa al-Bai'a' wa al-Ta'a... wa Kashf Talbis al-Hukam 'ala Talabat al-'Elm wa al-'Awam* (The Government, Allegiance and Obedience ... The Debunking of the Rulers' Deceptions of the Students of Religions and Laymen; no place or date), pp. 13, 28, 29.

50. Shaikh Nasir Bin Sulaiman al-'Omar, *al-rafida fi bilad al-tawhid* (The Rejectionists [i.e. the Shi'is] in the Land of Monotheism): see http://www.alsunnah.com/rafidah/1.htm. accessed on 17 February 2001.

51. The somewhat stilted language of the text is from Graham Fuller and Rend Rahim Francke's translation in *The Arab Shi'ia: The Forgotten Muslims* (New York, 1999), p. 184; also see: al-'Omar, *al-rafida fi bilad al-tawhid*.

52. *IOR-R15\5\1859*, dated 29 April 1927.

53. al-Khunaizi, *al-Da'wa al-Islamiyya 'ela Wehdat 'Ahlu al-Sunna wa al-Imamiyya*, vol. 1, pp. 170–71.

54. al-Hassan, *al-Shi'a fi al-Mamlaka al-'Arabiyya al-Saudiyya*, pp. 259–260.

55. Goldberg, 'The Shi'i Minority in Saudi Arabia', p. 233; Guido Steinberg, 'The Shi'ites in the Eastern Province of Saudi Arabia (al-Ahsaa), 1913–1953', in Werner Ende and Freitage Rainer (eds), *The Twelver Shi'is in Modern Times: Religious Culture and Political History* (Leiden, 2000).

56. Goldberg, 'The Shi'i Minority in Saudi Arabia', p. 234.

57. Steinberg, 'The Shi'ites in the Eastern Province of Saudi Arabia (al-Ahsaa), 1913–1953'.

58. *al-Shi'a fi al-Sa'udiyya* (The Shi'is in Saudi Arabia; London, 1991), p. 22.

59. James Piscatori, 'Ideological Politics in Saudi Arabia', in James Piscatori (ed.), *Islam in the Political Process* (Cambridge, 1983), p. 58.

60. *IOR-R\15\2\74*, dated 18 February 1924.

61. Dickson, *Kuwait and her Neighbours*, p. 302.

62. Ameen Rihani, *Ibn Sa'ud of Arabia* (London, 1928), pp. 234–5.

63. Abdul Rahim al-Harbi, *'Ahl al-Dar wa al-'Eman* (Abstract of a Book: *The People of Land and Faith*, unpublished manuscript), p. 24.
64. Yusif al-Khoei, *The Shi'is of Medina*, p. 5; quoted in Werner Ende, 'The Nakhawla, A Shi'ite Community in Medina Past and Present', in Koninklijke Brill, *Die Welt des Islams* (Leiden, 1997), issue no. 37, p. 329.
65. al-Harbi, *Mulakhas min Kitab 'Ahl al-Dar*, p. 24.
66. According to a PhD study published in Arabic in 2004, Najd holds 78% of executive power, compared with 17% for al-Hijaz, and 5% for the rest of the regions. See Muhammad b. Sunaitan, *al-Nukhab al-Sa'udiyya: Dirasa fi al-Tahulat wa al-Ekhfaqat* (Saudi Elites: A Study of Transformations and Declines; Beirut, 2004), pp. 176–9.
67. Robert Lacey, *The Kingdom* (London, 1981), p. 488.
68. Minnesota Lawyers International Human Rights Committee Report, 1996, Chapter IV.
69. B. D. Hakken reported from Bahrain in 1933: 'Many of the landowners have fled the country to escape punishment for non-payment since they have not been able to raise the required amount. The tax on date palms has been more than the sum realized on the sale of the dates at this time of depression.' He concludes, 'Religious hatred is [...] at the bottom of the matter.' B. D. Hakken, 'Sunni–Shi'i Discord in Eastern Arabia', *The Moslem World*, issue no. 23, 1933, p. 304.
70. Arend Lijphart, 'Power-Sharing Approach', in Joseph V. Montville (ed.), *Conflict and Peacemaking in Multiethnic Societies* (New York, 1991), p. 497.
71. Mordechai Abir, *Saudi Arabia in the Oil Era: Regime and Elites, Conflict and Collaboration* (Boulder, 1988), p. 153.
72. Lacey, *The Kingdom*, p. 488; Piscatori, 'Ideological Politics in Saudi Arabia'.
73. Goldberg, 'The Shi'i Minority in Saudi Arabia', p. 238.
74. James Buchan, 'Secular and Religious Opposition in Saudi Arabia', in Tim Niblock (ed.), *State, Society and Economy in Saudi Arabia* (Beckenham, 1982), p. 119.
75. http://www.ibnbaz.org.sa/Display.asp?f=Bz00654.htm. Retrieved on 22 March 2003
76. Shaikh Muhammad Ibn Ibrahim, *Fatawa Ibn Ibrahim* (Riyadh, n.d.), vol. 13, p. 248.
77. Kostiner, 'Shi'i Unrest in the Gulf', p. 175
78. Abir, *Saudi Arabia in the Oil Era*, p. 153.
79. *Sawt al-Taliya'* (The Voice of Vanguard), a quarterly magazine based in Baghdad, July 1973, issue no. 3, p. 29.
80. Piscatori, 'Ideological Politics in Saudi Arabia', p. 67.
81. al-Hassan, *al-Shi'a fi al-Mamlaka al-'Arabiyya al-Saudiyya*, vol. 2, pp. 307–10.
82. This caricature was widely circulated during the Shi'is uprising in 1979; also see Lacey, *The Kingdom*, p. 488.
83. The religious sanction (*fatwa*) was signed by four members of the Committee of the Scientific Research and Religious Jurisdiction, vol. 2, p. 372.
84. Ibid., p. 373.
85. This is based on a copy of a *fatwa* issued by Shaikh Abdulah b. Jibrin in 1991.
86. al-Hassan, *al-Shi'a fi al-Mamlaka al-'Arabiyya al-Saudiyya*, vol. 2, pp. 450–54.
87. Ibid., p. 453.
88. Sponsored by *Hai'at al-'eghatha al-Islamiyya* (al-Hasa, Saudi Arabia, n.d.), p. 46.
89. Nasir Abdulakarim al-'Aqil, *Muqadimat fi al-'Ahwa' wa 'al-Iftriaq wa al-bida'* (Introduction to Factions and Innovations; Riyadh, 1996), vol. 1, p. 27; vol. 2, pp. 49, 138; vol. 3, p. 12.
90. 'Abud b. Ali b. Dere, *Dahirat al-Gholuw fi al-Din ...al-'Asbab* (The Phenomenon of Religious Extremism ... the Causes; Qasim, 1998), introduction.
91. Shaikh Muhammad Ibn Ibrahim, *Fatawa Ibn Ibrahim* (Riyadh, n.d.), vol. 13, p. 213, dated 25/1/1386, 15 May 1966.

92. The Ministry of Education (Riyadh, 1977), p. 149.

93. al-Fawzan, Saleh b. Fawzan (Cairo, n.d.), pp. 87, 90, 95, 105–6, 113.

94. *al-Jazira al-'Arabiyya*, monthly magazine based in London, issue no. 21, October 1992, p. 16.

95. Muhammad 'Abdul Majid, *al-Tamieyz al-Ta'ifi fi al-Saudiyya* (Sectarian Discrimination in Saudi Arabia; Beirut, 1990), p. 99.

96. Turki Ahmad al-Turki and Abdul Khaliq al-Janabi were arrested on 10 March 1992 following their attempt to refute the accusation against Shi'is doctrine; *al-Jazira al-'Arabiyya*, issue no. 21, October 1992, p. 17.

97. Geoff Simons, *Saudi Arabia: The Shape of a Client Feudalism* (London, 1998), pp. 16–17.

98. Shi'is notables and *'ulama* presented these petitions to Crown Prince Fahad in 1975. See al-Hassan, *al-Shi'a fi al-Mamlaka al-'Arabiyya al-Saudiyya*, vol. 2, pp. 487–90.

99. Several petitions were sent between 1975 and 1985 to highly influential princes. See al-Hassan, *al-Shi'a fi al-Mamlaka al-'Arabiyya al-Saudiyya*, vol. 2, pp. 492, 494, 495, 497–9.

100. A petition presented by a number of Shi'is notables to the Minister of Finance, Prince Talal, in the 1960s demanded legal status equal to that of the Sunnis.

101. Mamoun Fandy, 'From Confrontation to Creative Resistance: The Shi'is Opposition Discourse in Saudi Arabia', *Critique*, Fall 1996, p. 4.

102. Joseph Kostiner, 'Shi'i Unrest in the Gulf', in Martin Kramer (ed.), *Shi'ism, Resistance and Revolution* (London, 1987), p. 175.

103. Fifteen mosques and *hussainiya*s were either destroyed or abandoned by the Saudi authorites. See *Huquq al-Ensan fi al-Mamlaka al-'Arabiyya al-Saudiyya* (Human Rights in Saudi Arabia; October 1989, sponsored by the International Committee for the Defence of Human Rights in the Gulf and Arabian Peninsula), pp. 208–9.

104. Ibid., p. 207.

105. *al-Riyadh* newspaper, issue no. 11701, 7 July 2000. For comparison, James A. Bill wrote in 1984 that there are 20,000 mosques and that another 2000 were to be built in the same year. James A. Bill, 'Resurgent Islam in the Persian Gulf', *Foreign Affairs*, Fall 1984, p. 117.

106. *al-Watan*, daily newspaper based in 'Asir, dated 18 December 2000.

107. *al-Riyadh*, issue no. 11701, 7 July 2000.

108. The *Hi'at al-'Amr bi al-ma'rouf wa al'nahi 'an al-munkar* in Qatif issued a decree, No. 6, dated 26 February 1984, that all Shi'is prayer callers in the Qatif region adhere to the legal *'Adhan* upon which both the Sunna and the Shi'is are agreed. See: *Huquq al-Ensan fi al-Mamlaka al-'Arabiyya al-Saudiyya*, p. 451.

109. *Sawt al-Taliya'*, August 1979, issue no. 20, p. 53.

110. According to a documentary report, the head of Dammam main post office ordered that 20 Shi'i books posted to the office be burned. See *Huquq al-Ensan fi al-Mamlaka al-'Arabiyya al-Saudiyya*, p. 452; see also: The Minnesota Lawyers International Human Rights, *Shame in the House of Saud* (Minneapolis, 1992), p. 102.

111. Amnesty International, Urgent Action dated 10 August 1989.

112. The Grand Mufti, Shaikh Muhammad b. Ibrahim, appealed to the crown prince of the time, Faisal, to issue a decree for sanctioning the killing of Shaikh al-Khunaizi, whom he described as 'a dirty person', as he deliberately caused chaos; this would be extinguished [by killing him]; failure to do this would encourage this sect to practise other innovations. Note No. 198, dated 24/7/1381, *Fatawa Ibn Ibrahim*, vol. 13, p. 250.

113. About 30 Shi'i activists were arrested in July 2000 at the conclusion of *'Ashura* ceremony. At least one Shi'i preacher was forced to cease religious activities including preaching on religious occasions, i.e. Muharram and Ramadan.

114. *Alyoum*, daily newspaper based in Dammam, issue no. 5208, dated 18 September 1987.

115. http://members.xoom.com_XMCM/aqidah/books/feraq/rafedah.htm, accessed on 25 February 2002.

116. http://www.hrw.org/wr2k1/mideast/saudi.html, accessed on 12 August 2002

117. Human Rights Watch Report 2002, http://www.hrw.org/wr2k2/mena7.html; Human Rights Watch Report 2003, http://www.hrw.org/wr2k3/mideast6.html

118. A. M. Thernstrom, 'The Right to Political Representation', in C. Fried (ed.), *Minorities: Community and Identity* (Berlin, 1993), p. 333.

119. Fuller and Francke, *The Arab Shi'is: The Forgotten Muslims*, pp. 185–6; also see: Bengio and Ben-Dor, *Minorities and the State in the Arab World*, p. 171.

120. *Huquq al-Ensan fi al-Mamlaka al-'Arabiyya al-Saudiyya*, pp. 212–13.

121. R. Harir Dekmejian, 'Saudi Arabia's Consultative Council', *Middle East Journal*, 1998, issue no. 52, p. 213.

122. Walker Connor, 'When Is a Nation', in Hutchinson and Smith (eds), *Nationalism* (Oxford, 1994), p. 154.

Chapter 2

1. Bryan R. Wilson, *The Social Dimension of Sectarianism* (Oxford, 1990), p. 48.

2. Emile Durkheim, *The Elementary Form of the Religious Life* (London, 1915), p. 261.

3. In September 1979, Ayatullah Khomeini decreed a *fatwa* for Shi'i pilgrims to Mecca and Medina, which made it obligatory for them to perform the common public prayer together with Sunni believers. See: Wilfried Buchta, 'Tehran's Ecumenical Society (*MAJMA' TAQRIB*): A Veritable Ecumenical Revival or a Trojan Horse of Iran?', in Rainer Brunner and Wenner Ende (eds), *The Twelver Shi'a in Modern Times* (Leiden, 2001), p. 334.

4. Walker Connor, 'Nation-Building or Nation-Destroying', *World Politics*, April 1973, p. 350.

5. Meredith B. McGuire, *Religion: The Social Context* (Belmont, CA, 1992), p. 36.

6. Durkheim, *The Elementary Form of the Religious Life*, pp. 256–7.

7. The Wahhabi *'ulama* launched a site on the Internet aimed at purging the Isma'ilis beliefs and attracting them to Wahhabism. See: http://www.khayma.com/najran.

8. The prominent Maliki scholar Saiyyd Muhammad 'Alawi al-Maliki (d. October 2004) was labelled *kafir* (infidel) by a Wahhabi scholar, because of his belief in the Prophet's birth festival. The Wahhabi scholar wrote a book entitled *Ma' al-Maliki fi Kufriatihi wa Dalalatihi* (A Refutation of Maliki Infidelities and Misleadings), introduced and expounded by Shaikh Ibn Baz, the former Grand Mufti of the country.

9. Hijazi scholars, notably Muhammad 'Abdu Yamani, the former Minister of Information, wrote books about the Prophet's family, one of which is entitled *'Allimu 'Abnaukum Hubba 'Ahlul Bayt* (Teach Your Children the Love of the Prophet's Family), published in 1994.

10. Charles Fried, in C. Fried (ed.), *Minorities: Community and Identity* (Berlin, 1983), p. 30.

11. Though discussed by the Shi'i rationalists (*usulis*) a long time ago, the concept of *marji' taqlid* was juristically formulated at the turn of the last century by Sayyid Muhammad Kadhim al-Yazdi in his landmark book *al-'Uruat al-Withqa* (The Firm Bond; Najaf, 1981), in which he states (question 7, p. 2): 'unless they are based on imitation of a *mujtahid*, the actions of an ordinary person are false'.

12. The only exceptional attempt to assign a *marji'* by the Shi'is was in the first quarter of the twentieth century. According to one source, Shaikh Hassan 'Ali al-Badr al-Qatifi exerted all efforts to encourage the Shi'is to follow the *mujtahid* of the time, Shaikh 'Ali Abu al-Hassan al-Khunaizi, the Shi'i judge during both the Ottoman and Saudi rules. Since then, the Shi'is began to follow the *marji's* in both Iraq and Iran. See Fouad al-Ahmad, *al-Shaikh Hassan 'Ali al-Badr al-Qatifi* (Beirut, 1991), pp. 101–4.

13. This story comes from several reliable Shi'i sources.

14. Shi'i jurisprudence covertly prohibits the marriage of Sunni men to Shi'i women, and not the reverse. This precept is based on the male-mastership principle (*Qawamiyat al-rajul 'ala al-mara*'), meaning the superiority of man over woman. By virtue of this *Qawamiyat*, a man may force his wife to embrace the sect to which he belongs. Although widely known, this *fatwa* is not recorded in Shi'i juristic books. It was strongly applied in the Eastern Province in the face of Wahhabi religious policies geared towards the imposition of Wahhabism on the Shi'is.

15. al-Hassan, *al-Shi'a fi al-Mamlaka al-'Arabiyya al-Saudiyya*, vol. 1, pp. 32–41.

16. McGuire, *Religion: The Social Context*, p. 178.

17. Durkheim, *The Elementary Form of the Religious Life*, p. 244.

18. Fried, in C. Fried (ed.), *Minorities: Community and Identity*, p. 27.

19. Eleanor A. Doumato, 'Gender, Monarchy and National Identity', *British Journal of Middle Eastern Studies*, vol. 19, no. 1, 1992, p. 36.

20. Goldberg, 'The Shi'i Minority in Saudi Arabia', p. 230.

21. James Piscatori, 'The Formation of the Saudi Identity: A Case Study of the Utility of Transnationalism', in John F. Stack, Jr (ed.), *Ethnic Identities in a Transnational World* (Westport, CT, 1981), p. 59.

22. Kostiner, Joseph, 'Transforming Dualities: Tribe and State Formation in Saudi Arabia', in Philip Khoury and Joseph Kostiner (eds), *Tribes and State Formation in the Middle East* (Berkeley, 1990), p. 226.

23. Muhammad al-Ruwaini, *Sukkan al-Mamlaka al-'Arabiyya al-Sa'udiyya* (The Population of Saudi Arabia; Riyadh, 1979), p. 94.

24. Lorimer, J. G., *Gazetteer of the Persian Gulf, Oman and Central Arabia* (Florida, 1908), vol. IIA, p. 664.

25. Gabriel Ben-Dor argues that, 'in the Arabian Peninsula a clear majority dominates'. Bengio and Ben-Dor (eds), *Minorities and the State in the Arab World*, p. 19.

26. Muhammad Ibn Ibrahim al-Saif, *al-Madkhal ela Dirasat al Mujtama' al-Sa'udi* (A Prelude to the Study of the Saudi Society; Riyadh, 1997), pp. 253-4.

27. In his refutation against Ghazi al-Qusaibi, Muhammad Said al-Qahtani argues against the former's view that, 'the Shi'is represent a big proportion of the population of the Kingdom' or that, 'the Rafida in our land is a neglected minority'. See: Ghazi al-Qusaibi, *Hatta La Takun Fitna*, ([In Order] to Avoid the Anarchy; Cairo, 1991), p. 154; Muhammad Said al-Qahtani, *al-Qusaibi Sha'ir al-'Ams wa Wai'z al-Youm* (al-Qusaibi [...] Yesterday's Poet and Today's Preacher; Chicago, 1991), p. 74.

28. Ghassan Salamé, 'Political Power and the Saudi State', in Albert Hourani, Philip Khoury and Mary C. Wilson (eds), *The Modern Middle East: A Reader* (London, 1993), p. 591.

29. Fatina Amin Shaker, *Modernization of the Developing Nations: The Case of Saudi Arabia* (Purdue University, University Microfilms, Michigan, 1972), pp. 122–4.

30. Kelly explains the regional sentiments among the 'Ashraf and several families of the tribes of Quraish. al-'Ashraf, he says, 'have never ceased to regard the al-Saud as other than interlopers, upstarts of undistinguished lineage and uncivilized ways who have usurped the guardianship of the *haramain*, the holy places, which rightfully belongs to the house of Hashim, and have deprived its members of their patrimony, the Hijaz itself.' J. B. Kelly, *Arabia, The Gulf and The West* (London, 1980), p. 273.

31. Shaker, *Modernization of the Developing Nations: The Case of Saudi Arabia*, p. 125.

32. The first consultative council in the country was established in Hijaz on 21 January 1924, based on a royal decree of Ibn Sa'ud. Hence, the Hijazi elite convened and selected 13 members headed by Shaikh 'Abd al-Qadir al-Shaibi, and formed what was entitled *al-majlis*

al-ahli, that is, the 'Communal Council'. Furthermore, he formulated in 1926 a constitution especially for regulating the affairs of Hijaz; it was called *al-ta'limat al-asasiyya lil-Hijaz,* the Basic Directives for Hijaz, the second article of which states that the 'Hijazi Arabia state is a monarchical, consultative and Islamic state; it is independent in its internal and external affairs'. However, neither the council nor the constitution was realized. See: Fahd al-Qahtani, *Sira' al-'Ajniha* (The Struggle of the Wings; London, 1988), p. 232; see also: Fouad Hamzah, *al-Bilad al-'arabiyya al-Sa'udiyya* (Riyadh, 1968), p. 99.

33. al-Shaikh 'Abd al-'Aziz Ibn Baz, *Naqd al-Qawmiyya al-'Arabiyya 'ala daw' al-Qur'an wa al-Sunna* (A Critique of Arab Nationalism in the Light of the Qur'an and the Sunna; Beirut, 1971), p. 63.

34. Manfred W. Wenner, 'Saudi Arabia: Survival of Traditional Elites', in Frank Tachau (ed.), *Political Elites and Political Development in the Middle East* (Cambridge, MA, 1975), p. 165.

35. *Area Handbook for Saudi Arabia,* issued by The American University (Washington, DC, 1971), p. 201.

36. Ernest Gellner discusses this topic at length in his book *Nations and Nationalism* (Oxford, 1983).

37. Piscatori, 'The Formation of the Saudi Identity: A Case Study of the Utility of Transnationalism', p. 105.

38. Salamé, 'Political Power and the Saudi State', p. 588.

39. Piscatori, 'The Formation of the Saudi Identity: A Case Study of the Utility of Transnationalism', p. 105.

40. Ibid., p. 131.

41. J. Joseph Nevo, 'Religion and National Identity in Saudi Arabia', *Middle Eastern Studies,* vol. 34, no. 3, 1998, pp. 38–9.

42. *Umm al-Qura,* the official newspaper, issue no. 64, 5/9/1344–19 March 1926.

43. 'Abd al-Jawad Muhammad Muhammad, a*l-Tatur al-Tashri'i fi al-Mamlaka al-'Arabiyya al-Sa'udiyya* (Legislative Development in the Kingdom of Saudi Arabia: Cairo, 1977), p. 65.

44. Ibid., p. 78.

45. 'Abdulfattah 'Abu 'Aliyyah, *'al-Islah al-Ijtima'i fi 'Ahd al-Malik 'Abdul'Aziz* (Social Reform in the Reign of King Abdul Aziz; Riyadh, 1976), p. 155.

46. Salamé, 'Political Power and the Saudi State', p. 591.

47. Fuller and Francke, *The Arab Shi'a: The Forgotten Muslims,* p. 10.

48. McGuire, *Religion: The Social Context,* p. 190.

49. F. S. Vidal noted (*The Oasis of al-Hasa,* Dhahran, 1955, p. 96) that, 'although Shi'ite children can be, and are, admitted to the main schools of Hofuf, their parents prefer to send them to receive a less formal type of education in one of the unofficial schools operated by Shi'ite divines in the *hussainiyas'.*

50. Ameen Rihani, *Ibn Sa'ud of Arabia* (1928), p. 39.

51. Doumato, 'Gender, Monarchy and National Identity', p. 36.

52. According to a survey by Walker Connor, only 12 out of 132 states can justifiably be described as nation-states. Walker Connor, 'The Question of Definition', in John Hutchinson and Anthony D. Smith (eds), *Nationalism,* p. 39.

53. Piscatori, 'The Formation of the Saudi Identity', p. 117.

54. Gellner, *Nations and Nationalism,* p. 4.

55. See: Andersen Benedict, *Imagined Communities: Reflections on the Origin and the Spread of Nationalism* (London, 1983).

56. George A. Lipsky, *Saudi Arabia* (New Haven, 1959), p. 311.

57. See: John Shotter, 'Psychology and Citizenship: Identity and Belonging', in Bryan S. Turner

(ed.), *Citizenship and Social Theory* (London, 1993), pp. 115–38.

58. Quoted in J. M. Barbalet, 'Citizenship, Class Inequality and Resentment', in Byan S. Turner (ed.),*Citizenship and Social Theory,* (London, 1993), p. 37.

59. Joseph J. Malone, 'Saudi Arabia', in *The Muslim World*, vol. 56, 1966, pp. 294–5; see also: *Area Handbook for Saudi Arabia*, p. 201.

60. Levion H. Melikian,'The Modal Personality of Saudi College Students: A Study in National Character', in L. Carl Brown and Norman Itzkowitz (eds), *Psychological Dimensions of Near Eastern Studies* (Princeton, 1977), p. 169.

61. Mai Yamani, 'Health, Education, Gender and the Security of the Gulf in the Twenty-First Century', in David E. Long and Christian Koch (eds), *Gulf Security in the Twenty-First Century*, The Emirates Center for Strategic Studies (Abu Dhabi, 1997), p. 269.

62. Ibid., p. 269.

63. Shaikh Safar al-Hawali, *Fasatadhkrun Ma-Aqul Lakum* (You Will Remember What I Say; September 1990); Shaikh Salman Bin Fahd al-'Awda, *Wailun Lil 'Arab Min Sharin Qad Iqtarab* (Distress for the Arabs as Evil Has Approached; September 1990). The lectures were recorded on cassettes and widely distributed during the second Gulf crisis.

64. *al-waha*, a quarterly magazine based in Beirut, issue no. 6, July 1997, pp. 4–5.

65. A petition advanced to King Fahad in January 1991 by 43 academics, politicians and notables from all over the country. *al-Jazira al-'Arabiyya*, issue no. 1, January 1991, pp. 5–6.

66. Mai Yamani, *Cradle of Islam: The Hijaz and the Quest for an Arabian Identity* (London, 2004).

67. Madawi al-Rasheed, *Politics in an Arabian Oasis: The Rashidis of Saudi Arabia* (1997; originally a thesis).

68. Soraya al-Torki, *Arabian Oasis City: The Transformation of Unayzah* (Texas, 1989; originally a thesis).

Chapter 3

1. See: www.shirazi.org.uk. Accessed on 10 September 2002.

2. See: Muhammad al-Shirazi, *Islamic Belief* (Kuwait, 1979); *al-Siyagha al-Jadida* (The New Reformulation; Beirut, 1988); *Al Sabil ela Enhad al-Muslimin* (The Path to the Revitalization of the Muslims; Beirut, 1986); *al-Hukum fi al-Islam* (The Rulership in Islam; Beirut, 1989).

3. *Muntalaqat al-Thawra al-Islamiyya fi al-Iraq* (The Principles of Islamic Revolution in Iraq; Tehran, n.d.), communiqué no. 19, p. 23.

4. See: 'Abdulghani' Abbas, *Tatalu' Umma ... Qira'a fi Fikr Ayatullah Sayyid Muhammad Taqi al-Mudarresi* (An Aspiration of a Nation, a Reading of the Thoughts of Ayatullah Muhammad Taqi al-Mudarresi; Qum, 1989).

5. Elie Kedourie, 'The Iraqi Shi'is and Their Fate', in Martin Kramer (ed.), *Shi'ism: Resistance and Revolution* (London, 1987), p. 135.

6. John Esposito, 'Political Islam and the West', *Joint Force Quarterly*, spring 2000, p. 51.

7. Lawrence G. Potter, *Islam and Politics: Egypt, Algeria and Tunisia* (New York, 1994), pp. 71–2.

8. Ali. R. Abootalebli, 'Islam, Islamists, and Democracy', *Middle East Review of International Affairs*, vol. 3, no. 1, March 1999, p. 16.

9. John Esposito, *The Straight Path* (Oxford, 1988), pp. 162–9.

10. Sayyid Hadi al-Mudarresi, the brother of Muhammad Taqi al-Mudarresi, was born in the holy city of Karbala in 1947. He became a popular preacher with a reputation for expertise in public preaching, delivering more than eight thousand sermons. He also authored

more than 200 books and pamphlets. He is considered one of the founding fathers of the MVM and the second highest leader of the Movement. While in Bahrain in the 1970s, al-Mudarresi founded the most powerful movement in Bahrain, called the Islamic Liberation Front (ILF), which derived its membership from the followers of leftist parties such as the Bahrain Popular Front (BPF) and the Bahrain National Front (BNF). He was appointed a deputy of Khomeini in Bahrain after the revolution but was dismissed from Bahrain for subversive activities. He then resided in Iran, where he continued actively to oppose the government of Bahrain. In December 1982, al-Mudarresi was accused of being involved in a coup d'etat attempt in Bahrain, leading to waves of arrest among the members of ILF and the abandonment of his Bahraini nationality. Relations between Iran and Bahrain deteriorated and H. al-Mudarresi lost his post as a deputy of Imam Khomeini. He then dissociated himself gradually from the Bahraini issue and concentrated on the cause of Iraq, to which he is now devoted. See: www.modarresi.org; Mansour al-Shaikh, *al-'Alama al-Sayyid Hadi al-Mudarresi ... Mawaqifahu wa Afkarahu* (Hadi al-Mudarresi ... His Stances and Thoughts; Beirut, 1991).

11. McGuire, *Religion: The Social Context*, p. 190.
12. According to Shi'i jurisprudence, the Sunna includes the sayings and practices of both the Prophet and the Twelve Imams. Sayyid Muhammad Baqir al-Sadr, *Durus fi 'Ilm al-'Usul* (Lessons on the Science of [Juristic] Principles; Beirut, 1986), p. 6.
13. Muhammad Taqi, al-Mudarresi, *Buhuth fi al-Qur'an al-Karim* (Research on the Holy Qur'an; Beirut, 1971), p. 13.
14. Ahmad Nasir (pseudonym), *al-Thaqafa ar-Risaliyya* (The Message-Oriented Culture; n.p, n.d), p. 126. The actual author of the book is Muhammad Taqi al-Mudarresi.
15. Hadi al-Mudarresi, *al-Ta'arruf 'Ala al-Islam* (Knowing Islam; Tehran, 1981), pp. 66–67.
16. Sayyid Qutb, *Milestones* (Indianapolis, 1990), p. 5.
17. Sayyid Qutb, *Fi Zilal al-Qur'an* (In the Shade of the Qur'an; Beirut, 1986), vol. 4, p. 891.
18. Qutb, *Milestones*, p. 15.
19. Ibid., pp. 9, 16.
20. See: Majid al-Nizari, *Abdul-Sahib al-Dakhil wa Bidayat al-Haraka al-Islamiyya al-Mu'asira* (The Emergence of the Contemporary Islamic Movement; Beirut, 1990), p. 23.
21. *Thaqafat al-Da'wa al-Islamiyya: al-Qism al-Siyasi* (The Literature of the Islamic Call: Political Section; n.p., 1985), vol. 1, p. 271.
22. Anonymous, *al-Din Hadara* (Religion Is a Civilization; privately published pamphlet), pp. 23-26.
23. Ibid., pp. 26–9.
24. Ibid., p. 30.
25. Ibid., p. 3.
26. Anonymous, *al-Risala Baina al-Ghayah wa al-Wasilah-2* (The Message: Between Aim and Means; privately published pamphlet), p. 19.
27. Anonymous, *al-Muslim baina Waqi'ihi wa Risalatihi* (The Muslim: Between [His] Reality and Message; privately published pamphlet), p. 5.
28. Anonymous, *al-Risala Baina al-Ghayah wa'al-Wasilah-1* (privately published pamphlet), p. 22.
29. Anonymous, *al-Eman wa al-Hayat* (Faith and Life; privately published pamphlet), p. 52.
30. Qutb, *Milestones*, p. 9.
31. In 1960, Imam al-Shirazi wrote a book entitled *Kaifa 'Arafta Allah?* (How Do You Know [the existence of] God?), based on an imagined dialectical discussion between a believer and a non-believer. In it, Shirazi rationally elucidates the fundamental creeds of Shi'i Islam: *tawhid*, God's justice, prophecy, the Imamate and the resurrection, with considerable

emphasis on the doctrine of *tawhid*.

32. al-Imam al-Marji' Sayyid Muhammad al-Shirazi, *al-'Aqai'd al-Islamiyya* (Islamic Creeds; Beirut, 1960), pp. 5–166. In the same vein, Hadi al-Mudarresi wrote a book in 1971 entitled *Alif Ba' al-Islam* (The Alphabet of Islam), to reintroduce Islamic doctrine to his Muslim readers.

33. Anonymous, *al-Din Darurah wa Manhaj* (Religion Is a Necessity and Programme; unpublished pamphlet).

34. Anonymous, *Risalat al-Anbiya'* (The Prophets' Message; privately published pamphlet), pp. 8–17.

35. See M. A. Amir-Moezi, *The Divine Guide in Early Shi'ism*, translated by David Streight (New York, 1994), pp. 134–9.

36. See: Sayyid Hossein Nasr, *Shi'ism: Doctrines, Thought, and Spirituality and Expectation of the Millennium: Shi'ism in History* (New York, 1988); Yann Richard, *Shi'ite Islam*, translated by Antonia Nevill (Oxford, 1995), p. 55.

37. On the development of Imami jurisprudence see: Juan R. Cole, 'Imami Jurisprudence and the Role of the Ulama: Mortaza Ansari on Emulating the Supreme Exemplar', in Nikki Keddie (ed.), *Religion and Politics in Iran* (New Haven, 1983), pp. 40ff.

38. Muhammad Taqi al-Mudarresi, *al-Mantiq al-Islami* (Islamic Logic; Beirut, 1977), p. 7.

39. Ibid., p. 12.

40. Ibid., p. 16.

41. Nasir, *al-Thaqafa ar-Risaliyya*, p. 73.

42. Ibid, pp. 74–6.

43. On various occasions, the author met students who joined religious seminaries sponsored by Muhammad Taqi al-Mudarresi, in Kuwait, Iran or Syria. The students expressed their disagreement with the curricula proposed by al-Mudarresi.

44. M. Momen, *Authority and Opposition in Twelver Shi'ism* (London, 1989), p. 62.

45. Ervand Abrahamian, *Khomeinism: Essays on the Islamic Republic* (Berkeley, 1993), p. 23.

46. 'Ali Shari'ati, *An Approach to the Understanding of Islam*; www.shariati.com. Accessed on 27 May 2002.

47. 'Ali Shari'ati, *On the Sociology of Islam*, translated from the Persian by Hamid Algar (Berkeley, 1979), pp. 97–110.

48. Anonymous, *al-Taliya' wa al-Muntalaqat al-Thawriyya* (The Vanguard and Revolutionary Principles; unpublished pamphlet), pp. 22–3.

49. Nasir, *al-Thaqafa ar-Risaliyya*, p. 8.

50. Ibid., p. 25.

51. 'Ali Shari'ati, *Intizar ... Madhab-i I'tirad* (Waiting ... The Religion of Protest; Tehran, 1971), quoted in John J. Donohue and John L. Esposito (eds), *Islam in Transition* (Oxford, 1982), pp. 297–304.

52. Hassan Musa al-Saffar, *al-Mahdi Amal al-Shu'ub* (Beirut, 1979), pp. 79–88.

53. Heinz Halm, *Shi'i Islam from Religion to Revolution* (Princeton, 1997), pp. 131–7.

54. Anonymous, *al-Haraka al-Shi'iyya ... Muquimatuha wa Tarikhuha* (The Shi'i Movement: Its Motives and History; unpublished pamphlet), p. 11.

55. See: Abrahamian, *Khomeinism*, pp. 26ff; Marvin Zonis and Daniel Brumberg, 'Shi'ism as Interpreted by Khomeini: An Ideology of Revolutionary Violence', in Kramer (ed.), *Shi'ism: Resistance and Revolution*, p. 57.

56. *al-Haraka al-Shi'iyya*, pp. 27, 29.

57. Hassan Musa al-Saffar, *A'immat Ahl al-Bayt ... Risalah wa Jihad* (The Imams of the Prophet's Family: A Message and Jihad; Beirut, 1977), pp. 92–3.

58. Ibid., pp. 16–22.

59. Henry Munson, Jr., *Islam and Revolution in the Middle East* (London, 1988), pp. 18, 231.

60. According to Abrahamian, Khomeini in the pre-1970s rarely used the word *shahadat*. See: *Khomeinism*, p. 27.

61. Shahrough Akhavi, 'Shariati's Social Thought', in Keddie (ed.), *Religion and Politics in Contemporary Iran: Clergy-State Relations in the Pahlavi Period* (New York, 1980), p. 140.

62. 'Ali 'Shari'ati, *Arise and Bear Witness*; http://www.shariati.com.

63. Hassan al-Saffar, *al-Hussain wa Mas'uliyat al-Thawra* (Kuwait, 1976), pp. 9–12.

64. While the Shi'is refer to Mu'awiya as a symbol of oppression, the Sunna refer to Pharaoh.

65. For the projection of Zainab, daughter of Imam 'Ali, in Karbala, on modern times, and on what role Muslim woman can play in social and political arenas, see: Hassan al-Saffar, *Mas'uliyat al-Mar'a* (Responsibility of Woman; Beirut, 1993), pp. 50, 52, 70, 72–3, 79, 85.

66. Amir-Moezzi, *The Divine Guide in Early Shi'ism*, p. 67.

67. Ibid., pp. 37–50.

68. al-Mudarresi, *Alif Ba' al-Islam*, p. 219.

69. Shaikh Ahmad al-Naraqi (d. 1829) is the Shi'i architect of *wilayat al-faqih*, which appeared in his juristic book entitled *'Awaid al-Ayam* (The Day-to-day References). In it al-Naraqi broadened the authority of jurist, who inherited nearly all the prerogatives of the Imams, including the institution and leadership of government. See: Fouad Ibrahim, *al-Faqih wa al-Dawla* (The Jurist and the State; Beirut, 1998), pp. 203–6.

70. Ibid., pp. 207–369.

71. 'Adil Hammuda, *Qanabil wa Masahif ... Qisat Tanzim al-Jihad* (Bombs and Cannon: The Story of the *Jihad* Organization; Cairo, 1985), pp. 172–3.

72. Qutb, *Fi Zilal al-Qur'an*, vols 5–7, p. 833.

73. Qutb, *al-'Adalah al-Ijtima'iyya fi'al-Islam*, p. 29.

74. al-'Alamah Jawad Kazim, *al-Qiyada al-Islamiyya*, (The Islamic Leadership; Beirut, 1970), p. 57.

75. Ibid., pp. 189, 106ff.

76. Ibid., p. 110.

77. Abul 'Ala al-Mawdudi, *Rights of Non-Muslims in an Islamic State*, pp. 2–3; see also 'Rights of Citizens in an Islamic State', in Abul 'Ala al-Mawdudi, *Human Rights in an Islamic State*.

78. Kazim, *al-Qiyada al-Islamiyya*, pp. 38–40.

79. Ibid., pp. 45–8.

80. Abu 'Ala Mawdudi, 'The Political Theory of Islam', in Donohue and Esposito (eds), *Islam in Transition*, p. 254.

81. The Koran (24:21), translated by N. J. Dawood (London, 1961), p. 289.

82. Kazim, *al-Qiyada al-Islamiyya*, p. 29.

83. Qutb, *al-'Adala al-'Ijtima'iyya fi 'al-Islam*, pp. 96–9.

84. Kazim, op. cit., pp. 35ff, 61, 117.

85. Hamid Algar, *Islam and Revolution* (Berkeley, 1981), pp. 27–8.

86. Kazim, *al-Qiyada al-Islamiyya*, pp. 21–2, 67, 88–9, 102, 113, 143–8.

Chapter 4

1. This slogan was chanted by a group of IRO members in 1985 during a Saudi propagandist exhibition called 'Saudi Arabia between Yesterday and Today' at Olympia in London.

2. R. K. Ramazani, 'Shi'ism in the Persian Gulf', in Cole and Keddie (eds), *Shi'sm and Social Protest* (New Haven, 1984), p. 45.

3. *Until the Dawn* (London, 1984), p. 14; *Intifadat al-Mantaqa al-Sharqiyya* (The Uprising of

the Eastern Province), p. 200.

4. This categorization is based on an analysis of a collection of petitions submitted by the Shi'i notables to the government between 1940 and 1990. The petitions were compiled by Hamza al-Hassan and annexed to volume 2 of his *al-Shi'a fi al-Mamlaka al-'Arabiyya al-Saudiyya'*.

5. A letter sent from G. S. Belham from Jeddah to Sir Anthony Eden. *ES1015/1/55,* dated 21 February 1955.

6. *Kalimat al-haraka al-Islamiyyah fi al-Jazira al-'Arabiyya* (The Discourse of Islamic Movement in the Arabian Peninsula), published by the Islamic Revolution Organization (London, 1986), p. 12.

7. *al-Thawra al-Islamiyya,* the organ of the IRO, issue no. 16, August 1981, p. 3.

8. *Country Profile 1992–93: Saudi Arabia,* The Economist Intelligence Unit (London, 1993), p. 30.

9. Arnold T. Wilson, *The Persian Gulf: An Historical Sketch from the Earliest Times to the Beginning of the Twentieth Century* (London, 1928), p. ix.

10. Frank J. Costa and Allen G. Noble, 'Planning Arab Towns', *Geographical Review,* vol. 76, no. 2, Thematic Issue: Asian Urbanization (April 1986), p. 162.

11. Madawi al-Rasheed, *A History of Saudi Arabia* (Cambridge, 2002), p. 96.

12. Richard. H. Sanger, *The Arabian Peninsula* (New York, 1954), p. 109.

13. Robert Vitalis, 'The Closing of the Arabian Oil Frontier and the Future of Saudi–American Relations', *Middle East Report,* no. 204, The Arabian Peninsula (July–September 1997), p. 19.

14. Ibid., p. 17.

15. Sanger, *The Arabian Peninsula,* p. 106.

16. Ibid., p. 108.

17. A. Brown, *Oil, God and Gold: The History of Aramco and Saudi Kings,* (Boston, 1999), p. 140; see also Sanger, *The Arabian Peninsula,* p. 107.

18. Benjamin Shwadran, *The Middle East, Oil, and the Great Powers* (New York, 1955), p. 351.

19. Vitalis, 'The Closing of the Arabian Oil Frontier and the Future of Saudi–American Relations', p. 10.

20. www.saudiaramco. com, accessed on 25 June 2002.

21. *Qafilat al-Zait* (The Caravan's Oil; 18 December 1984).

22. See: www.saudiaramco.com.

23. Ja'far al-Shaikh 'Abdullah, *al-Naft wa al-'Est'mar* (Oil and Colonization; London, 1983), p. 81.

24. Vitalis, 'The Closing of the Arabian Oil Frontier and the Future of Saudi–American Relations', p. 18.

25. Kostiner, 'Shi'i Unrest in the Gulf', p. 175.

26. Nadaf Safran, *Saudi Arabia: Ceaseless Quest for Security* (London, 1985), p. 95.

27. See: Ghassan Salamé, 'Political Power and the Saudi State', in Berch Berberoglu (ed.) *Power and Stability in the Middle East* (London, 1989), p. 81.

28. According to the Minister of the Interior, Prince Naif b. Abdulaziz (*Okaz,* a daily newspaper based in Jeddah, 8 October 1998), the total number of foreign labourers exceeded 7 million.

29. Khalid Bin Saeed, *Western Dominance and Political Islam: Challenge and Response* (New York, 1995), p. 83.

30. Michel G. Nehmem, 'Saudi Arabia 1950–80: Between Nationalism and Religion', *Middle Eastern Studies,* vol. 30, no. 4, October 1994, p. 941; Joseph Kostiner, 'State, Islam, and

Opposition in Saudi Arabia: The Post-Desert Storm Phase', in Bruce Maddy-Weitzman and Efraim Inbar (eds), *Religious Radicalism in the Greater Middle East* (Portland, Oregon, 1997), p. 79.

31. Jacob Goldberg, 'The Shi'a Minority in Saudi Arabia', in Cole and Keddie (eds), *Shi'ism and Social Protest*, p. 241.

32. Ibid., p. 239.

33. David E. Long, 'The Impact of the Iranian Revolution on the Arabian Peninsula and the Gulf States', in John L. Esposito (ed.), *The Iranian Revolution: Its Global Impact* (Miami,1999), pp. 105–6.

34. A royal decree, no. 217/23, issued on 11 June 1956, forbids the formation of political parties. See Helen Lackner, *A House Built on Sand: A Political Economy of Saudi Arabia* (London, 1978), p. 89.

35. David Easton, *A Systems Analysis of Political Life* (Chicago, 1965), p. 53.

36. Hassan al-Saffar, *Kaifa Naqhar al-Khawf* (How We Overcome Fear; Dallas, 1984), pp. 47–8.

37. Ibid., p. 25.

38. Ibid., p. 31.

39. Ibid., p. 91.

40. Ibid., p. 108.

41. *Until the Dawn*, p. 25.

42. *al-Thawra al-Islamiyya*, issue no. 54, October 1984, pp. 28–37.

43. R. K. Ramazani, 'Shi'ism in the Persian Gulf', p. 46.

44. Madawi al-Rasheed and Loulouwa al-Rasheed, 'The Politics of Encapsulation: Saudi Policy towards Tribal and Religious Opposition', Middle East Studies, vol. 32, no. 1 Jan. 1996, pp. 111–12.

45. *al-Thawra al-Islamiyya*, issue no. 10, January 1981, pp. 6–8.

46. Interview with Shaikh Tawfiq al-Saif, in London, October 2001.

47. Marvin Zonis and Daniel Brumberg, 'Shi'ism as Interpreted by Khomeini: An Ideology of Revolutionary Violence', in Martin Kramer (ed.), *Shi'ism: Resistance and Revolution* (Boulder, 1987), p. 48.

48. Hassan al-Saffar, *Mas'uliyat al-Shabab* (The Responsibility of Youth; Beirut, 1986), pp. 25, 34–35.

49. Olivier Roy, 'Islamists in Power', in Martin Kramer (ed.), *Islamism Debate* (Tel Aviv, 1997), pp. 82–5.

50. Muhammad Taqi al-Mudarresi, *al-'Amal al-Islami* (Islamic Action; Beirut, 1981), p. 15.

51. Muhammad Taqi al-Mudarresi, *al-Tahadi al-Islami* (Islamic Challenge; Tehran, 1990), p. 93.

52. Ibid., p. 105.

53. *Kalimat al-Haraka al-Islamiyya*, p. 30.

54. al Saffar, *Masu'lyat al-Shabab*, p. 45.

55. Hassan al-Saffar, *Fi'at al-'Amal al-Risali* (Message-oriented Action Groups; London, 1986), p. 25.

56. Ibid., p. 29.

57. Olivier Roy, 'Islamists in Power', p. 69.

58. Qutb clearly states that, 'the second aspect of this *din* as a practical movement is its progression stage by stage ... ', *Milestones*, p. 45.

59. *Manhaj Hizb al-Tahrir fi al-Taghiyeer* (The Program of the Tahrir Party for Change; private publication), p. 40; see also: Taqi al-Din al-Nabhani, *al-Takatul al-Hizbi* (Party Conglomerate; private publication), p. 36.

60. *Ikhwan al-Muslimin* played the democratic 'game' by supporting Hassan al-Banna as the *ikhwan* candidate for the January 1944 parliament; *hizb al-da'wa* literature shows that it adopts a strategy of four phases: intellectual, political, power struggle and proclaiming an Islamic state; MVM internal literature distinguished between revolutionary and *risaliyya* movements to which it allegedly belongs. See: Muhammad al-Taweel, *al-Ikhwan fi al-Barlaman* (Ikhwan in the Parliament; Cairo, 1992), p. 46; *Thaqafat al-Da'wa al-Islamiyya* (The Legacy of Islamic Da'wa; Iran, 1985), pp. 90ff.

61. Qutb, *Milestones*, p. 45.

62. *Fi al-Thawra*, 'About Revolution' (unpublished pamphlet by the IRO), pp. 53–5.

63. *al-Taly'a wa al-Muntalaqat al-Thawariyya* (Vanguard and the Revolutionary Principles; unpublished pamphlet), pp. 25–7.

64. al-Saffar, *Fi'at al-'Amal al-Risali*, p. 34.

65. Muhammad Taqi al-Mudarresi, *al-Ba'th al-Islami* (Islamic Renaissance; Tehran, 1984), p. 21.

66. *al-Taghiyeer wa al-Thawra al-Shamila Huwa al-Matloub* (Change and Comprehensive Revolution are Required; unpublished pamphlet), pp. 15–27.

67. Ibid., p. 22.

68. al-Mudarresi, *al-Ba'th al-Islami.*, p. 23.

69. Ibid, p. 23.

70. *Kalimat al-Harakah al-Islamiyya*, pp. 68–9.

71. Hassan al-Saffar, *al-Nidal 'Ala Jabhat al-Thaqafa wa al-Fikr* (The Struggle on the Cultural and Intellectual Front; London, 1983), p. 7.

72. *al-Muslim Bain' Waqihi wa Risalatihi* (The Muslim ... between Reality and Message; unpublished pamphlet), p. 5.

73. *Fi al-Thawra*; Ramazani, 'Shi'ism in the Persian Gulf', p. 45.

74. Hassan al-Saffar, *Ramadan ... Barnamaj Risali* (Ramadan ... A Message-oriented Programme; Beirut, 1986), p. 83.

75. Ibid., p. 9.

76. An interview with Shaikh Hassan al-Saffar in April 2001.

77. Ibid.

78. In political science, there are two main theoretical approaches to ideology. These Geertz identifies as the interest theory and the strain theory. Under interest theory, people 'pursue power'; under strain theory, they 'flee anxiety'. Interest theory's strength lies in the fact that it bases systematic cultural ideas on social structure, but its psychology is weak and unsubtle. Strain theory refers to 'personal tension' and social disarray; in it, motivation and context in relation to one another are well described. See: Clifford Geertz, 'Ideology as a Cultural System', in David E. Apter (ed.), *Ideology and Discontent* (New York, 1964), p. 52.

79. *al-Thawra al-Islamiyya*, issue no. 10, January 1981, p. 2.

80. Zonis and Brumberg, 'Shi'ism as Interpreted by Khomeini: An Ideology of Revolutionary Violence', p. 45.

81. *al-Thawra al-Islamiyya*, issue no. 8, November 1980, p. 1.

82. *Kalimat al-Haraka al-Islamiyya*, p. 76.

83. al-Mudarresi, *al-'Amal al-Islami*, pp. 144–5.

84. al-Saffar, *Mas'uliyat al-Shabab*, p. 15.

85. Ibid., pp. 36, 37.

86. al-Saffar, *Masu'liyat al-Shabab*, p. 55.

87. *Kalimat al-Haraka al-Islamiyya*, p. 83.

88. Ibid., p. 87.

89. *al-Thawra al-Islamiyya*, issue no. 15, July 1981, p. 8.

90. *Kalimat al-Haraka al-Islamiyya*, p. 30.

91. *Risalat al-ʿAnbiya'* (The Message of the Prophets; unpublished pamphlet), pp. 16–24.

92. *al-Sahafa Tuhawer al-ʿAlama al-Mudarresi* (The Press Interviews al-Mudarresi; Tehran, 1986), p. 70. The book includes a number of interviews with different newspapers and magazines.

93. al-Mudarresi, *al-ʿAmal al-Islami*, p. 263.

94. *Kalimat al-Haraka al-Islamiyya*, pp. 5–6.

95. Ibid., p. 165.

96. Muhammad Taqi al-Mudarresi, *Mustaqbal al-Thawra al-Islamiyya* (The Future of Islamic Revolution; Tehran, 1985), p. 23.

97. Ibid., pp. 167, 168.

98. *al-Sahafah Tuhawer al-ʿAlamah al-Mudarresi*, p. 183.

99. Ibid., p. 150.

100. al-Mudarresi, *Mustaqbal al-Thawra al-Islamiyya*, p. 19.

101. *Kalimat al-Haraka al-Islamiyya*, p. 111.

Chapter 5

1. An interview with Hamza al-Hassan in London in April 2002.

2. On 8 January 1980, the Islamic Union of Students of the Arabian Peninsula (affiliated with the IRO) organized a sit-in in front of the Saudi Embassy in London while another sit-in and hunger strike took place on 9–11 January in front of the South Bank Polytechnic on the 40th day of the uprising in the Eastern Province. See: Abdulrahman al-Shaikh, Saleh al-Dakhil and ʿAbdullah al-Zaier (eds), *Intifadat al-Mantaqa al-Sharqiya* (The Uprising of the Eastern Province; published by the Islamic Revolution Organization, Tehran, 1981), pp. 253–65.

3. Hassan al-Saffar, *al-Taʿadudiya wa al-Hurriyya fi al-Islam* (Plurality and Freedom in Islam; Beirut, 1996), pp. 184ff.

4. *al-Jazira al-ʿArabiyya*, issue no. 1, January 1991, pp. 2–3.

5. Interview with a leading member of the Reform Movement and a representative of the ICHR–GAP, 20 May 1993, *al-Jazira al-ʿArabiyya*, issue no. 29, June 1993, p. 18.

6. Madawi al-Rasheed, 'The Shiʿa of Saudi Arabia: A Minority in Search of Cultural Authenticity', *British Journal of Middle East Studies*, vol. 25, no. 1, May 1998, p. 12.

7. al-Saffar, *al-Taʿadudiya wa al-Hurriyya*.

8. See: *al-Jazira al-ʿArabiyya*, issue no. 29, June 1993, pp. 5–28.

9. See: *al-Jazira al-ʿArabiyya*, issue no. 13, February 1992, p. 42.

10. *al-Jazira al-ʿArabiyya*, issue no. 11, December 1991, pp. 37–9.

11. *al-Shiʿa fi al-Saudi ... alWaqiʿ al-Saʿb wa al-Tataluʿat al-Mashroua'* (The Shiʿis in Saudi Arabia: The Delicate Situation and Legitimate Pretensions; London, 1991), pp. 37–41.

12. This and subsequent ideas of al-Saffar set out in the following pages are from al-Saffar, *al-Taʿadudiya wa al-Hurriyya fi al-Islam*.

13. Interview with Tawfiq al-Saif in London, April 2002.

14. The report was written by Tawfiq al-Saif, Hamza al-Hassan and Abdul' Ameer Mosa and edited by Carmel Bedford, a member of Article 19.

15. *al-Jazira al-ʿArabiyya*, issue no. 10, November 1991, p. 19.

16. Ibid., pp. 20–27.

17. *al-Jazira al-ʿArabiyya*, issue no. 1, January 1991, p. 1.

18. Ibid.

19. *al-Jazira al-ʿArabiyya*, issue no. 3, March 1991.

20. In response to a letter sent by Minister of Interior Prince Naif on 9 September 1993 in regard to the alleged violations of Shaikh Safar al-Hawali and Shaikh Salman al-'Awda, Shaikh Ibn Baz wrote an extensive letter to Prince Naif following the 41st meeting of the Senior 'Ulama Committee in September 1993. Shaikh Ibn Baz said that the members of the Committee agreed to inform both al-Hawali and al-'Awda of the violations in their sermons, seminars and books. If they pledged to conform to state rules then they would be allowed to return to public preaching and religious learning; otherwise, they would be prevented from so doing. The Chamber of Religious Jurisdiction (*Dar al-Efta*'), the General Assembly of the Committee of Senior 'Ulama, no. 2/951, dated 3/4/1414– 19 September 1993. See: http://www.alsaha.com/sahat/Forum2/HTML/005476.html, accessed on 27 October 2004.

21. Key Salafi activists such as Shaikh Salam al-'Awda, Shaikh Safar al-Hawali, Shaikh 'Aiyd al-Qarni and others were arrested in September 1993 for provocative political activities. See: The Committee for the Defence of Human Rights in the Arabian Peninsula, http://www.cdhrap. net/text/legna/3.htm, accessed on 23 September 2004.

22. *al-Jazira al-'Arabiyya*, issue no. 12, January 1992, p. 3.

23. *al-Jazira al-'Arabiyya*, issue no. 18, July 1992, p. 47.

24. Fuller and Francke, *The Arab Shi'a: The Forgotten Muslims*, p. 188.

25. *al-Jazira al-'Arabiyya*, issue no. 21, October 1992, pp. 2–3, 4.

26. Among members of the *islahiyya* Movement who were in contact with al-Masa'ari were Ja'far al-Shayeb, the Chairman of the ICHR-GAP, 'Abdulamir Musa, the Managing Director of *al-Jazira al-'Arabiyya*, and the author.

27. Ibn Jibrin's *fatwa* was released in September 1991; *al-Jazira al-'Arabiyya*, issue no. 11, December 1992, p. 15.

28. A press conference held in Washington on 20 May 1993, *al-Jazira al-'Arabiyya*, issue no. 29, June 1993, p. 17.

29. Mancur Olson, *The Logic of Collective Action* (Cambridge, 1965), pp. 22ff.

30. Ibid., p. 52.

31. *al-Jazira al-'Arabiyya*, issue no. 1, January 1991, pp. 26–7, 40–41.

32. Interview with Shaikh Hassan al-Saffar, *al-Jazira al-'Arabiyya*, issue no. 17, June 1992, p. 19.

33. *al-siyasa*, Arabic daily newspaper based in Kuwait, 28 March 1992.

34. Interview with Shaikh Hassan al-Saffar, p. 18.

35. Fouad Ibrahim, 'Critical Reading of the Basic and *Shura* Orders', *al-Jazira al-'Arabiyya*, issue no. 14, 1992, p. 8. Articles of the Basic Order referred to are 26 and 37.

36. Ibid., pp. 8–9. Articles of the Basic Order referred to are: 5, 44, 50, 52, 56, 57, 60, 62, 68, 70, 73, 76, 79, 80.

37. *al-Jazira al-'Arabiyya*, issue no. 20, September 1992, p. 6.

38. An interview with Shaikh Hassan al-Saffar, *al-Jazira al-'Arabiyya*, issue no. 3, March 1991, p. 45.

39. Madawi al-Rasheed has successfully applied Scott's thesis on the arts of resistance to the *islahiyya* Movement in its search for authenticity. See: Madawi al-Rasheed, 'The Shi'a of Saudia: A Minority in Search of Cultural Authenticity', *British Journalism Middle East Studies*, vol. 25, no. 1, May 1998.

40. James Scott, *Domination and the Arts of Resistance: Hidden Transcripts* (London, 1990), pp. 9ff. Scott's thesis on the arts of contentious politics first appeared in *Weapons of the Weak* (1985).

41. Scott, *Domination and Arts of Resistance*, pp. 18–19.

42. Ibid., p. 2.

43. Ibid., pp. 206–7.

44. Mamoun Fandy, 'Sheikh Hassan al-Saffar and the Shi'a Reform Movement', in *Saudi Arabia and the Politics of Dissent* (London, 1999).

45. Fouad al-Ahmad (pseudonym of the present author), *al-Shaikh Hassan Ali al-Badr al-Qatifi* (Beirut, 1991).

46. Shaikh Hassan al-Saffar, *Shaikh Ali al-Biladi al-Qudaihi* (Beirut, 1990), p. 11.

47. Shaikh al-Saffar criticized al-Biladi's work for neglecting or belittling the importance of Shi'i scholars in the region, despite their remarkable roles in religious education, such as Shaikh Abdullah al-Ma'touq, one of al-Biladi's students. See: al-Saffar, *Shaikh Ali al-Biladi al-Qudaihi*, pp. 75–101.

48. Ibid., pp. 15–33.

49. Ibid., pp. 43–54, 113–16.

50. al-Ahmad, *Shaikh Hassan Ali al-Badr al-Qatifi*, pp. 44ff.

51. Ibid., pp. 93–133.

52. The author annotated the pamphlet and annexed it to the book; pp. 173–91.

53. Hamza al-Hassan, *al-Shi'a fi al-mamlak al-Arabiyya al-Saudiyya*, vol. 1, p. 7.

54. Ibid., p. 9.

55. See: al-Rasheed, 'The Shi'a of Saudia', pp. 125ff.

56. Ibid., pp. 15–26.

57. Ibid., pp. 26–72.

58. Ibid., pp. 378–91.

59. Muhammad Abdulmajeed, *al-Tamieyz al-Taifi f al-Saudiyya* (Sectarian Discrimination in Saudi Arabia; London, 1993), pp. 29–131.

60. *al-Shi'a fi al-Saudiyya … al-Waqi' al-Sa'b wa al-Tataluat al-Mashroua'*, pp. 45, 49–55.

61. Ibid., p. 47.

62. Scott, *Domination and Arts of Resistance*, pp. 216–17. Scott distinguishes between two forms of public declaration of defiance: raw and cooked declaration. While raw declarations come from subordinate groups who are subjected to indignities and relatively atomized by the process of domination, cooked declarations are more liberated from domination and surveillance.

Chapter 6

1. See: Michael Hudson, 'Arab Regimes and Democratization: Responses to the Challenge of Political Islam', in Laura Guazzone (ed.), *The Islamist Dilemma* (Reading and Ithaca, 1995) p. 231; Geoff Simmons, *Saudi Arabia: The Shape of a Client Feudalism* (London, 1995), pp. 24–5.

2. Abdul Latif al-'Amer (pseudonym), *al-haraka al-Islamiyya fi al-Jazira al-'Arabiyya* (The Islamic Movement in the Arabian Peninsula; London, 1988), p. 175.

3. 'Saudi deal curbs Shi'ite opponents', *New York Times*, 30 October 1993.

4. Michael Hudson, 'Arab Regimes and Democratization', p. 231.

5. Ibid.

6. Internal magazine, limited to the members of the Movement, issue 213, p. 52.

7. 15 January 1994, p. 56.

8. Ibid.

9. 24 September 1990.

10. Official letter signed by Prince Bandar on 17 October 1990.

11. Internal magazine (n.d.), issue no. 231, pp. 52–5.

12. Letter sent to Shaikh Abdul Aziz al-Tuwaijri in September 1991.

13. Letter dated 21 May 1991.

14. 20 September and 21 October 1993.
15. Shaikh Rashid al-Ghanoushi told the present author that he had indicated to al-Saif that, 'the presence of an Islamic movement inside its homeland should be a prime objective, since working from outside has little effect on internal issues in any given country'. London, 23 April 1999.
16. Tawfiq al-Saif was a member of a weekly seminar which used to be held at Shaikh Rashid al-Ghanoushi's house in London from 1991 and attended by a number of Islamists, both Sunni and Shi'is.
17. 19 April 1993.
18. Communiqué issued by ICHR–GAP on 29 July 1993.
19. Hamza al-Hassan, 9 January 1994.
20. London, 1 October 2002.
21. *al-Jazira al-'Arabiyya*, issue no. 15, April 1992, pp. 2–3; issue no. 24, January 1993, pp. 2–5.
22. *Qadaya al-'Usbu'*, Weekly Issues, issue no. 5, 3 November 1993, sponsored by the Preliminary Committee for the Permanent Conference of the Lebanese Dialogue, p. 9.
23. 25 March 1994.
24. *Risalat al-Haramain*, issue no. 45, October 1993, pp. 2–3.
25. *al-Nasr*, issue no. 35, October 1993, p. 56.
26. Ibid., p. 55.
27. *al-'Alam*, monthly magazine based in London, issue no. 209, 12 November 1993, p. 12.
28. *al-Nasr*, issue no. 35, p. 52.
29. Ibid., p. 50.
30. Reported in some Iranian newspapers, such as *Salam* (5 August 1993), and even by BBC World Service – Persian section.
31. Interview with Tawfiq al-Saif in London, 23 August 2002.
32. Hafiz al-Shaikh, 'Khatwa fi al-Ittijah al-Sahih wa Makhafat Ta'wil Ghair al-Sahih' (A Step in the Right Direction and the Fear of Misinterpretation), *Akhbar al-Khaleej*, daily newspaper based in Bahrain, 27 October 1993.
33. *al-'Alam*, issue no. 208, 12 November 1993, p. 12.
34. *Sawt al-Bahrain* (The Voice of Bahrain), issue no. 131, December 1993, p. 3.
35. Jane Mansbridge, 'What Does a Representative Do? Descriptive Representation in Communicative Settings of Distrust, Uncrystallized Interests, and Historically Denigrated Status', in Will Kaymlicka and Wayne Norman (eds), *Citizenship in Diverse Societies* (Oxford, 2000), p. 99.
36. This information comes from the archive of the Reform Movement.
37. Shaikh Abdullah b. Abdulrahman al-Ghadiyan was appointed by King Faisal as a member of the Senior *'ulama* Committee on the basis of a royal decree, no. 1/138, issued on 28 August 1970. al-Ghadiyan is also a lecturer at Islamic Law College, the head of the Legitimate Supreme Court in Khubar in Eastern Province, and a member of the Permanent Committee for Scientific Research and Religious Guidance. See: http://www.binbaz.org.sa/Display.asp?f=eng0241 and http://www.islamway.com/?iw_s=Scholar&iw_a=info&scholar_id=76, both accessed on 17 October 2004.
38. Information from the Saudi mediator in the dialogue between the king and the *islahiyya* Movement.
39. Letter sent by Shaikh Muhammad al-Saffar to the leader of the Reform Movement on 21 March 1994.
40. Letter sent by Sadiq al-Jabran on 1 March 1994.
41. Letter sent by a leader of the Reform Movement on 19 May 1993 to a representative of the

Movement in negotiation with the government.

42. Ibid.

43. Letter sent on 26 February 1994 by Muhammad Muhsin, a member of the Reform Movement. to the Central Committee.

44. Ibid.

45. Letter by Shaikh Hassan al-Saffar to Hamza al-Hassan on 9 January 1994.

46. Letter sent by Yahiya Quraish, a member of the Central Committee. on 2 April 1994.

47. According to Robert Hughes, the success of any movement to produce complaining victims would give power to the movement. Thus the positive victimhood promoted among the Shiʿis would be expected to lead to a growing number of complainants and accordingly to growing pressure on the government to realize the Shiʿi demands. See: Robert Hughes, *Culture of Complaint: The Fraying of America* (London, 1994), pp. 13ff.

48. Fuller and Francke, *The Arab Shiʿa: The Forgotten Muslims*, p. 19.

49. 'Saudi Deal Curbs Shiʿa Opponents', *New York Times*, 30 October 1993.

50. Letter to King Fahad, December 1990.

51. Letter to Central Committee, 9 January 1994.

52. Letter sent by Muhammad Muhsin, on 26 February 1994.

Chapter 7

1. Mordechai Abir, *Saudi Arabia in the Oil Era*, p. 154.

2. See: www.thulatha.com.

3. Daniel Horowitz, *Ethnic Groups in Conflict* (London, 1985), p. 578.

4. al-Saffar, Hassan, 'Ahadith fi al-Din wa al-Thaqafa wa al-Ijtima', (Sermons on Religion, Culture and Society; Beirut, 2002), p. 374

5. *al-Mawaqif*, (The Stances), a weekly magazine based in Bahrain, issue No. 1266, pp. 26–7

6. Hassan al-Saffar, *al-Tatur wa al-Tajdid al-Dini* (Evolution and Religious Renewal), sermon delivered on 9 Muharram 1416 (7 June 1995).

7. This is based on discussion among a group of leading members of the Movement in the period following the dialogue with the government in September 1993. Two books arose out of this, both dealing with the issue of religious authority in the Shiʿi school of thought. See: Fouad Ibrahim, *al-Faqih wa al-Dawla, Tatur al-fikr al-Siyasi al-Shiʿi* (Beirut, 1998); Tawfiq al-Saif, *Did al-Istibdad* (Anti-despotism; Beirut, 1999).

8. al-Saffar, 'Ahadith fi al-Din wa al-Thaqafah wa al-Ijtima', p. 319.

9. Robert Hughes's *Culture of Complaint* contends that we have developed into a culture of individuals arguing for their victim status, and that as the number of victims grows and the consistency of the search for resolution takes shape within our national identity, the very core of all that is valued and strong falls by the wayside.

10. Hassan al-Saffar, *al-Faʿiliyya aw 'Ejtirar al-Ghobn* (Activism or Remembering Repression), sermon delivered on 8 Muharram 1417 (25 May 1996).

11. Hassan al-Saffar, *al-Taʿlim wa al-Mustaqbal* (Education and Future); *al-ʿAmal Yasnau al-Waqe'* (Action Creates Reality), sermons delivered on 3 and 4 Muharram 1418 (10 and 11 May 1997) respectively; Hassan al-Saffar, *Bina' al-Kafa'* (Building Qualification), sermon delivered on 13 Muharram 1419 (9 May 1998).

12. Muhammad Mahfoud, *al-'Ahl wa al-Dawlah: Bayan Min 'Ajl al-Silm al-Mujtamaiʿ* (Nation and State, a Manifesto for Social Peace; Beirut, 1997), p. 41.

13. Robert Welson and Howard Wolpe, 'Modernization and the Politics of Communalism: A Theoretical Perspective', *American Political Science Review* 64, no. 4, December 1970, p. 1130.

14. *Ikhtilaf al-Madhhab, Hal Yamnaʿ al-Tazawuj* (Does Sectarian Difference Prevent

Intermarriage?), sermon delivered on 1/3/1422 (23 May 2001), www.saffar.org, accessed on 13 August 2001.

15. Ibid.
16. M. Mahfoud, *al-Umma wa al-Dawla, al-Rihan al-Jadid* (Nation and State, the New Stake), *al-Kalima*, issue 27, spring 2000.
17. Hassan al-Saffar, *Muqawimat al-Silm al-Ijtimai'* (The Pillars of Social Peace), sermon delivered on 10/2/1422 (3 May 2001), www.saffar.org.
18. Mahfoud, *al-Umma wa al-Dawla.*
19. Ibid.
20. Fandy, *Saudi Arabia and the Politics of Dissent*, p. 204; Hassan al-Saffar, *al-Hiwar wa al-'Enfitah Manhaj al-Mou'min* (Dialogue and Openness are the Method of the Believer), sermon delivered on 5/1/1418 (12 May 1997).
21. Fandy, ibid., p. 209.
22. Hassan al-Saffar, *al-Watan wa al-Muwatana, al-Huquq wa al-Wajibat* (Homeland and Citizenship, Rights and Obligations; Beirut, 1988), p. 11.
23. Hassan al-Saffar, *Hobu al-Watan min al-'Eman* (The Love of Homeland is Part of Belief), sermon delivered in Muharram 1416 (June 1995).
24. Tawfiq al-Saif, *'Eshkaliyat al-Dawla al-Haditha Min Manzour Fiqhi* (Problems of the Modern State from a Juristic Perspective), *al-Kalima*, issue no. 32, summer 2001, http://www.kalema.net/, accessed on 17 December 2003.
25. al-Saif, *Did al-Istibdad*, p. 329.
26. al-Saffar, *al-Watan wa al-Muwatana*, pp. 21–4.
27. Ibid., p. 25.
28. Muhammad Mahfoud, *Nahwa Mujtama' Ahli Arabi-Islami Jadid* (Towards New Arabian–Islamic Civil Society), *al-Kalima*, issue no. 23, 1999. http://www.kalema.net/.
29. Hassan al-Saffar, *al-Mujtama' al-Ahli* (Civil Society), sermon delivered on 9/1/1418 (16 May 1997).
30. Tawfiq al-Saif, *'Eshkaliyat al-Dawla al-Haditha Min Manzour Fiqhi.*
31. Muhammad Mahfoud, *Su'al al-Hurriyya fi al-Fikr al-Islami al-Mu'asir* (The Question of Freedom in Contemporary Islamic Thought), *al-Kalima*, issue no. 24, summer 1999, p. 27.
32. Muhammad Mahfoud, *Nazarat Hawla al-Wihda wa al-Ta'dud fi al-Fikr al-Islami al-Mu'asir* (Views on Unity and Pluralism in Contemporary Islamic Thought), *al-Kalima*, issue no. 21, autumn 1998, p. 27.
33. Ibn Taimiya Shaikh al-Islam Ahmad Taqi al-Din, *Minhaj al-Sunna fi Naqd Kalam al-Shi'a wa al-Qadariyya* (The Sunni Method in the Attack of the Theology of the Shi'is and Qadariyah [a Predestination-oriented sect]); (Riyadh, n.d.), vol. 4, pp. 6ff.
34. Muhammad al-Bahi, *al-Fikr al-Islami fi Taturihi* (Islamic Thought in its Development; Beirut, 1971), p. 140.
35. Richard, *Shi'ite Islam*, p. 119.
36. Hamid Enayat, *Modern Islamic Political Thought* (Austin, TX, 1983), p. 41.
37. Riyadh, 1988, pp. 153, 322, 327.
38. Muhammad al-Bahi argues that Wahhabism was the bridge through which Ibn Taimiyya's thought passed. See: al-Bahi, *al-Fikr al-Islami ...*, pp. 145ff.
39. Muhib al-Din al-Khatib, *al-Khutut al-'Arida* (Jeddah, 1960), pp. 9–10.
40. http://www.ibn-jebreen.com/fatawa/frame02.htm. accessed on 19 July 2002.
41. Shaikh 'Abdulaziz b. Ibn Baz, *Majmu' Fatawa wa Maqalat*, vol. 5, Question 7. www.binbaz.org.sa.
42. Muhammad Khalil al-Harras, *al-Haraka al-Wahhabiyya: Rad 'ala Maqal al-Doctur*

Muhammad al-Bahi fi Naqd al-Wahhabiyya (The Wahhabi Movement: A Refutation of an Article by Muhammad al-Bahi in Critique of Wahhabism; Medina, 1976), p. 44.

43. Shaikh Abdullah al-Fawzan, *Kitab al-Tawhid*, the first chapter; Ibn 'Uthimein, Muhammad b. Saleh, *'al-Qawl al-Mufid 'ala Kitab al-Tawhid* (Riyadh, 1985), vol. 1, pp. 5ff.

44. The most prominent example is Shaikh Hassan Farhan al-Malki, who authored a number of critical books under the title of *Nahwa Enqadh al-Tarikh al-Islami* (Towards Rescuing Islamic History). On 29/4/1422 (20 July 2001), Shaikh Humoud b. 'Aqla al-Shwu'aibi, a member of the Senior Wahhabi *'ulama* Committee, issued a *fatwa* urging that Shaikh al-Malki be prevented from writing, all his books be confiscated and that he be sacked and sued. http://www.saaid. net/Warathah/hmood/h35.htm, accessed on 29 March 2002.

45. Ibid.

46. Shaikh Nasir 'al-'Omar, *'Allahu 'Akbar Ghulibat 'al-Roum* (Great God, the Romans are Defeated), 18 April 2003. http://www.islamtoday.net/articles/show_articles_content. cfm?id=37&catid=39&artid=2099, accessed on 7 June 2002.

47. The crown prince's entourage, who took the lead in rebuilding relations with Iran, responded promptly to the provocative sermon, which offended Shaikh Rafsanjani enough to make him walk out of the mosque. It was claimed that the crown prince expressed his deep apology to his Iranian guest. Furthermore, Abdullah's entourage pleaded with Shi'i preachers in the Eastern Province to ignore the incident for fear of endangering the efforts made by both parties to rebuild their relations.

48. http://www.alsalafiyoun.com, accessed on 9 April 2001.

49. Shaikh Ibn Baz, *Majmu' Fatawa wa Maqalat*, vol. 5, Question 9, www.binbaz.org. sa; Shaikh Muhammad b. Saleh Ibn 'Uthiemin, *'Al'etidal fi al-Da'wa* (Moderation of Propagation), http://www.binothaimeen.com/cgi-bin/ebook/viewnews.cgi?category=26 &id=1035268240; Safar al-Hawali, *Jawab 'Amma Qaddamathu al-Taifa al-Shi'iyya Min Matalib Li-Wali al'Ahd* (A Response to the Shi'i Demands Submitted to the Crown Prince), http://www.almoslim.net/, accessed on 15 September 2003.

50. Abdullah al-Hamid, *Janahan Hallaqa bihima al-Islam: al-Hurriyya wa al-'Adala*, http:// www.arabrenewal.com/index.php?rd=AI&AI0=301.

51. Abdullah al-Hamid, *Fak al-'Ertibat baina Takfir al'Amal wa Taksir al-'Ashkhas* (The Separation between Excommunication of Actions and Destruction of Persons), *al-Hayat*, daily newspaper, issue no. 13635, 11 July 2000, p. 21.

52. Abdullah Nasir al-Subaih, *'al-jewar al-Makani wa al-Qawasim al-Mushtaraka* (Vicinity and Commonalities), 15 June 2003, http://islamtoday.net/articles/show_articles_ content.cfm?catid=39&artid=2405.

53. Hamzah al-Hassan, *al-Shi'a fi al-Mamlaka 'al-'Arabiyya al-Saudia*, vol. 2, pp. 404–5.

54. Salman b. Fahad al-'Awda, *'Ala Hamish al-intifada* (On the Margin of the Uprising), http://www.saaid. net/mktarat/flasteen/7.htm, accessed on 21 June 2003.

55. Sa'ad al-Faqih's view of the Shi'is is a bit vague. While he maintains a friendly relationship with Shi'i political activists in London, he refuses publicly to recognize the Shi'is as Muslims.

56. I put the question to Sa'ad al-Faqih during a gathering in Ramadan, at the house of Saeed al-Shihabi, a Bahraini political leader in London, on 10 December 2000.

57. Shaikh Salman al-'Awda was chosen as a spokesman by the participants of the National Dialogue in June 2003. He delivered a speech before the crown prince, in which he summarized the major issues that the conference encountered. www.islamtoday.net.

58. Muhammad Rida Nasrulla, 'Hadha Ma Jara fi Majlis al-Shaikh Ibn Baz', *al-Riyadh* daily newspaper, 18 June 2003.

59. www.alsaffar.org, accessed on 18 September 2004.
60. An interview with Shaikh Hassan al-Saffar by *al-Madina,* daily newspaper based in Medina city in the Western Province, which took place on 8 October 2004.
61. www.alarabiya.com, accessed on 20 September 2004.
62. Muhammad Mahfoud, *Nazarat Hawla al-Wehda wa al-Ta'dud fi al-Fikr al-Islami al-Mu'asir* (Views on Unity and Plurality in Contemporary Islamic Thought), *al-Kalima,* issue no. 21, autumn 1998, pp. 25–42; Muhammad Mahfoud, *al-'Ekhtilaf wa Ma'na al-Wehda* (Difference and Meaning of Unity), *al-Kalima,* issue no. 31, spring 2001, pp. 37–47; Muhammad b. Husain al-Tahir (pseudonym), *Mas'alat al-Wehda wa Ta'dud fi al-Waqi al-Islami* (The Question of Unity and Plurality in the Islamic Reality), *al-Waha,* issue no. 10–11, 1997, pp. 257–90.
63. *al-Waha,* issue no. 2, 1995, p. 156.
64. Ibid., p. 160.
65. *Nahwa Qira' Jadida lil-Shi'a* (Towards a New Reading of Shi'ism), *al-Waha,* issue no. 18, autumn 2000, pp. 52–7.
66. Hassan al-Saffar, *al-Ta'ifiyya wa Mustaqbal al-Watan* (Sectarianism and the Future of the Nation), sermon delivered on 4/1/1416 (2 June 1995).
67. Hassan al-Saffar, *al-Tanu' wa al-T'ayush* (Diversity and Coexistence; London, 1999), p. 36.
68. *al-'Amil al-Dini fi al-Thaqafa al-Wataniyya* (The Religious Factor in National Culture), *al-Waha,* issue no. 18, spring 2000, p. 5.
69. Hassan al-Saffar, *Thaqafat al-Silm al-Ijtimai' wa Akhlaqiatuh* (The Culture of Social Peace and its Principles), sermon delivered on 24/2/1422 (17 May 2001), p. 3.
70. al-Saffar, *'Ahadith fi al-Din ...,* p. 225.
71. *al-Madina* daily newspaper, issue no. 99, 4 February 2002, p. 2.
72. www.alarabiya.com, accessed on 20 September 2004.
73. *al-Waha,* issues no. 10, 11, 1st and 2nd quarter of 1997, pp. 257–90.
74. *al-Waha,* issue no. 12, spring 1997, pp. 128–51.
75. Hamid Enayat, *Modern Islamic Political Thought,* p. 30.
76. Ibid., pp. 30–31.
77. Wilfried Buchta, 'Tehran's Ecumenical Society' (*Majma' al-Taqrib*): A Veritable Ecumenical Revival, or a Trojan Horse of Iran?', in Rainer Brunner and Werner Ende (eds), *The Twelver Shi'a in Modern Times* (Leiden, 2001), p. 346.
78. Sayyid Muhammad Kazim al-Yazdi, *al-'Urwat 'al-Wethqa* (The Firm Bond; Beirut, 1990), pp. 61–2, Questions190–192, 200–203; 'al-Hurr al-'Amili, *Wasail 'al-Shi'a* (Qum, Iran, n.d.), Chapters 11 and 68.
79. Buchta, 'Tehran's Ecumenical Society', p. 333.
80. Abdullah Muhammad Ali, *Mu'jam Ma 'Allafahu 'Ulama al-'Umma al-Islamiyya Lil Rad 'Ala Khurafat al-Da'wa al-Wahhabiyya* (A Bibliography of the Writings of the Islamic Scholars in Refuting the Illusions of the Wahhabi Call), *Turathuna,* a quarterly magazine based in Qum, issue no. 17, 22 May 1989, pp. 146–78.
81. This is based on information obtained from various publishing houses in Beirut, some of which are owned and administered by Saudi Shi'is.
82. The question was put to a leading Shi'i preacher who subscribes to the Reform Movement, 12 May 2003.
83. http://www.alwahabiya.org/almoraqib.htm, accessed on 12 June 2003.
84. Murtada Mutahari, *al-Ejtihad fi al-Islam: Muhadarat fi al-Din wa al-Ejitma'* (Reasoning in Islam: Lectures on Religion and Sociology; Tehran, n.d.), vol. 2, pp. 54ff.
85. *al-Naqd al-Dhati wa Sultat al-'Awam* (Self-Criticism and the Authority of Common

People), *al-Waha*, issue no. 1, 1995, pp. 147–51; al-Tahir, *Mas'alat al-Wehda wa Ta'dud fi al-Waqi al-Islami*, pp. 266–69.

86. 12 May 2003.
87. I am indebted to Ja'ar al-Shayeb, a leading member of the Reform Movement, who spared no effort to make the questionnaire successful. He distributed leaflets among the Shi'i pilgrims and personally explained the technical aspects of the questionnaire and emphasized the importance of responding.
88. Bhikhu Parekh, 'Common Citizenship in a Multicultural Society', *Round Table*, 1999, 351, p. 449.
89. The full translation of the petition is given in the Appendix.
90. On 28 June 2003 some 1180 Isma'ili figures submitted a petition entitled 'The Homeland Is for All and All Are for the Homeland' to Crown Prince Abdullah, demanding justice, equality, religious freedom and civic liberties. See: *al-Hijaz*, a monthly magazine based in London, issue no. 9, 15 July 2003, pp. 25–7.
91. According to information obtained from al-Saffar in July 2000, he himself was granted land from the government to build a mosque; other Shi'i shaikhs were also granted land and licences to build mosques.
92. *al-Watan*, daily newspaper based in 'Asir, in the south of Saudi Arabia, 13 December 2001.
93. al-Rasheed, 'The Shi'a of Saudi Arabia: A Minority in Search of Cultural Authenticity', p. 137.
94. Claude Ake, *A Theory of Political Integration* (Homewood, IL, 1967), pp. 79, 118–19.
95. R. Dekmejian, 'The Liberal Impulse in Saudi Arabia', *Middle East Journal*, vol. 57, no. 3, summer 2003, p. 408.
96. Amira Kashgari, *al-Watan,* 20 January 2004. See: *Saudi Affairs*, issue no. 13, February 2004, pp. 36–9.
97. A spokesman of the State Department condemned the detentions as 'inconsistent with the kind of forward progress that reform-minded people are looking for'. BBC, 17 March 2004.
98. Saudi official television channel, 22 March 2004.
99. Information from one of the participants.
100. Mai Yamani, 'Arrests Make Mockery of Saudi Reform Talk: Empty Promises', *International Herald Tribune*, 23 March 2004.
101. *al-Hijaz*, issue no. 17, March 2004, p. 24.
102. R. Dekmejian, 'The Liberal Impulse in Saudi Arabia', pp. 400ff.
103. *Intifadat Skaka: Hal Tantaqil min al-Taraf ela al-Markaz* (Skaka Uprising: Will it Extend from the Periphery to the Core?), *al-Hijaz*, issue no. 16, 15 February 2004, p. 25.

Afterword

1. According to official reports published by the Saudi Press Agency on 12 December 2005, there was a steady increase in the revenues during the year 2005. The total expected revenues were estimated to be 555 billion riyals (U$=3.75 Saudi riyals), an increase of 275 billion riyals on forecast revenue, while total expenditure was estimated at 341 billion riyals.
2. The value traded during the period between summer 2005 and winter 2006 has reached unprecedented rates, the daily average being 36 billion riyals.
3. Jafar al-Shayeb, *New Saudi King and Challenge of Reforms*, 30 September 2005, http://www.saudishia.com/index.php?option=com_content&task=view&id=15&Itemid=30, accessed on 30 January 2006.
4. See: Madawi al-Rasheed, *Raheel al-Malik Fahad ... wa Muhasabat al-Marhala* (The Death

of King Fahad, and Rethinking the Stage), *al-Quds al-Arabi*, London, 15 August 2005.

5. *al-Hijaz*, issue no. 34, 15 August 2005, p. 5.

6. *Ibid.*

7. *al-Usbou'*, weekly newspaper based in Berlin, 18 August 2005.

8. See: http://www.saudishia.com/index.php?option=com_frontpage&Itemid=1; http://www.rasid.com, accessed on 31 January 2006.

9. http://alarabiya.net/Article.aspx?v=12491, accessed on 25 April 2005.

10. http://www.alwatan.com.sa/daily/2005!04!13/first_page/first_page02.htm, accessed on 31 January 2006.

11. www.elaph.com, accessed on 25 December 2005.

12. www.aljazeera.net, accessed on 8 August 2005.

13. Reuters, 11 August 2005.

14. Ibid.

Select Bibliography

Books

'Abbas, 'Abdulghani, *Tatalu' Umma. Qira'a fi Fikr Ayatullah Sayyid Muhammad*. Qum, 1989.

Abdulmajeed, Muhammad, *Al-Tamyeez al-Ta'ifi fi al-Sa'udiyya* (Sectarian Discrimination in Saudi Arabia). London, 1993.

'Abdulrahman al-Shaikh, Saleh al-Dakhil and 'Abdullah al-Zaier (eds), *Intifadat al-Mantaqa al-Sharqiya* (The Uprising in the Eastern Province). Tehran, 1981.

Abdulwahhab, Muhammad B., *Al-Radd 'Ala al-Rafida* (The Refutation of the Repudiators). Riyadh, n.d.

Abir, Mordechai, *Saudi Arabia in the Oil Era: Regime and Elites; Conflict and Collaboration*. Boulder, 1988.

Abrahamian, Ervand, *Khomeinism: Essays on the Islamic Republic*. Berkeley, 1993.

al-Ahmad, Fouad, *Al-Shaikh Hasan 'Ali al-Badr al-Qatifi*. Beirut, 1991.

Ake, Claude, *Theory of Political Integration*. Homewood, NJ, 1967.

Akhavi, Sharough, *Religion and Politics in Contemporary Iran: Clergy-State Relations in the Pahlavi Period*. New York, 1980.

Algar, Hamid, *Islam and Revolution*. Berkeley, 1981.

'Aliyah, 'Abdulfattah 'Abu, *'Al-islah al-'jtima'i fi 'Ahd al-Malik 'Abdul 'Aziz* (Social Reform in the Reign of King 'Abdul Aziz). Riyadh, 1976.

al-'Amer, Abdul Latif (pseudonym), *Al-Haraka al-Islamiyya fi al-Jazira al-Arabiyya* (The Islamic Movement in the Arabian Peninsula). London, 1988.

al-'Amili, al-Hurr, *Wasail al-Shi'a*. Qum, Iran, n.d.

Amir-Moezi, M. A., *The Divine Guide in Early Shi'ism*, translated by David Streight. New York, 1994.

Andersen, Benedict, *Imagined Communities: Reflections on the Origin and the Spread of Nationalism*. London, 1983.

Apter, David E. (ed.), *Ideology and Discontent*. New York, 1964.

An Approach to the Understanding of Islam, www.shariati.com.

Area Handbook for Saudi Arabia, issued by The American University. Washington DC, 1971.

al-Bahi, Muhammad, *Al-Fikr al-Islami fi Taturihi* (Islamic Thought in its Development). Beirut, 1971.

Barri, Abdulmeni'm, *Al-Shi'a al-Ethni 'Ashariyya fi Da'irat al-Dau'* (The Shi'a Twelvers in the Spotlight). Cairo, 1989.

ibn Baz, al-Shaikh 'Abd al-'Aziz, *Naqd al-Qawmiyya al-'Arabiyya 'Ala Dau' al-Qur'an wa al-Sunna* (A Critique of Arab Nationalism in the Light of the Qur'an and the Sunna). Beirut, 1971.

Ibn Bishr, *'Enwan al-Majd fi Tarikh Najd* (The Landmark of Glorification in the History of Najd). Riyadh, 1982.

Brown, A., *Oil, God and Gold: The Story of Aramco and Saudi Kings.* Boston, 1999.

Buchan, James, 'Secular and Religious Opposition in Saudi Arabia', in Tim Niblock (ed.), *State, Society and Economy in Saudi Arabia.* Beckenham, 1982.

Buchta, Wilfried, 'Tehran's Ecumenical Society (Majma Taqrib): A Veritable Ecumenical Revival or a Trojan Horse of Iran?', in Rainer Brunner and Werner Ende (eds), *The Twelver Shi'a in Modern Times.* Leiden, 2001.

Cole, Juan R., 'Imami Jurisprudence and the Role of the Ulama: Mortaza Ansari on Emulating the Supreme Exemplar', in Nikki Keddie (ed.), *Religion and Politics in Iran.* New Haven, 1983.

Connor, Walker, 'When Is a Nation', in Hutchinson and Smith (eds) *Nationalism.* Oxford, 1994.

Dekmejian, P. Harir, 'Saudi Arabia', in *Islam in Revolution: Fundamentalism in the Arab World.* Syracuse University Press, 1985.

Dere, Abud Ali, *Zahirat al-Gholuw fi al-Din ... al-'Asbab* (The Phenomenon of Religious Extremism ... the Causes). Qasim, 1998.

Dickson, H. R. B., *Kuwait and her Neighbours.* London, 1956.

Donohue, John J., and John L. Esposito (eds.), *Islam in Transition.* Oxford, 1982.

Durkheim, Emile, *The Elementary Form of the Religious Life.* London, 1915.

Easton, David, *A System of Analysis of Political Life.* Chicago, 1965.

Elahi Zahir, Ehsan, *Al-Shi'a wa al-Tashiu', The Shi'i and Shi'ism.* Lahore, 1985.

Enayat, Hamid, *Modern Islamic Political Thought.* Austin, TX, 1983.

Esposito, John L. (ed.), *The Iranian Revolution: Its Global Impact.* Miami, 1999.

Esposito, John L., *The Straight Path.* Oxford, 1988.

Fandy, Mamoun, *Saudi Arabia and the Politics of Dissent.* London, 1999.

al-Fawzan, Saleh b. Fawzan, *Kitab al-Tawhid* (The Book of Monotheism). Cairo, n.d.

Fi Dhikra Al-intifada (In Memory of the Uprising). London, 1985.

Fuller, Graham E. and Rend Rahim Francke, *The Arab Shi'a: The Forgotten Muslims.* New York, 1999.

Gause, Gregory, *Oil Monarchies: Domestic and Security Challenges in the Arab Gulf States,* published by Council on Foreign Relations. New York, 1994.

Ghannam, al-Shaikh al-Imam Hussain, *Tarikh Najd* (The History of Najd), annotated by Nasir al-Din al-'Asad. Beirut, 1985.

al-Gharaibah, Abd al-Kareem, *Qiyam al-Dawala al-Arabiyya al-Saudiyya* (The Rise of the Saudi Arabian State). Cairo, 1974.

al-Gharib, Abdullah Muhammad, *Dirasat fi 'Aqaid al-Shi'a* (Studies on the Shi'i

Doctrines). Riyadh, 1982.

Gellner, Ernest, *Nations and Nationalism*. Oxford, 1983.

Habib, John S., *Ibn Sa'ud's Warriors of Islam*. Leiden, 1978.

Halm, Heinz, *Shi'a Islam from Religion to Revolution*. Princeton, 1997.

Hamzah, Fouad, *Al-Bilad al-'Arabiyya al-Sa'udiyya*. Riyadh, 1968.

al-Harras, Muhammad Khalil, *Al-Haraka al-Wahhabiyya: Raddun 'Ala Maqal al-Doctur Muhammad al-Bahi fi Naqd al-Wahhabiyya* (The Wahhabi Movement: A Refutation of Dr Muhammad al-Bahi's Critique of Wahhabism). Medina, 1976.

al-Hassan, Hamza, *Al-Shi'a fi al-Mamlaka al-'Arabiyya al-Saudiyya* (The Shi'is in the Kingdom of Saudi Arabia). Beirut, 1993.

Helms, Christine Moss, *The Cohesion of Saudi Arabia: Evolution of Political Identity*. London, 1981.

Herb, Michael, *All in the Family*. New York, 1999.

Horowitz, Donald, *Ethnic Groups in Conflict*. London, 1985.

Hughes, Robert, *Culture of Complaint: The Fraying of America*. London, 1994.

Huquq al-Ensan fi al-Mamlaka al-'Arabiyya al-Saudiyya (Human Rights in Saudi Arabia), sponsored by The International Committee for the Defense of Human Rights in the Gulf and Arabian Peninsula. October, 1989.

Ibrahim, Fouad, *Al-Faqih wa al-Dawla, Tatur al-fikr al-Siyasi al-Shi'i* (Jurist and the State: the Evolution of Shi'i Political Thought). Beirut, 1998.

al-Jabhan, Ibrahim, *Tabdid al-Zalam wa Tanbih al-Niyam 'Ela Khatar al-Shi'a wa al-Tashi"u' 'Ala al-Muslimin wa al-Islam* (Diffusing Darkness and Awakening those who are Asleep to the Danger of Shi'a and Shi'sm to Muslims and Islam). Riyadh, 1988.

Ja'far al-Shaikh, 'Abdullah, *Al-Naft wa al-'Est'mar* (Oil and Colonization). London, 1984.

Jarallah, Musa, Al-Washi'a fi Naqd 'Aqa'id al-Shi'a (Critique of the Shi'i Doctrines). Cairo, 1935.

Kalimat al-Haraka al-Islamiyya fi al-Jazira al-Arabiyya (The Discourse of the Islamic Movement in the Arabian Peninsula), published by the Islamic Revolution Organization. London, 1986.

Kazim, al-'Alamah Muhammad Jawad, *Al-Qiyada al-Islamiyya* (The Islamic Leadership). Beirut, 1968.

Kelly, J. B., *Arabia, the Gulf and the West*. London, 1980.

al-Khatib, Muhib Al-Din, *Al-Khutuf al-'Arida*. Jeddah, 1960.

al-Khunaizi, Shaikh Ali Abu al-Hasan, *Al-Da'wa al-Islamiyya 'ela Wehdat 'Ahlu al-Sunna wa al-Imamiyya* (The Islamic Call for the Unity of the People of Sunna and the Imamiyya). Beirut, 1958.

Khuri, Fouad, *Tribe and State in Bahrain*. Chicago, 1980.

The Koran, translated by N. J. Dawood. London, 1961.

Kostiner, Joseph, 'Transforming Dualities: Tribe and State Formation in Saudi Arabia', in Philip Khoury and Joseph Kostiner (eds), *Tribes and State Formation in the Middle East*. Berkeley, 1990.

—— 'State, Islam, and Opposition in Saudi Arabia: The Post-Desert Storm Phase', in Bruce Maddy-Weitzman and Efraim Inbar (eds), *Religious Radicalism in the Greater*

Middle East. Portland, 1997.

Kramer, Martin (ed.), *Islamism Debate*. Tel Aviv, 1997.

Lackner, Helen, *A House Built on Sand: A Political Economy of Saudi Arabia*. London, 1978.

Lacy, Robert, *The Kingdom*. London, 1981.

Lijphart, Arend, 'Power-Sharing Approach', in Joseph V. Montville (ed.), *Conflict and Peacemaking in Multiethnic Societies*. New York, 1991.

Lipsky, George A., *Saudi Arabia*. New Haven, 1959.

Mahfoud, Muhammad, *Al-'Ahl wa al-Dawla: Bayan Min 'Ajl al-Silm al-Mujtamai'* (Nation and State, a Manifesto for Social Peace). Beirut, 1997.

Majmou'at al-Rasail wa al-Masail al-Najdiyya (The Collection of Najdi Letters and Jurisdictions), sponsored by Imam 'Abdulaziz al-Sa'ud. Egypt, 1928.

Manhaj Hizb al-Tahrir fi al-Taghiyeer (The Programme of the Tahrir Party for Change) (private publication).

Mansbridge, Jane, 'What Does a Representative Do? Descriptive Representation in Communicative Settings of Distrust, Uncrystallized Interests, and Historically Denigrated Status', in Will Kaymlicka and Wayne Norman (eds), *Citizenship In Diverse Societies*. Oxford, 2000.

al-Mawdudi, abu-l 'Ala, 'The Political Theory of Islam', in John J. Donohue and John L. Esposito (eds), *Islam in Transition*. Oxford, 1982.

McGuire, Meredith B., *Religion: The Social Context*. Belmont, CA, 1992.

Melikian, Levion H., 'The Modal Personality of Saudi College Students: A Study in National Character', in L. Carl Brown and Norman Itzkowitz (eds), *Psychological Dimensions of Near Eastern Studies*. Princeton, 1977.

The Ministry of Education, *Tarikh al-Dawla al-Islamiyya* (The History of the Islamic State). Riyadh, 1977.

Momen, M., *Authority and Opposition in Twelver Shi'ism*. London, 1989.

al-Mudarresi, Hadi, *Al-Islam Manhaj al-Hayat*. Beirut, 1973.

al-Mudarresi, Muhammad Taqi, *Buhuth fi al-Qur'an al-Karim* (Studies on the Holy Qur'an). Beirut, 1971.

—— *Al-Mantiq al-Islami* (Islamic Logic). Beirut, 1977.

—— *Al-'Amal al-Islami* (Islamic Action). Beirut, 1981.

—— *Al-Tahadi al-Islami* (Islamic Challenge). Tehran, 1990.

—— *Al-Ba'th al-Islami* (Islamic Renaissance). Tehran, 1984.

—— *Mustaqbal al-Thawra al-Islamiyya* (The Future of Islamic Revolution). Tehran, 1985.

Muhammad, 'Urabi Nakhlah, *Tarikh al-'Ahsa al-Siyasi* (The Political History of al-Hasa). Kuwait, 1980.

Munson, Henry, Jr, *Islam and Revolution in the Middle East*. London, 1988.

Nasr, Sayyid Hossein, *Shi'ism: Doctrines, Thought, and Spirituality and Expectation of the Millennium: Shi'ism in History*. New York, 1988.

Niblock, T., *Social and Economic Development in the Arab World*. London, 1980.

al-Nizari, Majid, *Abdul-Sahib al-Dakhil wa Bidayat al-Haraka al-Islamiyya al-Mu'asira* (The Emergence of the Contemporary Islamic Movement). Beirut, 1990.

Olson, Mancur, *The Logic of Collective Action*. Cambridge, 1965.

Piscatori, James, 'Ideological Politics in Saudi Arabia', in James Piscatori (ed.) *Islam in the Political Process*. Cambridge, 1983.

—— 'The Formation of the Saudi Identity: A Case Study of the Utility of Transnationalism', in John F. Stack, Jr (ed.), *Ethnic Identities in a Transnational World*. Westport ,CT, 1981.

Potter, Lawrence G., *Islam and Politics: Egypt, Algeria and Tunisia*. New York, 1994.

al-Qahtani, Fahad, *Sira' al-Ajniha* (The Struggle of Wings). London, 1988.

Qutb, Sayyid, *Fi Zilal al-Qur'an* (In the Shade of the Qur'an). Cairo, 1986.

Rabi, Uzi, and Joseph Kostiner, 'The Shi'is in Bahrain: Class and Religious Protest', in Ofra Bengio and Gabriel Ben-Dor (eds), *Minorities and the State in the Arab World*. London, 1999.

Ramazani, R. K., 'Shi'ism in the Persian Gulf', in Juan Cole and Nikki Keddie (eds), *Shi'ism and Social Protest*. London, 1985.

al-Rasheed, Madawi, *A History of Saudi Arabia*. Cambridge, 2002.

Richard, Yann, *Shiite Islam*, translated by Antonia Nevill. Oxford, 1995.

Rihani, Ameen, *Ibn Sa'ud of Arabia*. London, 1928.

Roy, Olivier, 'Islamists in Power', in Martin Kramer (ed.), *Islamism Debate*. Tel Aviv, 1997.

al-Ruwaini, Muhammad, *Sukkan al-Mamlaka al-Arabiyya al-Sa'udiyya* (The Population of Saudi Arabia). Riyadh, 1979.

al-Sadr, Sayyid Muhammad Baqir, *Durus fi 'Ilm al-Usul* (Lessons in the Science of Principles). Beirut, 1986.

Saeed, Khalid Bin, *Western Dominance and Political Islam: Challenge and Response*. New York, 1995.

al-Saffar, Hasan Musa, *'Ahadith fi al-Din wa al-Thaqafa wa al-ijtima'* (Sermons on Religion, Culture and Society). Beirut, 2002.

—— *Al-Tanawwu' wa al-Ta'ayush* (Diversity and Coexistence). London, 1999.

—— *Al-Ta'adudiyya wa al-Hurriyya fi al-Islam* (Plurality and Freedom in Islam). Beirut, 1996.

—— *Al-Mahdi Amal al-Shu'ub* (Mahdi, the Hope of the Peoples). Beirut, 1979.

—— *A'immat Ahl al-Bayt Risalah wa Jihad* (The Imams of the Prophet's Family). Beirut, 1977.

Safran, Nadaf, *Saudi Arabia: Ceaseless Quest for Security*. London, 1985.

al-Saif, Muhammad Ibn Ibrahim, *Al-Madkhal ila Dirasat al Mujtama' al-Sa'udi* (A Prelude to the Study of Saudi Society). Riyadh, 1997.

al-Saif, Tawfiq, *Didda al-Istibdad* (Anti-despotism). Beirut, 1999.

Salamé, Ghasan, 'Political Power and the Saudi State', in Albert Hourani, Philip Khoury and Mary C. Wilson (eds), *The Modern Middle East: A Reader*. London, 1993.

—— 'Political Power and the Saudi State', in Berch Berberoglu (ed.), *Power and Stability in the Middle East*. London, 1989.

Sanger, Richard H., *The Arabian Peninsula*. New York, 1954.

Sankari, Farouk A., 'Islam and Politics in Saudi Arabia', in Ali al-Din Hilal al-Dossouqi (ed.), *Islamic Resurgence in the Arab World*. New York, 1982.

Al Sa'ud, Faisal b. Mishal, *Rasail A'emmat Da'wat al-Tawhid* (Letters of the Imams of the Monotheist Call). Riyadh, 2001.

Schwartz, Steven, *The Two Faces of Islam: The House of Saud from Tradition to Terror.* New York, 2002.

Scott, James, *Domination and the Arts of Resistance: Hidden Transcripts.* London, 1990.

Shaker, Fatina Amin, *Modernization of the Developing Nations: The Case of Saudi Arabia.* PhD diss., Purdue University, 1972.

Shari'ati, 'Ali, *On the Sociology of Islam*, translated from the Persian by Hamid Algar. Berkeley, 1979.

—— *Intizar... Madhab-i I'tiraz* (Waiting... the Religion of Protest). Tehran, 1971, quoted in John J. Donohue and John L. Esposito (eds), *Islam in Transition.* Oxford, 1982.

al-Shirazi, al-Imam al-Marji' Sayyid Muhammad, *Al-'Aqa'id al-Islamiyya* (Islamic Creeds). Beirut, 1960.

—— *Islamic Belief* (Kuwait, 1979).

—— *Al-Siyagha al-Jadida* (The New Reformulation). Beirut, 1988.

—— *Al-Hukum fi al-Islam* (The Rulership in Islam). Beirut, 1989.

Shotter, John, 'Psychology and Citizenship: Identity and Belonging', in Bryan S. Turner (ed.), *Citizenship and Social Theory.* London, 1993.

Shwadran, Benjamin, *The Middle East, Oil, and the Great Powers.* New York, 1955.

Simons, Geoff, *Saudi Arabia: The Shape of a Client Feudalism.* London, 1998.

Steinberg, Guido, 'The Shiites in the Eastern Province of Saudi Arabia (al-Ahsaa), 1913–1953', in Werner Ende and Rainer Freitage (eds), *The Twelver Shi'a in Modern Times. Religious Culture and Political History.* Leiden, 2000.

Stockey, Robert W. (ed.), *The Arabian Peninsula.* California, 1984.

S}unaitan, Muhammad b., *Al-Nukhab al-Sa'udiyya.Dirasa fi al-Tahulat wa al-Ekhfaqat* (Saudi Elites: a Study of Transformations and Decline). Beirut, 2004.

Ibn Taimiyya, Shaikh Al-Islam Ahmad Taqi al-Din, *Minhaj al-Sunna fi Naqd Kalam al-Shi'a wa al-Qadariyya* (The Sunni Method in the Attack Against the Theology of Shi'i and Qadariyya). Riyadh, n.d.

al-Tami, Shaikh Ahmad b. Hajar, *Shaikh Muhammad b. 'Abd al-Wahhab, 'Aqidatahu al-Salafiyya wa Dawatahu al-Islahiyya wa Thana' al-'Ulama' 'Alaihi* (Shaikh Muhammad b. Abdulawahab, his Fundamental Beliefs and Reformist Call). Riyadh, 1999.

al-Taweel, Muhammad, *Al-Ikhwan fi al-Barlaman* (The Ikhwan in Parliament). Cairo, 1992.

Thernstorm, A. M., 'The Right to Political Representation', in C. Fried (ed.), *Minorities: Community and Identity.* Berlin, 1993.

al-Tunisi, Muhammad 'Abdulsattar, *Butlan 'Aqa'id al-Shi'a* (The Falseness of the Shi'i Doctrines). Cairo, 1983.

Tuwaimah, Sabir Abdulrahman, *Al-Shi'a, Mu'taqdan wa Madhhaban* (The Shi'i: Belief and Cult). Beirut, 1988.

Vidal, F. S., *The Oasis of al-Hasa.* Dhahran, 1955.

Wahbah, Hafiz, *Jazirat al'Arab fi al-Qarn al-'Eshreen* (The Arabian Peninsula in the Twentieth Century). Egypt, 1935.

al-Wardi, Ali, *Lamahat 'Ejtima'iyya min Tarikh al-'iraq al-Hadith* (The Social Aspect of

Modern Iraqi History). London, 1991.

Wenner, Manfred W., 'Saudi Arabia: Survival of Traditional Elites', in Frank Tachau (ed.), *Political Elites and Political Development in the Middle East*. Cambridge, 1975.

Wilson, Arnold T., *The Persian Gulf: A Historical Sketch from the Earliest Times to the Beginning of the Twentieth Century*. London, 1928.

Wilson, Bryan R., *The Social Dimensions of Sectarianism*. Oxford, 1990.

al-Yazdi, Muhammad Kadhim, *al-'Uruat al-Withqa*·(The Firm Bond). Najaf, 1981.

Yamani, Mai, 'Health, Education, Gender and the Security of the Gulf in the Twenty-First Century', in David E. Long and Christian Koch (eds), *Gulf Security in the Twenty-First Century*, The Emirates Center for Strategic Studies. Abu Dhabi, 1997.

—— *Cradle of Islam. The Hijaz and the Quest for an Arabian Identity*. London, 2004.

Zonis, Marvin and Daniel Brumberg, 'Shi'ism as Interpreted by Khomeini: An Ideology of Revolutionary Violence', in Martin Kramer (ed.), *Shi'ism: Resistance and Revolution*. Boulder, 1987.

Unpublished Documents

Prince Bandar, an official signed letter, 17 October 1990.

G. S. Belham, a letter sent to Sir Anthony Eden, ES1015/1/55, from Jeddah, dated 21 February 1955.

Al-Din Darura wa Manhaj (Religion is a Necessity and Programme) (pamphlet).

Al-Din Hadara (Religion is a Civilization) (private circulation).

Al-Eman wa al-Hayat (Faith and Life) (pamphlet).

Fi al-Thawra (About Revolution) (pamphlet).

Al-Haraka al-Shi'iyya ... Muquimatuha wa Tarikhuha (The Shi'i Movement: its Motives and History) (pamphlet).

al-Harbi, Abdul Rahim, *Mulakhas min Kitab Ahl al-Dar wa al-Iman* (Abstract of the Book of the People of Land and Faith) (manuscript).

Risalat al-'Anbiya' (The Message of the Prophets) (pamphlet).

Al-Risala Bayn al-Ghayah wa al-Wasila (The Message: Between Aims and Means) (pamphlet).

Al-Taghiyeer wa al-Thawra al-Shamila Huwa al-Matlub (Change and a Comprehensive Revolution are Required) (pamphlet).

Al-Tali'a wa al-Muntalaqat al-Thawariyya (The Vanguard and the Revolutionary Principles) (pamphlet).

India Office Records

IOR-R\15\5\27, dated 7 June 1913.
IOR-R\15\2\74, dated 18 February 1924.
IOR-R15\5\1859, dated 29 April 1927.
IOR-R\15\2\74, dated 10 August 1929.

Human Rights Reports

Communiqués of International Committee of Human Rights in the Gulf and Arabian

Peninsula, 1991–3.
Minnesota Lawyers International Human Rights Committee Report, 1996, Chapter IV.
2000 Annual Report on Religious Freedom: Saudi Arabia, issued by Bureau of Democracy, Human Rights and Labor, US Department of State, 5 September 2000.

Magazines and Newspapers

Akhbar al-Khaleej (daily newspaper based in Bahrain).
al-'Alam (weekly magazine based in London).
The Economist, 15 January 1994.
al-Hayat (daily newspaper based in London).
al-Hijaz (monthly magazine based in London).
al-Jazira al-'Arabiyya (monthly magazine formerly based in London; sponsored by the Reform Movement).
al-Mawaqif (weekly magazine based in Bahrain).
al-Nasr (monthly magazine based in Beirut).
New York Times, 30 October 1993.
Okaz (daily newspaper based in Jeddah).
Qadaya al-'Usbu' (weekly magazine; sponsored by Preliminary Committee for the Permanent Conference of the Lebanese Dialogue).
Qafilat al-Zait (The Caravan's Oil, a monthly magazine sponsored by Aramco).
Risalat al-Haramain (monthly magazine based in Qum, sponsored by Saudi *hizbullah*).
al-Riyadh (daily newspaper).
Salam (daily newspaper based in Tehran).
Saudi Affairs (monthly magazine based in London; the voice of the National Coalition for Democracy in Saudi Arabia).
Sawt al-Bahrain (Voice of Bahrain).
Time magazine, 24 September 1990.

Articles in Magazines

Abootalebi, Ali R., 'Islam, Islamists, and Democracy', *Middle East Review of International Affairs*, vol. 3, no. 1, March 1999.
'Al-'Amil al-Dini fi al-Thaqafa al-Wataniyya' (The Religious Factor in National Culture), *al-Waha* (editorial), issue no. 18, Spring 2000.
Ali, Abdullah Muhammad, 'Mu'jam Ma 'Allafahu 'Ulama al-'Umma al-Islamiyya lil Radd 'ala Khurafat al-Da'wa al-Wahhabiyya' (A Bibliography of the Writings of the Islamic Scholars in refuting the Wahhabi Call), *Turathuna*, [quarterly magazine based in Qum], issue no. 17, 22 May 1989.
Bill, James A., 'Resurgent Islam in The Persian Gulf', *Foreign Affairs*, Fall 1984.
Codevilla, Angelo M., 'Heresy and History', *The American Spectator*, 14 May 2004.
Connor, Walker, 'Nation-Building or Nation-Destroying', *World Politics*, April 1973.
Costa, Frank J., and Allen G. Noble, 'Planning Arab Towns', *Geographical Review*, vol. 76, no. 2, thematic issue: Asian Urbanization (April 1986).
The Country Profile 1992–93: Saudi Arabia, issued by The Economist Intelligence Unit.

London, 1993.

Dekmejian, R., 'The Liberal Impulse in Saudi Arabia', *Middle East Journal*, vol. 57, no. 3, Summer 2003.

—— 'Saudi Arabia's Consultative Council', *Middle East Journal*, 1998, issue no. 52.

Doumato, Eleanor A., 'Gender, Monarchy and National Identity', *British Journal of Middle Eastern Studies*, vol. 19, no.1, 1992.

Esposito, John., 'Political Islam and the West', *Joint Force Quarterly*, Spring 2000.

Fandy, Mamoun, 'From Confrontation to Creative Resistance: The Shiʻa Opposition Discourse in Saudi Arabia', *Critique*, Fall 1996.

Hakken, B. D., 'Sunni–Shia Discord in Eastern Arabia', *The Moslem World*, issue no. 23, 1933.

Ibrahim, Fouad, 'Nahwa Qira'h Jadidah Lel- Shiʻa' (Towards a New Reading of the Shiʻi), *al-Waha*, issue no. 18, Autumn 2000.

Mahfoud, Muhammad, 'Nahwa Mujtamaʻ Ahli Arabi Islami Jadid' (Towards a New Arabian-Islamic Civil Society), *al-Kalima*, issue no. 23, 1999.

—— 'Su'al al-Hurriya fi al-Fikr al-Islami al-Muʻasir' (The Question of Freedom in Contemporary Islamic Thought), *al-Kalima*, issue no. 24, Summer 1999.

—— 'Nazarat Hawla al-Wihda wa al-Taʻddud fi al-Fikr al-Islami al-Muʻasir' (Views on Unity and Pluralism in Contemporary Islamic Thought), *al-Kalima*, issue no. 21, Autumn 1998.

Malone, Joseph J., 'Saudi Arabia', *The Muslim World*, vol. 56, 1966.

Nehme, Michel G., 'Saudi Arabia 1950–80: Between Nationalism and Religion', *Middle Eastern Studies*, vol. 30, no. 4, October 1994.

al-Rasheed, Madawi, 'The *Shiʻa* of Saudi Arabia: A Minority in Search of Cultural Authenticity', *British Journal of Middle Eastern Studies*, vol. 25, no. 1, May 1998.

al-Saif, Tawfiq, ''Eshkaliyat al-Dawla al-Haditha Min Manzour Fiqhi' (Problems of the Modern State from a Juristic Perspective), *al-Kalima*, issue no. 32, Summer 2001.

al-Tahir, Muhammad b. Husain (pseudonym), 'Mas'alat al-Wehda wa Taʻaddud fi al-Waqiʻ al-Islami' (The Question of Unity and Pluralism in Islamic Reality), *al-Waha*, issue no. 10–11, 1997.

Vitalis, Robert, 'The Closing of the Arabian Oil Frontier and The Future of Saudi-American Relations, *Middle East Report*, no. 204, The Arabian Peninsula (July–September 1997).

Welson, Robert, and Howard Wolpe, 'Modernization and the Politics of Communalism: A Theoretical Perspective', *American Political Science Review*, vol. 64, no. 4, December 1970.

Websites

www.alarabiyya.com.
www.arabrenewal.com.
www.binbaz.org.sa.
www.binothaimeen.com.
www.bsos.umd.edu/cidcm/mar/saudishii.htm.
www.eia.doe.gov/emeu/cabs/saudi.html.

www.hrw.org.

www.ibn-jebreen.com/fatawa/frame02.htm.

www.islamicweb .com/beliefs/shia_population.htm 22/01/1421-2000.

www.islamtoday.net.

www.islamway.com.

www.kalema.net.

www.khayma.com/najran.

www.modarresi.org.

www.almoslim.net.

www.saaid.net/mktarat/flasteen/7.htm.

www.saffar.org.

www.alsalafiyoun.com.

www.saudiaramco.com.

www.shariati.com.

www.shirazi.org.uk.

www.state.gov.

www.alsunnah.com/rafidah.

www.thulatha.com.

www.alwahabiya.org/almoraqib.htm.

Interviews

Interview with Ali al-Ahmad, a member of the *islahiyya* movement, and chairman of the Saudi Institute in Washington, on 24 February 2002.

Interview with Hamza al-Hassan, chief editor of *al-Jazira al-'Arabiyya,* and member of the Central Committee of the *islahiyya* movement, on 19 April 2002.

Interview with Shaikh Hassan al-Saffar, a founding father of the *islahiyya* movement, in Syria, 28 April 2001.

Interview with Aramco employee M. Saleh al-Ahmad, on 16 July 2000.

Interviews with Ja'far al-Shayeb, chairman of the International Committee of Human Rights in the Gulf and Arabian Peninsula (ICHR–GAP) and a member of the Central Committee, on 27 April 2002 and 13 September 2003.

Interviews with Shaikh Tawfiq al-Saif, a founding father of the *islahiyya* movement, on 23 October 2001, 18 April 2002 and 23 August 2002.

The author interviewed two Aramco employees in London on 24 October 2000, who, for security reasons, preferred their names not to be revealed.

Index

Supreme Judicial Council, Saudi Arabia 38
Syria 145–6, 153, 154, 156

Tabdid al-zalam wa Tanbih (al-Jabhan) 226
Ibn Taimiyya, Shaikh al-Islam 18, 225, 227, 235
Talal, Prince 213
Talib, Abu 39
Taliban 213
Tehran 143, 144
Tehran Radio 121
Texas 148
Thernstrom, A. M. 41
al-Torki, Sorrya 70
Tuesday Intellectual Salon 216–7
al-Turabi, Shaikh Hassan 166
Turki, Faisal b. 24
al-Tuwaijri, Ahaikh Abdul Aziz 187, 188
Twelver Shi'is 22, 46, 54, 85

'ulama 155, 236
    see also Sh'is 'ulama; Wahhabi 'ulama
Umm al-Qura University, Medina 69
al-Umran, Shaikh Faraj 173
United Kingdom, London 11, 143–6, 153
United States 143, 144–5, 146–53, 182–3, 214, 253–4
    State Department 162, 164–5, 184, 232
'Universal Document of Muslim Human Rights' 160
'Urai'r, Abdulaziz 254
al-'Utaibi, Juhiman 27
bin 'Uthimein, Shaikh Muhammad 123

VOA (Voice of America) 151

al-Wahhab, Shaikh Muhammad Ibn 'Abdul 19–20, 22–3, 27, 43
Wahhabi 'ulama 29, 39–40, 110, 197, 225–6, 228–30
    Committee of Senior 'Ulama 27–8, 35, 40
    fatwa against Shi'is 197
Wahhabis/Wahhabism 18–25, 27, 28, 33–4, 36–7, 38, 47
    and Saudi regime 29, 58–63, 67, 105, 110, 160
    and Aramco employment 33–4
    Shi'i-Wahhabi divide 39–40, 48, 225–37, 246–7
    revivalist movement (1747) 42
    and islahayya members 215
WAMY 239
al-Wardi, Ali 19
Washington 143, 150–3, 180, 214
    State Department 162, 164–5, 184, 232
Weber, Max 78, 91
Welson, Robert 220–1
Wilson, Bryan R. 13, 46
World Association for Muslim Youth 239
World Muslim Charity Association 239

Yakun, Fathi 117
Yamani, Mai 70, 248–9
Yanbu 56
al-Yazdi, Sayyid Kadim 86

Zahir, Ehsan 'Elahi 227
Zaidi Shi'is 56, 61
Zonis, Marvin 123